The Lives of
Mentally Retarded People

Also of Interest

The Library and the Handicapped Child, Margaret Marshall

Early Development Hazards: Predictors and Precautions, edited by Frances Degen Horowitz

A Cybernetic Approach to the Assessment of Children: Toward A More Humane Use of Human Beings, edited by Mark N. Ozer

The Psychosocial Aspects of Drug Treatment for Hyperactivity, edited by Kenneth D. Gadow and Jan Loney

Impacts of Program Evaluation on Mental Health Care, edited by Emil J. Posavac

The Myths of Deinstitutionalization: Policies for the Mentally Disabled, edited by Joseph Halpern, Karen L. Sackett, Paul R. Binner, and Cynthia B. Mohr

The Lives of
Mentally Retarded People

Daryl Paul Evans

Westview Press / Boulder, Colorado

Paperback cover photo by Suzanne Burdick.

Published in 1983 in the United States of America by
   Westview Press, Inc.
   5500 Central Avenue
   Boulder, Colorado 80301
   Frederick A. Praeger, President and Publisher

Library of Congress Cataloging in Publication Data
Evans, Daryl.
   The lives of mentally retarded people.
   Includes index.
   1. Mentally handicapped. I. Title.
HV3004.E89 1983   362.3   82-10988
ISBN 0-86531-270-2
ISBN 0-86531-271-0 (pbk.)

Printed and bound in the United States of America

To Anne

Contents

Acknowledgments

Special thanks go to James Downton, Ray Cuzzort, Tom Mayer, Blaine Mercer, and David Armstrong. Each of these scholars would have approached the subject of mental retardation in manners unique to them, but as good teachers, they encouraged me to explore the topic in my own way. They guided me when I asked for direction, helped corral my restless aversion to discipline, employed me, critiqued my work, propped me up, and cared about me and the issues that are important to me.

I would also like to thank Karyn Zarley, who prepared the manuscript with steady competence; Edith King for her encouragement and advice; and Bob Fowler and Don Coloroso, friends who were always there when I needed them.

To Lynne Rienner, Dean Birkenkamp, Jude Biggs, Lynn Arts, Libby Barstow, and the other good people at Westview Press, I offer my appreciation for the sensitive interest they have taken in the subject matter of this work.

Singular gratitude is reserved for my wife, Anne, who supported the efforts leading to this book in manifold ways. Her professional commitment to handicapped people has created an atmosphere in our home that could be described in superlatives, but that, like so many things in our life together, is most deeply embedded in the ineffability of our love.

Daryl Paul Evans

Of the four baby birds in the barn, three had learned to fly and one stood on the floor, looking stupid and making flapping motions. Now and then, it would walk in the driveway, where it was dive-bombed by its siblings and snapped at by its parents. Then it would walk back into the barn again. The people in the house checked under the wheels of their cars to avoid running over the bird, and otherwise wished it well. On the third day, the children minced a worm and tried to feed the bird themselves. By the fourth day, one adult or another, thinking himself unwatched, would lean over the bird and mutter, and flap his arms in what he hoped was an exemplary way. On the fifth day, the bird was sitting on a high rafter of the barn with the rest of its family. It has not yet been seen to fly. Perhaps it walked up there.

—R. Adler[1]

1
Introduction

Method, Method, What do you
want from me?
You know that I have eaten
of the fruit of the subconscious.
                              —J. Laforgue[2]

One builds a magnificent palace, a wonder to behold, but goes on living in a
hovel next to it.
                              —S. Kierkegaard[3]

THE NAME GAME

In any discussion of mental handicaps, one of the first issues that must be resolved is, What do we call people who are retarded? Historically, the nomenclature of mental retardation has included terms such as idiot, imbecile, moron, and ament. Retarded people also have been designated feebleminded, mentally defective, mentally deficient, mentally subnormal, slow learners, developmentally delayed, exceptional, and a spate of other medical and educational terms. Today, it is a common conversational and journalistic practice to refer to people with mental handicaps as "the retarded." Such a designation reduces all of the human qualities of retarded people to a descriptive adjective—they are defined solely in terms of their handicap. This is akin to calling a person with kidney stones, "the stones." Another common practice is calling retarded people "retardates," which presumably makes the rest of us "normates." Many professionals in the field call retarded people "MRs." Yet we never refer to non-handicapped people as "NHs." A few individuals believe the appropriate term to be "intellectually handicapped." This designation is alluring, but its range of applicability would include many individuals who are not mentally retarded.

A few professionals suggest that the focus of the problem in mental retardation is behavioral. McAllister says, "There is no way to demonstrate that it is the mental apparatus that is 'retarded' since behavioral

1

rather than physical criteria have been used for evidence."[4] If this proposition is accepted, the result is a binary system of nomenclature and classification. It includes those people whose behaviors are typical and those whose behaviors are atypical. Many retarded individuals would, no doubt, fall into the latter category—along with a high percentage of the rest of the population.

The newest designation to come into vogue is "developmental disability." It has a nice ring to it, but it is not specific enough. Developmental disabilities include not only mental retardation but also cerebral palsy, epilepsy, autism, spina bifida, muscular dystrophy, and other significant neurological disorders. While some individuals who are mentally retarded have one or more of these other disorders, the various developmental disabilities are distinctly different. Thus the term developmental disability is confusing to a public already bewildered about what mental retardation is. Moreover, there is resentment among some developmentally disabled people at sharing the label. For instance, I have talked with some persons who have epilepsy who do not like being classified with those who are mentally retarded. "I may have a problem, but I'm not retarded, for heaven's sake." Always there is hierarchy.

As new euphemisms for mental retardation are created to supplant the ones that have become tainted, one wonders, Why the attention to names anyway? Sociolinguists like Whorf have argued for the importance of names. Whorf held that language is a tool that not only facilitates thinking, but also delineates the boundaries of thought.[5] Language *is* thought. If one accepts this theory, the names we attach to retarded persons have important consequences for our social attitudes regarding them.

Why do our designations tend to become pejorative so quickly? Because the relationship between words and social attitudes is reciprocal. For example, the word *idiot* is not inherently ugly. It was derived from the Greek, meaning "a private person" or "persons who did not hold public office."[6] It has become ugly because of social attitudes now underlying its use. Changing the names that are used to refer to retarded people may help improve the negative attitudes that often exist. But, if those attitudes were changed, it probably would not make much difference what we called such people, and we could all save a lot of time and confusion by not having to learn the latest vocabulary. The main thing is that we call them *people* and remember that "mentally retarded" is only an adjective.

METHOD, METHOD

This work is, in part, a field study, which is defined as an exploration of "human behavior in a natural setting where the investigator is known as such, but ideally attempts to conduct himself in a way that will not unduly influence the behavior of those being observed."[7] Field work is important because it can help us understand the distant provinces of our social web of interdependency. Although this web is huge, the action of any group, any "small world,"[8] on that web usually affects life for everyone in the other small interconnected worlds.

The communications media only give us thumbnail sketches of these small worlds, but the field sociologist can provide more detailed views because of lengthier and more intimate immersions in the groups under study. Field work aims at demystifying small worlds everyone probably knows about, but does not really know.

Mentally retarded people are good candidates for such studies. Conservative estimates put the percentage of retarded persons in our culture at 1 percent of the population,[9] although it is generally accepted that 3 percent of the total population is labeled as mentally retarded.[10] We shall discuss the controversy about labeling and the disagreement over incidence and prevalence figures in a subsequent chapter. What is important to consider now is that mentally retarded people constitute a sizable minority in our society—a minority that is unknown to most of our citizens. Gottwald's work illustrates that a very small percentage of the population possesses accurate information regarding mentally handicapped people.[11]

As it turned out, the seventies were an exciting time to examine the lives of mentally retarded persons, because there were so many changes going on as a result of the movement toward deinstitutionalization and the subsequent integration of a broad range of retarded people into communities from which they historically had been excluded. This *normalization* process, as it was called, was the focus of conversations among many of the special educators I came to know through my wife, Anne—a speech therapist who has worked with mentally retarded children. My interest was doubtless evoked as well by the usual morbid curiosity that seems to be reserved for retarded people. As a sociologist, I was fascinated by the normative landscape inhabited by retarded people, and there was something enchanting about the retarded individuals I met—an enchantment I would later be able to explain, but which, in its initial stages, drew me rather inexplicably to increase my contact with them.

Initially, it was my intention to limit the purview of this study to the educational environment of mentally retarded students, but the path to understanding educational issues had many branches. Consequently my inquiries moved from schools into homes and work places. I started out by spending my time with retarded people and their teachers and ended up meeting their parents, siblings, employers, friends, and all manner of other advocates, hangers-on, and adversaries. The major objective of my investigation became to understand the relationships mentally handicapped people maintain within their communities and the way that these individuals impact and are impacted by society.

During the period of the inquiry, my role was that of an active, known, participant-observer. As such, I explained my intentions to the non-handicapped "gatekeepers" in the settings I targeted for observation by telling them that I was interested in studying mental retardation. I asked them if they would let me watch what was going on. I was never refused. Indeed, I was encouraged to take part in the activities around me—a participation that doubtless became too earnest as I found myself serving on local boards of directors of developmental disability service agencies, on committees, and on state task forces responsible for planning services, most frequently as an advocate of retarded people. Here, I broke some of the cardinal rules of "scientific detachment," but although I played fast and loose with bias, it is my belief that the scope of the work was broadened.

In addition to the by-products of the field work that appear in this manuscript, I drew heavily on the body of quantitative and qualitative research appearing in the extensive literature on mental retardation. The literature review was done in the aftermath of my earliest concentrated observations in the field. Approaching the study in this sequence had the advantages of allowing me to go into the field without a lot of "theoretical baggage" and subsequently affording me an opportunity to check my observations against the empirical verities established by other scholars.

While in the field (which I have never really left in the last seven years), I was fortunate not to have to rely on a limited number of informants. People from all quarters of the field, including those who are mentally handicapped, were enthusiastic about discussing the issues. A simple explanation of the project typically led to a torrent of information on the subject of mental retardation. I did many formal interviews, but the most insightful remarks were often those that were unsolicited. This was, no doubt, because the volunteered information reflected the preoccupations of participants in the actual social settings.

One ground rule that facilitated the many confidences I became privy to was an assurance of anonymity, which I guaranteed each participant. As a result, no informants are identified in the manuscript, nor are there any anecdotes that reveal names or places. The settings where I observed have been given fictitious names, as have the localities of these places. The school that served as the primary focus of the study will be referred to as New Morning School and the town in which it is located I call Mountview. These are, in a sense, generic names, for while I spent much of my time in a single school, workshop, and residential facility, I visited numerous other mental retardation facilities in many different venues.

Whatever insights are brought to bear on the subject of mental retardation in this book are largely the result of the careful work of the many scholars who preceded me and the generosity with which so many good people shared their minds and hearts with me. For this, I will always be grateful, and I hope the story does them justice.

NOTES

1. Reprinted by permission of Random House, Inc., from R. Adler, *Speedboat*, New York: Popular Library, 1971, p. 51. Copyright © 1976 by Random House, Inc.

2. J. Laforgue, "Moralites Legendaires," in *Oeuvres Completes de Jules La Forgue*, Paris: Societe du Mercure de France, vol. 2, 1902, quoted in G. Bachelard, *The Poetics of Reverie*, New York: The Orion Press, 1969, p. 1.

3. S. Kierkegaard, quoted in P. L. Berger, *Invitation to Sociology*, Garden City, N.Y.: Doubleday, 1963, p. 154.

4. E.W.C. McAllister, "Thoughts on the Use of the Term Mental Retardation," *Mental Retardation*, 10:1972, p. 40.

5. B. L. Whorf, *Language, Thought, and Reality*, Cambridge, Mass.: M.I.T. Press, 1956.

6. D. L. MacMillan, *Mental Retardation in School and Society*, Boston: Little, Brown and Co., 1977, p. 32.

7. F. F. Hoult, *Dictionary of Modern Sociology*, Totowa, N.J.: Littlefield Adams and Co., 1969, p. 134.

8. J. Wiseman and M. S. Aron, *Field Projects for Sociology Students*, Cambridge, Mass.: Schenkman, 1970, p. 240.

9. R. E. Luckey and R. Neman, "Practices in Estimating Mental Retardation Prevalence," *Mental Retardation*, 14:1976, p. 16.

10. B. R. Gearheart and F. W. Litton, *The Trainable Retarded: A Foundations Approach*, St. Louis: C. V. Mosby, 1975, p. 26.

11. H. Gottwald, *Public Awareness About Mental Retardation*, Arlington, Va.: The Council for Exceptional Children, 1970, pp. 1–61.

2
The Basics:
Definitions, Diagnosis,
Causes, and Prevalence

I do not like the way the cards are shuffled
But yet I like the game and want to play.
—Eugene F. Ware[1]

Before we get into "the field," let me set the stage by explaining what mental retardation is and by exploring its history.

WHAT IS MENTAL RETARDATION?

A common-sense definition of mental retardation has three basic elements. First, mentally retarded people do not learn as quickly or as much as non-retarded people do. Second, mentally retarded people do not store information as well as non-retarded people. Third, mentally retarded people do not abstract very well, and thus find it difficult to use information applicable in one situation in another similar situation; that is, they have difficulty in situations calling for strategic behavior. The formal definition that is most widely accepted is more complex. *The Manual on Terminology and Classification in Mental Retardation* defines mental retardation as "significantly subaverage general intellectual functioning, existing concurrently with deficits in adaptive behavior, and manifested during the developmental period [birth to eighteen years of age]."[2] There is controversy surrounding various components of this definition.

Determination of Intellectual Functioning

A frequently discussed issue is the manner by which "significantly subaverage general intellectual functioning" is determined. It is based

7

largely upon the scores of IQ tests, the most commonly used of these being the Wechsler Intelligence Scales and the Stanford-Binet Intelligence Scale. These tests measure such things as general comprehension, visual-motor abilities, memory, concentration, vocabulary and verbal skills, judgment, and reasoning. The average score on IQ tests is 100. If a person's score on an intelligence test yields an IQ of 69 or below, he or she would be labeled as mentally retarded under most circumstances.

Intelligence tests are given a great deal of credence by some professionals, who may ignore their own clinical findings about a client or patient in deference to the power of IQ tests.[3] There is evidence indicating that IQ tests are more accurate than clinical findings in determining the intellectual level at which a person is functioning.[4] Conversely, the power of intelligence tests is looked upon circumspectly by many people in the field of mental retardation because of the shortcomings in the tests. For example, IQ tests are fallible. The information gleaned from them is based on inferences about intelligence, not precise indicators of how "smart" a person is. To make the point clearer, let us examine the differences in IQ scores, learning, and intelligence. *Learning* is a specific set of dynamic processes, including such things as practice, acquisition, attention, memory, and generalization.[5] Learning changes the way we characteristically respond in certain situations. *Intelligence* is an abstract quality—a set of options—that may permit faster and more refined learning, but is not synonymous with learning. Sometimes people assume an IQ score to be the same thing as intelligence. It is not. *IQ* is a statistical measure (the intelligence quotient) derived from a hypothetically distributed normal curve; it is a score. A normal curve assumes that intelligence is normally distributed throughout the population—that there are equal numbers of people at the upper and lower ends of the intelligence spectrum, with the bulk of the population being in the middle, yielding a so-called bell-shaped curve. Wortis and several other researchers after him have presented evidence that purports to show that intelligence scores are not normally distributed.[6] They suggest that a real representation of the distribution of IQ scores on a curve would be skewed toward the lower end of the continuum. That means that these researchers believe that there are more "slow" people, in absolute terms, than "bright" people. If their assertions are accurate, it could be argued that people should not be labeled as retarded because of their position on a hypothetically bell-shaped curve when the curve, if it were drawn to represent reality, would have no such symmetry.

There are other objections to IQ tests. For instance, they are said to report answers without attending to the process by which the responses are formulated. A very imaginative answer nonetheless may be an "incorrect" answer.

Occasionally, people being tested have attitudinal aversions to IQ tests. Some individuals find the tests absurd or impossible to attend to. An emotionally disturbed person might not be able to cope with the testing situation, but that does not mean he or she is mentally retarded. Or a mentally retarded person who is emotionally disturbed may score lower on such tests than he would subsequent to a reduction in the emotional problem.[7]

People with acuity problems, as well as those with emotional problems, can be discriminated against through the misuse of IQ tests. For example, a hearing- or visually impaired[8] person may not be able to participate adequately in the testing process.[9] Occasionally such impairments are not picked up by professionals before the child is tested for IQ, or if the tester is aware of the handicap, he or she may not be able to compensate for it accurately in determining IQ and the stigmatized identity of the client that may be attendant upon low IQ. Children with handicaps such as epilepsy sometimes take medications that reduce their faculties to such an extent that they score lower on IQ tests than they otherwise might.[10]

Even if a person being tested is in fact retarded because of demonstrable neurological deficiencies, there are other problems with IQ tests. For example, these tests typically require a level of verbal skill that many mentally retarded people do not possess.[11] A mentally handicapped person with poor verbal skills who functions effectively in other areas can be penalized. Indeed, certain combinations of tests may confuse the issue even more because different IQ tests are said to measure different abilities.[12]

The testing environment can also pose problems for retarded persons. IQ tests are occasionally administered by people unaccustomed to working with handicapped children. A tester who is a "stranger" can evoke a number of reactive effects when he enters the "special world" mentally retarded people inhabit—effects that can affect adversely a child's test performance. Moreover, testers occasionally enter the testing situation harboring prejudices about retarded children. In one experiment,[13] professional testers were asked to assess a group of subjects who had already been tested and found to have comparable IQs. This was unknown to the testers. When they were told before the assessment that the subject was from a middle-class home and had a history of doing well in school, the subject's IQ was found to be significantly higher then when the assessors were told the subject was from an impoverished background, with a poor history of performance in school. When people suspected of being retarded are tested, the score may turn out to be lower than it should be because the erroneous score more closely coincides with the tester's expectations. Such findings

intimate another widely voiced objection to IQ tests—that they discriminate against cultural and racial minorities.

The Cultural-racial Biases of IQ Testing. IQ tests are standardized, that
is, they are based upon the assumption that the people taking them
share similar socioeconomic, linguistic, and cultural opportunities. That
this is not the case may explain why certain ethnic groups have more
than their share of representatives labeled as mentally retarded. For
example, in 1972, although Spanish-surnamed children constituted only
13 percent of the total school population in the state of California, they
accounted for roughly 26 percent of the students in special classes for
retarded children.[14] In 1970, it was determined in the case of *Diana* v.
the State Board of Education[15] that as many as 22,000 Hispanic Americans
had been placed in classes for retarded people because of cultural biases
in the IQ tests that had acted as determinants of placement. Since that
time, efforts have been made to remedy the situation. IQ tests such as
the Cattell Culture Fair Test were developed. As a result of the litigation
Larry P. v. *Riles*,[16] it was determined that children had to be tested in
their primary languages or be provided with an interpreter and that
minority children already in special classes should be reevaluated.[17] In
late 1979, U.S. Judge Robert Peckham declared that IQ tests were
unconstitutional as they were being used in California, because they
discriminated against minorities and violated the Fourteenth Amendment's equal protection clause.[18] The judge ordered the tests stopped
in that state.

The law is interpreted so rapidly on matters relating to IQ, it is likely
that new cases will have changed the disposition of the aforementioned
judicial decisions by the time this work is in print. (Indeed, segments
of *Larry P.* v. *Riles* have already been challenged in court.) This fluidity
of the law does not, however, reduce the power IQ tests have in the
attachment of mentally handicapped labels—labels that are sometimes
inaccurate.

Adaptive Behavior

The second component of the definition of mental retardation refers
to deficits in adaptive behavior. Adaptive behavior is the ability of an
individual to meet the levels of personal independence and social
responsibility that are expected of all people of the same chronological
age in the same society.

In the earliest years of a child's life, self-help skills (such as toileting,
feeding, and dressing), speech and language skills, gross and fine motor
coordination, and socialization skills develop in a systematic manner
that reflects a child's maturation. If a child shows a delay in achieving
certain developmental milestones in any of these areas, this may be

indicative of deficiencies that can have serious consequences for his future development. For example, a child with delayed head control, a poor sucking reflex, extreme lethargy, or a lack of responsiveness to sounds and familiar people may show subsequent difficulties.[19] Schmitt and Erickson have shown an infant's failure to smile and/or sit up by himself as fairly cogent early indicators of later, and more significant, developmental delays.[20] Assessment of developmental milestones in younger children is often done through tests such as the Gesell Developmental Schedules, the Bzoch-League Receptive-Expressive Emergent Language Scale, and the Bayley Scales of Infant Development.

During a child's school years, academic achievement takes on added importance in determining adaptive behavior. With retarded people, particularly those who function at lower levels, the word *academic* must be used advisedly. With some retarded persons, academics do pertain to the three R's, but with many others, the academics being talked about are the so-called functional academics—such things as color identification, sign recognition, and other bare essentials. The Peabody Individual Achievement Test and the Wide Range Achievement Test both combine assessments of functional and formal academic skills. These kinds of assessment tools can also ascertain the degree to which an individual is able to gain knowledge from his experiences.

As a person approaches adulthood, adaptive behavior assessments tend to concentrate on his vocational and social skills and adjustment. This is usually a subjective determination, yet there are some adaptive behavior scales that presume to objectify the procedure to some extent. The Cain-Levine Social Competency Scale, the Vineland Social Maturity Scale, and the American Association on Mental Deficiency Adaptive Behavior Scale are probably the most widely used among these.

Adaptive behavior is a less controversial means of assessment than IQ. One reason for this is that adaptive behavior scales are more concerned with competence in real life situations than are IQ tests. Some people do object that the concept of adaptive behavior confuses a cause with an effect. Are people mentally retarded because they are socially incompetent, or are they socially incompetent because they are mentally retarded? On the whole, however, one hears few objections to the use of adaptive behavior scales. In fact, they can be used to qualify some of the cultural biases attributed to IQ tests. Mercer, one of the most outspoken opponents of IQ tests, has done some research that illustrates the mitigating effect of adaptive behavior tests on scores derived from IQ assessments. Mercer tested the IQs of a number of Anglo, black, and Chicano children. The blacks and Chicanos showed IQs significantly lower than those of the Anglos. The same people were then given adaptive behavior tests. While the Anglos' scores remained comparable to those they had received on the IQ tests, the blacks and Chicanos achieved adaptive behavior scores considerably in excess of those expected on the basis of their IQ scores. Indeed, on these measures, the minority people equaled the scores of the Anglos.[21] If adaptive behavior scales are reliable, Mercer's evidence would seem to provide a demonstration of the cultural biases in IQ tests. Zigler and Hartner hold that there is not a "simple and striking" relationship between social competence and IQ-test performance in IQ ranges from 50–75, but that there is a "striking and predictable" relationship between the two in individuals who are more severely retarded (IQs 0–40).[22]

The Developmental Years

The final element in the definition of mental retardation states that the subaverage intellectual functioning and deficits in adaptive behavior should manifest themselves during the developmental years. Conley objects to the use of this criterion because it excludes adults whose intelligence is impaired by senility, mental illness, or non-congenital brain damage.[23] Conley is apparently concerned that those people excluded from the definition cannot receive publicly supported services designed for retarded people, even though they are functionally retarded. Senile and mentally ill people can and do receive public aid. It is true, however, that a person who becomes retarded after the age of eighteen because of brain damage may find it more difficult to get remedial services than if he were congenitally retarded.

LABELING

Another issue associated with the definition of mental retardation that breeds a great deal of controversy is any use at all of the "retarded" label. Such labeling is found objectionable by certain professionals on five fundamental grounds.

First, labeling is said to lead to injurious self-fulfilling prophecies, especially in terms of the educational stimulation a person so labeled receives. In light of the findings of researchers such as Rosenthal and Jacobson,[24] the objection is well grounded. They found that if elementary teachers were led to believe children would go through a period of "intellectual blossoming," the children (whom the teachers did not know had been *randomly* selected as blossomers) would in fact make much greater gains on IQ-test performance than their classmates.

There is nothing in the Rosenthal-Jacobson research to indicate that students labeled as having little potential would necessarily show little progress, but many people infer that if proper stimulation breeds growth, a lack of stimulation will beget stagnation.

The second major objection to labeling people as retarded is the static nature of the label. Intellectual functioning can vary because of changes in a person's maturation level, fluctuations in emotional stability, educational growth, and so forth. Intellectual functioning is almost always a dynamic process, punctuated in a few cases with surges of development. It has been established that IQ scores tend to fluctuate for some individuals.[25] Yet it is often the *first* assessment, and the label that goes with it, that will define a "retarded identity" for life.

Third, an individual who is labeled as mentally retarded can get special rewards for playing the role associated with the label. Rowitz suggests that this problem may be connected with the need of school districts to keep their special education funding, which requires a certain number of people to be labeled as having special needs and to retain that label.[26] The suggestion, cynical as it seems, would make for an interesting inquiry.

A fourth objection to labeling is that it is used to preserve inequitable social conditions. This is done by labeling an individual child (frequently from a poor family or minority group) and thereby focusing problems which arise from social conditions on the individual. When this is done, it is generally assumed that the bearer of the label needs modification, when it may be the socially deprived conditions that occasioned the label that should be changed. It is easier to modify children than social structures.

Finally, labeling can mask individual, as well as social, problems. For example, if a person who has been labeled as mentally retarded is performing daily tasks at a low functional level, it may automatically be assumed that he is doing so only because he is retarded. This can lead people to ignore other factors that explain maladaptive behavior or inability to do tasks—things such as subtle deterioration in hearing, sickness, or assignment of inappropriate tasks.

There is another side to the labeling issue. On the basis of an extensive review of literature, MacMillan and his associates concluded that there is not enough empirical evidence to support the view that labeling retarded people ensures that they will stay at retarded developmental levels or regress.[27] There is, however, evidence that judgments of retarded children by non-handicapped children are influenced by demonstrated competence, not by the label "retarded."[28] Guskin asserts that labeling has been erroneously used as a synonym for stigmatization.[29] This perspective overlooks the negative connotations that are inherent in certain labels—the rhetorical clout we talked about earlier. Nonetheless, it can be argued there are reasonable, even necessary, uses of labeling.

One prolabeling position holds that special children need special education, and to get it (including the funds to support it), they must

TABLE 2.1   Labeling Schema of Mental Retardation

Category	Stanford-Binet	Wechsler	Standard Deviations from the Mean
Mild retardation	IQ 52–68	IQ 55–69	−3.3 to −2.0
Moderate retardation	IQ 36–51	IQ 40–54	−4.3 to −3.4
Severe retardation	IQ 20–35	IQ 25–39	−5.3 to −4.4
Profound retardation	IQ below 20	IQ below 25	−5.3 and below

be identified. The basis of this argument is that special education teachers are trained to give an intense level of stimulation *because* of the label. Such assertions are challenged by another view that suggests that special education teachers are vulnerable to negative self-fulfilling prophecies associated with the retarded label, so that special education actually can exacerbate the problems of special students.[30] Moreover, it has been argued, if the thrust of education were to deal directly with each student's individual behavior and needs, labels should be inconsequential in ensuring that the best instructional and remedial courses are followed in the classroom. Reality belies the idealism of this assertion. In groups, people do get compartmentalized; they are labeled.

An area in which labeling does seem to have some utility is in the identification of people by the *degree* of their retardation.

DEGREES OF MENTAL RETARDATION

The degree of a person's mental handicap is typically determined through his or her performance on an IQ test, although adaptive behavior may enter the picture in some locales. Table 2.1 illustrates a fairly common breakdown on the degrees of mental retardation.[31]

Currently, in public school systems, *mildly* retarded people are most often called *educable*. *Moderately* retarded students are commonly referred to as *trainable*.

Logically, the labeling of people by degrees of handicap ought to enhance the precision of communications among professionals who work in the field of mental retardation. This assumes widespread acceptance in principle of labeling and IQ-derived labels, both of which stand on shaky foundations with many professionals. My perception has been that most professionals in the field use the labels of degree even if they do not necessarily agree with the principles upon which they are based.

Labels of the varying degrees of mental handicaps do tend to demystify a common lay stereotype about mental retardation—that retarded people are an undifferentiated mass. Of course, retarded people are not all alike, but ironically, where schemas of labeled degree inject a note of heterogeneity into the term "mental retardation," the various categories of degree imply a certain homogeneity within themselves. This does not exist. Within any of the four major categories of degree (Table 2.1), there is enormous functional variation. That notwithstanding, most professionals seem to mean some of the same things when they are, for example, talking about a "moderately" or "trainable" retarded person (a TMR). Indeed, certain scholars have made tidy and instructive tables indicating the functional capacities that characterize the different degrees of mental handicap.[32]

CAUSES

People not only differ in the degree to which they are retarded; they also differ in the cause of their handicaps. The causes of mental retardation can be broken down into four primary categories: (1) genetic, (2) acquired physiological, (3) social environmental, and (4) unknown.

Genetic Causes

The simplest typology of genetic causes of mental retardation divides them into: (1) metabolic defects, such as phenylketonuria (PKU); and (2) chromosomal abnormalities, such as Down's Syndrome (once called mongolism).

Genetic defects occur in two primary ways. First, a parent who has a dominant defective gene (such as that for tuberous sclerosis) may pass it along to the child. Under these circumstances, the parent will manifest the genetic defect and has a fifty-fifty chance of passing it along to the youngster. Second, parents who are carriers of recessive defective genes can pass the genetic defect along to the child. The probabilities of this happening are much lower than when dominant traits are at issue. For one thing, both parents must have the recessive gene; if only one has it, the genetic material of the other parent will "cancel" the effects of the recessive gene. There is no way of looking at a person who is a carrier of a defective recessive gene and identifying him as such. The processes connected with genetic defects are complicated (over 100 different chromosomal abnormalities have been documented).[33] Rather than go into them here, the reader's attention is directed to *The*

Genetic, Metabolic, and Developmental Aspects of Mental Retardation,[34] and Prevention of Genetic Disease and Mental Retardation,[35] just two of many excellent books that explore the details of the etiology of mental retardation.

One other thing is noteworthy when one examines the causal link between mental retardation and genetic defects: mental retardation is a symptom, not a cause, of genetic defects. It is not a disease.

Acquired Physiological Causes

Acquired causes of mental retardation can occur before (prenatal), during (paranatal—sometimes referred to as perinatal, although the latter term specifically refers to the period from the twenty-ninth week of gestation to one to four weeks after birth), or after (postnatal) the birth of the child.

Prenatal Causes. A common prenatal cause of mental retardation is maternal infection. Some prenatal infections, such as rubella (German measles), immediately damage the fetus. If the mother contracts the infection during the first four weeks of pregnancy, the risk is 47 percent that the fetus will have problems.[36] Cytomegalovirus infections are now thought to be the most common viral causes of mental retardation. If the mother is infected, there is a 50 percent chance that the fetus will also "get" the damaging virus.[37] At least one prenatal maternal infection, syphilis, may not manifest its effects in the child until he reaches adolescence, when he begins to degenerate physically and mentally and to suffer seizures.

Physical agents such as prenatal irradiation, injury of the fetus through trauma, prenatal anoxia (often caused by compression of the umbilical cord, stopping the flow of oxygen to the fetus), or ingestion of toxic chemicals by the pregnant mother can also cause mental retardation. Virtually all drugs that a pregnant mother ingests pass through the placenta, thus entering the circulatory system of the fetus. One of the most alarming instances of maternal drug usage damaging children is seen in the Fetal Alcohol Syndrome. A child born of a mother with a history of alcohol abuse is likely to be jittery and poorly coordinated, to have a short attention span, behavioral problems, major craniofacial anomalies, and microcephaly, or to be mentally retarded.[38] Sells and Bennett studied twenty-three pregnant women who had a history of alcohol abuse and twenty-three pregnant non-alcoholics. The former group had an adverse pregnancy outcome in 43 percent of the cases, compared with a 2 percent adverse outcome for the control group. To wit, in the case of four of the pregnant alcoholics, the fetuses died prenatally. Six of this group's babies had Fetal Alcohol Syndrome.[39] It has been reported that in some regions of the country, Fetal Alcohol Syndrome is the "third most common cause of mental retardation."[40]

Maternal hormonal imbalances can also lead to mental retardation in children. Hypothyroidism (cretinism), which affects approximately 1 out of every 20,000 children, occurs if the mother does not have adequate quantitites of thyroid hormone thyroxine.[41]

Paranatal Causes. During birth, a number of things can go wrong and damage the child. He may suffer physical trauma, such as improper application of forceps to his head. His brain can be deprived of oxygen due to compression of the umbilical cord; this is called paranatal anoxia. Pelvic-head disproportions can lead to damaging compression of the child's skull as he passes through the birth canal. Asphyxia due to premature separation of the placenta is another fairly common paranatal cause of brain damage. Oversedation of the mother at birth can also retard a child. Another set of paranatal causes of retardation has to do with how long the birth takes. Prolonged labor (over thirty-six hours) and precipitous birth (under twenty minutes from the time the mother begins labor) are commonly associated with mental retardation.[42]

Premature birth, called a gestational disorder in medical literature, can be seen as both a prenatal (the factors that precipitate the premature birth) and a postnatal (the resulting damage taking place because of the newborn's inability to adapt to the nonuterine environment) cause of mental retardation. Premature infants are much more likely to be retarded than full-term babies.[43] Prematurity is associated with low birth weight. The lower the birth weight below six pounds, the greater the likelihood the child will be retarded.[44]

Very small babies are more prone to cerebral hemorrhage, hypoxia (deficiency of oxygen reaching body tissues), and immature renal function, among other things.[45] One significant and preventable cause of low-birth-weight babies is excessive smoking by the pregnant mother.[46] Mothers who have had fertility problems also run a special risk of giving birth to low-birth-weight infants.[47] Post maturity is another form of gestational disorder that is associated with mental retardation.[48]

Postnatal Causes. The postnatal causes of mental retardation are manifold. One common cause is postnatal anoxia, a subnormal oxygenation of blood and consequent brain damage. It often results from high body temperature, frequently the by-product of infections such as meningitis and encephalitis. Another symptom associated with infection that can be very dangerous to a child is severe diarrhea. This sometimes leads to a rapid loss of body fluids and a concomitant overabundance of salt in the child's system. The condition is called hypernatremic dehydration and can lead to brain hemorrhage in infants. Infant diarrhea is one of the leading causes of mental retardation in certain regions of the United States.[49] Brain tumors, electrical shocks, and traumas to the head are other common postnatal causes of mental retardation.

Many cases of damaging head trauma are not accidental. Kempe and his associates found that of 749 cases of child abuse they studied, 114 (28 percent) led to permanent brain damage.[50] Apthorp investigated 263 cases of child abuse that had been identified at the Children's Hospital of Los Angeles over several years. Of these cases, 138 involved head trauma, of which 79 were considered major and capable of creating permanent damage.[51] Not all such damage leads to mental retardation, but some children become retarded at the hands of abusive adults. More on this later.

After a child is born, the ingestion of certain toxins can lead to brain damage. A good case in point is lead poisoning, which has been estimated to retard between 6,000 and 8,000 people a year.[52] Until Public Law 91-695 (the Lead Based Paint Poisoning Prevention Act) was passed, the primary agent in retardation caused by lead poisoning was lead-based paint. Children, especially those living in slums, would eat bits of paint that had chipped off dilapidated walls and ceilings. In 1971, the American Academy of Pediatrics estimated that between 2 and 5 percent of the children living in urban slums showed signs of lead poisoning.[53]

Public Law 91-695 did not eradicate the problems of lead poisoning, though. For example, people living near freeways have been shown to have elevated levels of lead in their blood.[54] And this is just the tip of the iceberg: the whole environment is a chemical minefield. The continued pollution of our water, food, and air has deleterious effects on all of us—effects that may come to evince themselves with increasing regularity in the retardation of our children.

Social Causes

The social environment, as well as the physical, can retard people. For instance, a child's social milieu can be intellectually debilitating if he or she does not receive sufficient stimulation during the formative years. From research done on feral children[55] (children who have lived in the "wilds" and thus not been subject to human socialization) and from cross-cultural developmental inquiries,[56] it is apparent that, if a child reaches certain chronological milestones without having learned specific skills (talking is a good example), he will never learn those skills. Neglected children and physiologically normal children of mentally retarded parents are sometimes environmentally retarded due to understimulation.

Another connection between the social environment and mental retardation is apparent in a factor already alluded to—the relationship between socioeconomic status and intelligence test performance.[57] Cultural biases are inherent in some of the tests, but the extent to which those biases suppress IQ scores has not been ascertained precisely. In my opinion, the fact that more mentally retarded people come from the lower socioeconomic classes is not solely attributable to test biases. Certain predispositions of poor people and the living conditions to which they are subjected can lead to circumstances that retard their children's development.

For example, it has been shown that lower-class people characteristically have low levels of educational achievement and/or a lack of trust in education.[58] Lower-class parents may be unable or unwilling to motivate their children intellectually, and this can have an effect on the child's IQ-test performance. A high correlation is reported between parental encouragement of their children's learning and the scores these youngsters get on IQ tests.[59]

Other environmental factors help to explain the correlation between low IQ and poverty. Poor people frequently attend inferior schools. They either have second-rate health facilities or fail to use the good ones they have. Thus, prenatal care is often haphazard.

Lower-class women have a high incidence of chronic vascular disease, contracted pelvises, premature labor, toxemia, and malnutrition.[60] The latter is particularly disturbing, because a child born to a malnourished woman can suffer not only the neurological deficit occasioned by a poor intrauterine environment, but can then be "neurologically damaged" again in a malnourished postnatal environment.

Another biosocial factor that leads to retardation of babies in poor families is that the mothers tend to have their first pregnancy when they are very young and go on bearing children until they are relatively advanced in years.[61] Mothers below the age of sixteen and above the age of thirty-five are in high-risk categories, particularly with regard to problems arising from compressed birth canal for the younger women and to chromosomal abnormalities such as Down's Syndrome for women over thirty-five (although there has been a relative increase in the birth of Down's Syndrome children to mothers below the age of thirty-five since the late 1970s).[62] In 1970, Albee showed that of the 500,000 indigent mothers who delivered babies in public hospitals, one-fifth had some medical complications in pregnancy and birth.[63]

No one has thus far demonstrated irrefutably that poverty leads to mental retardation, only that there are correlates between poverty and retarding conditions. The point is that class-linked differences in IQ-test performance may not be attributable as much to biases in the tests as to inequalities in the society.

In some quarters, little stock is put in social-environmental explanations of the correlation between poverty and intelligence. A. R. Jensen is the chief spokesman of the hereditarian viewpoint, which holds that there are more retarded persons from the lower classes because of an inherent genetic inferiority among lower-class persons (the focus of Jensen's research has been black people[64]). There is scant scientific evidence to support the hereditarian viewpoint, but the environmental-heredity controversy persists.

Environmentalists contend that their viewpoint is substantiated in the distribution of different degrees of retardation by social class. A disproportionate number of *mildly* retarded people are from the lower socioeconomic classes, while those with moderate, severe, and profound degrees of retardation are proportionately represented among all socioeconomic levels.[65]

Moderate, severe, and profound degrees of retardation are generally associated with identifiable physical disorders, 40 percent being attributable to genetic disease, 20 percent to environmental causes such as perinatal infection and anoxia, and the rest being unexplainable.[66] Only 15 to 20 percent of the cases of mild retardation are clearly caused by "gross clinical findings," that is, something "wrong" with the person's body.[67] The implication is that environmental conditions are largely responsible for the remaining 80 to 85 percent of mild forms of mental retardation.

Hereditarians object to such reasoning, stating that the more severe types of mental retardation would be disproportionately high for lower socioeconomic groups (just as is the case with mild retardation) were it not for the fact that "the infant mortality rate is higher among lower social classes."[68] In other words, if their babies did not die younger than the infants of the more affluent classes, poor people would, according to the hereditarians, have a greater proportion of retarded children in all categories of severity. Environmentalists argue that, even if this were the case, it does not prove that poor people come from an inferior "gene pool."

Eaves and her associates discovered some interesting evidence to bolster the environmentalist viewpoint. They found that the effect of socioeconomic status on IQ does not start to manifest itself until children are between two and one-half and four years of age.[69] Toddlers seem to start out on an equal footing intellectually, but drift apart because of . . . something.

Hereditarians defend their viewpoint by citing the fact that a high proportion of parents of mentally retarded children are retarded themselves.[70] Garber found that the IQ of the mother was a more significant factor in predicting retardation among children than the mother's socioeconomic status.[71] In another study "the probability of having a retarded child was 14 times greater for the retarded mother than the controls."[72] Whether this is primarily a function of an inferior genetic heritage or the inadequate stimulation that low-IQ parents are able to provide for their offspring is debatable. When Heber found that mothers whose IQs were below 80 "contributed four-fifths of the children with IQs under 80,"[73] he was unsure whether this supported the environmentalist or the hereditarian viewpoint. So he put the issue to test. He selected a sample of eighty infants from "high-risk" families, placing half of the children in a full-time experimental day care program when they were three months of age. The other half acted as a control group. When the children were six and a half years of age, the IQs of both groups were tested. The mean IQ for the experimental group was 124; the mean for the control group was 94.[74]

There are other hereditarian arguments that stem from studies done on twins. In one such study, it was shown that twins who are reared apart from each other develop very similarly intellectually.[75] In another, the IQs of adopted children were shown to be more closely related to their biological parents than to those who adopted them.[76] Inquiries that show conflicting results with this study, say the hereditarians, do not take into account the fact that high-IQ children are usually placed with high-IQ adoptive parents.[77] The hereditarian arsenal is somewhat depleted when one examines Golden and Bridger's debunkery of the statistical presuppositions of both the twin and adoption studies.[78]

The most reasonable approach to the environmentalist-hereditarian controversy as it relates to mentally retarded persons is to give each side its due. It is possible that a disproportionate number of poor and retarded people do not come from particularly intelligent "stock." It is probable that, whether a person is genetically inferior in intelligence or not, if he lives in a poor intrauterine environment and is born into an impoverished social milieu, the deck is stacked against him.

What is conclusive is that a poor child has a much greater likelihood of being labeled as retarded than does a child from the middle- and upper-classes—from four[79] to fifteen[80] times as great a likelihood, depending upon which study one chooses to believe. Again, this tendency may not have as much to do with genetic heritage or environment as with the labeling process itself. For example, one investigation found that when people are matched for disability, those from the lower socioeconomic classes will be diagnosed as mentally retarded, while those of higher socioeconomic status will be diagnosed as having something else wrong with them.[81] Learning disability, autism, or emotional disorders would be relevant examples. Smith and Greenberg found that teachers discriminate against students of lower socioeconomic status in labeling them as retarded.[82] Mental retardation may not be the exclusive province of poor people, but they do seem to be given a priority on the label.

Unknown Causes

The final etiological category of mental retardation is that of unknown causes. There are approximately 250 known causes of mental handicaps, and yet, in from 75 to 85 percent of the cases that are labeled as retarded, no specific cause can be determined.[83] In pondering this figure, one gets some insight into the frustration that confronts so many parents and diagnosticians in dealing with mental handicaps.

DIAGNOSIS

The diagnostic sequence reflects some of the confusion occasioned by the complexity of etiology. While "significantly subaverage general intellectual functioning" is usually "objectified" through IQ tests and adaptive behavior scales, the suspicion that a child may be subject to intellectual deficits can arise even before his birth.

This suspicion is always present for parents who are in a high-risk category of having a retarded child. If, for example, a woman has had rubella in the early stages of her pregnancy, the risks are substantial that her child will have a handicap.

Certain technologies that fall under the generic heading of genetic counseling—things such as amniocentesis—can help a physician ascertain if a fetus will have genetic anomalies. More on this in a later chapter.

Physicians can frequently tell whether a child will have developmental problems immediately after the youngster is born. For example, newborns are typically given an Apgar test, which rates certain vital signs. Signs falling below acceptable limits on this test correlate with potentially handicapping conditions in the child's future. There are other tests given at birth such as that to detect the metabolic disorder PKU. Not incidentally, if PKU is detected early enough, most—if not all—of the damage it does can be prevented.

A physician can frequently just look at a baby and determine if the child has certain handicapping conditions. For example, a doctor can usually give a visual diagnosis of Down's Syndrome. This is not, however, the case for many other serious disorders. The persistent myth that retarded children (and adults for that matter) always look "retarded" is refuted by Menolascino, who cites cases in which severely and profoundly retarded children have "won photographic baby contests."[84] Visual diagnoses are, of course, verified with genetic testing. Indeed, such screenings are increasingly used for most cases in which the physician has suspicions that there is something wrong with a child.

As a child gets older, the diagnostic indications that he or she may be retarded hinge increasingly on the failure to reach developmental milestones. A child showing significant delays in these will usually be subjected to neurological assessments and to infant adaptive behavior tests and IQ tests. Although the predictive validity of the latter are questionable, as we have seen, Schmitt and Erickson hold that children who are diagnosed as mentally retarded early in life tend to be functioning at retarded levels three to six years later.[85] No one has, however, determined very rigorously how much of this is attributable to the self-fulfilling nature of the early labeling experience.

The newest organizational facilitant to the diagnostic process is the team approach. As we shall see, diagnostic teams are comprised of professionals who have expertise in virtually every aspect of a child's physical and social development.

Finally, by the time a child reaches school, he or she is generally the subject of routine intelligence testing, which can raise the issue of developmental delays that have been missed in other stages of the diagnostic sequence. Intelligence testing in the schools is no longer compulsory in certain locales, yet if a student is performing badly in his schoolwork, he will almost certainly be assessed. With the passage of Public Law 94-142 (the Education for all Handicapped Children Act of 1975), it is now incumbent on school districts to engage in child-find procedures. This means that the district or its representatives are required to develop strategies for identifying children with real or potential developmental delays who have not come to the attention of service providers. This is especially important for young children who require early intervention.

PREVALENCE OF MENTAL RETARDATION

The prevalence rates of mental retardation are just as puzzling as its etiology and as convoluted as the diagnostic spectrum in certain respects. For example, estimates of rates of retardation vary from "less than 1% to almost 20%."[86] The extreme variability in these estimates is largely a function of differences in criteria for identifying people with mental handicaps. Some estimates are based on census data, some on agency studies wherein professionals who provide direct care identify the retarded population, and some on sample surveys. Additionally, there are those prevalence figures based on statistical extrapolations from hypothetically posited normal curves. When these are used, well above 2 percent of the people living in the United States are found to be mentally retarded. According to the Stanford-Binet Test, 2.6 percent of the population have IQs below 69.[87] On the basis of the Wechsler,

2.2 percent of the people are considered to be mentally retarded.[88] In 1962, the President's Committee on Mental Retardation advocated a 3 percent figure, meaning there were 6.3 million retarded people in the United States.[89] As of 1976, thirty-nine states still accepted this figure as the correct prevalence rate.[90] (European rates fairly closely accord with the 3 percent figures as well.[91])

When the prevalence figures are broken down by labeled degree of mental retardation, mildly retarded people constitute 89 percent of the total population of mentally handicapped individuals, with moderately retarded people being 6 percent, severely retarded 3.5 percent, and profoundly retarded persons 1.5 percent.[92] The majority of people with IQs below 50 are multihandicapped, having any number of other physical disorders in conjuction with their mental handicaps.[93]

There is a burgeoning controversy about the accuracy of the 3 percent prevalence rate so widely accepted in the field of mental retardation. Tarjan and his colleagues believe that a 1 percent figure more closely reflects the reality of prevalence.[94] They give a number of reasons why they believe the lower figure to be more appropriate. First, they cite the familiar argument that IQs below 70 cannot be accurate barometers of mental retardation if they presuppose a symmetrical distribution curve where one may not exist. Second, diagnoses change, and many people labeled as mentally retarded at one point in their lives will not be considered as such at others. This has to do with age fluctuations in the labeling process. For example, fewer children are identified as mentally retarded during infancy and early childhood than when they are in school.[95] Tobias says that in many urban schools, over 50 percent of the children with IQs below 65 are not identified as retarded until after the fifth grade, this presumably happening as a result of the tests administered to sixth graders before they enter junior high school.[96]

In any case, after the years of compulsory formal education, the period when the highest prevalence of mental retardation is noted, the prevalence rates decline. After an adolescent who has been labeled as retarded in school leaves the academic setting, official case-finding agencies tend to lose track of him. When intellectual abilities are no longer a matter of "official" concern, many mentally retarded people are able to "slip back" into society, their handicaps going unnoticed. This is paralleled by another phenomenon that has less to do with age than with culture. I am talking about what has come to be called the "six hour retarded child," who adapts perfectly well to his own culture eighteen hours a day, but is "retarded" for the six hours he is in school.

The prevalence issue has been further complicated by a recently released census-based calculation done by Jones.[97] He indicates that only 0.43 percent of the population (866,320 persons) are mentally retarded. The empirical evidence to support this, the 1 percent, or the 3 percent figure is equally inconclusive. Given the murky nature of our definitions of mental retardation and the vague etiological and diagnostic qualities associated with mental handicaps, it is not too surprising that we are imprecise in our understanding of how many people are retarded.

COMMUNITY AND SEX PREVALENCE CHARACTERISTICS

The prevalence of mental retardation is differentially distributed on two demographic factors that have, so far, gone unmentioned: (1) community characteristics, and (2) sex. There is a general tendency for mental retardation to be proportionally more prevalent in rural than in urban areas.[98] These differences may be attributable to four factors associated with rural locations: (1) fewer educational opportunities, (2) overall lower level of environmental stimulation, (3) fewer remedial services, and (4) lower economic status of rural populations that subjects them to the covariations between mental retardation and poverty. The first and second of these factors are doubtless very inflammatory to rural people, who are proud of their schools and feel that the rural environment has a much richer kind of stimulation than the city. Nonetheless, migration studies show that intelligence test scores rise significantly when children move from rural to urban areas.[99]

There is a significant preponderance of mentally retarded males.[100] The figures are imprecise, but somewhere in the area of 55 to 70 percent of the people labeled as retarded are male.[101] Why? First, there are physiological factors such as recessive genetic tendencies that affect males more than females. A case in point is the recently discovered chromosomal abnormality, "Fragile X Syndrome," that only affects boys.[102] It is speculated that Fragile X Syndrome is second only to Down's Syndrome as a genetic cause of mental retardation.[103]

A second reason there is a disproportionate number of males who are mentally retarded is that boys are more vulnerable to complications in their mothers' pregnancies and to the effects of premature birth than are girls.[104]

Third, there are sociological explanations for the preponderance of retarded boys. Traditionally defined sex roles in our culture have, until very recent years, led to greater social acceptance of intellectual incompetence in women than in men. I am *not* suggesting that those role expectations were right, only that they have existed and that, as a result, the incompetence of men may have been more apparent and labelable.

REPRISE

Mental retardation is a concept fraught with complexities and controversies. In many ways, the basics have not even been agreed upon. The definition is multidimensional and parts of it generate controversy. The use of the concept as a label is not acceptable to all professionals in the field.

Mental retardation is not, as it is sometimes mistakenly believed to be, a homogeneous condition. There are many degrees of functional variation. There are many causes, some physiological, some social, some mysterious. And there is no hard and fast rule as to when a person will be diagnosed as mentally retarded—some diagnoses coming before birth, some as late as adolescence.

Finally, we do not really know how much of the population is retarded. In the first chapter of this work, it was suggested that mental retardation is a phenomenon that should receive more attention because retarded people constitute a significant minority. As we have seen, precise prevalence rates are hard to come by. If, however, we postulate the 3 percent prevalence rate, the immediate effect of mentally retarded people in our society can be seen. Even if only 0.5 percent of the population is mentally handicapped, retarded people are still a sizable minority. If we then add the people who live with retarded persons (Kurtz speculated on available data that the number could be as high as 15 to 20 million non-retarded individuals)[105] and the people who derive their livelihoods from working with retarded persons, the proportions of mental retardation as a social issue begin to become clearer. It is time that the issues surrounding mental retardation become a familiar component of the public consciousness.

NOTES

1. E. F. Ware, "Whist," in H. Felleman, ed., *Poems that Live Forever*, New York: Doubleday, 1965, p. 311.

2. H. J. Grossman, ed., *Manual on Terminology and Classification in Mental Retardation*, Baltimore: Gramond/Pridemark, for the American Association on Mental Deficiency, Special Publication Series no. 2, 1973, p. 11.

3. J. Adams, "Adaptive Behavior and Measured Intelligence in the Classification of Mental Retardation," *American Journal of Mental Deficiency*, 78:1973, p. 80.

4. R. A. Kurtz, *Social Aspects of Mental Retardation*, Lexington, Mass.: Lexington Books, 1977, p. 23.

5. K. G. Scott, "Learning Theory, Intelligence, and Mental Development," *American Journal of Mental Deficiency*, 82:1977, p. 325.

6. J. Wortis, "Poverty and Retardation: Biosocial Factors," *Mental Retar-*

dation—An Annual Review, 1:1970, p. 277; W. E. Stephens, "Mainstreaming: Some Natural Limitations," *Mental Retardation*, 13:1975, p. 40; R. C. Scheerenberger, "Mental Retardation: Definition, Classification, and Prevalence," in J. H. Rothstein, ed., *Mental Retardation: Readings and Resources*, New York: Holt, Rinehart, and Winston, 1971, p. 19; L. M. Dunn, ed., *Exceptional Children in the Schools: Special Education in Transition*, New York: Holt, Rinehart, and Winston, 1973, cited in F. W. Litton, *Education of the Trainable Mentally Retarded*, St. Louis: C. V. Mosby, 1978, p. 12.

7. A. T. Russell and P. E. Tanguay, "Mental Illness and Mental Retardation: Cause or Coincidence?" *American Journal of Mental Deficiency*, 85:1981, p. 573.

8. D. Ellis, "Visual Handicaps of Mentally Handicapped People," *American Journal of Mental Deficiency*, 83:1979, pp. 497–511.

9. R. B. Edgerton, *The Cloak of Competence: Stigma in the Lives of the Mentally Retarded*, Berkeley: University of California Press, 1967, p. 4.

10. K. D. Gadow and J. Kalachnik, "Prevalence and Pattern of Drug Treatment for the Behavior and Seizure Disorders of TMR Students," *American Journal of Mental Deficiency*, 85:1981, pp. 588–595.

11. L. G. Peters, "Concepts of Mental Deficiency Among the Tamang of Nepal," *American Journal of Mental Deficiency*, 84:1980, p. 356.

12. R. A. Kurtz, p. 23.

13. J. F. Jacobs and C. A. DeGraff, "Expectancy and Race: Their Influences on Intelligence Test Scores," *Exceptional Children*, 40:1973, p. 108.

14. A. Abeson and J. Zettel, "The End of the Quiet Revolution: The Education for All Handicapped Children Act of 1975," *Exceptional Children*, 44:1977, p. 118, quoting from F. J. Weintraub, "Recent Influences of Law Regarding the Identification and Educational Placement of Children," *Focus on Exceptional Children*, 4:1972, p. 4.

15. *Diana v. The State Board of Education*, Civil Action No. C-7037 R.F.P. (N.D. Cal., Jan. 7, 1970, and June 18, 1973).

16. *Larry P. v. Riles*, Civil Action No. 6-71-2270 343 F. Supp. 1036 (N.D. Cal., 1972).

17. A. Abeson and J. Zettel, p. 119.

18. "A Court Ban on IQ Tests," *Newsweek*, October 29, 1979, p. 59.

19. National Association for Retarded Citizens, *It Can Happen to Anyone*, Arlington, Texas: The Association, p. 10.

20. R. Schmitt and M. T. Erickson, "Early Predictors of Mental Retardation," *Mental Retardation*, 11:1973, pp. 27–28.

21. J. R. Mercer, "IQ: The Lethal Label," *Psychology Today*, September 1972, p. 47.

22. E. Zigler and S. Hartner, "The Socialization of the Mentally Retarded," in D. A. Goslin, ed., *Handbook of Socialization Theory and Research*, Chicago: Rand McNally, 1969, p. 1078.

23. R. W. Conley, "Mental Retardation—An Economist's Approach," *Mental Retardation*, 14:1976, p. 20.

24. R. Rosenthal and L. Jacobson, *Pygmalion in the Classroom: Teacher Expectation and Pupils' Intellectual Development*, New York: Holt, Rinehart, and Winston, 1968.

25. D. L. MacMillan, *Mental Retardation in School and Society*, Boston: Little, Brown and Co., 1977, p. 177.

26. L. Rowitz, "A Sociological Perspective on Labeling in Mental Retardation," *Mental Retardation*, 19(2):1981, p. 49.

27. D. L. MacMillan, R. L. Jones, and G. F. Aloia, "The Mentally Retarded Label: A Review of Research and Theoretical Analysis," *American Journal of Mental Deficiency*, 79:1974, pp. 241–261.

28. S. L. Guskin, "Theoretical and Empirical Strategies for the Study of the Labeling of Mentally Retarded Persons," *International Review of Research in Mental Retardation*, 9:1978, p. 140.

29. Ibid., p. 129.

30. H. D. Love and W. H. Osborne, *Early Childhood Education*, Springfield, Ill.: Charles C. Thomas, 1972, cited in H. D. Love, *The Mentally Retarded Child and His Family*, Springfield, Ill.: Charles C. Thomas, 1973, p. 38.

31. B. R. Gearheart and F. W. Litton, *The Trainable Retarded: A Foundations Approach*, St. Louis: C. V. Mosby, 1975. Table taken from pp. 22 and 23, except for standard deviations.

32. W. Sloan and J. W. Birch, "A Rationale for Degrees of Retardation," *American Journal of Mental Deficiency*, 60:1955, p. 262; H. Leland, "Some Thoughts on the Current Status of Adaptive Behavior," *Mental Retardation*, 2:1964, pp. 173, 175.

33. J. M. Berg, "Genetics and Genetic Counseling," *Mental Retardation and Developmental Disabilities*, 8:1976, p. 42.

34. R. F. Murray and P. L. Rosser, eds., *The Genetic, Metabolic, and Developmental Aspects of Mental Retardation*, Springfield, Ill.: Charles C. Thomas, 1972.

35. A Milunsky, ed., *Prevention of Genetic Disease and Mental Retardation*, Philadelphia: W. B. Saunders, 1975.

36. R. H. Michaels and G. W. Mellin, "Prospective Experience with Maternal Rubella and the Associated Congenital Malformation," *Pediatrics*, 26:1960, pp. 200–209.

37. C. J. Sells and F. C. Bennett, "Prevention of Mental Retardation: The Role of Medicine," *American Journal of Mental Deficiency*, 82:1977, p. 122.

38. Ibid., p. 121; The National Foundation/March of Dimes, *When You Drink, Your Unborn Baby Does Too!*, White Plains, N.Y.: The Foundation, n.d., p. 2.

39. C. J. Sells and F. C. Bennett, p. 121.

40. The National Foundation/March of Dimes, p. 3.

41. B. R. Gearheart and F. W. Litton, p. 47.

42. D.J.P. Barker, "Low Intelligence: Its Relation to Length of Gestation and Rate of Fetal Growth," *British Journal of Preventive and Social Medicine*, 20:1966, p. 61.

43. S. A. Perkins, "Malnutrition and Mental Development," *Exceptional Children*, 43:1977, p. 216.

44. R. Koch and J. H. Koch, "Retarded Children," *Psychology Today*, December 1976, p. 90.

45. J. B. Hardy, "Perinatal Factors and Intelligence," in S. F. Osler and R. E. Cooke, eds., *The Biosocial Basis of Mental Retardation*, Baltimore: Johns Hopkins Press, 1965, p. 50.

46. American College of Obstetricians and Gynecologists, *Cigarette Smoking and Pregnancy*, Bulletin no. 53, Chicago: Resource Center, ACOG, 1979.

47. C. M. Drillien, "Complications of Pregnancy and Delivery," *Mental Retardation—An Annual Review*, 1:1970, p. 293.

48. H. J. Grossman, p. 35.

49. M. Yoeli, G. P. Scheinesson, and B. J. Hargreaves, "Infectious Diseases in Etiology," *Mental Retardation and Developmental Disabilities*, 9:1977, p. 90.

50. C. H. Kempe, F. N. Silverman, B. F. Steele, W. Droegemueller, and H. K. Silver, "The Battered Child Syndrome," *Journal of the American Medical Association*, 181:1962, pp. 17–24.

51. J. S. Apthorp, "The Battered Child," in C. R. Angle and E. A. Bering, Jr., eds., *Physical Trauma as an Etiological Agent in Mental Retardation*, Omaha: National Institute of Neurological Diseases and Stroke, 1968, cited in M. Yoeli et al., p. 51.

52. R. S. Challop, "Estimation of Childhood Lead Poisoning in the United States," *Mental Retardation*, 9:1971, p. 46.

53. B. R. Gearheart and F. W. Litton, p. 32.

54. H. V. Thermas, B. K. Milmor, G. A. Heidbreder, and B. A. Kagan, "Bloodlevels of Persons Living Near Expressways," *Archives of Environmental Health*, 15:1967, p. 695.

55. I. Malson, *Wolf Children and the Problems of Human Nature*, New York: Monthly Review Press, 1972.

56. K. Dennis, "Children of the Creche: Conclusions and Implications," in A. M. Clarke and A.D.B. Clarke, eds., *Early Experience: Myth and Evidence*, London: Open Books, 1976.

57. R. Lapouse and M. Weitzner, "Epidemiology," *Mental Retardation—An Annual Review*, 1:1970, p. 208.

58. J. H. Meyerowitz and B. Farber, "Family Background of Educable Mentally Retarded Children," in B. Farber, ed., *Kinship and Family Organization*, New York: Wiley, 1966, cited in B. Farber, *Mental Retardation: Its Social Context and Social Consequences*, Boston: Houghton Mifflin, 1968, pp. 166–167.

59. B. Farber, *Mental Retardation: Its Social Context and Social Consequences*, Boston: Houghton Mifflin, 1968, pp. 85–86.

60. S. A. Perkins, p. 216.

61. Ibid., p. 215.

62. D. E. Zarfas and Lucille C. Wolf, "Maternal Age Patterns and the Incidence of Down's Syndrome," *American Journal of Mental Deficiency*, 83:1979, p. 358.

63. G. W. Albee, "Needed . . . A Revolution in Caring for the Retarded," in A. L. Strauss, ed., *Where Medicine Fails*, Chicago: Aldine, 1970, p. 34.

64. Two of Jensen's most expressive works are "A Theory of Primary and Secondary Familial Mental Retardation," *International Review of Research in Mental Retardation*, 4:1970, pp. 33–106; and *Genetics and Education*, New York: Harper and Row, 1972.

65. R. Lapouse and M. Weitzner, p. 209; F. W. Litton, *Education of the Trainable Mentally Retarded*, St. Louis: C. V. Mosby, 1978, p. 12.

66. J. Thoene, J. Higgins, I. Krieger, R. Schmickel, and L. Weiss, "Genetic Screening for Mental Retardation in Michigan," *American Journal of Mental Deficiency*, 85:1981, p. 339.

67. C. F. Benda, N. D. Squires, N. D. Ogonik, and R. Wise, "Personality Factors in Mild Mental Retardation. Part I: Family Background and Socio-Cultural Patterns," *American Journal of Mental Deficiency*, 68:1963, p. 38.

68. Ibid.

69. L. Eaves, J. Nuttall, H. Konoff, and H. Dunn, "Developmental and Psychological Test Scores in Children of Low Birth Weight," *Pediatrics*, 45:1970, p. 19.

70. C. F. Benda et al., p. 36.

71. H. Garber, "The Milwaukee Project: An Experiment in the Prevention of Cultural-Familial Mental Retardation—Intervention at Birth," in M. S. Bass and M. Gelof, eds., *Sexual Rights and Responsibilities of the Mentally Retarded*, Santa Barbara, Calif.: 1387 E. Valley Rd., 1975, pp. 70–86.

72. Ibid.

73. R. Heber and H. Garber, An Experiment in the Prevention of Cultural-Familial Mental Retardation, Madison: Rehabilitation Research and Training Center in Mental Retardation, University of Wisconsin, Progress Report, 1972, cited in B. Birns and W. Bridger, "Cognitive Development and Social Class," *Mental Retardation and Developmental Disabilities*, 9:1977, p. 212.

74. Ibid.

75. B. Farber, p. 90.

76. A. Kushlick and R. Blunden, "The Epidemiology of Mental Subnormality," in A. M. Clarke, and A.D.B. Clarke, eds., *Mental Deficiency: The Changing Outlook*, rev. ed., New York: The Free Press, 1965, p. 53.

77. Ibid.

78. M. Golden and W. Bridger, "A Refutation of Jensen's Position on Intelligence, Race, Social Class, and Heredity," *Mental Hygiene*, 53(4):1969, p. 651.

79. R. W. Conley, p. 21.

80. G. Tarjan, S. W. Wright, R. K. Eyman, and C. V. Keeran, "The Natural History of Mental Deficiency in a State Hospital," *A.M.A. Journal of Diseases of Children*, 96:1958, pp. 64–70.

81. W. L. Neer, D. A. Foster, J. G. Jones, and D. A. Reynolds, "Socioeconomic Bias in the Diagnosis of Mental Retardation," *Exceptional Children*, 40:1973, pp. 38–39.

82. I. L. Smith and S. Greenberg, "Teacher Attitudes and the Labeling Process," *Exceptional Children*, 41:1975, p. 323.

83. The President's Committee on Mental Retardation, *The Decisive Decade*, Washington, D.C.: U.S. Government Printing Office, 1970, p. 10; National Association for Retarded Citizens, *Facts on Mental Retardation*, Arlington, Texas: The Association, 1973; G. W. Albee, p. 29; K. G. Scott, p. 330.

84. F. J. Menolascino, "Emotional Disturbances in Institutional Retardates:

Primitive, Atypical and Abnormal Behaviors," *Mental Retardation*, 10(6):1972, p. 4.

85. R. Schmitt and M. T. Erickson, p. 27.

86. R. W. Conley, p. 20.

87. H. J. Grossman, p. 35.

88. Ibid.

89. B. R. Gearheart and F. W. Litton, p. 26.

90. R. E. Luckey and R. Neman, "Practices in Estimating Mental Retardation Prevalence," *Mental Retardation*, 14:1976, p. 17.

91. B. Farber, p. 63.

92. A. M. Clarke and A.D.B. Clarke eds., *Mental Deficiency: The Changing Outlook*, 3rd ed., New York: The Free Press, 1974, p. 2.

93. M. L. Rutter, "Psychiatry," *Mental Retardation—An Annual Review*, 3:1971, p. 195.

94. G. Tarjan, S. W. Wright, R. K. Eyman, and C. V. Keeran, "Natural History of Mental Retardation: Some Aspects of Epidemiology," *American Journal of Mental Deficiency*, 77:1973, pp. 369–379.

95. B. Farber, p. 69.

96. J. Tobias, "Vocational Adjustment of Young Retarded Adults," *Mental Retardation*, 8(3):1970, p. 14.

97. L. A. Jones, "Census-Based Prevalence Estimates for Mental Retardation," *Mental Retardation*, 17(4):1979, p. 199.

98. R. Lapouse and M. Weitzner, p. 211; B. Farber, p. 78.

99. B. Farber, p. 97; R. Lapouse and M. Weitzner, p. 211.

100. B. Farber, p. 73.

101. National Association for Retarded Citizens, "Defect in Sex Chromosome Reveals Why Retardation Effects More Males," *Mental Retardation News*, 28(5):1979, p. 1.

102. G. Turner, A. Daniel, and M. Frost, "X-linked Mental Retardation, Macro-Orchidism, and the Xq27 Fragile Site," *The Journal of Pediatrics*, 96:1980, pp. 837–841.

103. G. McBride, "Fragile X Chromosome Related to Mental Retardation in Males," *Journal of the American Medical Association*, 242:1979, p. 1829.

104. C. M. Drillien, pp. 280–297.

105. R. A. Kurtz, p. 71.

3
History:
Separate Worlds and
Intellectual Gatecrashing

. . . the offspring of the inferior, or of the better when they chance to be deformed, will be put away in some mysterious, unknown place. . . .
—Plato[1]

TARDOCIDE

Throughout history, social attitudes toward mentally retarded people have been characterized by a paradoxical mixture of cruelty and indifference. Some of the first literary references to mentally handicapped people appear in a Greek work dated 1552 B.C.[2] In this work, retarded people were called "monsters." The sentiments inherent in the term were often translated into social action. For example, the Spartan lawgiver, Lycurgus (ca. 900 B.C.), prescribed death for "idiots" in an attempt to keep Spartan society free of defectives.[3] This "cleansing" was usually effected by throwing the defectives off of cliffs or drowning them in the Eurotas River.[4] Another common practice was the abandonment of retarded people in the wilderness. While this may have assuaged the sensibilities of citizens queasy about murder, such ostracisms were tantamount to a sentence of death for many retarded persons who could not care for themselves under survival conditions.

DISPLAY

Some mentally retarded people avoided the consequences of tardocide or banishment by becoming the objects of display and amusement for the rich. As early as 4 B.C., there are records of wealthy Romans, such as Seneca, keeping retarded persons in their homes to amuse visitors.[5] The amusement value of "court defectives" did not lose its appeal quickly, either. The Aztec king Montezuma (ca. 1520) had a large "collection" of defective people. Montezuma is said to have housed them "after the manner of a modern park zoo."[6] As late as the seventeenth century, the monarch Philip IV of Spain (1621–1665) kept a sizable complement of mentally and physically handicapped people at his court. The lives of these people are chronicled in the works of Velasquez (1599–1660), Philip's court artist.[7] There is evidence that Philip treated his court "fools" compassionately, if there ever can be compassion in servitude. In virtually all cases, the human pets of the rich and powerful were functional beyond their amusement value, since they performed household duties—usually without remuneration.[8] It is ironic that the first step in the amelioration of retarded persons was the upward mobility of becoming slaves.

The display of retarded people was not entirely the province of the well-to-do. Foucault says that "insane" people were displayed during the early Middle Ages by chaining them to, or encaging them at, the city gates.[9] Although Foucault's choice of words is limited to "insane" people, it is not too bold to assume that some of these people were actually mentally retarded. One does find an occasional historical reference that distinguishes between mental illness and mental retardation. For example, during the reign of Edward I in England from 1272 to 1307, a distinction was made between "fools" and "lunatics." The king could take possession of the lunatic's property only during the period of his illness, while the fool's property "reverted permanently to the Crown."[10] For the most part, though, the histories of mentally retarded and mentally ill people seem to be so intertwined until the middle of the nineteenth century as to be synonymous. As we shall see, there is a modern stereotype that still erroneously equates the two.

The display of retarded people was given greater mobility in the early Middle Ages. During this period, in the rivers of the Rhineland and on the Flemish canals, "ships of fools" sailed from port to port exhibiting their cargoes of defective humanity to the fascination of the local citizenry.[11] These ships had the functional value of ostracizing retarded people without seriously eroding the amusement value that had come to be associated with them.

THE RELIGIOUS CURE

The great organized religions have had a somewhat checkered history with regard to their efforts on behalf of retarded people. There are some religiously based admonitions to treat retarded persons in a kindly manner. In the first Epistle to the Thessalonians, St. Paul recommended "charity for the feebleminded."[12] Saint Nicholas Thaumaturges advocated

the protection of mentally retarded people as early as the fourth century
A.D.[13] Clarke and Clarke point out that "the word 'cretin' is derived
from the French *'chrétien'* (Christian) and is testimony to the fact that
in early times severely handicapped were cared for by monastic communities."[14] In the *Koran*, one sees injunctions to believers to clothe
retarded people and speak kindly unto them.[15] Such sentiments notwithstanding, the destructive social effects of organized religion on the
lives of retarded persons have often eclipsed those that were salutary.

For instance, the Protestant Reformers relegated mental retardation
to a form of satanic unreason. Because retarded people were usually
thought to be "possessed," many were tortured or killed to exorcise
demons.[16] Indeed, since retarded people were thought to be the servants
of Satan, many clerics argued that they should be treated more harshly
than mere criminals, such as murderers.[17] A quote from Martin Luther
recapitulates the attitudes of many of his fellow reformers. He wrote,

> Eight years ago, there was one at Dessau whom I, Martin Luther, saw
> and grappled with. He was twelve years old, had the use of his eyes
> and all his senses, so that one might think that he was a normal child.
> But he did nothing but gorge himself as much as four peasants or threshers.
> He ate, defecated, and drooled and if anyone tackled him, he screamed.
> If things didn't go well, he wept. So I said to the Prince of Anhalt: "If
> I were the Prince, I should take this child to the Moldau River which
> flows near Dessau and drown him." But the Prince refused to follow my
> advice. Thereupon I said: "Well, then the Christians shall order the Lord's
> Prayer to be said in church and pray that the dear Lord take the Devil
> away."[18]

To Luther, this retarded boy was *masa carnis*, with the devil infusing
that part of him where his soul should reside. To kill him was, to
Luther, to destroy one more base of operations for Satan.

The same "Christian" attitude displayed by Luther was also pervasive
in Calvinistic New England. Retarded people (and those with mental
disorders) were often considered practitioners of witchcraft. Accordingly,
many of them were "tortured, hanged, and burned on this suspicion."[19]
Baker suggests that Catholics were not inculpable of excesses similar
to those of the Protestants.[20]

Even some of the scientific works of the sixteenth century occasionally
exhibited condemnatory religious overtones regarding retarded people.
Paracelsus, the most progressive physician-chemist of his time, in 1530
wrote what was probably the first "medical" work on mental retardation,
called "On the Begetting of Fools."[21] In it, Paracelsus mused about why
God would create beings unable to appreciate the sacrifice Jesus had

made on the cross and concluded that the reason humans, and not animals, have mentally retarded offspring is attributable to the Fall of Adam.[22]

In the wake of the excesses of the Reformation, there were some attitudinal and practical reactions of a religious origin that would begin to improve the lot of retarded persons. One attitudinal change occurred during the Renaissance, when the notion of retarded people as "divine gifts" came into prominence. Retarded children were sometimes called *les enfants du bon Dieu*. Unlike the Reformers, who viewed retardation as a sign of Providence meting out judgment to punish the wickedness of the retarded child's parents, some of the vanguard of the Renaissance viewed these children as "blessed" signs on the parents' houses. Tycho Brahe (1546–1601), the first great observational astronomer of the Renaissance, is said to have believed that retarded people kept counsel with God. Tycho reportedly kept a retarded (and probably epileptic) male as a close companion "in hopes that his mutterings would provide divine revelation."[23]

An impetus similar to that motivating Brahe had probably been operable several centuries earlier in the Belgian village of Gheel. Apparently a story circulated around Europe that several "idiots" had been cured while watching the slaying of a princess in Gheel. As a result, mentally retarded persons from all over Europe headed, or were sent, to Gheel with the thought of their being cured. Of course, the story was apocryphal, and Gheel became overpopulated with mentally handicapped people. In response to the dilemma occasioned by this, many of the wealthy people of Gheel took the surplus population into their homes, not only to provide cheap labor, but because of the belief that had sprung up, that retarded people were special children of God.[24] The Gheel experience probably represents the first instance in history wherein multitudes of mentally retarded people were treated in a relatively humane manner. It was, however, something of a historical aberration.

ASYLUMS

The first widespread practical advances on behalf of mentally retarded people came in the form of asylums designed to segregate and protect these individuals from the social brutalities that had beset them for centuries. The most important of these asylums were largely the work of clerics who had certainly heard of, if not internalized, the "divine gift" idea.

There is little agreement on when the first asylum was established. Some historians hold that the Hospital dels Folls, founded in Valencia in 1409 by a man named Bernardo Andreau, was the first.[25] Other historians credit Vincent de Paul (1576–1660) with establishing the first sanctuary, Bicêtre. This asylum, located in Paris, was founded in 1632, and whether or not it was the first of its kind, more is known about Bicêtre than the Hospital dels Folls.[26]

Bicêtre was not only a place of asylum for mentally retarded and mentally ill people, but for those who were blind, senile, invalid, epileptic, and poor.[27] (The first section exclusively for mentally retarded people was not established at Bicêtre until 1828.) The catchall nature of Bicêtre, and places modeled after it, would ultimately undermine any intended sanctuarial functions. With the approach of the eighteenth century, for instance, all manner of "deviants," including serious criminals, began to be placed in asylums; and with this, the asylums became places of confinement, not sanctuary. In fact, as confinement became the norm, the asylums became worse, in many respects, than some of the prisons.

By the middle of the eighteenth century, rumors were rampant about mysterious "fevers" that could infect asylum and prison visitors—fevers that would spread through residential areas adjacent to the asylums and prisons.[28] As a result of these claims, asylums were avoided, which resulted in malignant neglect of inmates by institutional officials. When the prison-fever panic did subside, the conditions within the asylums were found to rival some of Dante's more lurid descriptions. Emil Kraepelin describes the scene this way:

> Those who visited Bedlam in London in 1814 could see countless patients clad only in loose shrouds and chained by their arms or legs to the wall in such a way that they could stand upright or remain seated. One patient for 12 years wore rings around his neck and waist and was tethered to a wall because he had resisted attempts to control his movements by means of a chain manipulated from a neighboring room. The warden had also taken the precaution of lashing his arms to his sides.[29]

Such discoveries shocked many people, and efforts to improve conditions were made. Improvements in one area occasioned declines in others, though. For example, as the houses of confinement became more open, the practice of displaying retarded people made a comeback. In Bethlehem (Bedlam), "idiots" and "lunatics" were exhibited for the price of about a penny every Sunday. The annual revenue for these shows at Bethlehem in 1815 was £400, indicating an audience of approximately 96,000 people that year.[30] The visitors' curiosity was evoked, in part, by certain attendants who were particularly adept at getting the inmates to "perform dances and acrobatics with a few flicks of the whip."[31]

Indeed, the "keepers" often attained great popularity with the audiences. Retarded people had not come a very long way in eighteen centuries, although things soon would begin to change.

THE ENLIGHTENMENT AND
THE RISE OF SPECIAL EDUCATION

The impetus for this change came largely from the espousal of the cause of all oppressed groups by the likes of Locke, Condillac, Rousseau, Saint-Simon, Pestalozzi, Fellenberg, and the Encyclopedists. Where the clerics of the Reformation had tried to "cure" retarded people through exorcism, the sensualists, or sensationalists (as Locke and Condillac, especially, would come to be called), would seek "cures" through altering the environment, and thus the sensory stimuli, to which mentally retarded people were subjected. Sensationalist reasoning held that, as individual ills were socially caused, the malevolent imprints that the social environment had made upon retarded people could be erased. This idea was perhaps no more scientific than the thinking of the Protestant Reformers, but the practical ramifications of sensationalism proved beneficial to mentally handicapped people.

For example, it was in the spirit of sensationalist thought that the early nineteenth century saw Pereire develop a scientific method of instruction for deaf people. Braille made his contributions to helping blind persons. Pinel began to view insanity as curable through environmental manipulations. And finally, one of Pinel's associates, Jean Mark Gaspard Itard, took the first steps in implementing the sensationalist ideas with retarded people.

In 1798, a feral child was found in a forest near Aveyron, France. Pinel examined him and concluded that the boy was an "incurable idiot." Itard did not accept Pinel's diagnosis. Itard believed that people like Victor, as the boy was called, possessed reflexive powers that could be awakened through education. Thus, Itard began to work with Victor in an effort to cure him of his "idiocy." The process is described in Itard's *The Wild Boy of Aveyron*.[32] Itard worked with Victor for five years. The result of this effort was that the mute, asocial quadruped who had been found in the forest learned to "recognize objects, identify the letters of the alphabet, comprehend the meaning of many words, apply names to objects and parts of objects, make 'relatively fine' sensory discrimination. . . ."[33] Victor came to prefer "the social life of civilization to an isolated existence in the wild."[34]

Despite the strides made in Victor's socialization, when he reached puberty it is said he "broke out in a wild storm of passion,"[35] and Itard abandoned all hopes of curing him. The disconcerted Itard proclaimed the experiment a failure and placed Victor with a private family who provided the boy custodial care. Despite Itard's disavowal of his earlier hopes, the French Academy of Science formally recognized his contribution to a new philosophy of education. Although Victor was not cured, Itard had shown that even severe "mental defectives" could improve their social skills with proper training. A significant step toward special education and training for mentally retarded persons had been taken. The recognition accorded Itard signaled the beginnings of a change in the social currents regarding retarded people that had prevailed for nearly three millennia. Indeed, only two centuries before Itard's time, a Spanish physician named Juan Pablo had been driven from his homeland for merely trying to educate retarded children.[36]

In the wake of Itard's experiments, Johann Jacob Guggenbühl, a Swiss physician, developed another environmental approach to the cure of mental retardation. Unlike Itard, who emphasized fairly conventional educational methods, Guggenbühl focused his curative efforts on exposing retarded people to mountain air, intensive physical education, and proper diet. Guggenbühl practiced these therapies at an estate called Abendberg in Switzerland, which he had founded in 1842. It was the first institution established solely for the care and treatment of mentally retarded people.

Like Itard, Guggenbühl was hailed for his efforts, and his fame spread throughout Europe. But soon Guggenbühl's reputation acquired some blemishes. Evidences of fraud emerged at Abendberg. For example, children who had never had a mental handicap were displayed to visitors as "cured cretins."[37] Guggenbühl may have been only indirectly responsible for such misrepresentations: he was frequently absent from Abendberg on consulting and fund-raising junkets and may have been unaware of abuses that were creeping into the institution. Then again, Guggenbühl's seduction by his own notoriety may have inured him to such abuses. It has been suggested, however, that Guggenbühl's contribution to Abendberg's problems ran deeper than benign neglect. One author implies that Guggenbühl might have taken institutional monies for his own purposes.[38] In 1858 Abendberg was closed. Too much had been promised, too little delivered. The whole experience left many Europeans cynical and reluctant to sponsor similar efforts.

Guggenbühl was not the only individual associated with the nascent special education movement. In the same year Guggenbühl was founding Abendberg, one of Itard's students, Edouard Seguin, began his work. Seguin, often acknowledged as the founder of special education, attributed mental retardation to an infirmity of the nervous system that allowed the instincts to supersede the will. In 1837, Seguin established a school for retarded children in Paris, and in 1852 he became the leader at Bicêtre, the school Vincent de Paul had founded.[39] Here Seguin developed a sequential system of training and education for mentally retarded people that he called the Physiological Method. It was outlined in his book, *The Moral Treatment, Hygiene, and Education of Idiots and Other Backward Children*,[40] published in 1846. Seguin's system first trained the retarded child in the use of his muscular system, then focused on the nervous system. Seguin would first try to educate the senses, then help the child to develop abstract thought, which would facilitate the grasp of moral principles.[41] These ideas may seem both facile and grandiose to the modern reader. However, if one wants to get a sense of the sophistication of thought regarding retarded people during Seguin's time, one need only look at a compendium of the etiology of cretinism (the generic term for retardation at the time) published twenty-one years after Seguin's opus. Some of the causes listed (although all are not farfetched) were

> . . . drinking water, bad air, exposure of the neck to draught, vicissitudes of temperature, dietary faults, certain salts used in cooking, saltless food, cold water drunk while sweating, exclusive consumption of vegetables and milk, greasy food, parental drunkenness during procreation, lack of sunlight, exertion accompanied by tight clothes around the neck, waywardness, masturbation, inbreeding . . . [and] racial causes.[42]

In 1858, Seguin emigrated to the United States.[43] Here he found a fertile ground for his interests. Due to the efforts of men such as Samuel Gridley Howe (who had taught Ann Sullivan, Helen Keller's celebrated teacher[44]), certain localities in the United States already had begun to provide special education services for mentally retarded people. Howe, who was instrumental in getting Seguin to emigrate, had founded the first state-supported institution for handicapped persons in Boston in 1832.[45] It was called the Perkins Institute and, in its early stages, dealt primarily with blind and deaf children. Howe said that retarded children also might benefit from education and training, and in 1846 he was commissioned by the Massachusetts legislature to study the needs of the mentally handicapped population of that state. Howe reported back to the legislators that a state-supported education and training facility for retarded people was needed. On October 1, 1848, an experimental school for ten mentally retarded children was opened in a wing of the Perkins Institute.[46] Within three years, the successes of the school convinced legislators to provide regular funding. With these resources and the help of Seguin, Howe established a larger facility that came to be known as the Massachusetts School for Idiotic and Feebleminded Youth, which was seemingly successful in achieving some of its educational goals. For example, records indicate that between 1848 and 1869 the Massachusetts School for Idiotic and Feebleminded Youth discharged 365 of the 465 children who had been admitted, "many of them as self-supporting members of the community."[47] Seguin would help several other states organize special schools of their own.

THE AMERICAN ASSOCIATION ON MENTAL DEFICIENCY

In 1876 a convocation of the superintendents of many of the nation's special schools was held in Media, Pennsylvania. The purpose of the meeting was to organize the first professional group in the United States concerned exclusively with mentally handicapped people. Seguin was elected the organization's president, and it eventually came to be known as the American Association on Mental Deficiency. Its earliest publication, called *The Journal of Psycho-Asthenics*, would become the *American Journal of Mental Deficiency*, a highly respected publication in the field today.

One of the earliest projects of the association was to advocate the need for "special" classes within the framework of the public school system. The first class of this kind was opened on November 30, 1896, in Providence, Rhode Island.[48] By 1911, the U.S. Office of Education reported special classes in 220 cities.[49] The first training facility for teachers of special students, the New Jersey Training School for Feeble-minded Boys and Girls, was dedicated in 1905.[50] The special education movement was well underway.

The progress of this movement had been greatly facilitated by Alfred Binet's and Theodore Simon's development in France of a measure they called "intelligence quotient." This index, developed in 1896, was made public in 1905.[51] Its development fulfilled two important functions in the early days of special education. First, it could be used to illustrate that there were gradations of mental retardation. (The absolutism of mental retardation had actually been struck its first blow in 1866, when John Langdon Down dichotomized mongolism—now called Down's Syndrome—from other forms of mental retardation, thus showing differences in cause.[52]) Second, it gave educators a numerical index, and what most of them believed was an objective measure, to help them in determining the extent of a child's retardation. With this, the child could be placed in a class that was considered best adapted to his needs. For some children, this meant getting out of regular classrooms; for others, it meant getting into special classes in regular schools, where such classes existed.

SOCIAL DARWINISM'S CHALLENGE
TO SPECIAL EDUCATION

Despite the promise of the special education movement, there was still a great deal of opposition to it. One critic of Howe remarked that the report he had given to the Massachusetts legislature, which had led to the establishment of his first special school, was "for idiots as well as . . . concerning them."[53] Howe was caricatured in one publication as tilting at windmills.[54]

The *Providence Press* called that city's pioneering special education class "The Fool Class" in a sardonic article. Such raillery made the parents of many of Providence's mentally handicapped students unwilling to enroll their children.[55] Parental embarrassment was not, however, the only reason for this reluctance. Many of the earliest special education classes were not what they were represented to be. Frampton and Rowell explain that the first instances of special education in the United States "grew out of classes for incorrigible and truant boys."[56] Parents were reluctant to put their retarded children in these classes, not only because of the stigma attached, but because they were often nothing more than disciplinary units.

Special education faced some other problems. Segments of the public resisted the whole concept because special classes cost more than regular ones and usually did not produce very dramatic results. There was also a fear that if retarded boys and girls were allowed to attend the same classes, illicit procreation would result.[57] Moreover, many Americans were skeptical about the possibilities of educating retarded people. As Tredgold said in 1903, "In the present day, it is even questionable if such methods of so-called education are not carried a little too far; the training of imbeciles is in danger of becoming a popular fad and there is a tendency to allow it to run in lines which are altogether unsuited to the requirements and capabilities of these patients."[58]

In spite of the resistance, the number of special classes continued to grow until the 1930s, when the financial burdens of the Depression caused something of a decline in the trend.[59] However, the greatest impediment to the momentum of the special education movement came from a Social Darwinist doctrine called "eugenics."

In 1883, Francis Galton, Charles Darwin's cousin, introduced the concept of eugenics as "the science which deals with influences that improve the inborn qualities of the race."[60] The original thrust of the eugenics movement was an emphasis on the positive enhancement, even perfectability, of the human race through selective breeding. Soon though, the movement shifted its focus to "negative restrictions on so-called 'undesirables'. . . ."[61] In 1877, Richard Dugdale wrote a book about a degenerate family, *The Jukes,*[62] and in 1912, Henry Goddard published an exposition of the intellectual heritage of *The Kallikak Family.*[63] Although these books were aimed at demonstrating that deviance was hereditary, Goddard based his conclusions on some peculiar statistical inferences. (Martin Kallikak had been married twice, once to a "feebleminded" barmaid and once to a woman Goddard deemed a "respectable girl." Of the matching with the barmaid, 143 of 480 descendants were, in Goddard's estimation, "feebleminded." Of the marriage with the other woman, 496 of 496 were "respectable citizens," according to Goddard. From these figures, he concluded that 90 percent of all mental retardation is inherited.[64]) Both Dugdale and Goddard concluded that mental deficiency inevitably led to poverty, disease, moral degeneration, sexual promiscuity, and crime. Walter E. Fernald expressed the viewpoint quite succinctly to the Massachusetts Medical Society in 1912:

> The social and economic burdens of uncomplicated feeble-mindedness are only too well known. The feeble-minded are a parasitic, predatory class, never capable of self support or of managing their own affairs. The great majority ultimately become charges in some form. They cause unutterable sorrow at home and are a menace and danger to the community. Feeble-minded women are almost invariably immoral, and if at large usually become carriers of venereal disease or give birth to children who are as defective as themselves. The feeble-minded woman who marries is twice as prolific as the normal woman.
>
> We have only begun to understand the importance of feeble-mindedness as a factor in the causation of pauperism, crime and other social problems. Hereditary pauperism, or pauperism of two or more generations of the same family generally means hereditary feeble-mindedness. In Massachusetts there are familes who have been paupers for many generations. Some of the members were born or even conceived in the poor house. Every feeble-minded person, especially the high-grade imbecile, is a potential criminal, needing only the proper environment and opportunity for the development and expression of his criminal tendencies. The unrecognized imbecile is a most dangerous element in the community.[65]

An epiphenomenon of the writings of Dugdale, Goddard, and Fernald was something Kanner has called "the eugenic scare."[66] The results of the scare were threefold.

First, there was a challenge to the educational views championed by Itard, Seguin, and Howe. Charles Davenport, a prominent eugenicist (who would ultimately modify his eugenic views), held that, because mental deficiency was always hereditary, no amount of training could reduce it.[67] That which was genetically imprinted could not be environmentally altered. Special education was futile.

Second, there was a temporary reversal in the headway special educators had made in convincing many non-handicapped citizens that all "feebleminded" people did not need to live in institutions. Goddard wrote, "In considering the question of care, segregation through colonization seems in the present state of our knowledge to be the ideal and perfectly satisfactory method."[68] A retrograde back to the medieval philosophy of confinement was set in motion. In the last two decades of the nineteenth century and the first three of the twentieth, the impact manifested itself in several ways.

For one thing, institutions grew larger and their numbers increased. This was especially apparent in rural areas where so-called farms, or colonies, isolated retarded people from population centers. The rhetoric used to rationalize this new wave of separation can be seen in the comments of Kerlin. In 1885, he talked of "'villages of the simple,' made up of the warped, twisted and incorrigible, happily contributing to their own and the support of those more lowly,—'cities of refuge'— in truth; havens in which all shall live contentedly, because no longer misunderstood, not taxed with exactions beyond their mental or moral capacity."[69]

Another result was that institutions became custodial, the pervasive concern of administrators being to house residents as cheaply as possible. Because of this emphasis on economy, there developed an "institutional peonage." For example, in 1883 Fernald reported on one institution in which the per capita cost of housing "inmates" was reduced from $300 to slightly more than $100 per year. The report states that this was accomplished "largely from the fact that the work of caring for the low-grade children in the custodial department was done to a large extent by the inmates themselves."[70] If one ignored habilitation as the quid pro quo of institutionalization and further ignored the constitutional prohibitions against slavery, it might have been reasonably argued that the inmates Fernald was describing were engaging in productive labor, which justified the practice of using a captive work force for institutional peonage. In fact, though, there existed a great disparity in the potential and real productivity of retarded people who were institutionalized during the eugenic scare. Some insight into this may be gained in examining a statement made in *Education Magazine* by Henry Clapp in 1898. While Clapp suggested that the higher-grade inmates could do enough work to pay for their support in the institution, he also said that "in order to find exercise for them, they could be made to carry stones from one pile to another pile fifty feet away."[71]

The confinement philosophy also resulted in inmates being segregated by "sex, age, and ability level (and, in some states, by color)."[72]

Institutional trends were laced with hypocrisy. For example, even though custodial care, not education, was the stock-in-trade of many institutions, they were often euphemistically dubbed "schools."[73] The so-called hospitals were probably no more therapeutic than the schools were educational. As a matter of fact, in some of these institutions, the environment was decidedly unhealthy. White and Wolfensberger provide some sobering statistics: "Less than a third of those committed to the care of Elwyn School [Seguin had been the first president of Elwyn School, but later dissociated himself from it.[74]] lived to the age of twenty. Eight out of 625 made it to forty. The most common cause of death was tuberculosis, although a smaller percent died of consumption at Elwyn than statistics quoted for institutions as a whole across the country."[75]

The whole institutional philosophy of the eugenicists was a logical extension of their elitist views. Even though some of their arguments were put forth in bad faith, most of them probably did think that they were saving society from a downward spiral of genetic contamination. One wonders though if another factor was not at work. In *Diary of a Writer*,[76] Dostoyevsky suggested that it was through confining one's neighbor to an insane asylum that one was convinced of one's own sanity. Perhaps some of the eugenicists were attempting to confirm their own intelligence through a similar mechanism.

There was a third major effect of the eugenic scare. In 1911 a Committee of the American Breeder's Association pronounced, "We have decided that the mental have-nots in our midst, will, because they are maintained by private and official philanthropy, thrive and multiply and render helpless the dwindling remainder of the intellectual haves. We must get them out of circulation and curtail their propagation."[77]

Goddard had an even more "practical" answer to the procreation issue than elimination of retarded people through segregation in institutions. He believed all mentally retarded women should receive ovariectomies and mentally retarded males should be castrated.[78] An institutional official named Barr concurred. Because of improvements he perceived in the behavior of boys after castration, Barr "recommended that the operation be performed as soon as a person was found to be retarded."[79] One middle-western institution officially recorded 655 castrations between 1894 and 1944.[80] By 1926, twenty-three states had mandatory sterilization laws.[81] In a Supreme Court decision in 1927 (*Buck* v. *Bell*),[82] Justice Holmes wrote,

We have seen more than once that the public welfare may call upon the best citizens for their lives. It would be strange if it could not call upon those who already sap the strength of the state for these lesser sacrifices, often not felt to be such by those concerned, in order to prevent our being swamped with incompetence. It is better for all the world if, instead of waiting to execute degenerate offspring for crime, or let them starve for their imbecility, society can prevent those who are manifestly unfit from continuing their kind. The principle that sustains compulsory vaccination is broad enough to cover cutting the Fallopian tubes. . . . Three generations of imbeciles is enough.[83]

This decision was a catalyst for a frenetic period of sterilization of retarded people. Between 1925 and 1955, over 50,000 mandatory sterilizations were performed on persons said to be retarded or "deviant" in other respects.[84]

THE PARENT OR ADVOCACY MOVEMENT

A strong adversary relationship continued to exist between the eugenicists and Seguin's successors for the first half of the twentieth century. Although a good deal of the latter group's potentially productive energy was dissipated in skirmishes with the eugenicists, the controversy was not without beneficial effects. For one thing, the publicity the dispute generated brought the problems of mental retardation "out of the closet." People began to realize that mental handicaps were widespread. They saw that parents from any socioeconomic class, from any intellectual "gene pool," could have a retarded child. The luxury that society had enjoyed for centuries—that of locking away mentally handicapped people never to hear from them again—was diminished.

The popularity of Social Darwinism had also begun to decline. During the Depression, many members of the upper socioeconomic, "eugenically fit" classes became impoverished, undermining the economic and intellectual elitism of the "old eugenics." But the decisive decline in popularity of Social Darwinism came in the wake of World War II. Most Americans were appalled with Hitler's use of eugenic philosophy in forging his "ultimate solution," a horror that had affected retarded people as well as certain ethnic groups[85]—as many as 100,000 by some accounts.[86]

Other things happened in the late forties to undermine Social Darwinism and highlight the needs and potentialities of retarded people. First, there was an increasing public awareness that the genetic factors in mental retardation were very complex and that mental retardation was not always inherited. Indeed, with an increasing interest of social scientists in the problems of mental retardation, it became apparent that social factors such as the by-products of poverty could lead to the retarded label. Second, "the prediction of a fall in the national IQ level had been shown to be incorrect."[87] Third, there had been some marked successes of remedial programs undertaken in certain, still educationally oriented, institutions for mentally handicapped people.[88] Fourth, as is the case after most wars, a more tolerant attitude toward mild forms of deviancy developed. Fifth, retarded people became more accessible to the masses as a result of the postwar prosperity. The postwar economic boom made it easier for marginal workers to compete in the labor market. As a result, mildly retarded people who were employable in the private sector probably came to be seen as somewhat less of an economic threat to the working class than they had been before the war. In any event, some retarded persons got jobs in their communities. Such contact helped to reduce fears that had been spawned as a result of the isolation of retarded people from the rest of society. Sixth, after the war there were more retarded people than there had been before it. Medical advances had increased the life expectancy of many moderately and severely retarded individuals. Additionally, the absolute rise in the number of babies being born after the war resulted in an increase in the number of children being born with mental handicaps. Many of these babies were born to highly educated, articulate, and newly affluent portions of the population. Historically, the middle and upper classes had sequestered retarded children in institutions or at home because of the social stigma attached to retardation. The stigma had not been eradicated, but mental retardation was becoming a subject that could be discussed more openly. This, coupled with the fact that the care of certain retarded children was threatening the new affluence of their parents, caused some of these parents to unite in an advocacy effort that would undermine the widespread acceptance of Social Darwinist thought.

Local parent groups began to spring up throughout the country, and by 1950 representatives of these groups came together in Minneapolis to form the National Association of Parents and Friends of Retarded Children. The organization is now called the Association for Retarded Citizens. As of 1976, the association had 300,000 members and was the largest advocacy organization for retarded people in the United States.[89]

The focus of many of the earliest struggles of the so-called parent movement was the improvement of educational services for mentally handicapped students. A pivotal victory in this matter came in the Surpeme Court's ruling in *Brown* v. *The Board of Education*.[90] The case dealt primarily with the constitutionality of racial segregation, but the implications were more far-reaching. The Court's decision affirmed the right of all citizens to an equal education. With that principle enunciated, the path was laid for the passage of other legislation to address the educational rights that had so long eluded retarded people.

In recent years the scope of the parent movement, or advocacy movement as it is now called, has broadened to incorporate not only educational, but occupational, residential, and a host of other rights of retarded persons. The scope has broadened in another respect. Many of the earliest struggles of the parent movement were waged on behalf of mildly retarded people. This was logical since many of them were living in the community, and their greater visibility made their needs more apparent compared to those who were locked away in institutions. Moreover, society seemed to find it easier to respond favorably to appeals made on behalf of these most competent of "incompetents." In recent years, however, the activities of the advocacy movement have begun to encompass the needs of more severely retarded people.

Before the mid-1950s, the life options of moderately and severely retarded persons were very limited. For example, very few educational facilities for "trainable" children existed before 1953.[91] Consequently, these youngsters either made a go of it in public school classes designed for mildly retarded students (where such classes existed) or they stayed at home, receiving little or no specialized training. If the strain of a homebound arrangement became too intense for the child's family, he or she was usually institutionalized.

This has changed. Throughout the seventies, there was a strong movement toward getting moderately and severely retarded persons out of total institutions and into community-based residential, educational, and occupational settings. All of these changes were components of a process called the normalization movement.

NORMALIZATION/DEINSTITUTIONALIZATION

Although the normalization principle was first articulated in Sweden by Nirje in the late sixties, the idea was extended, refined, and popularized in the United States by Wolfensberger. He did this in an enormously influential book called *Normalization*, published in 1972.[92] In the book, Wolfensberger defines the principle as "the utilization of means which are as culturally normative as possible in order to establish and/or maintain personal behaviors which are as culturally normative as possible."[93]

The normalization principle represented a convergence of the thinking of the civil rights movement, the advocacy movement, and the social scientific conclusions inherent in works such as Goffman's *Asylums*.[94]

A central issue of this convergence focused on determining the appropriate reasons for institutionalizing a person. Proponents of normalization reasoned that if there was a quid pro quo for putting mentally retarded persons in institutions, it had to be habilitating them for integration into mainstream society. "Getting them out of the way" was not sufficient moral justification for institutionalization. If habilitation was the quid pro quo, it made little sense to house people in physical environments totally dissimilar from those found in the rest of the society. Advocates held that institutions created living conditions that only emphasized and exacerbated dissimilarities of retarded people from those who were not handicapped. And if these advocates needed an object lesson to illustrate this point or to provide a basis for saying what was being implied—that institutions are inherently bad places—they had it in Willowbrook.

Willowbrook, located in New York State, was the nation's largest institution for mentally retarded people. In a civil suit brought on behalf of Willowbrook residents in 1970, the following infractions of patient rights were cited by the plaintiffs:[95]

1. Most residents were confined for unspecified periods, usually until they "recovered."
2. Residents who should have been released were not.
3. No habilitation was occurring to justify the confinement of residents.
4. There were no individual habilitation plans for residents.
5. There were no periodic evaluations of residents to assess their progress and redefine goals and programs.
6. There were no educational programs provided for residents. In fact, virtually no stimulation of any kind was provided.
7. Services such as speech, occupational, and physical therapy were inadequate, if available at all.
8. The facility was overcrowded.
9. The residents had no privacy and there was an attendant absence of regulations that protected residents from theft. In the atmosphere that prevailed, personal property was nonexistent.
10. The residents were not protected against assault and injury, either by other residents or staff.
11. Experimentation was practiced on residents.
12. Residents were not given adequate clothing.
13. The diet in the facility was inadequate and the meals were rushed.
14. The facility was dirty.
15. Toilet facilities were not adequate to accommodate the institutional population.

16. Residents were segregated from those of the opposite sex.
17. Many residents were unwarrantedly confined to beds or chairs or kept in solitary confinement.
18. Many residents were denied grounds privileges and practically none were given passes.
19. Residents were not given help in reading, writing, or posting mail.
20. There was a paucity of bilingual staff; thus non-English-speaking residents had difficulty in communicating.
21. Residents were not compensated for work performed.
22. The facility was understaffed with professionals and paraprofessionals. The absence of proper supervision contributed to the fact that some residents died of such things as aspiration of food or vomit.
23. Medical facilities were inadequate.
24. Many of the professional staff were shown to be incompetent.

All in all, it was alleged by the plaintiffs that their First, Fourth, Eighth, Thirteenth, and Fourteenth Amendment rights had been violated. Although all the allegations were not proved, the plaintiffs "won" the case in a Consent Judgment against Willowbrook that took effect in 1975.[96] In approving the Consent Judgment, the judge wrote, "The consent judgment reflects the fact that protection from harm requires relief more extensive than this court originally contemplated, because harm can result not only from neglect but from conditions which cause regression or which prevent development of an individual's capabilities. . . ."[97] (The dubious consequences of the Consent Judgment are discussed in a later chapter.)

All institutions were not as bad as Willowbrook, but it became the embodiment of what was wrong with institutions in general. Some advocates railed against them as anachronistic residuals of a time when human warehouses were used to store hopeless people who were expected to live hopeless lives. Many of the eugenic arguments that favored institutionalization were seen to be hypocritical; modern pro-institutional ideas seemed shopworn and, as we shall see, were debunked empirically as well as rhetorically and theoretically. The momentum of normalization was very powerful in the seventies, and it was rare that an opponent of normalization or deinstitutionalization would voice his opinion publicly or in the literature.

One outspoken critic of the lengths to which normalization was being taken was Throne, who stated that the principle sought the right ends through the wrong means. According to Throne, if retarded people are treated as normal in remedial efforts, this will leave them functioning as retarded. Extraordinary means must be employed if retarded people are to be trained to act more normally.[98] Throne seems to have misunderstood normalization. If one examines Wolfensberger's definition, it is clear that what is being called for is "the utilization of means which are as culturally normative as possible."[99] All but the most radical proponents of normalization are comfortable with using specialized educational and training approaches where normal procedures are ineffectual in helping retarded people reach developmental goals. Conversely, it might be reasoned, to opt for non-normative methods of socialization when normal ones will do is tantamount to changing a tire by jacking up the wheel and trying to remove the car from it.

A second criticism of normalization is that it strives toward an undesirable human homogeneity, faulting normalization as an end. Mesibov suggests that emulating normalcy is not inherently good or satisfying to a retarded individual, especially in light of the "anxieties, uncertainties, and isolation" faced by the average person in modern society.[100] To be sure, atypical behaviors are the basis of most art, science, and other transcendent principles that propel civilization. What Mesibov overlooks is that the atypicality of retarded people is generally viewed as deviance and that the social response to this perception often heightens a retarded person's anxieties, uncertainties, and isolation.

A third criticism of normalization is that it is grounded in a fallacious sociological principle. Here, it is held that one of the verities implied in community placement of retarded persons is that public attitudes toward them will improve through mere physical and social proximity. It is argued that our society's experiences with racial integration belie this point[101]—indeed that propinquity intensifies antipathy. Even if the analogy between racial and intellectual prejudice were appropriate— and that remains to be demonstrated—there is evidence, for example, that non-handicapped neighbors living close to community-based residential facilities *do* develop more favorable attitudes toward the retarded persons living in them.[102]

Those on both sides of the propinquity argument may have reasonable, even verifiable, points, but they occasionally oversimplify the issue. Integrating retarded persons into "normal" neighborhoods, schools, and work places is, as we shall see, a very complex matter.

A fourth criticism of the normalization principle is that retarded people subjected to normal environments encounter risks they would not face under conditions completely tailored to their inadequacies. Mentally retarded persons are often vulnerable in non-sheltered situations, but the normalization principle does not eschew sheltered environments where they are the most culturally normal placements available. All of us take risks in sharing a community with each other, yet most persons prefer taking these risks to the shelter of an institution, such risks being an important and necessary requirement of human existence. (I am reminded of the story of a pool hustler who dies and finds that in his afterlife, every wish is granted. Every time he hits a cueball, for instance, all the other balls on the pool table go into the pockets. He quickly discovers that he is in hell.)

A fifth criticism of normalization, especially the deinstitutionalization component, is that no empirical base conclusively demonstrated that smaller, community-based, residential facilities were better for residents than institutions before the deinstitutionalization process was begun.[103] When one examines the literature on deinstitutionalization, it is notable that much of the empirical research exploring the possible virtues of community-based living for retarded persons was done after deinstitutionalization had become a *fait accompli.*

It could be argued that society had no way of knowing if normalization would work until it was tried. Of course, public policy usually guides, rather than being guided by, research in social experiments, and that is what normalization has been.

On the basis of my own field interactions with the earliest facilitators of normalization, it does seem accurate to assert that the movement was being guided more by moral than scientific convictions. Of the hundreds of professionals in the field of mental retardation I conversed with in the seventies, not one questioned the rectitude of the experiment, with the exception of a few comments made against mainstreaming in the schools. To some, the idea of normalization seemed self-justifying. A few probably succumbed to a bandwagon effect, but that should have come as no surprise. The normalization principle was a catalyst in a revolution of hope. Advocates could only presume to grasp the personal enrichment deinstitutionalization provided erstwhile confined human beings, or the growth engendered in retarded children who, because of the movement, escaped being "put away." The conventional wisdom among advocates had it that normalization led to independence, dignity, self-respect, and a feeling of belonging for retarded persons. This promise was realized often enough to justify the idea of normalization.

One did see retarded people who had been dismal parasitic beings in institutions transformed into contributing citizens with a sense of self-esteem when they moved into the community. These metamorphoses often occurred as a direct result of such things as increased community involvement—things that the structural constraints of institutions would have precluded.

The virtues of normalization have come under a more rigorous scrutiny of late. There is more data. The novelty has worn off. Everyone subjected to normalization was not miraculously transformed. The field of mental retardation has matured remarkably in the last decade. All that aside, the vanguard of the normalization movement created a special legacy: normalization did not always make a big difference for good or for ill, but where it worked, it was good.

NOTES

1. Quoted without reference in B. Blatt, *Christmas in Purgatory*, Boston: Allyn and Bacon, 1966, p. 46.

2. B. R. Gearheart and F. W. Litton, *The Trainable Retarded: A Foundations Approach*, St. Louis: C. V. Mosby, 1975, p. 1.

3. Ibid.

4. M. W. Barr, *Mental Defectives: Their History, Treatment, and Training*, Philadelphia: Blakiston, 1913, p. 24.

5. Ibid.

6. E. Horsfield, "Mental Defectives at the Court of Philip IV of Spain as Portrayed by the Great Court Painter Velasquez," *American Journal of Mental Deficiency*, 45:1940, p. 152.

7. Ibid.

8. M. W. Barr, p. 24.

9. M. Foucault, *Madness and Civilization: A History of Insanity in the Age of Reason*, New York: New American Library, 1965, p. 68.

10. A. M. Clarke and A.D.B. Clarke, "Criteria and Classification of Subnormality," in A. M. Clarke and A.D.B. Clarke, eds., *Mental Deficiency: The Changing Outlook*, rev. ed., New York: The Free Press, 1965, p. 14.

11. M. Foucault, p. 7.

12. N. Bernstein, "Intellectual Defect and Personality Development," in N. Bernstein, ed., *Diminished People*, Boston: Little, Brown and Co., 1970, p. 182.

13. B. R. Gearheart and F. W. Litton, p. 2.

14. A. M. Clarke and A.D.B. Clarke, p. 13.

15. M. W. Barr, p. 25.

16. L. M. Dunn, "A Historical Review of the Treatment of the Retarded," in J. H. Rothstein, ed., *Mental Retardation: Readings and Resources*, New York: Holt, Rinehart, and Winston, 1961, p. 14; M. E. Frampton and H. G. Rowell, *Education of the Handicapped*, vol. 1, *History*, Yonkers, N.Y.: World Book Co., 1938, p. 167; H. D. Love, *The Mentally Retarded Child and His Family*, Springfield, Ill.: Charles C. Thomas, 1973, p. 186.

17. L. Kanner, *A History of the Care and Study of the Mentally Retarded*, Springfield, Ill.: Charles C. Thomas, 1964, p. 6.

18. M. Luther, *Colloquia Mensalia*, London: W. Du-Gard, 1652, p. 387.

19. W. Wolfensberger, *Normalization*, Toronto: National Institute on Mental Retardation, 1972, p. 14.

20. H. J. Baker, *Introduction to Exceptional Children*, New York: The Macmillan Co., 1953, p. 199.

21. P. F. Cranefield, "Historical Perspectives," in I. Philips, ed., *Prevention and Treatment of Mental Retardation*, New York: Basic Books, 1966, p. 3.

22. Ibid.

23. M. W. Barr, p. 25.

24. B. R. Gearheart and F. W. Litton, p. 1

25. E. Horsfield, p. 155.

26. M. Foucault, p. 42.

27. L. Kanner, p. 46.

28. M. Foucault, p. 202.

29. Cited without reference in B. Blatt, p. 87.

30. M. Foucault, p. 68.

31. Ibid.

32. J. Itard, *The Wild Boy of Aveyron*, New York: Monthly Review Press, 1972 (first published in 1801).

33. L. Kanner, "Itard , Seguin, Howe—Three Pioneers in the Education of Retarded Children," *American Journal of Mental Deficiency*, 65:1960, p. 4.

34. Ibid.

35. Ibid.

36. B. R. Gearheart and F. W. Litton, p. 2.

37. Ibid., p. 5.

38. L. Kanner, *A History of the Care and Study of the Mentally Retarded*, p. 29.

39. M. E. Frampton and H. G. Rowell, p. 174.

40. E. Seguin, *The Moral Treatment, Hygiene, and Education of Idiots and Other Backward Children*, New York: William Wood, 1846.

41. M. E. Frampton and H. G. Rowell, p. 174.

42. L. Kanner, *A History of the Care and Study of the Mentally Retarded*, p. 92.

43. M. E. Frampton and H. G. Rowell, p. 174.

44. P. F. Cranefield, p. 10.

45. H. D. Love, p. 46.

46. National Association for Retarded Citizens, *The Parent/Professional Partnership, Book I: The Right to Education*, Arlington, Texas: The Association, 1976, p. 3.

47. C. S. Raymond, "The Development of the Program for the Mentally Defective in Massachusetts for the Past One Hundred Years (1848–1948)," *American Journal of Mental Deficiency*, 53:1948, cited in W. D. White and W. Wolfensberger, "The Evolution of Dehumanization in Our Institutions," *Mental Retardation*, 7:1969, p. 5.

48. L. Kanner, *A History of the Care and Study of the Mentally Retarded*, p. 112.

49. M. E. Frampton and H. G. Rowell, p. 185.

50. L. Kanner, *A History of the Care and Study of the Mentally Retarded*, p. 115.

51. Ibid., p. 122.

52. Ibid., p. 97.

53. L. Kanner, "Itard, Seguin, Howe—Three Pioneers in the Education of Retarded Children," p. 9.

54. Ibid.

55. L. Kanner, *A History of the Care and Study of the Mentally Retarded,* p. 115.

56. M. E. Frampton and H. G. Rowell, p. 185.

57. G. M. Boehme, "Proceedings on Public School Classes for Feeble-Minded Children," *Journal of Psycho-Asthenics,* 14:1909–1910, p. 86.

58. B. Farber, *Mental Retardation: Its Social Context and Social Consequences,* Boston: Houghton Mifflin, 1968, p. 30.

59. National Association for Retarded Citizens, p. 5.

60. L. Kanner, *A History of the Care and Study of the Mentally Retarded,* p. 128.

61. H. A. Bender, "A Geneticist's Viewpoint Towards Sterilization," *Amicus,* Feb., 1977, p. 45.

62. R. L. Dugdale, *The Jukes,* New York: Putnam, 1888.

63. H. H. Goddard, *The Kallikak Family: A Study in the Heredity of Feeble-mindedness,* New York: Macmillan, 1912.

64. H. D. Love, p. 47.

65. A. M. Clarke and A.D.B. Clarke, pp. 16–17.

66. L. Kanner, *A History of the Care and Study of the Mentally Retarded,* p. 133.

67. M. E. Frampton and H. G. Rowell, p. 182.

68. L. Kanner, *A History of the Care and Study of the Mentally Retarded,* p. 132.

69. W. D. White and W. Wolfensberger, "The Evolution of Dehumanization in Our Institutions," *Mental Retardation,* 7:1969, p. 7.

70. W. E. Fernald, "The History of the Treatment of the Feeble-Minded," *Proceedings of the National Conference on Charities and Correction,* 1893, cited in ibid., p. 6.

71. H. L. Clapp, "Special Schools for Feeble-Minded Children," *Education Magazine,* 19:1898, cited in W. D. White and W. Wolfensberger, p. 8.

72. A. A. Baumeister and E. C. Butterfield, eds., *Residential Facilities for the Mentally Retarded,* Chicago: Aldine-Atherton, 1970, cited in National Association for Retarded Citizens, p. 56.

73. S. K. Thurman and R. L. Thiele, "A Viable Role for Retardation Institutions," *Mental Retardation,* 11:1973, p. 21.

74. W. D. White and W. Wolfensberger, p. 7.

75. Ibid., p. 8.

76. Cited without reference in M. Foucault, first page of preface.

77. L. Kanner, *A History of the Care and Study of the Mentally Retarded,* p. 135.

78. R. Perske, "About Sexual Development," *Mental Retardation,* 11:1973, p. 6.

79. W. D. White and W. Wolfensberger, p. 9.

80. R. Perske, p. 6.

81. H. D. Love, p. 48.

82. *Buck* v. *Bell, Supreme Court Reports,* Number 584, U.S. 200, 1927.

83. E. Ferster, "Eliminating the Unfit—Is Sterilization the Answer?" *Ohio State Law Journal,* 27:1966, p. 595, quoting ibid.

84. S. J. Brackel and R. S. Rock, eds., *The Mentally Disabled and the Law,* Chicago: The University of Chicago Press, for the American Bar Association, 1971, chap. 6, pp. 207–225.

85. The President's Committee on Mental Retardation, *Silent Minority,* Washington, D.C.: U.S. Government Printing Office, Dept. of Health, Education, and Welfare, 1973, p. 1.

86. W. Wolfensberger, "The Extermination of Handicapped People in World War II Germany," *Mental Retardation,* 19(1):1981, p. 3.

87. A. Kushlick and R. Blunden, "The Epidemiology of Mental Subnormality," in A. M. Clarke and A.D.B. Clarke, eds., *Mental Deficiency: The Changing Outlook,* rev. ed., New York: The Free Press, 1965, p. 63.

88. A. M. Clarke and A.D.B. Clarke, "Criteria and Classification of Subnormality," p. 18.

89. National Association for Retarded Citizens, p. 6.

90. *Brown* v. *The Board of Education,* 347 U.S. 483, 493, 74 S. Ct. 686, 691, 98 L. Ed. 873, 1954.

91. H. D. Love, p. 50.

92. W. Wolfensberger, *Normalization: The Principle of Normalization in Human Services,* Toronto: National Institute of Mental Retardation, 1972.

93. Ibid., p. 28.

94. E. Goffman, *Asylums: Essays on the Social Situation of Mental Patients and Other Inmates,* Garden City, N.Y.: Doubleday, 1961.

95. P. Roos, "Testimony of Dr. Philip Roos in *Wyatt* v. *Stickney,*" pp. 455–490 and "Testimony of Dr. Philip Roos in *New York State Association for Retarded Children* v. *Rockefeller,*" pp. 591–610, in B. J. Ennis and P. Friedman, eds., *Legal Rights of the Mentally Handicapped,* New York: Practicing Law Institute—Mental Health Law Project, 1974.

96. C. A Hansen, "Willowbrook," *Mental Retardation and Developmental Disabilities,* 9:1977, p. 12.

97. Judge Judd's comments on the Willowbrook Consent Judgment are recorded in ibid.

98. J. M. Throne, "Normalization Principle: Right Ends, Wrong Means," *Mental Retardation,* 13:1975, p. 23.

99. W. Wolfensberger, p. 28.

100. G. B. Mesibov, "Alternatives to the Principle of Normalization," *Mental Retardation,* 14:1976, p. 31.

101. Ibid.

102. L. S. Kastner, N. D. Reppucci, and J. J. Pezzoli, "Assessing Community Attitudes Toward Mentally Retarded Persons," *American Journal of Mental Deficiency,* 84:1979, p. 142.

103. M. J. George and A. A. Baumeister, "Employee Withdrawal and Job Satisfaction in Community Residential Facilities for Mentally Retarded Persons," *American Journal of Mental Deficiency,* 85:1981, p. 639.

4
The Education of Mentally Retarded People: Models and Methods

The true, sound, and strong mind is the mind that can embrace equally great things and small.

—J. Boswell[1]

SPECIAL SCHOOLS

The cornerstone of the normalization movement has been the education and training through which many mentally handicapped individuals have learned to live, work, and play in their respective communities. New Morning School, the site of most of my observations, is a *special school*. Its students are mentally handicapped, and the school itself is separated geographically from schools for children who have not been labeled as mentally retarded.

The practice of segregating mentally retarded students into schools of their own has been changing, especially since the passage of Public Law (P.L.) 94-142, the Education for All Handicapped Children Act of 1975. P.L. 94-142 mandated that a child who is mentally handicapped be educated in a setting that is "the least restrictive environment" for him. For many mentally retarded youngsters, this means integration into schools, if not classrooms, with non-handicapped children—a phenomenon called mainstreaming.

While it may be somewhat anachronistic to discuss special-school settings in the age of mainstreaming, I am not certain that special schools—even those predominantly for moderately retarded students—will be eradicated by mainstream education. As we shall see in a later chapter, the efficacy of mainstreaming remains to be irrefutably demonstrated. There are intense pressures in opposition to mainstreaming in some quarters, accompanied by rumors that efforts will be mounted to rescind P.L. 94-142—the legal basis of mainstream education.

Whether special schools are good and essential for most moderately and severely retarded students or are separate and unequal educational relics, they were crucial in the evolution of the normalization movement. And they are still with us, some doubtless providing educational services for youngsters who belong in mainstream situations, others very adequately meeting the broadest range of educational and social needs of their handicapped students.

Special schools have been the central repositories of the ascendent special education philosophy of the last three decades. That philosophy has been based on the premise that mentally retarded persons are limited in the quantity of information they can internalize; therefore, the information passed along in school must be the most essential the society has to offer. The primary goal has been to help retarded people reach their highest levels of functional competence. This is achieved through the transmission of skills in learning domains that help retarded persons to survive, lead productive and personally fulfilling lives, and fit into their communities. The fundamental learning domains include: (1) self-care skills, such as personal health and hygiene; (2) physical skills, such as gross and fine motor movements; (3) communication skills; (4) social and affective skills; (5) other cognitive skills, including the so-called functional academics; (6) recreational and leisure-time skills; and (7) vocational skills.

In the time it has taken to complete this study, I have visited numerous special schools and mainstream settings. New Morning School was typical of the others in its staff philosophy, educational methodologies, student demographics, physical setting, and history.

New Morning School was founded in the early sixties under a grant by the U.S. Commissioner of Education. Two teachers, both without experience in special education, were hired to instruct approximately 20 moderately retarded students, ages six to sixteen. Classes were held in a dilapidated building. Until the very recent past, hand-me-down facilities have typified the educational surroundings of moderately and severely retarded students in most special schools. As was the case with many other special schools in the seventies, New Morning increased its staff, moved to new facilities, and expanded the age range and number of clients served. By 1982, New Morning enrolled approximately 100 moderately and severely retarded students and 6 who were more profoundly retarded. It had a staff of thirty-five.

WELCOME TO A DIFFERENT WORLD

The ambience of most special schools is similar to that found at New Morning. It is a memorable experience for an "outsider" to enter one of these schools for the first time. My formal introduction to observation at New Morning School came when the director handed me a piece of paper headed "Ground Rules for Observers," which said to be unobtrusive and stay out of the teachers' way. My informal introduction came from one of the teachers who said to me, "This is a different world." She was right.

As schools go, New Morning was a culture shock. It was noisy. The classrooms were often chaotic. The building itself was clean, bright, and new. Yet the spontaneous nature of a *few* of the students' bladders, bowels, noses, and mouths introduced me to a constellation of sights and smells not usually associated with school. I say "a few" because such spontaneity is not typical in most of the students, despite certain stereotypes to the contrary.

Many of the first impressions I had of New Morning were surrealistic. Some of the students were engaging in repetitive, seemingly purposeless behavior such as pacing or rocking their heads. On the first day of observation, I stepped into one classroom and saw an adolescent walking around the periphery of the room, sucking his thumb, making peculiar noises, sniffing a stuffed animal, stopping periodically at the coatrack to masturbate. When he came close to me and looked into my eyes, he responded as though he were looking at something other than another human being. It was chilling.

Although such behavioral extremes are atypical, many of my first impressions were based on them, rather than all the less conspicuous, more normative behavior that was going on around me. Predictably, the most unusual things were the most fascinating. This can create problems for retarded persons. Non-handicapped people who have not spent much time around retarded people often fail to realize what a great proportion of their behavior is normative. When we focus on the inevitable extremes of their behavior, we come away with jaundiced images of them.

The older students at New Morning had a particularly eerie effect on me. The younger students were cute and lovable for the most part, but many of the older students seemed ominously weird. A number of other neophyte observers in the setting said that they felt the same way. This perplexed the staff at the school, to whom the older students seemed very mature relative to those who were younger and not as well socialized.

One would expect the New Morning students to be inured to observers. Multitudes of outsiders volunteer and observe at the school. But while I was busy observing the students, they noticed me as well. Indeed, many of them had developed special uses for newly arrived onlookers. To the younger students, I was a new playmate. There was no way to avoid playing with them. It undermined my "detachment" and embarrassed me; but in the end, I skipped, I danced, I sang, and engaged in genuine exasperation as they pilfered my pen and mutilated my field notes.

The older students took notice of me as well. The attention ranged from a shy giggle from behind a half-closed door to a magisterial demand that I identify myself and explain my notes. Practically everybody said, "Hello." Most of the males shook my hand. A couple of the older women became verbally amorous with me in their inimitable, woman-child fashion. This led to some jocular conversations between me and some of the staff. In retrospect, I wonder what the psychological dynamic is that causes normal people to view making love with a retarded person as something ludicrous. I believe that in pondering that notion we can probe the depths of many of our other attitudes regarding mentally retarded people; indeed, many of our attitudes in general.

The people who most reacted to my presence at the school were volunteers. Now and again, they would stage scenarios for me that involved getting the students to perform—a kind of "lion tamer syndrome." Clearly, they were trying to elicit some feedback from someone (anyone) for activities about which they were fundamentally uncertain. The teachers were usually too busy to pay much attention to volunteer performances, and I was there, seemingly not retarded, and holding a clipboard—one of our society's most potent symbols of authority.

The students at New Morning School possessed a whole range of perceptual abilities and communicative styles. Some attended to comments directed at them; some did not. Some conversed quite clearly, while the speech of many others was difficult or impossible to understand. Some did not try to talk at all. A few repeated things people said to them (echolalia). Several had a private gibberish, and some repeated a repertoire of nonsensical sentences that apparently meant something to them. At first, the communication patterns of these students made me nervous. I did not know what to say to the student who said hello fourteen times in succession. I did not know what to do when someone sought my attention by pulling my hair. I assumed that when a retarded child wanted to be picked up, I should automatically oblige. I was not sure what the consequences of my faux pas would be, yet I was preoccupied with responding appropriately to a lot of communication that I had no experiential basis for evaluating.

Almost everything at New Morning School was somewhat different than things were on the "outside." Several students were strapped in wheelchairs to keep them from falling over. A few of them wore helmets to protect them in the event of an epileptic seizure. Some of the students communicated with each other and their teachers in sign language.

Of all my earliest impressions, the most vivid was the way some of the students deviated from the spatial norms I had been accustomed to on the outside (Hall calls such personal territoriality "proxemics"[2]). Within ten minutes of my arrival at the school, I had been hugged, poked at, and had my hand shaken several times. I wanted to tell them to stop.

As the first days of observation passed, many of my own apprehensions and annoyances diminished. I had met a number of friendly and courteous kids. I got used to people touching me. I discovered that many of the students' behaviors required no particular pattern of response. If I interacted in a less than optimal way, no one seemed to be devastated. I began to feel at ease with the students and tried to come across as very erudite to the "new" observers.

My feelings for the students warmed for some other reasons as well. For one thing, there was something about the innocence in the smiles of many of them. It was very . . . pure.

Then, too, the solicitous attitude most of the students had toward each other was quite engaging. That is not to say that some of them were not rude, indifferent, or downright mean to their classmates. But most were very helpful to other students. If somebody needed his wheelchair pushed, another student would do it. If someone were upset, a friend would try to soothe him. I did not expect to see this with retarded people. Greenfeld calls it a "community of kinship among all the maimed."[3]

I was also charmed by the way some of the students misconstrued things. For instance, one youngster gave a special interpretation to a sex education lesson. His teacher had been showing the class explicit nude pictures of men and women. After showing the class a picture of a naked man, the teacher produced another photo of the same man; only this time, the man pictured had an erection. The teacher asked the class if anyone noticed any differences in the first and second pictures. One boy raised his hand and pointing to the man's tumescence said, "Yeah, it's upside down."

The New Morning students arrived at school at 8:30 A.M.; they left by 2:30 P.M. They had a half hour for lunch, which many of the older students helped to prepare and serve as part of their vocational training. Judging by the enthusiasm with which the students entered school in the morning and the generally good spirits most maintained during the day, they liked being there.

The school had eleven different classes—twelve, counting a preschool that was in operation for half a day. The preschool class was not operated by the public school system, but was conducted in the same building as the rest of the classes. Until New Morning became a public school, the preschool class was a part of New Morning administratively as well as geographically. (Under provisions of P.L. 94-142, public school systems are not mandated to provide preschool education.) Because the preschool class was part of the school during the period of most of my observations, I will treat it as an integral part of the New Morning experience.

The age ranges were broader in classes at New Morning than the age distributions by grade one sees in regular schools. For example, the first primary grade had students six to nine years of age; the second, ten to twelve years. This kind of age distribution progressed through the intermediate, prevocational, and vocational classes—the latter having students from eighteen to twenty-one years of age. There were also two so-called basic skills classes for students who functioned at levels below those necessary to participate in any of the other classes. Although the students in a given class at New Morning were all within a four-year age range, many did not look it. Attenuated physical development makes it difficult to judge the age of some retarded people.

Age is not a particularly good barometer of a retarded person's intellectual abilities, either. Some New Morning students mastered fundamental life skills at a young age, while others were still bewildered by very simple things when they were ready to graduate. Since a few of the students would never have graduated from the school if achievement were the main criterion, they were moved to higher grades on the basis of age rather than ability. Profound developmental differences were thus apparent within all of the school's classes. One example of such developmental heterogeneity could be seen during a holiday visit to the school by Santa Claus. Some of the younger students did not buy the whole masquerade and said as much, while many of the older students were clearly enraptured and reacted with a very "young" exuberance. As a rule, however, the older students did act more maturely.

Of the many notable aspects of the instructional environment at New Morning School, six things were most conspicuous: (1) the individualized approach taken toward students, (2) the dialectic between openness and structure in the classrooms, (3) the complex simplicity of instruction, (4) the staff's adherence to an instructional perspective called the developmental model, (5) the use and misuse of behavior modification, and (6) the pragmatic methodological emphasis of the staff. Let us examine each of these in its turn.

INDIVIDUALIZED EDUCATION

The wide range of abilities and differential rates of progress of the New Morning students necessitated a specialized approach to teaching each of them. Many of the things that a teacher of non-handicapped children can take for granted were absent at the school. For example, one eight-year-old child had eaten baby food all of her life because she could not swallow solid food. One of the school's staff ate lunches with the child over a period of three years in an attempt to help the child swallow solid food, and that began to correct the situation.

Every class had a teacher and an aide. Because of the favorable student-teacher ratio (6:1 including aides), the students were able to receive considerable individual attention, which was designed to provide learning activities ideally suited to each student's skills and needs.

Although individualized instruction was considered a necessary educational element at New Morning, group instruction also took place. Teachers were especially insistent on appropriate behavior from students during group learning periods. As mainstreaming became more viable in Mountview, group activities were increasingly emphasized at New Morning to prepare some of its students for integration into normal schools, where individualized instruction was typically less common and group activities the norm.

OPEN VERSUS STRUCTURED CLASSROOMS

The issue of balancing openness (child-directed activity) and structure (teacher-directed activity) in the classroom presented staff members at New Morning with an interesting problem. Many of the classes, especially those with younger students, were to a large extent open. In some cases, the spontaneous emotions of the students did not make this a matter of teacher choice, although most teachers managed to avoid anarchy with a continual attentiveness to the students.

The advantages of deliberate openness were that: (1) while some students were busy directing their own activities, the teacher was free to provide individualized instruction for others; and (2) certain students were free to do what interested them, giving them valuable experience in self-direction. This process was facilitated by the multitude of learning devices that lay about every classroom—attractive and colorful items, many of which looked like toys.

The primary disadvantages of an open instructional approach were that: (1) some of the students were not physically and/or intellectually able to select and pursue an activity for a significant period of time, and (2) open classrooms did not provide the established routine that some of the students seemed to need in order to learn most effectively. Many retarded people do not understand their environment very well in the first place. One facilitant of this understanding is to make the environment as predictable as possible. A number of the students at New Morning became very irritable or "lost" when their routines were altered. (Cohen et al. found a similar phenomenon with retarded people who were in institutions.[4]) Thus, the staff members at New Morning had to maintain an uneasy balance between openness and structure in their classrooms.

COMPLEX SIMPLICITY

Another conspicuous aspect of the instructional milieu at New Morning was the complex, yet simple appearing and concrete nature of the teaching. Because mentally retarded people have difficulty abstracting, they are, for the most part, limited spatially to their immediate environment and temporally to the present. A few of them do have very strong future or past orientations. In fact, some literally dwell in the future or the past. But the majority of the students at New Morning School were always "in" the present, which required that teaching be made relevant to the immediate spatiotemporal environment. Hence, students were given continuous and immediate feedback on their performances in class, and most learning experiences were designed to stimulate the senses directly and immediately rather than abstractly.

The staff at New Morning was always devising ways to make facile tasks even easier for the students. Take the example of putting on a coat. Many retarded children cannot put their coats on one sleeve at a time. A few of them are not well enough coordinated to find a sleeve behind their backs. Some others, because they cannot see the sleeve, do not take for granted that it is there. So, to make the job of putting on a coat easier, the coats were laid on the floor; the child put a hand in each armhole; and the coat was brought up over his head as his arms slid into the sleeves of the garment.

Because everything had to be made to appear uncomplicated to the students, outsiders often could not discern the degree of difficulty that went into teaching a particular task. Frequently, I found, the New Morning staff put an enormous degree of thought into teaching very simple things, which made such instruction look a great deal easier than it was.

To help the process of simplification, the New Morning staff constructed many so-called task analyses. In a task analysis, something such as the act of washing one's hands is broken down into its most elemental components, keying on the necessary sequence those minute components must follow if the task is to be performed. Once the task analysis is constructed (many are available in prefabricated form in special education texts and the like), the instructor can use the guidelines of the analysis to teach the targeted skill to a student, giving him as many steps at a time as he is able to grasp. This is sometimes referred to as precision teaching. It is amazing to see how many complicated operations are involved in even the simplest gesture. (And it has occurred to me that observing the sequential simplicity of instruction at a place like New Morning School would prove very informative to sociologists interested in ethnomethodology—the study of the formal phenomena that underlie the informal methods whereby people attend to ordinary or commonplace actions and activities.)

THE DEVELOPMENTAL MODEL

The sequential nature of instruction at New Morning School intimated the stated philosophical viewpoint of most of the school's staff—the so-called developmental model. This model arose out of the pioneering child-development studies of Charles Darwin.[5] Darwin's account of the development of one of his children aroused interest in this area. Subsequent work by Bayley,[6] Gesell,[7] Griffiths,[8] and Frankenburg and Dodds[9] has provided normative data about child development such as the rate and sequence of development of the average child, based on studies of large numbers of infants and young children.

A simplified version of the developmental model holds that humans are constantly changing in a sequential and predictable manner. Recognition that the life of an individual is constantly changing is subject to little controversy, except, that is, when the concept of change is applied to mentally handicapped people. Because they are slow, it is sometimes assumed that they are fixed physical, mental, and psychological entities, which, in effect, implies that they are not alive at all. This intimates a paradox that developmentally oriented special educators confront. While mental retardation as a definitional and classificatory phenomenon is static, the developmental model is a dynamic perspective. To repeat an earlier assertion, if a teacher is really using developmental growth as a primary goal for a student, it should be immaterial whether the youngster is classified as moderately retarded, severely retarded, or retarded at all. Development is the key to growth, not label. And yet developmentally oriented special educators find both the static and the dynamic components of this paradox inescapable in their work.

Sequential development lies at the heart of the developmental model. For example, a child must learn to match shapes before he can identify them. He must learn parallel play (playing beside but not with another person) before he can learn cooperative play. It is easier for a child to learn to take a shoe off than to put it on.

Piaget's ideas have, for the most part, provided the theoretical basis for the developmental model and have been utilized extensively in approaches to early childhood education. He theorized that there are four discrete stages of development: (1) the sensorimotor stage (birth to one and one-half years); (2) the preoperational stage, subdivided into the preconceptional (one and one-half years to four years) and the intuitive (about four years to seven years); (3) the stage of concrete operations (about seven to eleven years); and (4) the stage of abstract operations (about eleven years onward).[10]

According to Piaget, the development of certain cognitive structures is a prerequisite for particular kinds of learning, and each of his stages has different structures attendant upon it. For example, a child who is in the stage of concrete operations has the ability to classify—form hierarchies of classes of concrete objects through his understanding of inclusion relations. These include "the relations of parts to the whole, of the whole to the parts, and the parts to the parts."[11] A child at this developmental stage could form the following type of hierarchy: brown horses, horses, animals.

According to the developmental view, retarded people appear to go through Piaget's stages of intellectual development in essentially the same sequence as non-handicapped people. Usually, they just go through them at a slower pace. Moreover, as was mentioned earlier, mentally handicapped people usually do not become as sophisticated in the stage of abstract operations as most non-handicapped people. Indeed, depending on the severity of retardation, certain retarded persons do not acquire the cognitive structures and operations of the *earliest* stages.

The developmental model can be used both diagnostically and remedially. Diagnostically, if a child fails to reach certain developmental milestones within certain chronological periods, this signals an alert for potential problems. If, for example, a baby does not respond as actively as he should, never smiles, never reaches for toys, cries all of the time, or is exceedingly passive, he can be said to be showing signs of a developmental delay.

One of the major strengths of the developmental model may also be one of its major drawbacks. The very timetables that help to identify problems frequently become problematic themselves. Many individuals adhere so rigidly to the dates by which developmental milestones should be reached that they become overly concerned if a child is a little late in arriving at one of them. The dates for these milestones are based on averages, and many non-handicapped children do develop skills much later than the arithmetic mean would dictate. Thus, when a child is somewhat late in arriving at a developmental step, he should be watched carefully and stimulated in that area, but the lateness should not be equated with a retarding condition. Remedially, the developmental model can be used to help special educators plan the sequence in which skills ought to be taught to those students who are, in fact, mentally retarded (those who will suffer a protracted developmental delay).

Despite the seemingly uniform philosophical underpinnings of the developmental model, there are many differences in the way in which special educators approach its use. For one thing, there is not universal agreement on some of the finer points of developmental sequencing; "even among experts, there are differences of opinion about exactly which skill or activity follows another."[12]

Furthermore, all proponents of the developmental model do not see eye-to-eye on the pace at which the model ought to be implemented as a form of remediation. Some developmentalists are adamant that retarded persons be allowed to develop at their own rates,[13] while other self-proclaimed developmentalists hold that developmental expectations for retarded children ought to be accelerated. For example, Throne holds that if retarded children are pushed to exceed rates immutably associated with developmental milestones, they will get a head start that can diminish the intellectual disparity between themselves and non-handicapped children.[14] This assertion ignores one of the simplest components of Piaget's theory: children must be ready to learn before learning can take place.

While there is no evidence that developmentally delayed children ought to be pushed faster than they logically can be expected to go, there is data indicating that we ought to start pushing as early as we can—that early intervention is more effective in earlier attainment of developmental tasks than no intervention at all.[15]

Despite the popularity of the developmental model, it does have detractors. Its theoretical polarity has been called the "difference theory."[16] This theory holds that mentally retarded persons do not always go through all the same developmental stages as non-handicapped people—that neurological problems not only slow the pace of developmental sequencing, but create completely different types of developmental beings with their own developmental sequences and their own cognitive landscapes.

The controversies between developmental and difference perspectives are a Pandora's box of complexity. Let it suffice to say they exist, and that if one accepts the developmental rather than the difference model, the primary implication for special education settings is clear: special educators ought to have a deep understanding of early childhood development and the sequencing of events that development usually takes. It is futile for a teacher and frustrating for a child if sequential degrees of difficulty are not taken into account in instructional efforts. Indeed, if a child is taught out of the logical sequence, he may not only fail to learn what is being taught, but regress to earlier stages out of sheer frustration. Despite this, Stainback and her coauthors[17] hold that many special educators do not possess much information about childhood development. Several New Morning staff members, as well as those from other special schools, told me without solicitation that there were deficiencies in this area of their training.

BEHAVIOR MODIFICATION

A frequently discussed and controversial intervention strategy used at New Morning School was behavior modification. Most staff members were either firm in their support of, or opposition to, its use.

Put simply, behavior modification is a systematic attempt to develop, maintain, or extinguish observable behaviors. With behavior modification, the situational conditions of a learning environment are seen to supersede intangibles such as attitude or intrinsic motivation. Behaviorists believe it is inconsequential to change something as impalpable as an attitude when all that is manifest in human interaction is behavior. Thus, in the school setting, the behaviorist tries to arrange the consequences of a student's behavior so that the behavior can be controlled or "shaped."

Two justifications for the use of behavior modification techniques were suggested by staff members at New Morning School. First, these techniques are ubiquitous, and, second, they work. The ubiquity argument holds that reinforcement psychology is seminal in all learning. As one New Morning staffer said, "Behavior modification is the way mankind molds its society." Another said, "We are all using it all the time without knowing it."

There is a sizable body of literature supporting the claim that behavior modification, properly employed on retarded persons, can help them progress toward developmental goals.[18] In spite of this demonstrated effectiveness, behavior modification is not without its critics.

At New Morning School there were a few staff members who would not use behavioristic techniques at all, and others who would set up reinforcement schedules only in situations where a student would respond to no other method. This last-resort quality bore mute testimony to the power of behavior modification.

Criticisms of behavior modification voiced most frequently at New

Morning School were typical of those that one hears in nearly any setting when behavioristic techniques are discussed. Some teachers said that their colleagues only used behavior modification to pacify unruly students, not to engender any growth in them. Other staff members said that "programming" retarded children only served to stifle what creativity they did happen to possess. The most frequently mentioned criticism was that behavior modification deals only with symptoms of a student's disorder, not with the causes.

The ethical integrity of using any technique purely as a pacifier in an educational environment is questionable; but when one saw the behavior of some of the more disruptive students at New Morning, it was understandable that a teacher might adhere to any effective pacification technique available. More than once, I witnessed teachers use every resource in their repertoire of mollification to no avail. Behavior modification may, at times, be used as a psychological straitjacket, but be the least of many other evils.

I believe, however, that if one reads between the lines of the pacification criticism, what is really being objected to are control tactics in general. Behavior modification is, after all, a very deliberate manipulation of one human being's interpersonal environment by another. Proponents of behavioral engineering try to shine a different light on this criticism. They say that the main reason that the control issue receives such unrelenting critical attention is that the successes of behavioristic techniques are conspicuously and immediately apparent. Roos holds that our society is replete with attempts to control human behavior, singling out such things as child rearing, advertising, politics, psychotherapy, and *education*.[19] The implication here is that all educational techniques are control oriented. The difference in operant and non-operant techniques, according to the behaviorists, is that the latter's rhetoric of control is less explicit than that of behavior modification and that behavior modification is more successful in achieving its goals. If non-operant techniques were as effective as behavior modification, hold the behaviorists, the critics of behaviorism's control tactics would be more muted. They may be right on this account, yet there is a critical distinction between behavior modification and other educational techniques. For instance, when one uses a non-operant technique such as play therapy in an educational setting, the control resides with the child, who guides the process of intervention. Further, with behavior modification, nothing about the technique itself determines the values governing its use. It is this quality that makes people uneasy about behavior modification—it gives the method an aura of control for control's sake. This aspect of behavior modification is especially unnerving in special education settings in light of evidence that illustrates that some teachers are "more concerned with maintaining power over students than in transmitting knowledge and skill. . . ."[20] Behaviorists might retort to criticisms of their purported value neutrality by pointing out that theirs is not the only technique that can be applied with equal effectiveness by autocrat or saint.

Despite criticisms of behavior modification as control technology, the method can be innocuously powerful when competently applied to certain objectives likely to be associated with the remediation of mental retardation. If, for example, behavior modification is the only way to extinguish a child's self-destructive tendencies, such as head banging or pica (the ingestion of inedible substances), then critics cannot fault its use. If behavior modification is the *only* method that will stop a person from being severely socially disruptive—bullying or striking others, for example—it is not only unobjectionable to use the method, but ethically negligent not to do so.

Even if the situational variables can justify the control elements of behavior modification, this still does not answer the criticism that the technique is stifling to the creativity of people upon whom it is used. In the case of many mentally retarded persons, the potential for creativity is doubtless quite meager, diminishing somewhat the indictment inherent in the criticism. That notwithstanding, behaviorism does view the learning process as extrinsically motivated. The mechanistic behavioral view that all learning is motivated by its consequences leaves little room for creativity and its cousin, curiosity, in the learning process, and where these factors are viewed as irrelevant, they will not be cultivated.

The third major criticism leveled at behavior modification by some of the New Morning staff was its atomism—its focusing on isolated symptoms while ignoring the whole person and his total environment. Indeed, say critics, not only does behavior modification deal exclusively with symptoms, but when the technique is used to eradicate those that are undesirable, one maladaptive symptom may be substituted for another. With behavior modification, a child can be programmed to stop doing something that is inappropriate; but, the critics argue, the factors that influenced the child to act inappropriately in the first place are not changed one whit.

THE USE AND MISUSE OF BEHAVIOR MODIFICATION

Positive reinforcers were the prevalent mode of reinforcement in evidence at New Morning School. Tangible rewards were typically used, bits of food or candy being particularly effective with many of the younger and lower-functioning students. These rewards were given immediately in response to student behaviors the teachers deemed desirable. With retarded persons, positive reinforcement must often be concrete and immediate to be effective. Other rewards that were used to reinforce students were paste-on stars, check marks, "happy faces," and, in one of the intermediate grades, money. In this class, if the students exercised appropriate table manners at lunch, treated each other with a modicum of respect throughout the day, did not disrupt the class, and so on, they received a penny every day. At the end of the week, the students would spend their accumulated pennies on candy and inexpensive toys in the homeroom store. Although this method of reinforcement was not immediate, many of the students did participate and their behavior could be changed or "shaped" by the system. It also had the advantage of teaching the students lessons in deferring gratifications.

Not incidentally, behavior shaping has a very specific meaning in the jargon of behavior modification. The method uses a positive reinforcement schedule to reward successive approximations of a desired response. If, for example, one wants a child to sit at his desk, but he insists upon leaving the building, the youngster is rewarded when he comes back to the building, when he walks through the classroom door, and when he finally sits at his desk. In precision teaching, one can see how task analysis and shaping can be combined.

The aforementioned positive reinforcers have many uses in behavior modification programs designed for mentally retarded populations, but such rewards can become problematic when not used carefully. For example, food rewards, especially the candy and sweet breakfast cereals that were often used as positive reinforcers at New Morning, were not appropriate for some students. Many of them had weight or blood-sugar problems. It was a mistake to give them sweets, yet they felt slighted when they saw classmates gettings sweets as rewards they could not have. Further, there were some students who would go to great lengths to get a snack—even feigning inability to do a task so they could eventually get a treat when they did do it.

Arbitrary rewards such as happy faces can be problematic too, because they reinforce a child with something that does not naturally exist in normal environments. The school is geared to the normalization principle, and one does not usually get happy faces for appropriate behavior in mainstream society. Moreover, while arbitrary reinforcers may be very good instruments in the acquisition phase of a behavior-shaping program, they tend to lose their value in the maintenance stage. This occurs when behavior trainers keep students on token reward systems too long without tapering off the rewards.[21] Some teachers prefer to go with what has worked and are reluctant to reduce the frequency of reward. Indeed, some increase the frequency and overreward students—

this despite clear evidence that retarded persons profit most from behavior modification programs based on intermittent reward schedules.[22]

There is another reason that token rewards should be tapered. If they are not, the students can be transformed into beggars or petty extortionists. As one New Morning teacher who uses them put it, "Token rewards are a flagrant form of bribery." One can imagine the scenario of a child who has taken his expectations for rewards home to uncompliant parents who refuse to continue the payoff.

Many of the older students and higher-functioning younger students at New Morning were not reinforced by the use of token rewards. Most of them were well enough socialized to be satisfactorily reinforced by words of praise from staff members. Tramontana did an interesting piece of research that shed some light on the effectiveness of praise versus token rewards in behavior-shaping programs. He found that, despite the fact that praise increases in effectiveness as intellectual level increases, "candy was the more effective reinforcer regardless of intellectual level."[23] Aside from the gastronomical implications of this finding, it is suggestive of a social-psychological characteristic of certain mentally retarded persons.

While some retarded individuals may be motivated by the self-satisfaction of performing tasks, others share no such motivational value. For example, Bernstein reports one study in which retarded children scored lower than normal youngsters in a concept-switching task when the only reward was the satisfaction of giving a correct response. But when toys were given as rewards, the retarded children performed comparably with the non-handicapped children.[24] Bernstein wonders aloud about how many of the differences in performance between retarded and non-handicapped youngsters are actually attributable to differences in incentive values. Probably not many; but it is an interesting question, worthy of further research.

A number of New Morning's antibehaviorists said that their strongest immediate aversion to behavioristic techniques stemmed from uninformed usage by their colleagues. A lack of sufficient knowledge of behavior modification resulted in some misuses of its techniques. For example, some of the behavior modifiers at the school were uncertain about the terminology of behaviorism. Terms such as *negative reinforcement* (the increase in a behavior as a result of the removal of an aversive stimulus) and *punishment* (the decrease in a behavior as a result of application of an aversive stimulus) were confused occasionally. Confusion in terminology can lead to miscommunication among professionals. The jargon of the technique is also applied to euphemize unorthodox and/or uninformed reinforcement practices. An example of confusion on this matter at New Morning was evident in a teacher who had put a rubber band on a child's wrist, snapping it to extinguish certain behaviors, and mistakenly calling this punishment negative reinforcement.

In some instances, behavior modification programs were not applied with the proper degree of consistency at New Morning School. Some behavior modification programs (and other intervention strategies for that matter) were not given sufficient time to work. Certain staff members frequently phased operant programs for the same student in and out and occasionally failed to coordinate their efforts with colleagues who had professional contact with the student. Inconsistency in teaching methods threatens the predictability in environment that most retarded people seem to need. Indeed, it has been suggested that consistency in the application of *any* educational technique with retarded persons may be more important to the learning experience than the technique itself.[25]

Another thing that must be guarded against in using behavior modification with retarded people is the creation of undesirable epiphenomenal behaviors. One New Morning staff member told an anecdote about a student who was being conditioned to nod her head in the two manners that convey affirmation and negation in our culture. In response to a certain stimulus, the conditioner used his hand to help the child nod her head in the appropriate manner. At last the time had come for the child's first nodding solo, and, sure enough, while she responded with the appropriate gesture, she did so by moving her head with her hand. This was harmless enough, but given mentally handicapped people's difficulty in interpreting the world, uninformed use of operant techniques with them invites the creation of unforeseen and potentially dangerous or embarrassing residuals.

A related issue is teaching "conditioned" children to adapt to the changed significance of cues. As I have said, retarded people have a hard time adapting the information relevant in one situation to another similar situation. So, for instance, a child conditioned to use the toilet properly may become confused when he is prohibited from doing so in the models at the plumbing store—a circumstance that befell one of New Morning's students.

The misuses of behavior modification techniques that have been discussed so far are not, on the basis of my observations, limited to New Morning School. They were typical in all settings I observed where operant techniques were applied by people who did not have extensive training in, and experience with, the methods.

It is easy to see why some special educators misapply behavior modification techniques. On the surface, behavior modification seems a simplistic technique, and people tend to jump to unwarranted conclusions about their own skills with the technique on the basis of its apparent simplicity. Behavioristic techniques are really very complex, though, and the appropriate utilization of them is not easy. Because the moment-by-moment demands of students in special education settings are unrelenting, it is understandable that many special educators have seized upon behavioristic techniques even if these educators do not fully understand the techniques or cannot implement them appropriately. A cultism has developed around behaviorism, with many of its strongest advocates touting it as a miracle-producing panacea. And in a profession as frustrating as special education can be, one empathizes with educators who grasp at easy solutions, especially when they face no-progress situations, parental pressures, high expectations from administration, and recurrent disciplinary problems with students.

AD HOC SPECIAL EDUCATION

While behavior modification or its variants were widely used techniques at New Morning, and while the staff talked of the developmental model as the only acceptable theoretical base, most of the intervention strategies seemed to be *ad hoc*. Staff members might make an occasional comment about Skinner's methods or Piaget's theories, but they were not wont to expostulate upon their own educational philosophies. I believe the sentiments of many of the staff were embodied in the motto of one teacher who was less equivocal than her colleagues in responding to my probings about theories, methods, and guiding principles. She said, "If it works, I use it." The pragmatism of this statement may sound methodologically capricious, but every staff member at New Morning was legally required to answer the question, If it works to do what?

Each teacher and specialist at New Morning School was required by the mandates of Public Law 94-142 to write an Individual Education Plan for every student with whom that person had professional contact. The Individual Education Plans (IEPs as everyone called them) removed some of the ambiguity associated with *ad hoc* pragmatism. In the IEP, the special educator must state:

- The levels at which the child is currently functioning in all relevant developmental areas.
- The style of learning the child uses, with an examination of the strengths and weaknesses of that style.
- What educational and special services the child will need.
- Short-term objectives.
- The materials needed to achieve those objectives.

- Longer-term, or annual, goals.
- When the services will begin and how long they are likely to be needed.
- A statement or description that justifies the educational environment in which the child has been placed as the "least restrictive environment" available to achieve educational goals.
- All of those who will have responsibility for implementing the plan.
- Some mode to monitor the effectiveness of the IEP in facilitating the child's development.

In developing the IEPs, a representative of the child's school other than a teacher should participate, along with specialists, the child's parents, and where necessary, the child.

The Individual Education Plans yield a format that shows what will be done with a student and why. The process of developing an IEP ensures that special educators will attempt to communicate with parents and makes it more likely that professionals will communicate with each other. IEPs address the much ballyhooed issue of accountability.

Most of the professionals I observed and conversed with seemed to take the Individual Education Plans seriously, but the existence of these plans was somewhat incongruous with the *ad hoc* pragmatism of many of them. The IEPs are supposed to pin down very specific educational goals. But to the ultrapragmatic special educator, who constantly modifies not only methods, but goals, the IEP can become a time-consuming annoyance. A few of them commented that they were not going to change their fluid instructional approaches in deference to what they viewed as the static expectations inherent in the IEP. Thus, while the IEP adds the important dimension of specifying educational goals, it does not typically force the educational process to deviate very far from the old "if it works, use it" philosophy. It is clear that IEPs are often more static than the realities they are supposed to reflect, although the converse is sometimes true as well.

DISCIPLINE

Because mentally retarded students have difficulty in learning social norms, they frequently break "the rules" in school. Thus, discipline is a focal concern of special education, and the issues surrounding it are manifold and complex. For example, the staff members at New Morning had to decide whether to impose sanctions on a child purely on the basis of his behavior, or whether there were circumstances associated with the youngster's handicap that mitigated the behavior. Some students may be unruly because they have come to school sick. Many have difficulty in communicating illnesses to parents. Some students take medications that leave them very sensitive on certain days. A few students have hyperkinetic days that are precipitated by irregular patterns of brain activity, reducing their impulse control. A number of retarded pupils never learn the rules of society well enough to conform to them in anything other than a random way. And nearly all of the children are easily frustrated by their difficulty in learning—venting this frustration by misbehaving. These kinds of circumstances, while mitigating obdurate behavior, are usually difficult, if not impossible, for a teacher to uncover.

When discipline is clearly warranted, however, the New Morning staff must weigh the quality of disciplinary responses. What methods of discipline should be employed? Does one discipline all recalcitrant children in the same fashion, or should responses be tailor-made? There was little consensus on these questions among the New Morning staff; however, they did agree on three things that should not be done. First, withdrawal of love should never be threatened. Second, uncompliant children should never be ridiculed publicly. Third, one must never strike a child.

For the most part, the staff at New Morning adhered to these rules, although a few of them confessed to having near misses with regard to physical aggression. Some staff members said they had shaken children's shoulders; one said she had pinched a student. Another said, "I sometimes respond to a child the way they respond to me." This teacher admitted to having bitten a biter to "give him a taste of his own medicine." Two other staff members told me that they got demonstrably angry with certain students. "After all," explained one, "if normalization is something other than a fad, these students must get practice in experiencing real responses to their actions; they cannot be over sheltered."

A disciplinary factor that all of the New Morning staff supported was the notion that students must have the limits of acceptable behavior very specifically, almost tediously, outlined for them. Because the students do not understand moral abstractions very well, a teacher wastes time in describing negative sanctions that are likely to result from hypothetical situations. Some of the more intelligent students may profit from such lessons, but with most, discipline must be germane to situations that arise *in* school. Where punishment is used, it must be meted out very quickly after transgressions occur so that the student can understand the connection between the inappropriate behavior and the responses designed to discourage it. With many of the New Morning students, any delay at all in disciplinary response was too long. Thus, an observer had to recognize that a quick disciplinary reaction was not necessarily an overreaction.

It was also worth noting that some students responded to discipline in fictive ways. Several New Morning staffers described students who had learned to use certain expressions of contrition in purely instrumental ways. One teacher cited the example of a student who had a very difficult time understanding the dynamics of diminishing returns associated with overuse of the phrase "I'm sorry." He received just enough intermittent reinforcement to keep using it, but never seemed to be genuinely contrite. It is easy to teach retarded people to say they are sorry. It can be very difficult to help them understand why they should be sorry.

Whether they believed in behavior modification or not, most of the New Morning staff used it in disciplinary matters. One widely practiced method of dealing with misbehavior at the school was to try to "extinguish" the behavior by ignoring it—a process sometimes referred to as *extinction*.

Many children who do not possess enough competence to control their environments with appropriate behavior learn that they can have some control if they misbehave. Behaviorists view any reaction to such behavior as reinforcing. Thus, if one does not respond to the behavior, it will purportedly atrophy and die. Extinction is a difficult method to employ, and it has certain liabilities.

First, the behavior modifier who chooses to use extinction should know that reinforcement can be extremely subtle. As Murdock says, "Frequently, just a glance, a moment's eye contact, physical nearness, etc. are strong enough reinforcers to strengthen or at least maintain some behaviors. It is almost impossible to eliminate such subtle reinforcers."[26] And there is almost always somebody around (often a volunteer) who, noting that the behavior is being ignored, will unwittingly and with the best of intentions, reinforce it.

Second, a teacher can easily botch extinction procedures through inappropriate responses to what has been called an "extinction burst" in a child. When a teacher first employs extinction techniques, the person being conditioned will often intensify the behavior the teacher is attempting to extinguish. If the teacher responds by discontinuing the extinction process, that usually reinforces the very behavior it was designed to eliminate.

Third, extinction should never be used to eliminate dangerous behaviors. That should have been a matter of common sense. Sometimes, it was not.

Fourth, when one ignores behavior, he may be ignoring the legitimate needs of the child. Even if behavior can be eradicated by ignoring it, if one does not get at the cause of persistent misbehavior, the impulse that occasions the behavior will manifest itself in other ways. This is a bit like ignoring the protests of a child who is afraid of the dark. If ignored long enough, the child discontinues his protests, but he will still be terrified.

Fifth, if a person ignores behavior he finds annoying, it may only magnify his response when it does come. Not only do we have the hazards of overreaction in this case, but we see a very powerful reinforcement of the behavior designated for extinction.

Sixth, it is easy to set students on the wrong path by ignoring persistent misbehavior. New Morning School's discipline should parallel the social control mechanisms the students will encounter in the community. On the "outside," misbehavior will not be ignored.

The disciplinary device most frequently employed at New Morning was isolation. Each classroom, except those used by the vocational classes, had an adjoining "time-out room." These rooms were small. Some of them provided a view of the classroom, others did not. The rooms were virtually bare, so there was little in them to stimulate a student who was being isolated. The logic behind "time-out" is that students prefer to participate cooperatively in the activities of the classroom, no matter how disdainful of them, rather than be removed from the situation to an unstimulating environment. According to behaviorists, brief social deprivation should make the students more malleable to subsequent social reinforcement. Much of the literature on this point is cited in Baran.[27]

One New Morning teacher told me that the logic of time-out does not always apply. There are, she said, some children for whom isolation is quite rewarding. They so enjoy being isolated from the group that they deliberately misbehave to make it into the "slammer." Indeed, some New Morning teachers actually used their time-out rooms as rewards. (Nolley et al. found that isolation can be rewarding as well as punishing to mentally retarded subjects,[28] while Favell and her colleagues have shown restraint to be a powerful positive reinforcer for some mentally retarded persons.[29])

Although the vocational classes at New Morning did not have time-out rooms, the older students were occasionally disciplined by isolation. If they were behaving inappropriately, the students were usually asked to leave the room and return when ready to participate cooperatively with the group. These students rarely left the school when "kicked out" of their classrooms, even though there were no restraints to prevent them from doing so. On those occasions when a student did leave the school for any length of time, the tension level rose among the staff.

I was at New Morning during two of these tension-filled days. The first time, a boy who had been disciplined by a teacher left the school to find his father, who lived somewhere in an adjoining state. Another time, a couple of the older students went out for a romp. This caused great consternation because they were of the opposite sex and old enough to reproduce. When the students returned, I watched a very circumspect policeman lecture them on how much trouble they had caused everyone. They looked and acted dutifully remorseful, but one could tell that they had had a marvelous day, and, by the way, an innocent one.

At first blush, isolation seems a harmless way to control students who misbehave. In fact, since most of the transgressions that necessitate discipline are disruptive, isolation seems ideal. One wonders, however, if the practice cannot be too easily misused. First, it is an effective way of pacifying a classroom. And when isolation is used solely for that purpose, the reinforcement is more teacher oriented than student oriented.

Second, isolation may have an especially sharp edge for some retarded people, when it is equated with punishment. A few of them conclude that, in view of their lives of relative isolation from the community, they are continuously being punished—a conclusion that could have unfortunate psychological consequences, albeit an abstraction that eludes most retarded people.

Besides isolation, the other forms of punishment used at New Morning generally translated into a student's loss of accumulated tokens, or a tongue-lashing by a teacher. There were four main circumstances in which punishment was used: first, when a staff member became so exasperated that an outburst became virtually unavoidable; second, when a student's inappropriate behavior was so frequent that there was no appropriate behavior to reinforce positively; third, when a child physically endangered someone; and fourth, when the child became exceedingly self-abusive.

Punishment is risky business. There is always the possibility that punishment can create emotional problems in the person being punished. For example, punishment may suppress appropriate as well as inappropriate behaviors to the extent that a child who has been punished will avoid all settings in which he has been punished and all meaningful contact with the persons associated with the punishment.

Punishment also begs for more punishment. If behavior that is targeted for elimination is not punished consistently, the intermittent reward that accompanies the inconsistency will reinforce the behavior.

THOUGHTS

There is a great deal of room for innovation in the field of special education. Special educators seem to be an open-minded group, encouraged by the difficulties of their jobs to try new ideas on the basis of the practical merit inherent in those ideas.

As an outsider to the educational setting and a stranger to retarded people, I entered the field mistakenly believing that special education was predicated only on the elimination of inappropriate behavior. There was some of that. But one of the vital signs of the special education settings I observed was the emphasis on cultivating appropriate behaviors. The tacit sociological understanding special educators seemed to possess was that the more competent a student can be made to appear, the more eccentricities will be tolerated in him by society. That ethos probably goes a long way in explaining many of the successes of normalization.

NOTES

1. J. Boswell, *The Life of Samuel Johnson*, Chicago: University of Chicago Press, 1952, quoted in L. C. Henry, ed., *Best Quotations*, Greenwich, Conn.: Fawcett, 1966, p. 149.

2. E. T. Hall, *The Hidden Dimension*, Garden City, N.Y.: Doubleday, 1951, p. 1.

3. J. Greenfeld, *A Place for Noah*, New York: Holt, Rinehart, and Winston, 1978, p. 89.

4. H. Cohen, J. W. Conroy, D. W. Frazer, G. E. Shelbecker, and S. Spreat, "Behavioral Effects of Interinstitutional Relocation of Mentally Retarded Residents," *American Journal of Mental Deficiency*, 82:1977, p. 17.

5. C. Darwin, "A Biographical Sketch of an Infant," *Mind*, 2:1877, p. 285.

6. N. Bayley, "Mental Growth During the First Three Years," *Genetic Psychology Monographs*, 14:1933, p. 1.

7. A. Gesell, *Studies in Child Development*, New York: Harper, 1948.

8. R. Griffiths, *The Abilities of Babies*, London: University of London Press, 1954.

9. W. K. Frankenburg and J. B. Dodds, "The Denver Developmental Screening Test," *Journal of Pediatrics*, 71:1967, p. 181.

10. M. Woodward, "The Application of Piaget's Theory to Research in Mental Deficiency," in N. Ellis, ed., *Handbook of Mental Deficiency*, New York: McGraw-Hill, 1963, p. 299.

11. H. Ginsburg and S. Opper, *Piaget's Theory of Intellectual Development*, Englewood Cliffs, N.J.: Prentice-Hall, 1979, p. 121.

12. J. Mather, *Make the Most of Your Baby*, Arlington, Texas: National Association for Retarded Citizens, 1974, p. 7.

13. R. Perske, "About Sexual Development," *Mental Retardation*, 11(1):1973, p. 7.

14. J. M. Throne, "Normalization Through the Normalization Principle: Right Ends, Wrong Means," *Mental Retardation*, 13(5):1975, p. 24.

15. S. B. Morgan, "Development and Distribution of Intellectual and Adaptive

Skills in Down Syndrome Children: Implications for Early Intervention," *Mental Retardation*, 17(5), 1979, p. 249; B. Connolly and F. Russell, "Interdisciplinary Early Intervention Program," *Physical Therapy*, 56:1976, pp. 155–158.

16. A. G. Kamhi, "Developmental vs. Difference Theories of Mental Retardation: A New Look," *American Journal of Mental Deficiency*, 86:1981, pp. 1–7.

17. S. Stainback, W. Stainback, and S. Maurer, "Training Teachers for the Severely and Profoundly Handicapped: A New Frontier," *Exceptional Children*, 42:1976, p. 205.

18. L. S. Watson, "Behavior Modification of Residents and Personnel in Institutions for the Mentally Retarded," in A. A. Baumeister and E. Butterfield, eds., *Residential Facilities for the Mentally Retarded*, Chicago: Aldine, 1976; N. G. Haring and E. L. Phillips, *Analysis and Modification of Classroom Behavior*, Englewood Cliffs, N.J.: Prentice-Hall, 1972, cited on page 65 of J. Y. Murdock, "Behavior Modification," in F. Litton, *The Education of the Trainable Mentally Retarded*, St. Louis: C. V. Mosby, 1978, pp. 65–91; J. Y. Murdock, "Behavior Modification," in F. W. Litton, *The Education of the Trainable Mentally Retarded*, St. Louis: C. V. Mosby, 1978, p. 65; J. M. Throne, "Deinstitutionalization: Too Wide a Swath," *Mental Retardation*, 17(4):1979, p. 173.

19. P. Roos, "Human Rights and Behavior Modification," *Mental Retardation*, 12:1974, p. 4.

20. D. L. MacMillan and S. R. Forness, "Behavior Modification: Limitations and Liabilities," *Exceptional Children*, 37:1970, p. 293.

21. Ibid, p. 296.

22. W. I. Gardner, *Behavior Modification in Mental Retardation: The Education and Rehabilitation of the Mentally Retarded Adolescent and Adult*, Chicago: Aldine, 1976.

23. J. Tramontana, "Social Versus Edible Rewards as a Function of Intellectual Level and Socioeconomic Class," *American Journal of Mental Deficiency*, 77:1972, p. 33.

24. N. Bernstein, "Intellectual Defect and Personality Development," in N. Bernstein, ed., *Diminished People*, Boston: Little, Brown and Co., 1970, p. 178.

25. H. C. Gunzburg, "The Education of the Mentally Handicapped Child," in A. M. Clarke, and A.D.B. Clarke, eds., *Mental Deficiency: The Changing Outlook*, 3rd ed., New York: The Free Press, 1974, p. 655.

26. J. Y. Murdock, p. 83.

27. S. J. Baran, "TV and Social Learning in the Institutionalized MR," *Mental Retardation*, 11(3):1973, p. 37.

28. D. Nolley, D. Boelkins, L. Kocur, M. K. Moore, S. Goncalves, and M. Lewis, "Aversive Conditioning Within Laws and Guidelines in a State Facility for Mentally Retarded Individuals," *Mental Retardation*, 18(6):1980, p. 297.

29. J. E. Favell, J. F. McGimsey, M. T. Jones, and P. R. Cannon, "Physical Restraint as Positive Reinforcement," *American Journal of Mental Deficiency*, 85:1981, pp. 425–432.

5
The Education of Mentally Retarded People: Settings and Sources

What Wisdom can you find that is greater than kindness?
—J. Rousseau[1]

Adopt the pace of Nature: her secret is patience.
—R. W. Emerson[2]

SETTINGS

Each class at New Morning School had its own character. There were differences in instructional content, social expectations, ambience, and a host of other factors at every level. Some of these factors will be discussed in this chapter.

The Preschool (Ages Three Through Five)

The first task of the preschool teacher, once preliminary assessments had been completed, was to get certain students to attend to the world around them. This was not a problem for those students who were either inherently attentive, or were veterans of infant stimulation and/or toddler programs. The latter had been going to school, in a manner of speaking, since infancy. A few of the preschool children, on the other hand, were making their first apparent contacts with the external realities of "the real world" and had to be eased into it.

There are numerous reasons why retarded persons can have trouble attending to the world around them. For example, a couple of the students in the preschool who were originally suspected of being mentally retarded were later found to be autistic—autism being the most mysterious, difficult to diagnose, and etiologically vague of the developmental disabilities. It is posited that the apparent lack of responsiveness to external stimuli that characterizes autism may result from an inability to inhibit attention to internal stimuli. The word autism comes from the Greek, *autos,* meaning self.

A few of New Morning's preschoolers took medications that aggravated their inattentiveness. For example, some anticonvulsive drugs taken by the children with seizure disorders made them very drowsy.

A few of the children did not seem to be able to distinguish between what are generally considered to be relevant social stimuli and those stimuli "normally" viewed as socially irrelevant. A person, a chair, a rock . . . they all seemed to be of the same order to some of the children in the preschool.

One of the empirically supported elements of "special education folk wisdom" holds that retarded people have short attention spans.[3] Another is that where the attention span is long, it is also very narrow. Some students became engrossed in an object or person, so strongly riveting their attention there that they could not be distracted; others were too easily distracted. The volatile attention spans of most of the children in the preschool and many of those in more advanced grades were the primary reason why, in virtually all of the classes, lessons tended to be brief—seeming fragmentary, at times, to outsiders.

One of the earliest realities the preschoolers had to attend to was the assessment process, whereby their needs and abilities were ascertained. The children who had been in infant stimulation and toddler programs were no strangers to assessment. And all of the children had been through a diagnostic assessment before being enrolled in school, although these were cursory in the case of some of the youngsters.

Increasing the students' attention spans and assessment of their respective needs were preludes to another important educational component of the preschool experience. The socialization process began in the preschool. This is especially important for retarded people who will eventually be living in the community. Frequently, they are given only one chance to deviate from community norms before they are institutionalized in a "state school" or, as we shall see later, a prison.

The first phase of the socialization process concentrated on cultivating the student's cooperative abilities. To that end, all the preschoolers— and the students in every other class—received continuous feedback on their adequacies as group participants. Minimally, they were taught to not be chronically disruptive.

The preschool students were also taught grooming and cleanliness skills. For some of them, their training in personal hygiene at New Morning was the first of its kind. A few of them were neglected at home. For example, one boy who had not had the benefit of the early hygiene offered at New Morning nearly lost all of his teeth to gum disease generated by neglect. The parent with whom the child lived

ressing and feeding, along with
preschool. Sometimes the training
Jew Morning's students were still
adolescence. One of the criticisms
of significant resources on students
ntal achievement than to be toilet
e were a small number of New
p measurable benefits from the
al education asserts that everyone
est functional capacities. Further,
learning certain skills (taken for
warrants the expenditures.[4]
d deal of their time playing. The
simple motor acts, such as riding
as practically no thematic play—
g. And there was little interaction
among the children.

Ancillary Services

The preschool students began to receive help from the school's specialists, including speech-language, music, and occupational therapists as well as a physical education specialist.

Speech Therapy. Many mentally retarded people have serious speech and language problems. Ninety percent of retarded persons with IQs below 50 and approximately 45 percent of mildly retarded individuals are impaired in their development of language.[5] As was indicated earlier, children who reach certain chronological milestones without learning skills such as speech may never learn those skills. Because of this, it is crucial that the speech therapists begin their work as early as possible with the New Morning students. Current research shows that there is a period sometime around the second birthday that is critical to the remediation of a child's deficits in speech if these are the result of environmental deprivation.[6] Thus, for some students, the earliest intervention at New Morning may not come soon enough. Indeed, intervention prior to the age of three may be the only way to help certain children avoid serious developmental deficits. It is a curious irony that compulsory education is mandated *after* the most important developmental period of a child's life, but that compulsory assessment and intervention are not mandated *during* this period.

A few of the younger students at New Morning received both individual and group therapies from the school's speech clinicians. The school did not have enough clinicians on staff to service most of the older students (fifteen through twenty-one). It is fairly common for young adults who are retarded to be excluded from ancillary services in limited resource situations. While it is not usually verbalized, some service providers justify this situation with the belief that older students would not benefit from such services anyway. There are doubtless situations in which this is the case; however, Gunzburg has found that retarded people above the age of sixteen may not only benefit from intensive educational stimulation, but are frequently more receptive to it than they might have been in their earlier years.[7] Gilbert and Hemming show that the language development of mentally retarded persons does not cease at maturity.[8] Thus, both early *and* continued speech-language stimulation have been shown to be developmentally important to retarded persons.

As with other aspects of development, a child's speech-language skills go through a certain sequence. For example, the process of a baby learning his first word starts with a cry. He then experiments with different noises, such as cooing and gurgling, and sounds, such as vowels, consonants, syllables, and diphthongs. The infant will use these sounds when people are talking and playing with him or when he is playing by himself. Next, the baby imitates the noises and sounds he has made and gradually shifts to imitating the intonation and melody patterns he hears others use. Finally, the baby will try to name a familiar object by attaching some of the sounds he can make to the object.

A youngster must learn to *understand* and *use*: (1) the sounds and sound sequences of his language system, (2) the system's vocabulary, (3) word endings, and (4) sentence structure, in addition to the variety of ways language is used for communication. A mentally retarded child will progress through the developmental sequences that make up each of these components of language more slowly than a non-handicapped youngster. Most mentally retarded children will never develop age-appropriate language skills.

There are three primary aspects of language development; a disturbance in any of these, alone or in combination, can lead to communication disorders. First, there is receptive language. Before someone can respond appropriately, he must have perceived accurately and attached appropriate meanings to his perceptions. This requires that all the receptive mechanisms work properly, meaning that the child must not only hear, which is a purely physiological process, but *listen*, which is a lot more. Even simple listening requires these steps: (1) auditory awareness: being aware of environmental sounds; (2) auditory focusing: determining where a sound is coming from; (3) auditory figure-ground: the ability to discriminate and focus on one sound to the exclusion of all others in the sound field; (4) auditory discrimination: being able to tell the differences in sounds; (5) auditory memory: the ability to remember what one has heard; (6) auditory sequencing: correctly repeating a sequence of items to oneself; and so on.[9] These are only a few of the skills a child needs to understand spoken language. This understanding, which is receptive language, is a very complex process. Then add the second major component of communication development—association— and the plot thickens.

Although association involves many complicated processes, the term primarily refers to mastery of the skills involved in directing the "internal dialogue." It is the communication we have with ourselves. It has even been suggested that human speech developed not so much for communication with others but as a means to control the individual's own information retrieval system.[10]

Neurological problems render some retarded children deficient in the associative elements of language. No one is quite sure what it is like inside the minds of children with poor associative powers, but it must be a hodge-podge. When the child attempts to process a well-ordered social reality with such a mind, the result is doubtless very confusing and frustrating.

Assuming a child has the abilities to attach meaning to the perceptions he processes and sufficient associative and/or cognitive capacities to have something to communicate, he must be able to express his communications. This is called expressive language and is the third major element of language development.

One of the components of expressive language is the ability to produce the sounds of the speaker's culture. Some people cannot produce intelligible sounds at all. Many of them omit sounds that are crucial to word formation or substitute one sound for another. A few distort sounds so badly that they cannot be understood. When speech-language clinicians cannot teach a child to speak intelligibly, he is sometimes taught to use sign language. This strategy has been shown to be an effective receptive and expressive language tool, and it has the benefit, in some cases, of helping the youngster to become more *vocally* expressive.[11]

Another alternative to spoken language that has been used with retarded children is a communication board. These boards, which the youngsters carry with them, bear images such as pictures, printed words, or other symbols. When the child wants to express a certain idea that symbolically appears somewhere on the board, he simply points to it. Children who learn to use sign language (unless they are hearing-impaired) or a communication board are in a sense bilingual—their receptive language being verbal and their expressive language manual or graphic.

It was initially very difficult for me to grasp what many of the students at New Morning understood or were trying to communicate. I found myself smiling, nodding in affirmation, and saying yes to a lot of communications that were unintelligible. What was even more difficult to understand was the staff's apparent sixth sense in grasping these communications. With time, however, one can come to understand messages that are, at first, incomprehensible. This comes with a training of one's ear, and a knowledge of what certain children are capable of saying. I learned another trick. The children often understood each other even when no one else could. One teacher went so far as to say that some of the students "intuit the emotions of others." Dubious as I was about such telepathy, I certainly spared no effort in using the more articulate students as translators.

The importance of communication skills to retarded people cannot be overestimated. Aside from causing the frustrations of not being able to express oneself, poor communications focus a great deal of social stigma on one. Cross-cultural studies indicate that verbal skill is the basis of the mental retardation label in many modern *and* preliterate societies.[12] More specifically, in our society the degree of a person's handicap is usually determined on the basis of his ability to communicate with a tester—the effects of the labels that arise from this interaction often determining what role a person will play in society for the rest of his life.

Occupational Therapy. In addition to speech-language therapy, a few of the preschoolers at New Morning began to receive the help of the occupational therapist. Occupational therapists are concerned with promoting improvement in a retarded child's sensory awareness (tactile, auditory, visual, kinesthetic, and so forth), as well as enhancing the youngster's motor planning and bodily movements, among other things.

As with speech, the physical development of a child follows a certain sequence. The infant will learn to sit unsupported after he learns to balance his head upright, extend his spine, and bear weight on his arms in front of his body. Development always proceeds from gross movement patterns to finer movement patterns. Gross motor skills require the use of the larger muscles, while fine motor skills use the smaller muscles—for example, kicking a ball versus buttoning a shirt or fastening a zipper. Another principle of the physical development of a child is that movements are coordinated in the upper regions of the body before they are coordinated in the lower regions. Thus, head control is achieved before leg control. And finally, development of control over the trunk of the body precedes control over the extremities.

For example, control of shoulder movements occurs before control of the fingers.

As is the case with speech, if specific physical milestones are not reached by certain chronological periods, they may never be attained. For example, ophthalmologists report an interesting fact about a disorder called strabismus. If an individual has strabismus of one eye, that eye is focused to one side and is relatively ineffectual for use in normal vision. In order to correct the condition, the properly focused eye must have a patch over it, forcing the defective eye to be focused forward. If the procedure of patching the unaffected eye is not done by the time a child reaches the age of four, "no useful perceptions can ever be developed in it [the defective eye] despite the fact that organically it is a perfect organ of vision."[13]

Occupational therapists are wont to emphasize the fact that sensorimotor neurological development always precedes cognitive development. Thus, the occupational therapist at New Morning saw her efforts as the common denominator underlying all other development of the students at the school. This view was shared by New Morning's physical education specialist.

Physical Education and Physical Therapy. The physical education specialist was concerned with three main elements of the students' development: (1) basic movements, (2) perceptual-motor skills, and (3) physical fitness. The first two areas were in the domain of the occupational therapist as well, although the physical education specialist was more concerned with gross motor skills, while the occupational therapist put more emphasis on fine motor skills.

As is the case with non-handicapped populations, physical fitness for mentally retarded persons focuses on such things as strength, flexibility, muscular and cardiovascular endurance, balance, agility, speed, general coordination, and reaction time. That physical fitness is important to the New Morning students is borne out by two facts: first, retarded people are two to five years behind national norms on motor performance; second, poor physical fitness is characteristic of retarded persons.[14]

The ramifications of these facts are critical. The physical eccentricities of many mentally retarded people are the focus of their stigmatization in the community. In addition, poor physical condition may adversely affect a child's capacity to learn. While the literature on humans does not go so far as to draw causal conclusions between poor fitness and low IQ, one study done on laboratory animals showed that an enriched program of motor stimulation promoted "cerebral cell growth and the complexity of the dendritic connections."[15] (The latter are the conduits of synaptic energy.)

It was noteworthy that New Morning School did not have a gymnasium despite the fact that it was a new facility. The students took their indoor physical education in a cafeteria. The physical education specialist attributed this to an oversight on the part of planners who, she said, "did not know retarded kids could get around at all, much less have physical education."

There was an oversight in one element of the personnel policy at the school as well: New Morning had no physical therapist on the staff. The need for a physical therapist was frequently mentioned by teachers and other therapists. Children who had severe balance and mobility problems as a result of cerebral palsy or spina bifida (two developmental disabilities that sometimes accompany mental retardation) could have profited from the skills of a physical therapist to complement what the other motor specialists were able to do. The fact that there was no physical therapist at the school was, in part, symptomatic of an issue raised by both the occupational therapist and the physical education specialist.

They said that too little emphasis was given to the physical domain of the students. The occupational therapist held that much of the "academic" information disseminated to the students at school was misinterpreted, ignored, or forgotten by them anyway. Further, she said that the physical afflictions of many of the students adversely affected their learning abilities and their capacity to put academic acquisitions into practice. Predictably, all the specialists at New Morning thought that more emphasis should be placed on their specialty, and probably they all were right.

Music Therapy. The preschool students at New Morning also began to receive help from the music therapist. She went from classroom to classroom with a bag of small rhythm instruments, supplying many of the students with what appeared to be the energy peaks of their days. The students, almost without exception, participated in the music period even if they did not know the words to the songs being sung or they were in wheelchairs and could only move certain parts of their bodies to the dances being done. (I do not, by the way, mean to imply that retarded people have a natural or exaggerated sense of rhythm.) Music therapy was more than fun, though. Through music, the therapist helped the students develop a variety of skills: auditory-perceptual, visual-perceptual, language, and gross and fine motor skills, to name only a few. Music therapy occasionally contributed to a reduction in erratic behavior associated with hyperactivity and helped certain students learn to participate in groups. The music therapist also tried to cultivate the special skills of those children who showed promise on particular musical instruments. Some of them were fairly adept musicians.

Basic Skills

After finishing their stint at New Morning's preschool, those students who were not assessed as being mentally retarded (remember: the preschool would enroll virtually any child suspected of having a handicap) typically went on to other schools that had classes designed specifically to meet the needs associated with their handicaps or disorders. These included classes for language-impaired, learning-disabled, hearing-impaired, autistic, or emotionally disturbed students.

Most of the preschoolers who were still assessed as being mentally retarded moved up to the earliest of the school's primary classes, while those students who were so severely retarded that they could not benefit from participation in the primary grades went on to New Morning's basic skills classes. With the passage of such laws as the Rehabilitation Act of 1973, which set the tone for emphasis on services to those individuals with the most severe handicaps, and the Education for All Handicapped Children Act of 1975, which mandated educational opportunities for *all* handicapped children, an increasing number of severely and profoundly handicapped children began to be enrolled at New Morning in the late seventies. Indeed, during the last decade, in the whole field of mental retardation a remarkable amount of attention was paid to severely and profoundly retarded children. Prestigious journals were dominated by research on severe and profound levels of mental retardation.[16] The American Association for the Education of the Severely and Profoundly Handicapped was founded in 1975.

The basic skills teachers at New Morning did many of the same things that were done in other classes at the school, but at a slower rate and with more repetition. Emphasis was put on such things as response to environmental stimulation; grasping objects; sucking, swallowing, and chewing; bodily balance and movement; imitations; vocalization; and (where possible) self-feeding, dressing, toileting, walking, talking, and social-recreational behavior.

The basic skills students received ancillary services, although these were modified. For example, the speech-language clinician did a great deal of feeding-training (helping the children learn how to eat without choking, for example) in addition to some elementary speech-language therapy. Until the recent past, it was not widely believed that severely and profoundly retarded persons could profit from ancillary services such as speech therapy. Recent practice has proven this assumption wrong.[17] One inquiry, for instance, has shown that some severely retarded youths and adults can improve their language skills through "the application of systematic instructional techniques and reinforcing strategies."[18]

Such findings create hope among professionals involved in teaching severely and profoundly handicapped children. Now and again, though, I observed such earnest hope inspired in a teacher that he lost touch with the realistic capabilities of his students. While hope must spring eternal in such professionals if educational breakthroughs are ever to be achieved, overamplified expectations about students occasionally created problems, especially in the basic skills settings. For example, collaborating colleagues, such as specialists, became annoyed and frustrated when they were expected to perform miracles on the basis of the ill-founded hopes of the occasionally benighted basic skills teacher.

One notable feature of the basic skills teachers at New Morning was their adamance, when interacting with administrators and colleagues, in maintaining that basic skills classes were not dumping grounds of custodial care. This attitude was understandable. Special education's history is steeped in a tradition of giving the least help to the children who need it most. As we shall see, the education of severely and profoundly retarded youngsters has become one of the most volatile political issues in special education today.

The Primary Grades (Ages Six Through Twelve)

In the primary grades at New Morning, the training in self-help, socialization, communication, and motor skills that characterized the preschool was combined with instruction in "functional academics." The more basic academics included such things as learning to identify colors, shapes, numbers, and letters. The higher-functioning primary students began to learn to read, write, and do elemental calculations. The students were also instructed in weather recognition, telling time, calendar reading, and sign identification. Here, they were taught to understand the meaning of essential signs such as Don't Walk, Exit, Danger, Stop, Poison, Private, Flammable, and so on.

The repetitiveness seen in the games of the preschoolers was still typical in the play of the primary students, but the games began to take on more thematic content. There was more role-playing, and the primary students also seemed to be more curious than most of the preschoolers.

Common sense tells us that mentally retarded children are likely to be less curious than those without handicaps. This is a difficult issue to pursue because empirical barometers of curiosity are not widely agreed upon. Some investigators use responsiveness to external stimuli. For example, Webster says that retarded people are "responsive if stimulated, but they do not tend to seek external objects except in terms of some rather immediate direct gratification."[19] The teachers at New Morning tended to use the quantity and types of questions their students asked as indicators of curiosity. Several of the staff told me that their students were just as curious as normal children in terms of the number of questions they asked. According to the teachers, the students just asked different kinds of questions than non-handicapped children of the same age. For example, the younger students at New Morning asked numerous identification questions, seeking to know "What?" or "Who?"—queries that could be answered briefly and concretely. They rarely asked descriptive questions like "How?" or causal questions like "Why?"—questions that would be frequently asked by non-handicapped children of the same age. This changes for many of the students as they get older, but one must remember that curiosity is very abstract, because it is based upon the assumption that that which has presented itself is not complete and requires further investigation. It is suggested by one author that special educators will often describe a child as exploring or curious when the child is simply following hyperactive impulses.[20] Perhaps, but not in all cases. Many of the students I observed seemed to savor their explorations with genuine curiosity.

Not incidentally, when some of the New Morning students asked ostensibly causal questions like "Why?," it was not always an expression of curiosity. A period of exaggerated negativism usually characterizes the social development of most normal preschool children—a phenomenon sometimes referred to as the "terrible twos." This stage, although often annoying to parents, is a positive step in social self-discovery and the development of self-sufficiency in the child. Most retarded children go through the same stage. The difference is that, because of delayed development, the negativistic period usually comes later (about six or seven years of age) and lasts longer for retarded children. If a primary student at New Morning School happened to be in this phase, the context in which the question "Why?" was asked was often a challenge to his teacher's authority—a test of the teacher's limits of tolerance. This posed real problems for the staff members at the school. While they worked to accustom their students to authority and tried to foster self-sufficiency, they had to be careful not to stifle the incipient stages of causal curiosity. Sometimes it was very difficult to separate obstinacy from wonder.

There were other factors that complicated the curiosity issue for staffers. For example, it was easy for them to become inured to the questions some students asked. To one girl, "Can I stay here?" was not really a query about the permissibility of her staying; it was just her way of establishing communication. She said "Can I stay here?" six times within the first minute of our meeting (such repeating is called perseveration). After assuring her six times that it was all right if she stayed, I realized that it did not matter how I responded. A lot of students asked nonsense questions; many perseverated. These factors may distort the intentions of legitimate inquiries made by the youngsters, so that teachers must be very careful when they tune in and tune out.

The socialization process was continued in the primary grades. Two instances of this could be seen in the way students were taught to respect other persons' spaces and property. The primary students were, for example, shown that it was not acceptable to walk into a bathroom when someone else was using it. This was clearly confusing to some of them, because their teachers frequently walked in on the students when they were in the bathroom. A number of the students needed help in the bathroom, though—one of the extra duties special educators must assume.

The sanctity of private property was a frequently discussed aspect of the socialization process that began in the primary grades. Practically everything belonging to the students was labeled with their names. This helped them recognize their names when written and grasp the notion of ownership. Private-property lessons, especially the idea of not helping oneself to someone else's property, were stressed in all the grades at New Morning. This helped students with poor impulse control and an acquisitive nature to keep out of trouble. There were also some students who, responding to property lessons, would obsessively avoid touching things that belonged to other people, demonstrating the literal way that certain retarded people interpret ideas.

The Intermediate Grades
(Ages Thirteen Through Sixteen)

When the students entered the middle-range grades at New Morning, they were expected to comport themselves more as though they were in a traditional classroom. They were given work periods during which they were expected to perform specified tasks, with a modicum of silence, at their own desks.

They were also expected to defer certain gratifications. This was very difficult for some of the students. As Thompson points out, compared to people without handicaps, retarded persons are much more willing to accept immediate and small rewarding outcomes rather than delayed and more substantial rewards.[21] (This quality is typical of some primitive peoples as well.[22])

Functional academics became more sophisticated in the intermediate grades. The students were given lessons in numerical concepts such as lengths, measurements (for instance, quarter, half, dozen), and amounts (pair, twice, increase, decrease). A few of the students learned to read. The instruction here was focused on using information in telephone directories, bus timetables, and newspapers. Some higher-functioning students began to read for pleasure. This became an inexpensive source of enjoyment for those individuals who eventually "went out on their own."

Despite the potential inherent in functional academics, they are occasionally looked upon negatively. The reader will remember the overemphasis on them mentioned earlier by one New Morning staff member. Hirshoren and Burton suggest that even if limited academic skills can be taught to select "trainable" retarded persons over protracted periods of time, we should be cautious about generalizing these findings.[23] On the basis of her research, Warren says, "Results indicated that as a group, trainables [moderately retarded people] do not attain a level of academic skill in reading and arithmetic that could be considered of any degree of usefulness."[24] If one takes the lowest common denominator of students in any of New Morning's classes, there might be support for the assertions of skeptics regarding academics for retarded persons. However, many of the students at the school clearly profited from the academics. These students should not be denied, and as long as they are in a school where they receive individualized instruction, they need not be.

Socialization in the intermediate grades began to focus on the "rough edges" of the students. For example, in recognition of the fact that some retarded persons are predisposed to stand too close to, or be too physically demonstrative with, other people, the teachers tried to cultivate culturally acceptable spatial boundaries in their students. Shaking hands is considered an acceptable substitute to the embraces many of the students dispense with abandon, and this is one of the reasons why many retarded people will shake a stranger's hand. Incidentally, I believe that the reason retarded people tend to be physically demonstrative may not be solely attributable to an inherent lack of inhibition. Some of them learn it: retarded children are handled a great deal, especially when people are trying to help or direct them, and they are not usually asked first if hands may be laid on. It is natural that they imitate this license with others, and even more natural that they become confused when they suddenly discover it is "wrong."

The socialization process in the intermediate classes began to assume an ethical complexity for the staff that was not present in the earlier grades. There was little controversy as to whether the younger students should learn cooperation, or respect for other people, their property, and their space. The issues endemic to socialization in the upper grades were less cut and dried. For example, the staff members faced philo-sophical and practical ambiguities regarding such things as how compliant with authority their students should be trained to be, or how the students should be taught to deal with competition. These questions are significant and we shall discuss them, but first, it is important to understand why many of the staff members at New Morning were so circumspect about the approaches they took with their students on value-laden issues.

Special educators possess extraordinary power over the socialization of most of their students. A few of New Morning's students were not socialized at home. Some of their parents imparted little information pertinent to the socialization process, perhaps because they underrated the child's ability to assimilate this information; a few of the parents did not know how to relate to their retarded children or simply did not like them well enough to spend any time with them. Some of the students' parents were retarded themselves and not equal to the socialization task. Religions and peer groups did not seem very important elements in the socialization process of most of the students. Where these factors, or family, had minimal effects on socialization, the educational setting (and the TV[25]) took on an unusually powerful significance in the process.

If there were vacuums in the students' interpersonal lives, their teachers were the only "significant others" to interact with them frequently enough to fill these voids. And when potent methods such as behavior modification were applied to this captive audience—who, the reader will remember, seldom asked "Why?"—the power of the staff was additionally increased.

Add to this certain features of the typical retarded individual's personality, and we see a further intensification of the special educator's power. For one thing, retarded people tend to be very compliant with non-handicapped adults. It has been shown, for instance, that interviews with retarded persons, in which they are allowed to agree or disagree, are invalid for scientific purposes because the respondents will almost always say yes to questions whether they want to or not—this as a means of obtaining social approval.[26] Other research has shown that retarded people tend to have lower self-esteem than non-handicapped persons and that individuals with low self-esteem are highly suggestible to value modeling of people with higher-esteem positions.[27] Further, when a retarded person does assimilate an idea, he will almost mechanically conform to it. A special educator told a story about watching a retarded man crossing a street. The man waited on the street corner while the light was red and no traffic was coming. The light turned green and the retarded pedestrian began to cross the street . . . right into the path of an oncoming car, which he saw was going to run the light. And why not? The rules were with him even though his compliance with them led to a near miss. As one New Morning teacher said, "The whole life of the retarded is based upon habits that are hard to come by, and not easily extinguished once formed. It's all they've got; even their concept of self is habitual."

Social aphorisms fill the void created by retarded people's inability to carry on reflexive discourse about moral subtleties. And the New Morning staff was often the sole determinant of which aphorisms would be transmitted. Prominently displayed on the bulletin board of one classroom was the following: "How to Look, How to Talk, How to Act, *How to Think.*" How were retarded people taught to act and think at New Morning School? Take two examples mentioned earlier: compliance with authority and attitudes toward competition.

Retarded people usually rely on normal adults to help them make decisions. Even mentally retarded children live in a world where most of their significant others are non-handicapped adults, since, as we shall see, they have a few friends. This reliance, coupled with retarded persons' predisposition toward compliance and meager powers of discrimination, lead to some special problems with regard to the authority issue. For instance, does one teach mentally retarded children to obey all adults as legitimate authorities? Or must the adult possess some symbol of legitimation? If so, what symbols? Several New Morning staff members told me that nearly anyone wearing any kind of uniform could command the obedience of their students. I saw an example of a parallel phenomenon when I was out one afternoon with a friend of mine who is mentally retarded. We were at a camera store in which all the salespersons but one were wearing T-shirts with the name and logo of the store on them. As it turned out, the only person not wearing one of the shirts was the owner of the store—a very knowledgeable photographer. My friend would not let the man serve us, waving him away, and pointing to someone wearing the proper T-shirt.

There is also the problem of what criteria can be used to help retarded persons discriminate appropriate demands from inappropriate or exploitative ones made by legitimate authorities. In the work place, for example, retarded individuals may be asked to do things that are unsafe or morally questionable. More on this later.

As more mentally handicapped persons achieve a greater degree of independence, the philosophical and practical issues surrounding their relationship to authority will become more acute. And it is the individuals who act as the primary socializers—the educators—who will have to make the difficult value judgments regarding how their students will be taught to comply with authority.

Another issue infused with complex value questions was the manner in which the New Morning students were taught to relate to competition. During my earliest observations at the school, the students were conspicuously non-competitive. For example, I attended a swimming meet in which a little boy, finishing last in a race by about six minutes, jumped out of the water and threw his one semifunctional hand up in victory. Competition has changed a lot since then at New Morning. During my last visits, students were being taught to compete seriously, the sense of competition being especially keen when associated with events such as track and swim meets, basketball and football tournaments, and Special Olympics. Many of the students who participated in these activities had internalized a passion for winning. Some went into depressions if they did not win; a few became aggressive or petulant.

Parents often exacerbated their offspring's anxiety levels by vicarious participation in the sports events, exhibiting conspicuous disappointment when their child was on the losing side. In this way, they were like the parents of many non-handicapped children. With a few, though, it seemed as if the obsession with their child's winning had a lot to do with providing the parents something compensatory for the child's handicap. The competitive trend became so powerful at New Morning that certain students began to be excluded from participation in Special Olympics because they were not proficient enough athletes, thus defeating the whole purpose of Special Olympics.

Several members of the New Morning staff said they were alarmed by the burgeoning competitive trend at the school. The proponents of competition at New Morning said that it facilitated learning. One study shows that under "certain, very limited conditions, relating to very specific tasks, competition may facilitate performance."[28] Advocates of competition also argued that competitive victories may be the first, and sometimes the only, contact with success these students will have.

Competition also began to be more manifest in the classrooms of New Morning over the years. Along with this, a number of students became preoccupied with giving correct answers to questions posed by teachers. Some changed from rather indifferent participants in class recitations into frenetic, edge-of-the-chair, "Me, teacher, me," hand wavers. Conversely, there were students who became less active in class than they previously had been. A few who were not very academically competitive to start with adopted a reticent style in the classroom. They would not answer questions publicly that they could answer privately, because they seemed to be afraid of making fools of themselves. Such dynamics are not restricted to handicapped children, and many of the New Morning students were shy, competition or not. There are, however, other values that must be questioned in teaching mentally retarded children to compete.

Is it fair to teach them to compete in a world in which they probably cannot win? It is one thing when retarded persons compete against each other, quite another when they compete in less-protected circumstances. Nurturing the competitive thrust in retarded people who will be entering the community may give them a more accurate picture of mainstream norms, but it also can lead them toward collisions with their thresholds of frustration—toward crises of competence. It can be argued that competition affects all of us that way; but, as we shall see, the psychological vulnerabilities of mentally retarded people make the dangers greater for them.

Certain staff members suggested that the problems associated with competition could be minimized if the students were pitted against inanimate objects such as the clock or were simply encouraged to better their old levels of accomplishment. The problem with this kind of competition is that it is directed toward abstract goals. If one does not conceptualize the concept of time very effectively, running a mile in five minutes and twenty seconds, rather than five minutes and thirty seconds, cannot be nearly as rewarding as outrunning someone else. The important issue special educators face is that of providing meaningful and concrete successes for students within competitive contexts, while minimizing some of the unfortunate byproducts of competition.

The Prevocational and Vocational Grades
(Ages Seventeen Through Twenty-one)

In the prevocational and vocational classes at New Morning, there was an extension and refinement of the self-help, communication, physical, social, and academic skills that began in the earlier grades. Domestic skills such as sewing, shopping, cooking, laundering, using the phone, finding addresses, using public transportation, and handling money received increasing attention. The older students began to get more sophisticated training in human development and sexuality than they had in the intermediate grades. They also learned about family living and apartment life in the school's built-in apartment, which had a living room, dining area, kitchen, bedroom, bathroom, and laundry and utility room. Community awareness was also stressed, including such things as contact with police and fire officials and use of the public library.

The prevocational and vocational students frequently took field trips. Not only did this give them practice in community living, but because their appearance in Mountview became more commonplace, the students lost some of their "geek" status. One staff member made an interesting comment about field trips, saying, "It is all well and good that we go into the community, but it seems that every time we do, it's in large groups. . . . We usually end up 'herding' the students." The teacher said that such field trips would accord more closely with the normalization goals of the school if the students were taken on outings in groups proportional in size to those of normal people when they go out.

The older students were encouraged to develop hobbies and cultivate leisure-time skills. In line with this, many of them were given an opportunity to manage part of their own time during the day. They were required to complete specified tasks within these self-managed time blocks; a few of them learned that if they were efficient in completing a job, there was some extra time for leisure activities.

The immersion in vocational training also included teaching the students about punctuality. They learned to fill out applications. The school acquired more tools every year, which allowed the students to get valuable experience in manual arts. Some of them entered janitorial training programs or learned to sort objects. Many of the jobs these people would take after graduation involved janitorial and sorting skills.

Commencement

By the time they were ready to graduate, most of the students had achieved a degree of academic skills roughly comparable to those of an average third grader. Their social skills were typically better than this. Many students did much better than the norm; some worse. A few graduates had not progressed appreciably since they entered the program, although this was rare.

Regardless of their level of achievement, students were graduated from New Morning when they were twenty-one years old. They had a graduation ceremony similar to that held in most high schools, with speeches, diplomas, and the like.

After graduation, a few of the lowest-functioning students were institutionalized, although that is becoming exceedingly unusual. As a rule, the slowest of them either remained at home or entered so-called life enrichment or skills development programs. These were continuations of training in elemental educational and occupational skills—sort of postgraduate programs in basic skills. Such programs were not developed in Mountview until the late seventies; they reflected the increasing concern for direction of the normalization principle toward more severely retarded people.

New Morning's higher-functioning graduates usually went to work in sheltered workshops. A few got jobs in the community. Regardless of where they ended up, the students shared one thing; they had had a school, a place where they were not looked upon as useless or problematic because of their handicaps.

SOURCES

Boy Talk

One of the most conspicuous characteristics of the staff at New Morning was the imbalance between men and women. There were only two men—a teacher and an aide—out of a staff of thirty-five people when I began my observations. I wondered aloud about this, and got varied responses from staff members.

A few of them believed that men had little inclination to work with retarded children because of a stigma attached to male special educators unless they work in colleges, in programs for adult retarded people, or in administration. Another staff member said that, as society changes its norms of "manliness," more men will enter the field of special education as classroom teachers. Some of the staff believed women to be innately better suited to the task of educating mentally handicapped children. One said that there are more women in special education environments because "women tend to put up with more than guys," although she allowed that this may be because the "female role has been defined that way." One of her colleagues said that it is "the innate nature of the female of the species to be a caretaker." Her coworkers would probably have taken umbrage at this characterization of their vocation, as "caretaking" is antithetical to every tenet of the normalization principle. There may have been some wisdom in her perceptions, though. One investigation showed that women were more accepting of disabilities such as mental retardation than men.[29] Another body of research indicated that male children were more inclined to reject mentally retarded children their own age than were female children.[30]

One of the major reasons men have shied away from classroom teaching of mentally retarded students probably has nothing to do with innate gender characteristics. I believe that men, especially those who are the sole financial support for families, have avoided special education because of economic considerations. Until the recent past, salaries for special educators have been very low in some localities. For example, the starting salary at New Morning School for a person with a master's degree was $5,800 per school year in 1975. This has gone up significantly in the last few years to a base salary of $12,500 in 1981, although it is still prohibitively low for a breadwinner—man or woman. As such inequities reflect our society's bias toward downgrading the importance of occupations and professions that are dominated (on the staff level, anyway) by women, further inquiry would be warranted to determine why special education has been considered a woman's field.

Since my earliest observations at New Morning, one more male teacher and another male aide have come to the staff, as well as a male social worker. This trend is important and promising. If, for example, a child has a poor relationship with his or her own father, the school setting may be the only place where the youngster spends enough time to establish more than a superficial relationship with a significant male. This is particularly important to boys, who need male role models other than those they see on TV. The reader will also remember that there are more mentally retarded males than females; for example, there was a consistent 5:3 male to female ratio of students at New Morning between 1973 and 1981. A school's commitment to the normalization principle should be reflected in its staffing procedures. Presumably, graduates will not enter a world comprised predominantly of women, so special education students should be given considerable practice negotiating their realities with men.

Special Educators

It was only a quarter of a century ago that states began to develop certification standards for special educators.[31] Those guidelines, designed mainly for educators of mildly retarded students, were not appropriate for teachers of those with more severe handicaps. With the increased need for educators of moderately, severely, and profoundly retarded students generated in the wake of the normalization movement, certification standards for these teachers have been developed rapidly in the last few years.[32]

Today, most professionals entering the field of special education have been certified through undergraduate and graduate training in universities with special education and/or mental retardation programs. But the seventies was a period of transition in this regard. For example, most of the staff members who came to work at New Morning School before 1977 had degrees in fields totally unrelated to special education and subsequently earned their certification in night school and summer programs.

While a few New Morning staff members had relatives who were mentally retarded, most of them had their first taste of special education when they volunteered at the school. After that, they were hired as teacher aides, were certified, and filled teaching positions as they opened. Such patterns are not atypical. Gottfried and Jones found that 40 percent of the people who went to work in the field of "exceptional children" had previous volunteer or other personal experience with such children.[33]

It is easy to see why people are attracted to special education once they get a little experience. Mentally retarded children are captivating. I do not mean to mystify them, but some inexplicable attraction tends to develop between retarded children and almost anyone who has more than a few contacts with them. Most are delightfully spontaneous in their expression of loving emotions, although this can be a dual-edged sword. Most need the kind of extensive help that appeals to anyone with strong nurturing instincts. This was demonstrated in one study that showed that the most effective teachers of trainable mentally retarded children were those who had personality needs such as succorance, nurturance, and affiliation on the Edwards Personal Preference Schedule.[34]

Because retarded people are less tied to the superficialities of social posturing, one learns to drop one's social guard around them—making the world much less a "stage." Retarded people can also be enchanting in the way they perceive things. For example, I was at a cemetery with a retarded friend, and we were talking about death. His best friend and roommate had just died, and he wanted a little clarification on the idea of the soul. I tried to explain to him what philosophers and theologians had said, in terms he could understand, but seemed to be getting nowhere. Finally, he looked at me and said, "You mean the soul is like air?" Yeah.

There was another reason I was attracted to certain retarded children and adults whom I got to know in the course of doing this study. I think the "high" I often experienced after spending a day with retarded persons came from a juxtaposition of my comfortable "normalcy" to their handicaps. One needs to share some life with retarded people to realize one's own good fortune in not being mentally retarded in a world that puts such a premium on intelligence.

The Frustrations of Special Educators

Despite the highs one can experience in working with mentally retarded people—no matter what the cause of the elation—special education can be a very frustrating profession. The New Morning staff all mentioned that they had been frustrated by the slow, often erratic, progress of many of their students. It can be difficult to formulate realistic expectations for moderately retarded people. There are not many miracles, and overexpectation is frustrating to teacher and student alike. So special educators learn to find satisfaction in mini-triumphs—as one teacher put it, "We must learn to judge progress on an infinitesimal scale."

A special educator always faces the frustrating problem of deciding with whom to spend his time in class. Is it advisable to exert a lot of energy on a low-functioning youngster when the same energy can be spent with much greater return on many of the more intelligent students? For example, does one spend equal time and resources on a retarded student who is eventually likely to move into the community and another student whose maximum functional potential may be at the six-month level of development? The introduction of the basic skills classes into New Morning's curriculum has made this issue less acute, yet there are still some low-functioning students in each of the non-basic skills classes, and it is difficult to know just how much time to give them. Some of these youngsters do not reach their stride until they are older, relative to the higher-functioning students. When they do, the quantum of progress can, on rare occasions, be sudden and significant. Prognostic tools are, however, vague on the probability of such fortuitous events. Spending a lot of time on a "very slow" student is a gamble.

There are some other frustrations of a temporal nature. For example, how long should a teacher persevere with a program? Is a year long enough? How many repetitions are adequate? There is no hard-and-fast rule. Some staffers told me that they continuously reformulated old approaches and instituted new ones; one teacher said that she frequently found herself switching from an unsuccessful approach to "its exact opposite." Here, a teacher's frustration can become a student's as well.

Some of the staff were frustrated by the way they believed themselves to be perceived in the community. They said they were exasperated at being told, "It must be horribly depressing to work with retardates." They were also nonplussed by some of the images society has of the intellectual capacities of special educators. When special education was very young, it was often the case that regular educators were handed the responsibility of teaching retarded students. Although never stated as policy, school administrators often assigned the people they believed to be the dullest teachers to work with the dullest students. Such was not always the case, but it happened with enough frequency to establish a stereotype that still has some credence in the community. While there may be no malicious intent, lay persons occasionally refer to special educators as "retarded teachers," rather than teachers of retarded children. (Parents of retarded children are also called "retarded parents" with some frequency.) An unfavorable reaction to this may be just semantic nit-picking, but some special educators find it offensive. And it is not only their intelligence that is impugned. Sometimes social perceptions have more sting. It has, for example, been suggested that deviant persons drift into employment where they can work with deviant clients.[35]

There is no evidence that special educators tend to be marginal in an intellectual or any other sense. Indeed, one group of researchers has asserted that the less competent students are, the more competent the teachers must be.[36]

The depth of feeling New Morning teachers experienced over anything that seemingly diminished the image of their profession was apparent in staff reaction to an administrative proposal that the school hire a full-time art teacher. To my surprise, this suggestion was resisted vehemently by several staff members, who said enough attention was already paid to arts and crafts in the school's classes. When further pressed upon their aversion to an arts teacher, it became clear that some of the opponents were reacting to personal antipathies for what could best be described as "artsy-craftsy" special education or, as H. D. Love called it, "the handiwork philosophy."[37] From the turn of the century until the mid-fifties, many special education programs consisted not so much in educating mentally handicapped children, as in immersing them in a world of captivating baubles designed primarily to keep them occupied. Those staff members opposed to the idea of an art teacher based their opposition on a reluctance to give New Morning the appearance of slipping back into the custodianism of "the handiwork" era, even though none would deny that arts and crafts are important things for retarded students to learn.

Another complex and often frustrating factor involved in being a special educator is carrying on amicable relationships with the parents of retarded children. These parents sometimes have unrealistic hopes for their children and unreasonable expectations of teachers. For example, when a child is placed in a class for retarded children, parents may view the class as "remedial" in the sense that it is erroneously seen as an opportunity for the student to be brought quickly to the levels of his normal peers.[38] There is also the possibility of disagreements on goals between parents and special educators. Sometimes teachers may be more inclined to stress academic goals and future orientations, while parents may be interested only in the most practical and immediate objectives,[39] or vice versa.

Parents and teachers occasionally develop competitive attitudes toward each other with regard to youngsters, the parent being threatened that a stranger can handle his child better than he can, the teacher feeling threatened that so many parents are excellent special educators. Now and again, a parent will offer an encouraging word; unfortunately, the converse is often true.

Sometimes parents refuse to accept staff diagnoses of a child's problems and a teacher's suggested course of remedial action. The parents may begin to "shop" for other evaluations. Naturally, parents should not unquestioningly accept teacher evaluations. No one can blame them for looking for the best services for their children; but excessive shopping behavior can be destructive to the parent-professional relationship and to the child's progress.

The parent-professional relationship reaches its nadir when a parent publicly or privately assaults a teacher's reputation. In line with this, the parent may find people outside of the school setting who suggest all manner of remedial methods alternative to those espoused by the classroom teacher. Sometimes the interventions suggested by these outsiders are well intentioned, but the individuals in question are often amateurs or professionals who have no experience in working with retarded children. It is not uncommon for parents to incur wasted expenses in such situations, and the children are confused by the difference in what they get in and out of school. In the long run, even if the parent is proven wrong, the assault on the teacher's ego may significantly diminish his or her predisposition to be candid with the parent in the future or to interact in other constructive ways. All of the New Morning staff members had been involved in counterproductive, frustrating, ego-shattering incidents provoked by a parent's failure to form realistic expectations of his child. Most of the teachers bore their frustration in silent deference to the difficulties that parents of retarded children face.

When the parent-professional relationship deteriorates, it is usually the child who suffers most. For example, a parent may deemphasize effective remedial techniques in the home, which impedes progress in school. The staff at New Morning spent a maximum of six hours a day with students, five days a week. These students were usually with their parents or guardians the other eighteen hours and on weekends, holidays, and during the summer. The home can be a very powerful educational environment—more effective than school, according to one study.[40] Thus, the client-oriented teacher frequently endures relationships that she or he disdains in the hope of securing essential home-front co-operation—sometimes to no avail.

One New Morning teacher facetiously confided that she was considerably more frustrated by the actions and attitudes of her colleagues than she ever could be by parents or students. A modest amount of friction is to be expected in any social setting. One feature of a special education environment that may make it somewhat more contentious than would be expected in ordinary circumstances is that a multitude of professionals and paraprofessionals must coordinate their efforts in achieving amorphous goals that are frequently very difficult to attain. Moreover, the professionals who need to coordinate their efforts so closely often hold diametrically opposed perspectives on one or more elements of a child's needs and how to meet them. In the context of explaining why there was not more coordination among the staff at New Morning School, one teacher said,

If you were to ask all of the teachers at the school where any one child were going, you would be likely to get as many different answers as there are teachers. I think the reason we haven't coordinated more is because we like to do what we feel best at, and avoid any chance at group criticism, to maintain our self-confidence. Criticism might pop our respective bubbles. Ego is tenuous here with our teachers anyway, because it is a high-frustration job.

One of the school's veterans observed that her frustrations were intensifying. As the school increased in prominence and adopted the public school system's rules of accountability, it became the object of greater scrutiny from the outside. This gave frustrating emotions a sharper edge. What were once private bungles became much more public.

In line with this, another thing that several New Morning staff members identified as frustrating was what one of them described as an "inundation in paper work." The IEPs and other accountability measures did not seem excessive, and the content was far from superfluous in most cases. However, a point raised earlier does bear repeating. Special education administrators of the future must recognize the enormous temporal and energy demands retarded children put on teachers. A concern for accountability is essential, but great care must be taken not to require that special educators spend so much time writing up what they are planning to do, and what they have done, that no time is left to *do* anything.

How did the special educators at New Morning cope with their frustrations? One of them said she conferred with much greater frequency with her colleagues. Several others said that they continually went back to college.

A commonplace coping mechanism was what I call the delusion of progress. A few of the teachers were always on the verge of some great breakthrough with a student or were able to discover in children significant improvements that, judging by even the most infinitesimal standards, were undiscernible.

Another coping strategy was apparent in the black humor that is an important survival skill in most human service professions. Sometimes in the teachers' lounge at New Morning, staff members would make humorous, but disparaging, remarks about a student's "intellect" or about retarded people in general. (I never heard anyone tell a "retarded" joke per se.) These staffers would doubtless have become incensed if an outsider had made fun of their students, but sometimes the frustrations were so great, all that was left to do was laugh. And *everyone* did.

One teacher, who had worked for years with non-handicapped

children before coming to New Morning, said she had "a good deal less frustration working with retarded youngsters than with the normal ones." "The latter," she went on to say, "are all expected to be at certain levels of achievement at certain times. At least with the retarded kids, the expectations are ambiguous." For other teachers, such ambiguity was a source of frustration in itself. Another teacher remarked that whenever she despaired at her own "inadequacies in helping a kid," she realized "how terribly frustrating it must be to be the kid."

Other Occupational Hazards

Frustration was not the only occupational hazard the New Morning staff faced. Some syndromes associated with retardation increase a person's vulnerability to infections. For example, children with Down's Syndrome are very susceptible to upper respiratory infections.[41] The absenteeism rate of New Morning students was much higher than that of students in regular schools in Mountview. Because some of New Morning's students did not have enough control over their bodies to inhibit a generous passage of germs or because they were not socially adept enough to care, illnesses were often passed on to teachers. Most of the rookie staff members found themselves with many minor sicknesses for the first few months. The veterans either built up resistances or got used to it. It was part of the job.

Another hazard was the noise level. It hurt my ears to be around the more stentorian students at the school. One teacher told me he was concerned that he, or some of his students, might suffer hearing losses as a result of the verbal excesses of some of the very loud and shrill students. This is highly unlikely; but a steady diet of such noises does jangle the nerves of students and teachers alike, and some of the students were already hyperkinetic.

There was another physical hazard presented by some of the most aggressive students, that of minor injuries to teachers. A director of one residential facility in Mountview received a serious and permanently debilitating injury as a result of the actions of one of his clients who attended New Morning. Most retarded people are passive, but occasionally the hyperaggressive stereotype is seen.

While some students were so strong and aggressive that they posed a threat to classmates and staff, others were so fragile that they represented a different kind of threat. As more low-functioning and multihandicapped students enrolled in New Morning, this new occupational hazard became increasingly apparent. Some of these students, for example, had a difficult time swallowing and had very bad gag reflexes. Many of the teachers and specialists responsible for them were chronically unnerved at the thought of feeding the youngsters for fear that they would aspirate some food and choke to death. Teachers who were responsible for moving a skeletal student who lacked muscle tone and control were concerned that they might break one of his bones. The recruitment of a part-time nurse to the staff mollified some of the concerns. The fact remains, though, regular special educators are not adequately trained to deal with the medical problems of some of their students—a situation that will doubtless play itself out in a horror story followed by equally dreadful litigation.

Emotional involvement with students was another problem that complicated the lives of some staff members. A few teachers obviously had a special fondness for certain students and did not like others. Various staff members related to the problem of emotional involvements in different ways. One teacher stated that "no one who has the problem of emotional involvement should get into this business." Her colleague observed that such involvement is "inevitable," and a desirable inevitability at that. She said, "The longer you are out of school, the less bookish and more human in your approach you become. This cannot help but lead to intense emotional involvements with students."

Nearly every staff member had what one called "favorite kids," although some of them said they were reluctant to admit it. Part of the reason for this, one teacher explained, was that many of the students were attuned to displays of favoritism. The "teacher's pet" phenomenon elicits many of the same negative peer reactions for retarded students that it does for those who are not handicapped.

According to one teacher, "Favoritism is an inevitability in working with these children, because teachers who have large ego investments are naturally going to work more with children who give them the greatest results." Not always, though. Two other teachers said that they liked the students who presented the greatest challenge—"the brats," as one called them.

Favoritism can pose another problem that was not intimated by the New Morning staff. Zigler and Hartner say that some retarded people may take longer than they really need to learn something if they are in the presence of a very loving teacher.[42] The student sometimes becomes more motivated to satisfy his needs for affection than to complete the learning task. Conversely, it must be remembered that an affective bond with a teacher makes her a much more potent reinforcer.

All of the New Morning staff admitted not liking certain students; one told me that she "hated" a particular boy. When such animosity developed, most of the staff said they simply related to the students in question in a perfunctory manner, "just going through the motions with them," as one put it. It used to be the case at New Morning that if a teacher could not cope with a child, arrangements were made to separate the antagonists. Under school policy that was in effect until 1977, a student could be moved up a grade if it met with the approval of that class's teacher. I am aware of only one case in which this happened, and it was said to have worked out nicely. The original teacher had more peace of mind, and the student was exposed to more mature role models. Such arrangements probably could still be made, but probably would not be. Teachers received many evaluations from administrators in the public school system. A demonstrated inability to work with a particular student would be looked upon as a professional failure and go into the teacher's file. This is just one instance in which the progressive bureaucratization of the special education system has diminished some useful flexibility.

Perhaps the greatest problem staff members faced in relating to their emotions vis-à-vis students was taking student behavior personally. It is patronizing to be indifferent to a person's behavior just because he is retarded. A student must feel that his actions have consequences on other people's feelings. This requires a personal, but somewhat detached, touch from teachers, which is easier said than done. One teacher told me that she took "much of the kids' behavior very personally." A colleague of hers said, "Much of my emotional involvement comes from my own investment of ego, not only in the success of the children, but in their evaluations of me as a person. It is very important that my students love me." Given the mercurial nature of the emotions of many of the New Morning students, such an attitude borders on masochism.

The personal rewards of being a special educator must be immense, because the "dues" are high. The staff of New Morning School had to decide the right course of action for each student; implement a multiplicity of programs; be patient enough to wait for, and then be satisfied with, modest, somewhat minute, degrees of progress; determine when a course of action had failed; endure many failures; and engage in constructive relationships with parents, many of whom are frustrated themselves. These are all done in a frenetic, sometimes hazardous, environment, for moderately low pay, without many emotional strokes. To hear most special educators talk of it, the rewards more than compensate for the dues they pay.

NOTES

1. J. Rousseau, *Emile ou de l'éducation*, Paris: Garnier-Flammarion, 1966, p. 39.

2. R. W. Emerson, quoted in L. C. Henry, ed., *Best Quotations*, Greenwich, Conn.: Fawcett, 1966, p. 172.

3. D. G. Ullman, "Breadth of Attention and Retention in Mentally Retarded and Intellectually Average Children," *American Journal of Mental Deficiency*, 78:1974, p. 647.

4. The President's Committee on Mental Retardation, *Silent Minority*, Washington, D.C.: U.S. Government Printing Office, Department of Health, Education, and Welfare, 1973, p. 12.

5. N. Bernstein, "Intellectual Deficit and Personality Development," in N. Bernstein, ed., *Diminished People*, Boston: Little, Brown and Co., 1970, p. 171.

6. W. Dennis, *Children of Creche*, New York: Prentice-Hall, 1973, cited in J. L. Northern and M. P. Downs, *Hearing in Children*, Baltimore: Williams and Wilkins, 1974, p. 74.

7. H. C. Gunzburg, "Further Education for the Mentally Handicapped," in A. M. Clarke, and A.D.B. Clarke, eds., *Mental Deficiency: The Changing Outlook*, 3rd ed., New York: The Free Press, 1974, p. 670.

8. K. A. Gilbert and H. Hemming, "Environmental Change and Psycholinguistic Ability of Mentally Retarded Adults," *American Journal of Mental Deficiency*, 83:1979, p. 457.

9. F. W. Litton, *Education of the Trainable Mentally Retarded*, St. Louis: C. V. Mosby, 1978, p. 119.

10. J. Greenfeld, *A Place for Noah*, New York: Holt, Rinehart, and Winston, 1978, p. 227.

11. P. Hobson and P. Duncan, "Sign Language and Retarded People," *Mental Retardation*, 17(1):1979, p. 37.

12. L. G. Peters, "Concepts of Mental Deficiency Among the Tamang of Nepal," *American Journal of Mental Deficiency*, 84:1980, p. 356.

13. J. L. Northern and M. Downs, *Hearing in Children*, Baltimore: Williams and Wilkins, 1974, p. 73.

14. F. W. Litton, p. 162.

15. B. Levine and A. Birch, "Physical and Occupational Therapy," *Mental Retardation and Developmental Disabilities*, 9:1977, pp. 133–134.

16. H. C. Haywood, "What Happened to Mild and Moderate Mental Retardation?" *American Journal of Mental Deficiency*, 83:1979, p. 430.

17. American Association on Mental Deficiency, "The Right to Life—Proposed Statement," *Mental Retardation*, 11(6):1973, p. 66.

18. L. K. Snyder, T. C. Lovitt, and J. O. Smith, "Language Training for the Severely Retarded: Five Years of Behavior Analysis Research," *Exceptional Children*, 42(1):1975, p. 13.

19. T. E. Webster, "Problems of Emotional Development in Young Retarded Children," *American Journal of Psychiatry*, 120:1963, p. 40.

20. Ibid.

21. T. Thompson, "The Behavioral Perspective," *Hastings Center Report*, 8(3):1978, p. 30.

22. E. T. Hall, *The Silent Language*, Greenwich, Conn.: Fawcett, 1959, p. 23.

23. A. Hirshoren and T. A. Burton, "Teaching Academic Skills to Trainable Mentally Retarded Children: A Study in Tautology," *Mental Retardation*, 17(4):1979, pp. 178–179.

24. S. A. Warren, "Academic Achievement of Trainable Pupils With Five or More Years of Schooling," *Training School Bulletin*, 60:1963, p. 85.

25. S. J. Baran and T. P. Meyer, "Retarded Children's Perceptions of Favorite Television Characters as Behavioral Models," *Mental Retardation*, 13(4):1975, p. 28.

26. C. K. Sigelman, E. C. Budd, C. L. Spanhel, and C. J. Schonrock, "When in Doubt, Say Yes: Acquiescence in Interviews with Mentally Retarded Persons," *Mental Retardation*, 19(2):1981, p. 57.

27. S. J. Baran, "TV and Social Learning in the Institutionalized MR," *Mental Retardation*, 11(3):1973, p. 37.

28. Z. Stoneman and P. A. Keilman, "Competition and Social Stimulation Effects on Simple Motor Performance of EMR Children," *American Journal of Mental Deficiency*, 78:1973, p. 98.

29. J. L. Tringo, "The Hierarchy of Preference Toward Disability Groups," *Journal of Special Education*, 4:1970, p. 303.

30. H. Goodman, J. Gottlieb, and R. H. Harrison, "Social Acceptance of EMR's Integrated Into a Nongraded Elementary School," *American Journal of Mental Deficiency*, 76:1972, p. 417.

31. R. P. Mackie and L. Dunn, *College and University Programs for the Preparation of Teachers of Exceptional Children*, Washington, D.C.: U.S. Office of Education, 1954.

32. R. J. Simenson and M. G. Redding, "State Certification of Teachers of the Mentally Retarded," *Mental Retardation*, 10(6):1972, pp. 21–23; National Association for Retarded Citizens, *The Parent/Professional Partnership: Book I: The Right to Education: Where are We and How Did We Get There?*, Arlington, Texas: The Association, 1976, p. 14.

33. N. W. Gottfried and R. L. Jones, "Career Choice Factors in Special Education," *Exceptional Childlren*, 30:1964, pp. 218–223.

34. R. B. Blackwell, "Study of Effective and Ineffective Teachers of the TMR," *Exceptional Children*, 39:1972, p. 143.

35. W. Wolfensberger, "The Principle of Normalization and Its Implications for Psychiatric Services," *American Journal of Psychiatry*, 127:1970, p. 292.

36. E. Sontag, P. J. Burke, and R. York, "Considerations for Serving the Severely Handicapped in the Public Schools," *The Education and Training of the Mentally Retarded*, 8(2):1973, p. 23.

37. H. D. Love, *The Mentally Retarded Child and His Family*, Springfield, Ill.: Charles C. Thomas, 1973, p. 178.

38. Ibid., p. 26.

39. National Association for Retarded Citizens, *The Parent/Professional Partnership: Book III: The Partnership: How to Make It Work*, Arlington, Texas: The Association, 1976, p. 8.

40. M. S. Shearer and D. E. Shearer, "The Portage Project: A Model for Early Childhood Education," *Exceptional Children*, 39:1972, p. 217.

41. B. Henker and C. K. Whalen, "Pyramid Therapy in a Hospital for the

Retarded," *Proceedings of the 77th Annual Convention of the American Psychological Association,* 4:1969, pp. 779–780.

42. E. Zigler and S. Hartner, "The Socialization of the Mentally Retarded," in D. A. Goslin, ed., *Handbook of Socialization Theory and Research,* Chicago: Rand-McNally, 1969, p. 1084.

6
The Social Psychology of Mental Retardation: Stigma, Stereotype, and Adaptation

Sweet are the uses of adversity
Which like a toad, ugly and venomous
Wears yet a precious jewel in his head.
　　　　　　　　　—W. Shakespeare[1]

PLANES OF SOCIAL IMAGERY

How does being mentally retarded translate into everyday experience with the "normal" world? Among the many stereotypes applied to persons who are retarded is the belief that they are blissfully ignorant, "jolly imbeciles." This notion is probably derived from the public's contact with people who have Down's Syndrome. There are certain cherubic facial features associated with Down's Syndrome, and children with the syndrome are frequently cheerful, although, as Menolascino has shown, the opposite is often the case.[2]

Linked with the jolly imbecile stereotype is the tendency of some non-handicapped individuals to attribute a low degree of emotional affect to handicapped persons—or, as Davis puts it, to see them as "devoid of normal sentiments."[3] This parallels a long-standing societal predisposition to impute diminished powers of sensory acuity to "the retarded."

Throughout history, it was widely held that retarded and insane persons could, because of their "animal nature," withstand physical hardships (such as extremes of temperature) that would kill a normal person.[4] In truth, the sensory acuity misconception was a convenient justification for social acquiescence to the squalid and inhumane conditions in asylums. The attribution of diminished emotional sensitivity to retarded people is, in part, an extension of the physical myth.

Mentally retarded persons probably do not worry about some of the ponderous issues that non-handicapped people face. This happens partially because their levels of internal dialogue are not very sophisticated; partially because they do not project very far forward or backward in time, and thus do not harbor many problems of the past or fear those of the future; and partially because their short attention spans may distract some of them from ruminating over things that are anxiety-producing. This is not to say that they are invulnerable to anxiety. The severity of the distress is relative to the mind experiencing it. Little problems to "big minds" can be big problems to "little minds." Some retarded people do dwell on regrettable pasts or unseemly futures. Moreover, because they are retarded, these people face a multiplicity of difficulties that "normal" people do not. Thus, *some* of them become emotionally disturbed.

There are numerous studies illustrating that the incidence of emotional disturbances in mentally retarded persons is disproportionately greater than in those who are not handicapped.[5] (Menolascino found retarded boys much more likely to be mentally disturbed than retarded girls.[6]) Craft[7] and Rutter[8] found that one-third of the retarded people they investigated had emotional problems (as high as 50 percent for retarded individuals residing in institutions[9]).

Such evidence does not stand alone in belying the credibility of the "blissful ignorance" stereotype. For example, Berman found that ten of the thirty retarded persons who were referred to him for counseling talked of wanting to commit suicide.[10] While conducting my study, I was apprised of several attempted suicides in the Mountview area—one by a teenage girl. In talking to mentally retarded adults, I found suicide to be a frequently discussed topic. It is not difficult to comprehend why these people may experience depression and other psychological difficulties when one considers certain social and physiological elements of their lives.

THE ANTECEDENTS OF EMOTIONAL INSTABILITY

Our culture's priorities are reestablished in delivery rooms every day. One of the first questions a parent invariably asks about a newborn is, "Is the baby OK?" Retarded children are not OK, and the social stigma associated with their incompetence has a particularly sharp edge for them. They are not stigmatized for what they *do* so much as for what they *are*. As Edgerton says, "The MR's stigma is closest to what we call the soul. Of all the attributes of man, mind is the quintessence; to be found wanting in mental capacity—in general intellectual competence—is most devastating of all possible stigmata."[11]

Moreover, community attitudes reflect a pathological antipathy for mental retardation. For example, when Tringo asked respondents to rate twenty-one "disabilities" according to their level of acceptability, mental retardation was ranked well behind things such as heart disease, stroke, tuberculosis, and cancer.[12]

All but the most oblivious retarded children must become aware of some all-encompassing difference that sets them apart from everyone else. For example, non-handicapped persons frequently talk very slowly and loudly when addressing retarded people, and the tone of such communication is almost always humorless or infused with artificial levity, compulsive loquaciousness, or awkward solemnity.[13]

Normal people will frequently tolerate uncomfortable physical behavior, such as unsolicited touching, by a retarded person—behavior they would never brook in ordinary social intercourse. This only exacerbates the problem by encouraging it. Other "normals" will tolerate no touching whatsoever from retarded persons.

It is also interesting to watch non-retarded people communicate with mentally handicapped individuals who have articulation disorders that make them difficult to understand. I have rarely heard a non-professional, non-handicapped person ask a retarded individual to repeat himself. After a brief moment of embarrassed fumbling, the former almost always answers uncomprehended questions as if he understood them. Retarded people must get confused at having others repeatedly answering questions they have not asked.

Some "normals" patronize retarded persons. I fell prey to a patronization ritual of my own. Whenever I went on community outings with one of my retarded friends, I made sure to let salespersons at stores, people at parties, anyone who might be observing, know that my companion was from a "special setting." Sometimes I did this to facilitate more sensitive interactions between the handicapped and non-handicapped persons. But in many circumstances, I did it a trifle too quickly— to dissociate myself from the handicap. I seemed to need to let people know that I could be much more discriminating in my choice of friends and was just doing the retarded person a favor by going out with him.

Subtle rejecting behaviors are frequently directed at retarded persons. One morning, for example, I sat across from a street corner where a group of retarded people were waiting for a bus. Virtually every individual who approached the group took a detour to the other side of the street. Maybe the retarded group did not notice. Maybe people had always crossed to the other side of the street. After the group boarded the bus, nearly every passerby took the route where the retarded people had been sitting. On another occasion, I watched a swimming pool all but vacated when a group of retarded youngsters came to swim. Maybe they did not notice that, either.

There are some forms of social rejection that *cannot* be ignored. One young retarded man told me, "They say, 'There goes the nut,' or they say, 'There goes the stupid.'" A middle-aged man said, "They still make fun of me, and to make fun of me, you know, is not right. When they make fun of me it makes me feel terrible."

What are the effects of such social rejection on the emotional development of mentally handicapped persons? There is evidence that retarded individuals rate themselves almost exactly as other people do, and that the self-image of most retarded persons is low.[14] For instance, mildly retarded school-age adolescents see themselves to be negatively regarded by their non-handicapped peers[15]—this same age cohort having negative perceptions of "their bodies, their moral-ethical selves, their personal worth, adequacy as persons, family selves and social selves."[16] Goffman simplifies the feelings of many retarded persons: "I am inferior. Therefore people will dislike me and I cannot be secure with them."[17]

And where there is not scorn, there is often pity for retarded persons— not the pity born of compassion, but that which views them as something to be regretted. There is no question that the lives of some retarded people are pitiful by any measure; but most, despite the many difficulties they face, can lead modestly satisfying lives by popular standards. They can, however, lead these lives only if negative societal reactions to the mental handicap do not become "more crippling than the handicap itself."[18]

What are the other crippling social factors that erode the emotional stability of retarded people? For one thing, they must face a confusing array of contradictory stereotypical imagery. "Retardates" are said to be blissfully ignorant, yet pitiful. The same non-handicapped persons who view them as "jolly imbeciles" in the abstract, often transform them into "thieves," "sexual deviants," even "homicidal maniacs" when they want to move into "normal" neighborhoods.

Another damaging double stigma is the equation of mental illness with mental retardation. Many retarded people do have emotional problems, but a substantial majority do not. The belief that mental illness and mental retardation are synonymous was the most pronounced deficiency in public awareness I encountered in the course of doing this study. For example, I was talking to a man about my work, and he said, "I can really appreciate what you are doing. My wife had a nervous breakdown once." The erroneous equation of mental retardation with mental illness is borne out in numerous inquiries.[19] Given the historical parallels of mental retardation and mental illness and the proven statistical elevation of emotional disturbances in retarded people, the misconception is understandable. However, if retarded people are treated as though they are mentally ill, significant restrictions are placed on their lives, already devoid of many of the choices available to other persons. The mental illness-mental retardation stereotype can also become a self-fulfilling prophecy. One of the most frequently stated attitudes of some of the higher-functioning students at New Morning School was that it was a place for "crazies."

Those retarded individuals who once lived in poor institutional settings typically bear indelible emotional scars that can lead to problems on the outside. One woman who had had a long institutional career described her experiences in one such place this way: "They punished me quite a bit. I was in isolation quite a bit 'cause I was a bad girl. I was in cuffs for a while—you know, handcuffs. I was in ice packs. . . ."

Many retarded people have physical handicaps that undermine their emotional well-being. For example, one inquiry showed that 50 percent of a group of Down's Syndrome children who had been diagnosed as emotionally disturbed displayed abnormal electroencephalograms (EEGs), while only 13 percent of a control group of Down's children showed irregular EEGs.[20] Such cerebral dysrhythmia is probably a significant etiological factor in emotional disturbances of mentally handicapped people.

Some retarded individuals take medications that make them vulnerable to emotional disturbances. Prolonged use of certain drugs can lead to toxicity that can, in turn, cause neuropsychiatric symptoms, including dementia.[21] If a retarded person takes several drugs, these can have untoward synergistic effects. Many of the New Morning students became quite disoriented when they were being taken off one medication and put on another or when dosages were changed.

Then there are retarded children who are frequently hospitalized because of ailments associated with their retardation. Imagine the trauma of repeated trips to an environment where one is separated from loved ones and subjected to pain, often with the medical focus being an affliction that may have already been the subject of ridicule on the "outside."

For many retarded persons who have convulsive disorders such as epilepsy, there are anxieties about public seizures and the accompanying embarrassment. And retarded epileptics have a compound stigma.

Other physical problems can assail a retarded person's ego as well. Some have sensory-perceptual handicaps that make it difficult for them to adapt to the social environment appropriately. If they cannot differentiate stimuli very well or have difficulty integrating them into a cohesive whole, they occasionally misinterpret and overreact in ordinary social interactions with non-handicapped persons or peers.

Many retarded people have motor problems that lead them to move their bodies in an abnormal fashion or engage in repetitive movements. Poor motor control has been shown to correlate negatively with peer acceptance.[22]

Although some retarded people are beautiful by popular standards, others are ugly by the same standards. The devastating effects of being homely in a society that places strong emphasis on superficial aesthetics is too often underestimated. Romer and Berkson have demonstrated that physical attractiveness is a good predictor of sociability among retarded persons.[23] An incident relevant to this matter, which occurred at New Morning School, is illustrative. One of the older female students returned from a visit to a beauty shop in a state that could be conservatively described as euphoric. I was surprised. I did not expect them to want to be attractive—an all too common social misconception that militates against many retarded people being given a chance to be attractive. This attitude explains why retarded persons are frequently clothed in hand-me-downs, why some dentists counsel parents against orthodontia for their retarded children, why retarded people in many institutions are shorn.

Some mentally retarded people are vulnerable to emotional problems because of difficulties occasioned by speech and language handicaps. While causal direction is not implied, Rutter demonstrated a significant association between "language retardation" and "psychiatric disorders."[24] A speech clinician told me, "When language disorders combine with intellectual deficits, the result can be profound feelings of inadequacy, confusion, frustration, and isolation on the part of the child."

Many mentally handicapped people also have emotional stresses related to their arrival at certain biological milestones. This is especially apparent in the difficulties a mentally retarded adolescent encounters when he reaches puberty. As he matures physically he must negotiate the difficult and confusing period, with all its socially-stifled impulses, equipped with the mind of a child.

Retarded people often suffer profound instability in their interpersonal relationships. While some retarded children are fortunate enough to have close ties with parents or siblings, those who do not can be impacted very badly,[25] resulting in depression and severe ego deficits.[26]

If family relationships are poor, then retarded people usually find themselves relying on bonds with teachers, counselors, volunteers, staff at community-based residential settings, institutional attendants, and/or other retarded persons to satisfy most of their emotional needs. Understandably, they come to depend heavily on such relationships and suffer intense and chronic depression at being separated from one of those significant others. And separations are commonplace.

Premature deaths probably separate many friends. Exact death rates are difficult to come by because IQ is not recorded on death certificates, but the mortality rate for retarded people is higher than it is for the general population.[27] Nine New Morning students died of complications associated with their handicaps between 1973 and 1981—a mortality figure highly disproportionate to that of other schools in Mountview.

A second factor contributing to the transitory interpersonal relationships of some retarded persons is the rapid turnover rate of residential staff members. It is reported that a retarded resident might have to adjust to as many as twenty new institutional attendants over a six-month period.[28] Staff in community-based residential settings have very high turnover rates as well.[29] Volunteers, both in institutional and community-based residential and educational settings, come and go with great frequency, too. Many people who volunteer to work with mentally handicapped persons fail to recognize how much the latter come to depend upon them and how painful it can be when a volunteer-friend suddenly disappears.

A third factor that contributes to instability of the interpersonal relationships of retarded people is "the residential shuffle." It is not uncommon for a retarded person to be moved between institutions or community-based residences or back and forth between both for his whole life. This does more than continuously separate him from loved ones. It forces him to adjust constantly to new physical and interpersonal environments. It creates anxiety about the future, and accentuates feelings of helplessness. It subjects him to what Coffman and Harris have described in some detail as "transition shock."[30] The comments of one retarded man intimate this phenomenon:

> Sometime in the 1920s my folks moved to Colorado. Then in my sixth year they put me in a home [names the institution] and I grew up there. I guess my folks had me put there because they was too poor to take care of me. Those kids wouldn't leave me alone there; they were mean to me and I ran off from there about nine times—from that institution—and they filed charges against me and sent me to [another institution]. Some authorities from juvenile court I think—there's four men with yellow hair—they asked me a bunch of questions and then they said, "Send him to [names institution]." I was in there seventeen years. It was better, but you couldn't get out . . . unless an attendant was with ya; they're the ones that carry the keys. All the doors are locked there all the time. Well, after seventeen years, they sent me to [a third institution]. I was there thirteen years and they *shipped* me to [still another institution].

Compared to some of his peers, this man had led a moderately sedentary existence. Nevertheless, just about the time he was able to call one of these places home, he was "shipped" elsewhere. Some retarded people are shuffled constantly and at much shorter intervals. In either case, a retarded person subjected to the residential shuffle becomes conditioned to expect that interpersonal relationships will not be abiding and becomes wary about forming them in the first place. Romer and Berkson have shown that occupational, as well as residential, placements often tend to be of limited tenure.[31] Thus, there seems to be an "occupational shuffle," having some of the same destructive effects on social networks as its residential counterpart.

FRIENDS

Even when there is stability in the residential environment, there are factors that contribute to a retarded person's relative isolation from significant others. Some mentally retarded adults have been shown to have friendly dyadic relations in special residential settings, even when they are severely handicapped and/or limited in communication or social skills.[32] However, many others spend virtually all of their free time engaged in very solitary activities, such as watching television, even when they live in a residential facility shared with numerous peers.[33] These individuals have frequently spent the whole day at sheltered workshops and the like, working alongside the same people they live with in the evening. It is not surprising that they may not seek out each other's company even if there are strong feelings of mutuality among them.

Those retarded individuals who move into apartments of their own in the community get away from an immersion in relationships with particular peers, but some of them do not fare very well in the friendship department either. It is reported that, while they like independent living, one of the things they complain of is not having enough friends.[34]

Mentally retarded children also face special problems in the formation and maintenance of friendships. One New Morning teacher put the issue this way: "They don't have friends because they don't have much in the way of self-concept. So they don't value the esteem of others." This may be true in some cases, yet many of the New Morning students who had friends in the school setting had very few, if any, out of it. They did not have the opportunities to do so. There are several reasons for this.

The younger New Morning students seldom came together socially outside of the school setting. A conspicuous case of such separation was evident in the lives of the school's two most notorious chums. I asked the parents of each child why the youngsters never got together outside of school. The father of one boy looked perplexed. He said that it had never occurred to him that the boy might like to have an outing with his friend. In my experience, it was not unusual for parents to have fairly limited views of the social proclivities of their retarded youngsters. The mother of the other boy said that her son picked up too many of his friend's bad habits. This statement could doubtless apply to the interaction among any children. For them, half the fun of having friends is picking up their bad habits.

Several of the New Morning School staff told me that their students' parents did not get the children together outside of school because of the parents' own psychological vulnerabilities. According to one teacher, "These parents have enough trouble facing comparisons of their children with normal youngsters. It is more than many of them can take when the kid doesn't even stack up well with other retarded children." Because they fear such comparisons, these parents avoid promoting situations in which they can be made.

At first, I believed such reasoning to be farfetched. But as time wore on, I witnessed more than a few encounters between parents in which comparisons were made between their handicapped youngsters. Occasionally, these parents were very defensive and quick to call to one another's attention that *their* child did not have a particular problem that beset the other's youngster. It did not take much prodding to escalate such conversations into competitive encounters or transform empathy into condescension.

Another reason frequently given by parents as to why their children did not have more opportunities to get together with each other outside of school was that the youngsters were too difficult to supervise. Understandably, some of the children will become overly excited the first few times they visit each other outside of the school setting. Many times, it is difficult to cope with the energy level and demands of a single retarded child; most parents do not encourage groups. Moreover, retarded friends occasionally stimulate a latent exploratory instinct in each other. The children may wander away, and for mentally handicapped youngsters, being lost on the block can be as frightening as being lost in the woods, and as dangerous. The wanderers may not understand real hazards such as traffic, especially if they have been sheltered and have had no practice in negotiating such dangers.

While mentally handicapped youngsters can be difficult to supervise in their extracurricular activities, this is not always the case; and the need for close supervision of older, more mature, retarded youths should be the exception rather than the rule. Nonetheless, parents and professionals often fail to recognize that retarded people can enjoy each other's company without someone planning all their time for them or watching their every move. Many retarded youths and adults are inconvenienced and demeaned by too much supervision.

Retarded youngsters also face special problems in developing associations with non-handicapped friends. Normal children rarely choose a retarded child as a playmate.[35] Younger retarded children usually do not have the motor abilities to keep up with normal children their own age, and never the cognitive capacities. The retarded child may be difficult to communicate with, or boring. Moreover, the non-handicapped child faces the tendency for "a stigma to spread from the stigmatized individual to his close connections."[36]

Parents of normal and retarded children are often reluctant to let their youngsters interact. The former may fear for the safety of their children because of the purported emotional volatility of retarded persons. In certain cases, this fear is well founded; more often, it is not. Some parents of non-handicapped children are concerned that their youngsters will emulate inappropriate behaviors of retarded kids, and a few are said to fear that the retardation itself may be "contagious" (this according to several parents of New Morning students). Other parents of normal children worry that their youngsters will do or say something to the retarded child that may become a source of familial embarrassment.

Retarded and non-handicapped children can become friends, though. One New Morning student told me, "I know a couple of friends of mine. One, he understands about me being mentally retarded and him and I get along so well."

One of the problems retarded persons face in cultivating friendly interactions with non-handicapped people is that the former are usually not very stimulating company. They may have a lot of engaging idiosyncracies, but it does not take very long to exhaust the conversational repertoires of most mentally handicapped persons. Here I believe the problem does not stem so much from the handicap, as from the fact that retarded persons are not exposed to experiences that give them the material of good conversation. One summer, several New Morning teachers took a group of the school's older students to the desert of southern Utah. I encountered them on their way back to Mountview and stopped to see how the trip had gone. The bus in which they were riding was abuzz. In the course of a conversation with one group of the travelers, I asked if they were glad to be going home. The four of them shouted that they were. Hadn't they had a good time? "Oh, no," one assured me, "we are glad so we can show people our trip." Then they produced a number of books they had purchased and gave me a thirty-minute presentation about the desert. Until this time, I had never seen a couple of these young people converse, and yet on this day, they not only spoke, but were charming. The difference: they had something to talk about.

Whether the relationships are developed with handicapped or non-handicapped peers, retarded children need friends. They need them to use as sounding boards in the process of growing up. They need someone with whom they can conspire against adults as they try to assert their independence. They need them to diminish boredom, because, contrary to certain misconceptions, retarded people do get bored. And most importantly, retarded youngsters need friends to reduce the loneliness and isolation that is so common to many of them. That loneliness was highlighted to me in the comment one woman made, "I didn't have many friends in special education. I was more or less alone, like an alone kind of kid because the rest of the kids would always make fun like in junior high. All they did was make fun. They didn't seem to wanna understand. It made me feel really torn up inside."

DEFENDING AGAINST THE STIGMA

How does a retarded person respond to that "torn up" feeling? What kind of defense mechanisms do retarded people develop? Most retarded persons must rely on very simple psychological tactics or, as Sternlicht suggests, the more primitive defense mechanisms such as repression, regression, fixation, denial, undoing, and isolation.[37]

Not only are the defensive styles of retarded people very simple, but a single style can become pervasive. For example, some of them may opt for the role of retarded Uncle Toms. They wear happy and acquiescent masks to cover a chronic sense of inferiority. These are the perennial mascots, what Goffman called the "in-group deviants."[38] In light of this, it is apparent that the "jolly imbecile" stereotype is not totally the invention of non-handicapped people.

Another defensive strategy employed by some individuals is to deny their retardation. One of the most shopworn methods of denying a mental handicap is to try to "pass" as normal. There are many ways retarded persons try to pass. Edgerton found that *mildly* retarded people will attempt to facilitate their passing by marrying a non-retarded spouse.[39] Mildly retarded schoolboys were found to disavow their participation in special classes when talking to strangers.[40]

Moderately retarded people, because of their more serious limitations, usually have difficulty in passing. Despite this, many try. Of those I met, some did so with object symbols (sometimes referred to as disidentifiers). For example, a few of New Morning's students carried a pocketful of pens even if they could not write or wore wristwatches although they could not tell time. Some devoted themselves to mastery of facts that would make them sound precocious. Two examples of this were memorization of sports statistics or the dates of historical or personal events. (This memorization was not always in order to pass, though. Some retarded people are very interested in sports. And those who have been moved around a lot to various educational, residential, or occupational settings have to know essential, sometimes arcane, biographical information—especially dates that many non-handicapped persons would not know in reference to their own lives.)

Another method retarded people used to direct attention away from their handicap was to ask questions compulsively. Most who did this did not listen to the answers. It was just that in being on the asking rather than answering end of an interaction, they did not have to display what they knew or did not know.

A few of the retarded people were coy in the denial of their handicap. One man, in responding to a query about whether he had ever been called mentally retarded, said, "Oh, I hope not." A colleague had the following interaction with a retarded women:

> "Let's see. Do you know what mental retardation is?"
> "Someone that's near-sighted?"
> "Have you ever been called mentally retarded?"
> "No, but I been called a 'retard.'"
> "How does that make you feel?"
> "Terrible."
> "How come?"
> "I don't like to be called a 'retard' because I know that I'm near-sighted and I don't like to be called anything else."[41]

The predominant passing mode used by most of the people I encountered was apparent in unrealistic domestic and occupational aspirations. Many talked about the cars they would drive, the houses they would own, the children they intended to raise. A few wanted to become policemen, doctors, or nurses. Example: "I want to be a nurse. I would go to school for four years. That's how ambitious I am." In some cases, such comments were reflections of very real aspirations, although most were primarily efforts to appear more a part of the social mainstream. These people were usually aware of the limitations on their aspirations as a result of conversations with parents and teachers. One New Morning teacher said that it was one of her more joyless and ironic tasks to get students to emulate normalcy, while "keeping their pipe dreams just pipe dreams."

When retarded persons successfully pass, they enter the realm of what Goffman has called "phantom normalcy."[42] There are degrees of phantom normalcy, and each has its risks. The moderately successful passer fools some of the people some of the time or is led to believe he does. Periodic reinforcements of the success of his subterfuge can delude him, leading him to believe his social acceptance to be greater than it is. When this delusion is quashed, he typically feels a painful sense of betrayal. Other phantom passers just get confused by the many normal voices, some telling them how much like everyone else they are, some how different they are, some both things. The marginality of the moderately successful passer can be emotionally distressing in another way. While in his quasi-normal role, the marginal passer is asked to assume the pervasive, and oftentimes negative, social attitudes regarding the "deviant" group from which he has passed, despite being expected to remain a part of that group. Consider the feeling of a brain-damaged woman who, when asked if she had any of the same problems of her retarded brother, responded by saying, "No, his is a lot different . . . um . . . his is a lot different. He had brain damage when he was a baby."

The most successful passers are in the most awkward position. They may shroud their handicap better than the moderately successful phantom normals, but they are always at risk of being "found out" and discredited, a situation that breeds constant anxiety. Moreover, they are privy to what non-handicapped people really think about "retardates."

Another defensive tactic is apparent in those mentally retarded persons who try to deny that their retardation is really a handicap by glorifying it. One man said that being retarded did not really mean much in his life, other than that it allowed him "to do more than other people." Another held, "If we're mentally retarded and such, we are proud of that." A woman said, "I'm doing more than anyone can do."

While some retarded persons deny their retardation in an effort to protect themselves, others use their handicapped identity to a different advantage. For instance, early in my observations at New Morning School, a thirteen-year-old boy astutely panhandled a pack of chewing gum from me. He sensed my transparent uneasiness at being around the students. He saw that I was fawning over all his classmates. Thereupon, he longingly looked at my gum, glanced at me in a doleful style not rivaled by any picture of starving fourth worlders, stuck out his hand, and took his gum. My "conscience money." (At the turn of the century in Brazil, retarded children were regarded as a blessing to poor families because they made such effective mendicants.[43]) When I wondered aloud if the boy was always this adroit in using the handicap to control his environment, his teacher answered that he was. He had learned that a mixture of retardation and audacity could be very rewarding.

Where audacity works for one person, inhibition works for another. The primary defense of many retarded people is excessive reserve. They avoid all behavior that might upset others or cause them to laugh. Some become very skittish, going to great, sometimes absurd, lengths to avoid contact with normal people. The inhibited style also manifests itself in a restriction of wonder, an indifference to the acquisition of new experiences, a profound passivity. "If they are going to ridicule me, I'm not going to try." Some retarded people just play possum, or something else. When a retarded woman was asked if she had gone to school, she said, "I was too dumb. I didn't know how to say my numbers. So I played hooky."

Retarded persons may adopt the passive style for a number of reasons. For some, it is a mask that covers aggression. For others, it is a reaction to feelings that it is futile for them to try to control their environments. We are all confronted with tasks that we are intellectually ill equipped to handle. For retarded people that problem is chronic; as a result, some of them become anxious and fearful. This may partially explain why, as a rule, retarded persons show more anxiety than non-handicapped people.[44] Eisenberg describes a "catastrophic reaction"—sweating, tremor, rapid heart beat, rapid breathing—that many retarded children suffer when they find themselves faced with "unfamiliar situations, tasks that tax their abilities, or disapproving attitudes toward them."[45] Indeed, retarded persons are said to be "much more highly motivated to avoid failure than to achieve success."[46]

Anxiety about failure causes some retarded people to carry their passivity to the point of acting totally helpless. And this helplessness is often reinforced. For example, negative feedback from teachers has been shown to exacerbate helplessness in retarded students—students who are more likely than those without handicaps to get such feedback.[47] Conversely, non-handicapped people can be overly solicitous to retarded persons, and parents may treat them as infants—both of these practices inviting helpless responses. That some retarded adults are subject to such treatment is apparent in the comment of one mentally handicapped woman:

> My mom wanted me to come to our home state and coddle me like as if I didn't know nothing and I couldn't stand that. . . . When I go she doesn't treat me like an adult, when I go and visit. And yet they understand I'm a young lady, but they just won't. They don't accept the fact that I can do things, you know, for myself. They don't accept the fact that I'm a young lady and can do things.

The passive or helpless roles that many retarded people assume compound the inherent difficulties they already have in learning. There is evidence to show that after retarded people experience a failure, many become unable to solve a simple problem that they previously had been able to solve.[48] When their ego structure breaks down, retarded people come to distrust their own solutions to problems and develop an "other-directed style." They depend on others to make most of their decisions in an effort to minimize the ambiguity of dealing with novel situations. Some become rigid in their thinking,[49] adopting the habitual personality structures mentioned earlier. Such inflexibility typically precludes these people from finding solutions to ever-changing emotional conflicts and frustrations. Further, a morbid fear of novelty may actually precipitate emotional crises.

Some retarded persons make use of a defensive outlet not heretofore associated with them. They get drunk. The sparse data on the subject is inconclusive about the magnitude of the drinking problems of retarded people. Survey results on alcohol treatment programs throughout the country indicate that the problem is not unknown,[50] although it is not clear whether it is increasing in the wake of deinstitutionalization.[51] Of the many mentally retarded adults I know, only a handful drink even when given the opportunity, and rarely to excess. With the more permissive attitudes associated with normalization and community placement, there was, however, more of a predisposition on the part of mentally handicapped persons living in relatively independent residential settings to go out "for a few beers." There was at least one mentally handicapped Mountview resident who had repeatedly gotten into trouble for alcohol-induced disruptive behavior both in and out of her residential facility. Thus, while alcohol abuse among retarded persons may not become a sizable problem in the immediate future, it will probably become a more visible one.

Not every defensive style reveals itself in denial, inhibition, or the auto-aggression of something such as drunkenness. A few retarded people turn their aggression outward. Their limited repertoire of defense mechanisms against aggressions[52] contributes to this. Retarded persons frequently find it easier to "act out" their aggressions than to verbalize them or abstract them in other ways. Consequently, they attack sources of frustration directly. One woman said that when she is referred to as "mentally retarded," she gets "mad." "And I've hit 'em for it. . . . I think it should be handled, not ignored."

The aggressive tendencies of a few retarded individuals are heightened by the fact that they derive their role models from television shows.[53] While television has been shown to be a powerful agent of socialization for non-handicapped children, its influence may be even greater on mentally retarded youths because of their higher levels of dependence, generally low levels of self-esteem, and relative isolation.[54] Baran and Meyer reported that the majority of shows retarded children watched "contained regular 'doses' of violence."[55] Talkington and Altman found that mentally handicapped children modeled the aggressive behavior they saw on televison[56]—as was the case in studies conducted with non-handicapped children.[57] While all these inquiries have been done with children, it does not stretch the imagination too far to assume that there may be parallels with retarded adults. And television is omnipresent in residential settings for retarded children and adults; ironically, it is often there as a pacifier for residents.

Predictably, the retarded person who adopts a rude or aggressive style to protect himself from real social rebuffs sometimes uses it when the situation lends itself to congenial interaction. As is the case with all bullies, the defense mechanism intensifies the problem that necessitated it in the first place, creating an infinite regress.

The vital aspect of the defenses of retarded persons is the rigor with which they are employed. This alone should dispel stereotypes that hold retarded people to be emotionally insensate. While a few retarded individuals are oblivious to all but the most arrant social cruelties, most sense the disgust, the pity, the trepidation, and the ridicule of which they often become the objects. One little girl at New Morning School said it best in her response to some people who were laughing at her "retardedly cute" behavior in a patronizing way. She stopped what she was doing, turned to the people, and said, "Don't laugh; you know I have feelings too."

PSYCHOTHERAPY FOR RETARDED PERSONS

The "feelings" of retarded people do not always get much or very good attention when they are hurt. When I arrived at New Morning School, it purportedly had a part-time psychologist. Most of the school's staff did not know who he was—a significant factor, since they were responsible for making counseling referrals. There were other periods, one lasting a year and a half, when the school had no psychologist. In 1977, New Morning got a half-time psychologist; but this professional functioned, to a large extent, as a tester, providing colleagues with data from standardized instruments such as IQ tests. The psychologist conducted a few ongoing therapeutic programs for those students with emotional problems, although these were rare at New Morning, as they are in most educational and residential settings for retarded persons.

There are at least two major reasons why retarded children and adults often have to go it alone or settle for perfunctory psychotherapeutic services when they have emotional problems. First, limited resources usually siphon funds for special services into "tangible" areas such as education, living space, and occupational opportunities. Second, and more importantly, the psychotherapeutic profession has been largely indifferent to the needs of retarded people, there being a "severe shortage" of psychotherapists trained to provide services for mentally retarded clients.[58] This is a baffling phenomenon in light of the fact that all eight of the charter members of the American Association on Mental Deficiency were psychiatrists.[59]

The organized efforts that *have* been made to attend to the emotional problems of retarded persons have proved to be less than overwhelming successes. For example, in 1958 funds were set aside by the National Institute of Mental Health to train psychotherapists to work with mentally retarded people.[60] Nothing much came of it. In 1963, the American Psychiatric Association approved a program to combat the psychiatric problems involved in mental retardation. The association said, " . . . it is incumbent on the American Psychiatric Association to strengthen its own leadership role in the field of mental retardation, and to work with other medical specialists and physicians generally toward more concentrated concern with retardation."[61] The merit of the intentions inherent in this rhetoric was undeniable. By 1965, fewer than 1 percent of the certified psychiatrists in the nation were attached to state institutions for retarded people, and most of these professionals worked on a "relatively inactive consultant basis."[62] Research shows that psychiatrists prefer to do their therapy with people of normal intelligence.[63]

The tone of the psychotherapeutic community's attitude toward retarded persons was probably set in 1904, when Freud addressed the College of Physicians at Vienna. He said, "Those patients who do not possess a reasonable degree of education and a reliable character should be refused. The qualification which is the determining factor of fitness for psychoanalytic treatment is—whether the patient is educable."[64] Contemporary theorists such as Rogers have been cited for similar prejudices.[65] In fact, most non-behavioral techniques of modern psychotherapy do require introspection, retrospection, and interpretation, which are difficult operations for most retarded persons. As Colodny and Kurlander say, retarded people do not play "the talking game" very well.[66] There is no question that this creates difficulties for the non-behavioral therapist who has to try to understand the emotional problems of a retarded person from the latter's viewpoint. Such intersubjectivity requires that the therapist bridge an enormously wide intellectual gap—something that traditional training has not prepared him or her to do.

The by-products of such ill preparation can be dangerous, especially if therapists eschew not only long-term psychotherapeutic relationships with mentally retarded clients, but crisis intervention as well. A social worker related a relevant incident to me. One of her clients—a retarded adolescent—was embroiled in a psychotic incident that the social worker "could not handle" and believed called for immediate psychiatric intervention. She took the young man to a large, highly respected, crisis center. After "a three-hour wait" in an anteroom of the clinic, during which several other walk-in cases were treated by therapists, and a seemingly interminable "runaround," the social worker decided to take the somewhat becalmed youngster home and "hope for the best." A few days later, the boy raped his little sister. He has subsequently threatened the life of a worker at the residential facility to which he was sent after the rape, using a knife to back up the threat. Perhaps this would have happened even if the boy had received the intervention he needed. Perhaps not.

Psychotherapists are not the only reluctant partners in counseling relationships with retarded people. More than a few mentally handicapped individuals deny their emotional problems. Many of them, particularly those persons who have had bad familial and institutional experiences, learn to hide their feelings. They are distrustful of strangers and very circumspect when anyone begins to probe. Some go through their crises in a solitary way, neither asking for nor receiving help, or receiving "help" they have not asked for in the form of drugs. Sometimes these drugs do resolve behavioral problems with no apparent ill effects on the client. Sometimes they only mask the causes of the problems by eliminating the symptoms of the disturbance. Now and again drugs designed to reduce emotional problems actually intensify them. It has been shown that many retarded persons, like their non-handicapped peers, are "very sensitive to hints that drugs are given to punish or control them."[67]

An alternative to the use of "chemical straitjackets," purely behavioral therapies, or techniques based upon the problems of clients with normal intelligence would be the development of psychotherapy designed to meet the special needs of mentally handicapped persons. Much work needs to be done in this area, and a great deal of cooperation will be required from representatives of the psychotherapeutic and special education communities.

Before new psychotherapies for retarded people can be developed, however, better psychodiagnostic techniques are needed. The application of an appropriate therapy first requires that the clinician have some inkling of the etiological basis of the emotional disturbance. For example, does the problem emanate from physiological or social-psychological antecedents or a combination of the two? Psychological profiles on the New Morning students rarely shed much light on this as these profiles were derived largely from the interpretation of the students' performance on IQ and adaptive behavior tests. The nature and cause of emotional problems cannot be deduced from the results of such tests. Personality inventories such as the MMPI (Minnesota Multiphase Personality Inventory) are not useful in their applications to mentally handicapped populations. Thus psychotherapists and special educators who wish to develop and apply special psychotherapies do not have indexes that provide rough approximations of physical versus social-psychological factors in the etiology of the psychiatric disorders of their retarded clients.

In some cases, it cannot even be ascertained whether a person labeled as retarded actually is retarded or instead has a severe psychosis that impedes an otherwise normal intelligence. One New Morning teacher addresssed the problem this way: "I don't know whether this kid is retarded or if he's schizophrenic. Sometimes I think he's just schizophrenic." There is evidence that a chronic psychosis can lead to a permanent depression in intelligence.[68]

In the absence of adequate etiological guideposts, professionals frequently grope blindly for answers to the psychiatric riddles posed by retarded clients. For example, a few of the New Morning staff became amateur psychologists developing their own diagnostic tools. One staff member said that she assumed, "When problems emerge in the kids who are functioning at higher levels, these problems are probably emotional." The risk in this reasoning is that physical maladies, of which behavioral extremes may be symptomatic, could go untreated.

Another staff member maintained that she could best discern the difference between an emotional and an organic affliction because emotional problems made erratically periodic appearances, while physical problems were chronic. This overlooked the lingering nature of some emotional problems and the periodicity of certain physiological conditions.

Even if psychologists and special educators had better psychodiagnostic and therapeutic techniques, many of them, especially the educators, would be loath to get involved in counseling retarded students. When the parents of these children hear about such interventions, many feel threatened. As we shall see in the next chapter, parents of mentally handicapped youngsters frequently suffer neurotic reactions to their children's handicaps that, in turn, contribute to emotional problems in the children. These parents resent any implications by teachers or other professionals that highlight such contributions.

There is an encouraging sign in the area of diagnostics for retarded people. In the early 1970s the diagnostic-team approach to evaluating retarded people came into vogue. That is when Mountview's developmental and evaluation clinic got its start. Team members include:

1. a pediatrician, responsible for evaluating the medical history and current health status of the client
2. a neurologist, who does cranial nerve examinations, checks the sensory and motor systems, runs electroencephalograms, and so on
3. a public health nurse, who helps compile the client's medical history and interviews the child's family to ascertain how his health, nutritional, educational, and emotional needs are being met
4. a social worker, who supports the family by helping them cope with stress they feel regarding the child, helps the family maintain the primary decision-making responsibilities on behalf of the child, and provides the rest of the team with information about the individual needs of the family members and the social needs of the family unit
5. a psychologist, whose primary concern is to determine the degree of intellectual development of the child and make appropriate recommendations for therapeutic interventions where the need can be ascertained
6. a psychiatrist, who works closely with the psychologist as a diagnostician
7. a speech, language, and hearing evaluator.

Every factor relevant to the retarded child's handicap is scrutinized by these professionals, and the psychological profiles on the New Morning children who had been assessed by this team were usually more comprehensive and incisive than those of the students who had not had the team assessment.

In addition to a brightening diagnostic scene, there are some tentatively encouraging signs in the therapeutic area. First, hypnosis has been used successfully with retarded people to remediate emotional problems.[69] Second, family counseling has become more widespread and helps parents create a better emotional environment for their retarded children at home. Third, we see the development of important programs of psychotherapeutic aid to retarded persons, such as Chicago's Mental Health Program of the Institute for the Study of Developmental Disabilities.[70] Fourth, interview or "discussion therapy" has been found to be useful in helping retarded adolescents and young adults with their emotional maladjustments.[71]

DISCUSSING RETARDATION WITH
RETARDED PERSONS

The process of discussing mental handicaps with retarded people is complex and requires a great deal of delicacy. Two of the more controversial issues in this regard at New Morning School concerned *when* such discussions should take place and *who* should be responsible for conducting them.

The question of when retardation is discussed with a mentally handicapped child is not a purely chronological matter, since the range of emotional maturity of retarded children of the same age is enormous. What is certain is that some children recognize themselves as "different" very early in life. Retarded children with normal brothers and sisters are probably the first to discover some essential eccentricity in themselves as they compare the differing ways they and their siblings are treated by parents and peers.

All of the New Morning School staff agreed that discussions of mental handicaps were not appropriate with young children. Although the youngsters may sense their differences, even the higher-functioning children who are younger than eight or nine years old do not have the cognitive development to understand the explanation of why and how they are different. Beyond agreement on that point, the New Morning staff members were of varying opinions on when such discussions should begin. There were two philosophies, one preventive and one reactive. Advocates of the preventive approach argued that a child should have his handicap discussed with him as soon as he is capable of understanding, and before he has a bad social experience precipitated by the handicap. Others opted for a more reactive approach, holding that retardation should be discussed with a handicapped person only after an unpleasant social experience necessitated it. A couple of the staff said that such discussions had never crossed their minds one way or the other.

The staff members advancing the preventive approach said that retarded people need realistic understandings of their handicaps now more than they ever have in history. Because of the normalization movement, most mentally handicapped people are more subject to emotionally painful interactions on "the outside." If a retarded person is not fortified prior to a regrettable experience, the accompanying embarrassment and shame can be compounded by a sense of betrayal.

Proponents of the reactive approach argued that discussions of mental retardation were not fortifying for people with mental handicaps. To talk about retardation before a discussion is necessitated by a bad experience may in fact generate emotional problems that otherwise would not have existed—creating, for example, an intensified lack of self-esteem. At least, if the discussion comes as a result of an unpleasant incident on the outside, it can be held in a specific context and illustrated with concrete instances fresh in the retarded person's mind. Thus he need not rely on abstract mental projections into some hypothetical future.

Accompanying the problem of when retardation should be discussed is that of who will do the discussing. Some parents cannot do so very aptly because they are retarded themselves, although it might be argued that they make the best teachers. Other parents do not accept their children's handicaps and will not address them. Some do not know what to say or could not get the words out if they did. The parent who becomes overwrought in such discussions only confirms the stigma associated with the handicap in the child's mind.

Several New Morning staff members said that, under conditions where parents could not or would not discuss a child's handicap with him, and no one else better qualified was available, they would assume the responsibility.

At New Morning, the teachers of the vocational classes shouldered these responsibilities. In those sessions I attended, euphemisms for "mental retardation" were never used. Mental retardation was usually equated with an inability to do the thinking and work some other people can do. Many lessons were prefaced by comments such as "Some of you will be able to learn to do this, and some of you will not." One of the vocational teachers said of her relationship with the students, "The secret is to let them know your own limitations and help you overcome them. Then they are less sensitive to their own and more willing to accept help with them."

In addition to emotional bolstering of students, this teacher gave them physiological referents associated with their handicaps. In classes where "body parts" were discussed, the teacher explained brain damage and the causes and consequences of it. The approach to this discussion was very candid, and most of the students attended to what was being said with no apparent shock or dismay. It probably helped some of them to achieve a better understanding of themselves.

In the last few years, the oldest students at New Morning have also participated in psychodramas focusing on their handicaps and community responses to them. This not only desensitizes them to social rebuffs, but sensitizes them to their own inappropriate behaviors around non-handicapped people.

For mentally handicapped adults living in Mountview, there are counseling sessions in some of the city's residential facilities—usually group therapies conducted by consulting psychologists. Occasionally, mental retardation is mentioned in these. There is also a program of adult education for retarded citizens that as part of its curriculum offers self-awareness classes in which the students talk about their handicaps.

Listening to retarded people discuss their handicaps can be strange and emotionally wrenching. Like the rest of us, their self-assessments are frequently indulgent and can be quite bitter. But one always comes away with the feeling that one has been made privy to some special, rarefied, and often delightful realm of knowledge. To wit:

> Some people always tease 'bout us mentally retarded guys. Why don't you stop and think about it. Mentally retarded is something handicapped inside your brain. I have a little trouble learning. If you stop and think about what you're doing, you're hurting the mentally retarded, plus you're hurting yourself. I love to play sports, just like anybody else—like any normal kids. I'm a nice guy. I laugh at some things.

Occasionally, the remarks are more acerbic: "Sometimes they make fun of us. They still make fun of me. That's not right. It makes me feel terrible. I'll make fun of them too, just to make it even."

These comments convey a sense of the combination of anger and vulnerability these people feel, both of which can be reduced with a little help from their friends. Retarded persons can be helped to find and enjoy experiences that inspire self-confidence and stifle passivity and senseless inhibition. They can be helped to conquer the urge some of them have to blame all of their shortcomings on their handicap. They can be directed to appropriate outlets for their aggressions. They can learn not to be suspicious of all non-handicapped people, yet react appropriately when they are victimized. Here, they must be neither flippant nor grave. For retarded people, a candid understanding of their handicaps and a willingness to talk about them forthrightly with non-handicapped persons may be their most disarming protection against some of the things that hurt them.

NOTES

1. W. Shakespeare, *As You Like It*, Act II, Scene I, New York: New American Library, 1963.

2. F. J. Menolascino, "Psychiatric Aspects of Mongolism," *American Journal of Mental Deficiency*, 69:1965, pp. 653–660.

3. F. Davis, "Deviance Disavowal: The Management of Strained Interaction by the Visibly Handicapped," *Social Problems*, 9:1961, pp. 120–132.

4. W. Wolfensberger, *Normalization*, Toronto: The National Institute on Mental Retardation, 1972, p. 18.

5. S. Chess, "Emotional Problems in Mentally Retarded Children," in F. J.

Menolascino, ed., *Psychiatric Approaches to Mental Retardation,* New York: Basic Books, 1971, p. 55; J. G. Dewan, "Intelligence and Emotional Stability," *American Journal of Psychiatry,* 104:1948, p. 553; F. J. Menolascino, "Emotional Disturbances in Mentally Retarded Children: Diagnosis and Treatment Aspects," *Archives of General Psychiatry,* 19:1968, p. 464; I. Philips, "Psychopathology and Mental Retardation," in S. Chess and A. Thomas, eds., *Annual Progress in Child Psychiatry and Child Development,* New York: Brunner/Mazel, 1968; also in *American Journal of Psychiatry,* 124:1967, p. 29; A. T. Russell and P. E. Tanguay, "Mental Illness or Mental Retardation: Cause or Coincidence?" *American Journal of Mental Deficiency,* 85(6):1981, pp. 570–574; I. Philips and N. Williams, "Psychopathology and Mental Retardation: A Study of 100 Mentally Retarded Children: I. Psychopathology," *American Journal of Psychiatry,* 132:1975, pp. 1265–1271.

    6. F. J. Menolascino, "Emotional Disturbance and Mental Retardation," *American Journal of Mental Deficiency,* 70:1965, pp. 248–256.

    7. M. Craft, "Mental Disorder in the Defective: A Psychiatric Survey Among Inpatients," *American Journal of Mental Deficiency,* 63:1959, p. 833.

    8. M. L. Rutter, "Psychiatry," *Mental Retardation—An Annual Review,* 3:1971, p. 192.

    9. Ibid.

    10. M. I. Berman, "Mental Retardation and Depression," *Mental Retardation,* 5(6):1967, p. 20.

    11. R. B. Edgerton, *The Cloak of Competence: Stigma in the Lives of the Mentally Retarded,* Berkeley: University of California Press, 1967, p. vii.

    12. J. L. Tringo, "The Hierarchy of Preference Toward Disability Groups," *Journal of Special Education,* 4:1970, pp. 295–306.

    13. F. Davis, pp. 120–132.

    14. C. C. Carr and J. A. McLaughlin, "Self Concept of Mentally Retarded Adults," *Mental Retardation,* 11(6):1973, p. 59.

    15. H. Von Bracken, "Attitudes Concerning Mentally Retarded Children," presented at the meeting of the First Congress of the International Association for the Scientific Study of Mental Deficiency, Montpellier, France, September 1967, cited in I. Bialer, "Emotional Disturbance and Mental Retardation: Etiologic and Conceptual Relationships," in F. J. Menolascino, ed., *Psychiatric Approaches to Mental Retardation,* New York: Basic Books, 1970, p. 82.

    16. H. A. Collins, G. K. Burger, and D. Doherty, "Self-Concept of EMR and Non-Retarded Adolescents," *American Journal of Mental Deficiency,* 75(3):1970, p. 289.

    17. E. Goffman, *Stigma: Notes on the Management of Spoiled Identity,* Englewood Cliffs, N.J.: Prentice-Hall, 1963, p. 18.

    18. H. D. Love, *The Mentally Retarded Child and His Family,* Springfield, Ill.: Charles C. Thomas, 1973, p. 187.

    19. S. L. Guskin, "The Perception of Subnormality in Mentally Defective Children," *American Journal of Mental Deficiency,* 67:1962, pp. 53–60; S. L. Guskin, "Measuring the Strength of the Stereotype of the Mental Defective," *American Journal of Mental Deficiency,* 67:1963, pp. 569–575; S. L. Guskin, "Theoretical and Empirical Strategies for the Study of the Labeling of Mentally Retarded Persons," *International Review of Research in Mental Retardation,* 9:1978,

p. 135; H. Gottwald, *Public Awareness About Mental Retardation*, Reston, Va.: The Council for Exceptional Children, 1970; P. M. Hill and A. L. Hill, "MR Knowledge of Undergraduate and Graduate Students," *Mental Retardation*, 14(3):1976, p. 27; R. Latimer, "Current Attitudes Toward Mental Retardation," *Mental Retardation*, 8(5):1970, p. 32.

20. F. J. Menolascino, "Psychiatric Aspects of Mongolism," p. 659.

21. K. R. Kaufman and L. Katz-Garris, "Epilepsy, Mental Retardation, and Anticonvulsant Therapy," *American Journal of Mental Deficiency*, 84(3):1979, p. 257.

22. I. Bialer, "Emotional Disturbance and Mental Retardation: Etiologic and Conceptual Relationships," in F. J. Menolascino, ed., *Psychiatric Approaches to Mental Retardation*, New York: Basic Books, 1970, p. 79.

23. D. Romer and G. Berkson, "Social Ecology of Supervised Communal Facilities for Mentally Disabled Adults: II. Predictors of Affiliation," *American Journal of Mental Deficiency*, 85:1980, p. 241.

24. M. L. Rutter, p. 198.

25. I. Philips, "Children, Mental Retardation, and Emotional Disorder," in I. Philips, ed., *Prevention and Treatment of Mental Retardation*, New York: Basic Books, 1966, p. 116.

26. I. Philips, "Psychopathology and Mental Retardation," *American Journal of Psychiatry*, 124:1967, p. 30.

27. B. W. Richards, "Health and Longevity," *Mental Retardation and Developmental Disabilities*, 8:1976, p. 168; B. Farber, *Mental Retardation: Its Social Context and Social Consequences*, Boston: Houghton Mifflin, 1968, p. 92.

28. R. D. King, N. V. Paynes, and J. Tizard, *Patterns of Residential Care: Sociological Studies in Institutions for Handicapped Children*, London: Routledge and Kegan Paul, 1971, cited in E. S. Zaharia and A. A. Baumeister, "Technician Turnover and Absenteeism in Public Residential Facilities," *American Journal of Mental Deficiency*, 82:1978, p. 581.

29. M. J. George and A. A. Baumeister, "Employee Withdrawal and Job Satisfaction in Community Residential Facilities for Mentally Retarded Persons," *American Journal of Mental Deficiency*, 85:1981, pp. 639–647.

30. T. L. Coffman and M. C. Harris, Jr., "Transition Shock and Adjustments of Mentally Retarded Persons," *Mental Retardation*, 18(1):1980, pp. 3–8.

31. D. Romer and G. Berkson, "Social Ecology of Supervised Communal Facilities for Mentally Disabled Adults: III. Predictors of Social Choice," *American Journal of Mental Deficiency*, 85:1980, p. 250.

32. S. Landesman-Dwyer, G. Berkson, and D. Romer, "Affiliation and Friendship of Mentally Retarded Residents in Group Homes," *American Journal of Mental Deficiency*, 83:1979, p. 578.

33. S. Reiter and A. M. Levi, "Leisure Activities of Mentally Retarded Adults," *American Journal of Mental Deficiency*, 86:1981, p. 203.

34. R. L. Schalock, R. S. Harper, and G. Carter, "Independent Living Placement: Five Years Later," *American Journal of Mental Deficiency*, 86:1981, p. 175.

35. M. L. Rutter, p. 196.

36. E. Goffman, p. 30.

37. M. Sternlicht, "Personality—One View," *Mental Retardation and Developmental Disabilities*, 8:1976, p. 193.

38. E. Goffman, p. 142.

39. R. B. Edgerton, chap. 4, pp. 144–177.

40. R. Jones, "Labels and Stigma in Special Education," *Exceptional Children*, 38:1972, p. 564.

41. Interview conducted by Linda Hill, University of Colorado at Boulder, 1975.

42. E. Goffman, p. 122.

43. M. W. Barr, *Mental Defectives: Their History, Treatment and Training*, Philadelphia: Blakiston, 1913, p. 25.

44. I. Bialer, p. 76; R. Snyder, "Personality Adjustment, Self-Attitudes, and Anxiety Differences in Retarded Adolescents," *American Journal of Mental Deficiency*, 71:1966, p. 40.

45. L. Eisenberg, "Psychiatric Implications of Brain Damage in Children," *Psychiatric Quarterly*, 31:1957, p. 75.

46. E. Zigler, "Familial Mental Retardation: A Continuing Dilemma," *Science*, 155:1967, pp. 292–298, cited in N. Bernstein, "Intellectual Deficit and Personality Development," in N. Bernstein, ed., *Diminished People*, Boston: Little, Brown and Co., 1970, p. 178.

47. S. M. Raber and J. R. Weisz, "Teacher Feedback to Mentally Retarded and Nonretarded Children," *American Journal of Mental Deficiency*, 86:1981, p. 148.

48. E. Zigler and S. Hartner, "The Socialization of the Mentally Retarded," in D. A. Goslin, ed., *Handbook of Socialization Theory and Research*, Chicago: Rand McNally, 1969, p. 1089.

49. H. W. Stevenson and E. Zigler, "Discrimination Learning and Rigidity in Normal and Feebleminded Individuals," *Journal of Personality*, 25:1957, pp. 699–711.

50. C. H. Krishef and D. M. DiNitto, "Alcohol Abuse Among Mentally Retarded Individuals," *Mental Retardation*, 19:1981, p. 153.

51. Ibid, p. 154.

52. G. H. Pearson, "The Psychopathology of Mental Defect," in C. L. Stacey and M. F. DeMartino, eds., *Counseling and Psychotherapy with the Mentally Retarded*, Glencoe, Ill.: The Free Press, 1957, p. 136.

53. J. V. Fechter, "Modeling and Environmental Generalization by Mentally Retarded Subjects of Televised Aggressive or Friendly Behavior," *American Journal of Mental Deficiency*, 76:1971, p. 267.

54. T. P. Meyer, "Children's Perceptions of Their Favorite TV Characters as Behavioral Models," *Educational Broadcasting Review*, 7:1978, p. 28.

55. S. J. Baran and T. P. Meyer, "Retarded Children's Perceptions of Favorite Television Characters as Behavioral Models," *Mental Retardation*, 13(4):1975, p. 29.

56. L. W. Talkington and R. Altman, "Effects of Film-Mediated Aggressive and Affectual Models on Behavior," *American Journal of Mental Deficiency*, 77(4):1973, pp. 420–425.

57. S. J. Baran, "TV and Social Learning in the Institutionalized MR," *Mental*

Retardation, 11(3):1973, p. 36; A. Bandura, D. Ross, and S. Ross, "Transmission of Aggression Through Imitation of Aggressive Models," *Journal of Abnormal and Social Psychology*, 63:1961, pp. 575–582; A. Bandura, D. Ross, and S. Ross, "Imitation of Film-Mediated Aggressive Models," *Journal of Abnormal and Social Psychology*, 66:1963, pp. 3–11; O. J. Lovaas, "Effect of Exposure to Symbolic Aggression on Aggressive Behavior," *Child Development*, 32:1961, pp. 37–44.

58. S. Reiss, "Psychopathology and Mental Retardation: Survey of a Developmental Disabilities Mental Health Program," *Mental Retardation*, 20(3):1982, p. 128; S. Reiss, G. W. Levitan, and J. Szyszko, "Emotional Disturbance and Mental Retardation: Diagnostic Overshadowing," *American Journal of Mental Deficiency*, 86(6):1982, p. 567.

59. H. Potter, "Mental Retardation: The Cinderella of Psychiatry," *Psychiatric Quarterly*, 39:1965, p. 540.

60. I. Philips, "Psychopathology and Mental Retardation," *American Journal of Psychiatry*, 124:1967, p. 29.

61. American Psychiatric Association, "Psychiatry and Mental Retardation," *American Journal of Psychiatry*, 122:1966, p. 1305.

62. H. Potter, p. 538.

63. J. G. Dewan, p. 552; S. E. Slivkin and N. R. Bernstein, "Group Approaches to Treating Retarded Adolescents," in F. J. Menolascino, ed., *Psychiatric Approaches to Mental Retardation*, New York: Basic Books, 1970, pp. 448–449.

64. H. C. Gunzburg, "Psychotherapy," in A. M. Clarke, and A.D.B. Clarke, eds., *Mental Deficiency: The Changing Outlook*, 3rd ed., New York: The Free Press, 1974, p. 712.

65. M. Sternlicht, "Psychotherapeutic Procedures With the Retarded," *International Review of Research in Mental Retardation*, 2:1966, p. 280.

66. D. Colodny and L. F. Kurlander, "Psychopharmacology as a Treatment Adjunct for the Mentally Retarded: Problems and Issues," in F. J. Menolascino, ed., *Psychiatric Approaches to Mental Retardation*, New York: Basic Books, 1970, p. 378.

67. R. D. Freeman, "Use of Psychoactive Drugs for Intellectually Handicapped Children," in N. Bernstein, ed., *Diminished People*, Boston: Little, Brown and Co., 1970, p. 284.

68. A. T. Russell and P. E. Tanguay, p. 573.

69. M. Sternlicht, "Psychotherapeutic Approaches with the Retarded," p. 325.

70. S. Reiss, pp. 128–132.

71. M. Sternlicht, "Psychotherapeutic Approaches with the Retarded," p. 285.

7
The Family:
Parents and Siblings
of Retarded People

The White Coat Gouges
My Soul with
the dull knife
of the word. "Retarded."
　　　—J. C. Higgens[1]

No Place Vast Enough
To Escape from Known Truth
　　　—J. C. Higgens[2]

　　I cried when I was first told that my mother died. I didn't get to go to my mother's funeral either. My brothers got a car but they couldn't come after me; there wasn't no chance. The nurse was the one that told me my mother died. I suppose I'd a been worried all the more if I'd a went to her funeral.

So goes the account of a mentally retarded adult. One senses the forced resignation of an encompassing separateness. This man's brothers live twenty miles from him. Such accounts are not uncommon in the lives of mentally retarded people. But what of their parents?—their siblings? What must it be like for them? One mother answers this way,

　　Much has been written about its ego-shattering impact, its dislocation of normal values, the dark veil of hopelessness it casts over the whole family; but nothing I have thus far seen begins to describe this shattering blow, and even more important the subtle, psychological, social, . . . and even physical changes it brings about to affect the parent-child, parent-parent, parent-society relationships.[3]

Raising a mentally retarded child is a very difficult matter for many parents.

THE PHASES OF ACCEPTANCE

A commonly employed method of exploring life in families of mentally handicapped youngsters is tracing the sequence of events parents of these children typically pass through as they establish a relationship with the retarded child. One frequently cited model has parents going through the following stages: (1) awareness, (2) recognition, (3) the search for a cause, (4) the search for a solution, and (5) varying degrees of acceptance.[4] The model is instructive. It is, however, an overgeneralization to assume that all parents of retarded children go through each of these phases. For example, some parents get bogged down in one phase or another. A few move directly from recognition to rejection. Others "accept" a retarded child before they begin to look for solutions to any problems that might result from the handicap. It is worth being mindful of such things as one reads this chapter. It will deal primarily with the problematic aspects of the familial environment of mentally retarded children, and one liability of the problematic approach is that it overlooks those parents and siblings who enjoy amiable, relatively trouble-free relationships with family members who are mentally retarded. It ignores the many parents who approach the task of raising a retarded child in a calm, committed fashion and make living with the youngster look easy and enjoyable. Indeed, as a result of their relationships with retarded children, some parents become more emotionally mature, or closer and more intimate with friends and family, or better all-around parents. Thus the exploration of the difficult aspects of rearing a retarded child that follows in this chapter is not meant to apply to all parents of mentally handicapped children, although I would venture that even the most splendid parents have experienced some of the feelings described.

The Phase of Awareness

Sometimes "the feeling" comes shortly after the child is born; sometimes it takes years. "Awareness" as it is used here denotes the first inklings parents have that their child is different in some significant way from other children. As we have seen, these inklings are often the result of the child's failure to reach such developmental milestones as smiling, sitting up, walking, or talking. The suspicions of the awareness phase are quite precise sometimes. In fact, it is a fairly common occurrence for parents to suspect mental retardation before any confirmation is made by professionals.[5]

The Phase of Recognition I: The Informing Interview

Whether the diagnosis of a mental handicap confirms suspicions of the awareness phase or comes as a complete surprise to parents, the result is usually the same. The discovery that one's child is mentally retarded is an indelible and stunning experience. One mother is quoted as saying "I had the feeling that everything in the world had ended . . . for me. Nothing worse could happen. It would be better if the whole family could be wiped out. I got hysterical. It's something you just don't get over. . . . It's crushing."[6] The father of a retarded child says, "I submit that, in many cases, being told that one's child is retarded may well be the most severe shock that one may experience in a normal lifetime full of trying experiences."[7]

Although the informing interview (the pivotal diagnostic encounter between physicians and parents) should occasion great delicateness, the process is occasionally haphazard, insensitive, even cruel. An example was revealed to me by a social worker who was counseling a young couple who had been informed of their child's handicap in a less than ideal fashion. The couple had taken their newborn to see a pediatrician in response to some suspicions related to his slow development. During the visit, the doctor did not raise the subject of mental retardation. As the parents were leaving the physician's office, he purportedly handed them a book on the subject and said, "Here, you should read this; you'll probably be needing it." Waskowitz provides an account of similar harshness: "The doctor said our child was a mongolian idiot over the telephone. He acted as though it was your problem buddy."[8] The callousness evident in these stories is not common, and as we shall see in a later section of this chapter, physicians are sometimes unfairly cast in the role of the "heavies" in meeting their diagnostic responsibilities. Some doctors, however, do handle the informing interview poorly. This is not only manifest in undue harshness, either.

For example, many parents report frustration at the circuitous approach doctors take in apprising them of a child's mental handicap. Common parental complaints I heard while in the field were that doctors equivocated by: (1) not saying anything about mental retardation at all, (2) circumlocuting and/or misemphasizing certain elements of the handicap, (3) using very abstruse language, (4) playing guessing games, or (5) pushing the responsibility for the informing interview off on other professionals.

The assertion that occasionally doctors do not mention mental retardation even when it is "obvious to them that there is something wrong" was a primary complaint of the mothers of retarded children surveyed by Anderson and Garner.[9] Diagnostic circumlocution through misemphasis was discussed by Anderson, who suggested that if a child is multihandicapped, the physician may emphasize one disability to the parents (cerebral palsy, for example), while ignoring the mental handicap.[10]

I asked several pediatricians how they told parents about a child's retardation. Three of the physicians most adamant that they "leveled with" parents or were "straight shooters" were also most predisposed, according to their accounts, to use language such as "genetic anomaly" or "chromosomal abnormality" to approach the subject of mental retardation. They left me with the impression that they used such medical jargon with little elaboration or clarification—an impression supported anecdotally by Svarstad and Lipton.[11] In the presence of a parent who is awed or intimidated by the doctor and will not follow up with questions about the ramifications of a genetic anomaly, the informing interview can be conducted without imparting much salient information.

One pediatrician also confirmed "the guessing game approach." He said, "I keep dropping clues to the parents until they tell *me* the child is retarded."

Some physicians purportedly pass off the responsibility for the informing interview to other professionals through referrals *ad infinitum.* Waskowitz reported the sad saga of a parent who went from a pediatrician who said the woman's retarded son "would be all right," to a neurologist who said the boy was "nearsighted," to an orthopedist who found that the child's "feet were quite flat."[12] In a recent study, 88 percent of sixty-nine physicians surveyed said they provided diagnostic information on the handicap immediately after the birth of the retarded child.[13]

Another complaint voiced by parents of mentally handicapped children is that doctors do not give them adequate information about mental retardation once the diagnosis has been made. In a survey of sixty physicians and 175 parents conducted by Kelly and Menolascino, it was shown that while 71 percent of the physicians said they gave materials on mental retardation to parents, only 10 percent of the parents said they received such materials.[14]

Parents of mentally retarded children also contend that physicians fail to give them referrals to appropriate social service agencies in the wake of a diagnosis of mental retardation. Eighty-one percent of the physicians surveyed by Kelly and Menolascino said they referred parents to the Visiting Nurse Association, while only 3 percent of the parents said they had ever been referred there.[15] The same survey showed that disparities between the accounts of doctors and parents existed with regard to referrals to all local service agencies.

A failure to make proper referrals may exist, in part, because physicians do not bother to learn about local services. In a study conducted in the early sixties, Olshansky and Sternfeld found that only 27 percent of the general practitioners they contacted could identify the activities, location, or sponsorship of local agencies that provided services to mentally retarded persons.[16] Much more recent studies indicate that the situation has not greatly improved.[17]

A few physicians avoid persistent pleas for information and referrals by getting the child out of their sphere of responsibility; they automatically advise parents to institutionalize their retarded children. In the late 1950s, Waskowitz reported the following parental account:

> When Johnny was about two years of age, a doctor was called about another sibling and casually commented that Johnny was mentally retarded. The doctor referred him to the hospital where the opinion was that the child was a mongoloid, very retarded, and that the best thing for us to do was to put him in an institution because he would forget us very quickly, and if we had other children, it would have an effect on the whole family, particularly that our children would be embarrassed because of Johnny. . . .[18]

Modern doctors have many more service referral options available to them than did the physicians of the late fifties and early sixties. Precise data is not available on their referral patterns with mildly and moderately retarded children. But as late as 1975, automatic institutionalization was still the course preferred by 80 percent of those surveyed by Kelly and Menolascino when the child was severely or profoundly retarded.[19] A recent study by Adams has shown this to have changed radically, only 13.5 percent of a population of physicians recommending institutionalization for severely and profoundly retarded children.[20]

Another problem between parents of retarded children and their physicians was highlighted in the Kelly and Menolascino survey. They found that 57 percent of the parents with whom they talked were dissatisfied with doctors' attitudes toward their retarded youngsters.[21] Most of the mothers in another survey believed that the doctors wanted them out of the office as quickly as possible after the informing interview, and that in subsequent visits "the doctors were not as interested in their retarded child's injuries and illnesses as they were in normal children's."[22]

In the matter of the informing interview, insensitivity, equivocation, and the dissemination of misinformation by doctors is inexcusable. In fairness to the physicians, however, there are mitigating circumstances that explain the way some of them deal with parents of mentally handicapped children. For instance, there are a number of reasons doctors might equivocate in diagnostic encounters with parents. Physicians are often puzzled about whether a particular set of parents should be told without delay about their child's mental handicap or should be told slowly and circuitously. Some parents want to know about the handicap candidly and quickly. Svarstad and Lipton present the following excerpt from a postinforming interview: "The way he just came right out, point blank, and said it. . . . It sort of shocked me into accepting reality. . . . I'm the kind of person that the more you give me the run-around, the less I like you. . . ."[23] Other parents prefer a very gradual preparation. Waskowitz reported the following parental account: "The doctor was very tactful. He implied things right along. . . . Not until two or three years later did he really tell me the child was seriously defective and had to be in an institution. He prepared me well."[24] Carr's inquiry dispels some of the ambiguity on direct versus circuitous processes of informing parents about their children's mental handicaps. In reviewing literature on the subject, he found that between 60 and 90 percent of parents favored the immediate approach, while between 1 and 7 percent preferred to be informed of the handicap at a later date than they actually were.[25]

The physician takes a chance in every informing interview of breaking the news of a mental handicap to someone not equipped to handle it. McDonald and her colleagues found that 13 percent of the sixty-nine physicians they surveyed held parental emotional stability to be the most salient variable in the diagnostic information they disseminated.[26] The results of mistaken judgment on this account can be devastating. One of the physicians with whom I consulted described telling a woman that her newborn was brain-damaged. She had a psychotic response despite no previous history of emotional problems. The woman was institutionalized in 1963 and was still in an institution as of 1980. One can understand why this doctor became circumspect in subsequent informing interviews, even to the point of equivocation or evasiveness.

To make matters worse, the odds of choosing the appropriate approach to the informing interview are reduced by a structural factor involving the boundaries of a physician's professional responsibility. If the handicapping condition is diagnosed in the early postnatal period, parents may be given the news by a stranger. Obstetricians relinquish responsibility for the newborn's welfare to a pediatrician immediately after all routine paranatal procedures have been completed. In the case of the first-born child, the obstetrician has typically seen the mother a few times during her pregnancy and has usually met the child's father only briefly, if at all. If it is the couple's first child, they may not have met the pediatrician who is responsible for the informing interview. Some pediatricians consult with the family doctor and/or obstetrician to get some kind of psychological profile on the parents before giving them the news. Even at that, it is a rare doctor who has developed a deep enough understanding of the parents' emotional status to break the news with the required subtle sensitivity.

Physicians also face another problem in their timing of the informing interview. There is some evidence that children diagnosed as mentally retarded very early in the postnatal period have a particularly difficult time because their parents have negative interactive predispositions toward them from the outset. The parents recoil from the child before they have a chance to get to know him and his capabilities.[27]

Another reason doctors equivocate in the informing interview is, quite simply, that it is very difficult for them to break the news about something as potentially devastating as a mental handicap. All too often, in the welter of their own confused outrage, parents fail to give doctors as much empathy as they expect from them. In the immediate aftermath of the informing interview, excessively emotional parental responses are understandable, including berating the physicians who did the telling. Those parents who experience a lingering anger at their doctors might diminish it by imagining themselves being given the responsibility for telling another parent his child is retarded. A good instance of parental performance in this regard is apparent in an anecdote related by Gordon and Ullman. A remiss physician left the responsibility of telling a mother about her child's mental handicap up to the youngster's father. The father in this case was unable to break the news to the mother for three months.[28]

Diagnostic equivocations by physicians are justified in assessing rare or subtle forms of retardation, forms similar to other afflictions, or those that manifest themselves slowly. Doctors are torn between expressing potentially ill-founded suspicions or waiting until they are certain a developmental delay exists and is likely to be permanent. Here, a physician finds himself in a "no win" situation. If he raises unconfirmed suspicions, parents want answers the doctor cannot give. If he does not raise them and the child has a retarding condition, the youngster is denied the amelioriative effects of early intervention. An error in either direction has manifold negative consequences.

Sometimes parents exaggerate the diagnostic vaguenesses of physicians. One doctor who had been the object of a great deal of parental invective in Mountview because of alleged diagnostic equivocations admitted that when he began his practice it was "nearly impossible" for him to tell parents their child was retarded. He said that he has "toughened up" in recent years, and despite this, many parents still do not listen to him, "because they don't want to hear" what he tells them.

There is no doubt that some parents disregard straightforward diagnoses. For example, one inquiry demonstrated that prior to counseling, 52 percent of a sample group of parents of mentally handicapped children "were willing to admit they were originally appraised of the retardation by medical doctors." This was increased to 71 percent after counseling.[29]

While a few parents "do not hear" the diagnosis of their children's mental retardation, others do not understand what they do hear or erroneously translate the information given them. For instance, they equate all mental retardation with the most severe forms of the condition even if their child is mildly or moderately handicapped and his level of functioning inconsistent with their stereotypical visions of what a retarded person is like.[30] Other parents may go to the opposite extreme, denying the existence of the handicap as it has been diagnosed. Such denial can be exacerbated by peculiar characteristics associated with certain retarding conditions. For example, "spasticity" resulting from reduced forebrain inhibition can lead certain infants to turn over on their own, months ahead of normal timetables, thus making the child appear developmentally advanced to the parent.[31] Naturally, this makes acceptance of the retarded diagnosis difficult. In the informing interview, physicians ought to clarify the fact that there are degrees of mental retardation and explain anomalous physiological symptoms to allay the possibility of parental misunderstandings.

Doctors must also be attuned to the tendency some parents have to translate diagnostic explanations into whatever they want to hear. When a physician says that a child is "slow," a few parents take that to mean the youngster will "catch up," although the intent of the euphemism is fairly clear.

Even when doctors explain mental retardation in very simple, complete, understandable terms, certain parents will find the physicians' diagnostic performances unacceptable. To some parents, it makes no difference what is said or how. According to Meadow and Meadow, a diagnosis of nearly any handicapping condition evokes parental dissatisfaction with the diagnosing physician.[32] In talking with mothers of mentally handicapped children, Anderson and Garner found a high degree of satisfaction about physicians' interactions with the youngsters *before* the diagnosis of mental retardation was made. *After* the diagnosis, though, there was a precipitous drop in this satisfaction.[33] Some of these mothers said the dissatisfaction resulted from the feeling that the doctor gave the child a cursory examination or did not explain adequately why the diagnosis was made.[34] For others, the dissatisfaction was doubtless a protest of the diagnosis itself.

It is difficult to know how much credence to give the parental allegation that doctors do not provide adequate postdiagnostic information about mental retardation. Some physicians probably avoid disseminating the facts in the vain belief that the "laity" could not understand anyway. It is known that doctors tend to give more specific, complete, and candid explanations on handicapping conditions to parents perceived as having a greater capacity to comprehend medical explanations—this typically being based on the physician's informal assessment of the parents' socioeconomic status.[35] There are, however, cases in which parents of retarded children complain about the amount and quality of information their physicians give them about mental retardation even though the doctors have done an adequate job. What some of these parents may really want is not just information and support, but a "total handling of the problem" by the physician.[36]

In many cases doctors do not provide information on retarding conditions to parents, not because they *will not*, but because they *cannot*. Most established physicians have little experience in diagnosing mentally retarded children.[37] Despite the fact that mental retardation is "the most handicapping of all childhood disorders,"[38] one large survey showed that fewer than 25 percent of a sample of fourth-year medical students had received any formal instruction about it.[39] This study was conducted in the late sixties, but its findings are probably still germane. Indeed, with the increasing expectations that physicians in training must learn more and more technical information just to "keep up," the time devoted to understanding the needs of special medical interests such as retarded people is further eroded. As Schwartz suggests, "The amount of attention paid to mental retardation in the medical school curriculum is a message to the student about the relative importance of this condition in his future work."[40] What many physicians must do once they begin to practice is develop trial-and-error procedures for conveying diagnostic information on mental retardation.[41] This kind of dangerous experimentation with volatile human issues is one of the great shortcomings of modern medicine.

Experience has, by the way, shown that short-term training can help doctors avoid certain pitfalls in their dealings with mentally handicapped children and their parents. In the late 1970s, a cooperative program between Children's Hospital National Medical Center in Washington, D.C., and the Experimental Preschool Model Demonstration Program of the National Children's Center was begun.[42] Each pediatric resident was required to spend twelve hours at the preschool during the second or third year of his residency training, with the thought that the experience would enhance his knowledge and sensitivity about mental retardation in several targeted areas, such as behavior, terminology, assessment, psychology, communication with parents and teachers, and community resources. The doctors participating in the program rated dealing with the parents of mentally handicapped children as the most important thing they expected to learn,[43] dispelling to some extent the notion that physicians are indifferent to the needs of these parents. In the end, the physicians increased their knowledge in all of the areas that had been targeted. Indeed, they more than doubled their competence in "gaining understanding of community resources available for handicapped children."[44] Helping parents make the best of community services that are available is one of the greatest kindnesses a doctor can show someone who has just learned his child is mentally retarded. That is what reason would dictate, anyway, but it is not always the case. In a recent article, Waisbren expressed surprise that the availability of public services for handicapped youngsters and their parents did not necessarily diminish the "internal strain experienced by parents with a very young developmentally disabled child."[45] Doctors may be gentle and handle the informing interview and all subsequent parental encounters flawlessly. Services may be the best available in the country. What remains, though, what will always remain for these parents, is the profound shock of discovering that they have a retarded child.

The Phase of Recognition II: Mourning and Denial

Some parents respond to the informing interview by going into mourning or something akin to it. One mother said, "It's like someone came and told you your child was dead."[46] Several researchers suggest that the mourning may not be completely figurative.[47] During pregnancy, parents create a vision of the "ideal child" they are going to have. The birth of a defective child is tantamount to the death of the ideal child. Several parents and siblings of retarded children told me that the name that had been picked out for the baby was changed when it was discovered he or she was retarded. To compound parents' stress, there is no time for them to mourn adequately the death of the ideal child because the retarded baby demands immediate attention. Moreover, the whole process of mourning the one child and caring for the other comes at a time when the parents, particularly the mother, may be physically depleted.

Recognition of the handicap comes rapidly for some parents. For others, it never comes. A few parents try to deny the existence of the handicap by engaging in what has been termed "shopping behavior." They go from doctor to doctor looking for a diagnosis other than mental retardation. Shopping behavior is understandable and may be fruitful on occasion. Oftentimes, though, it ends up costing the family a lot of money, time, and energy, and it diverts parental attentions from the child's most acute needs.

Just because a parent makes repeated visits to an array of professionals does not mean he or she is "shopping." In some cases, several different consultations are necessary to piece together the diagnostic mosaic, especially where there are multiple handicaps. Numerous and repeated consultations are transformed into shopping behavior when a parent demonstrates an inability to resolve a resolvable problem.[48] Keirn found that fewer than 3 percent of the parents he studied were, by this definition, "shoppers."[49]

The Phase of Searching for Causes

Recognition of a child's mental handicap typically precipitates a parental probe for causes. In some instances, the search is a rational effort to effect a cure or avoid similar handicaps in future children. In other instances, the parents are looking for something or someone to blame for the handicap or their own feelings about it.

It is not uncommon for physicians to be scapegoats. As we have seen, ill will can result from faux pas committed by doctors in the diagnostic process. Further, a few physicians probably do bear responsibility for the handicapping condition or are seen to in the eyes of certain parents.[50] Occasionally, though, unculpable doctors become the focus of the anger, confused exasperation, and guilt of parents, just as ancient messengers were sometimes put to death when they brought bad news.

The scapegoating may be reciprocal. Physicians are trained in reversing illnesses. The irreversibility of most forms of mental retardation evokes feelings of helplessness in doctors, which leads some of them to exaggerate the unwillingness of parents to follow directions.

Not all parental externalizations of blame are directed at doctors. Some parents blame their spouses for the child's handicap. One variation of this is apparent in the following account: "Mrs. S. wanted to know from where Martha's condition came. She commented that it could not come from her family since everybody on her side was 'college material.' She thought that it must therefore come from Martha's father who was not an educated man, 'just a truck driver.' She often blamed her husband for Martha's condition."[51] The cycle of accusations and counteraccusations this creates gives rise to severe stress on a marriage, worsening any difficulties the parents had in coping with the child in the first place. It is very risky business to pin the blame for a retarded child on one's doctor or mate. A parent will usually be dependent on both of them to help raise the retarded youngster.

It is not uncommon for the retarded child himself to become the object of parental anger. "How could you be this way?" Such hostility can, in turn, set off an emotional chain reaction. Parental anger leads to guilt, which, of course, is heightened because the child is handicapped. To compensate for this guilt, the parents overindulge and/or overprotect the child. The overindulged child will act in such a way as to anger the parents further and the cycle will begin anew: only on this round, every emotion is intensified. Meanwhile, the child is sensing his parents' displeasure because he cannot be what they want. In order to protect himself from the anxiety he feels, he becomes withdrawn or aggressive, either of which increases parental negativity, and further perpetuates the whole cycle. It is an infinite regress that, along with the other stresses of raising a retarded child, can lead to psychopathological reactions by parents.

Some parents dream of killing their children, as in the account of this over-protective mother: "I dreamed that my child was lying in my arms and I was loving him, just as I do when I am awake. And then a hand with a pistol came through the window, and my poor little baby was shot through the head. I tried and tried to save him, but I could not keep him from dying."[52]

The repressed impulse to kill the child comes out in daydreams as well:

> . . . [A]fter reading several accounts of successful heart and kidney transplants, a mother of one retarded child and several normal ones found herself thinking that if anything ever happened to her retarded child she would want the vital organs made available as transplants. At first, she was puzzled because she was thinking of this only in terms of her retarded child and not in terms of the rest of her family. Then the implication of these thoughts became clear and she realized that she partly wanted her child to die.[53]

Olshansky concludes that the question frequently asked by parents of retarded children—"What will happen to my child if I die?"—is a displacement of the parents' death wish for the child.[54] Historically, such death wishes were less figurative than they are now. It was once the case that babies diagnosed as mentally retarded at birth were immediately institutionalized. Parents would then put an obituary in local newspapers and tell friends and family the child was stillborn or died shortly after birth.[55]

A few parents contemplate killing their retarded children.[56] Greenfeld describes the decision to kill his son Noah as follows:

> A horrible weekend. I thought continually that soon I will have to kill Noah. The monster that has long been lurking in him increasingly

shows its face. And just as the day may come when I can no longer bear to take care of him, I could not bear to see him mistreated—or maltreated—in a state hospital. . . . Killing him would be a kindness. His brain has stopped working; he has not been functioning anyway. I dread it but I see myself killing my son not as a myth but as a fact. . . .

There is a man from Santa Barbara who killed his brain-damaged son a few years ago. He put a gun to the boy's head and squeezed the trigger, then called the police. He's in prison now. But he'll get out eventually.[57]

Not all parents of retarded children externalize the blame for the handicap. Some become enveloped in a cloud of guilt and self-recrimination. Weller et al. state that guilt is the most pervasive of all parental reactions to a retarded child.[58]

Self-blame, despite repeated assurances from physicians that the handicapping condition was no one's fault, inspires many parents to propound their own, sometimes esoteric, causal explanations. Some believe they are carriers of a genetic contaminant.[59] Rosen found the majority of mothers in his survey "would not want to have more children for fear that the next would be mentally retarded."[60] Two-thirds of the mothers Holt talked with felt the same way.[61] The mother of a mentally retarded youngster told me, "After we had our boy, the thought of another child terrified and sickened me. I could not have sex with my husband for several years."

A few parents manage both to externalize and internalize the blame for a child's retardation. They attribute it to an angry god. One mother writes,

> Heaven's wrath
> descends
> on me.
> What have
> I done to
> invoke Your
> rage?[62]

A few parents believe they are given the child by God as a test of their faith.

Some of the more bizarre etiological speculations parents advance manage to combine genetic and spiritual explanations for retarding conditions. Emde and Brown report the fantasies of a mother who believes she has given birth to a Down's Syndrome child as a form of atonement for "knowing too much by carrying the genes of another civilization within [her]. . . ."[63] The same woman propounds a modified

Karmic principle that suggests that if individuals hate retarded people, they are likely "to come back as that kind of a person. . . ."[64]

Other parents confused about the cause of their child's developmental delays and learning difficulties attribute them to inadequacies in the way they treat him.[65] This is most likely to happen when the informing interview is vague and the parent insecure. Indeed, the incredulity, confusion, shame, guilt, and loss of self-esteem some parents feel at the recognition of their children's mental handicaps are extensions of preexisting conditions. For these parents, having a retarded child is merely an affirmation of feelings of inferiority and inadequacy they already had. One mother says, "I always thought of myself as a failure until I got pregnant, and then I felt I was just as good as anyone else. But after the child came, I realized that I had failed in everything, and I didn't want to live anymore."[66]

If parents have no accurate etiological information and have not identified some blameworthy subject, their response to the recognition of the child's mental handicap may be a generalized self-pity: "Why me?" "Why did this have to happen to us?" "It isn't fair." The feeling that an injustice has been done causes these parents to become resentful of anyone who has been more fortunate—that is, anyone whose baby is not retarded.[67] In fact, resentment can lead to a generalized hostility by the parent toward other normal adults because of the way they respond to the child's defects when the youngster is "displayed." Hart describes it this way:

> One interesting example occurs again and again in *No Time for Tears*, a book written by . . . the . . . mother of a hydrocephalic son. Pictures of the child show a youngster unlike any that most people have ever seen and one who would consequently attract attention anywhere. The mother admits that she had to force herself to look at him and touch him and that this baby she wanted so much became repulsive to her. However, there is no anger toward him. It is interesting that at this point she begins to take the child out to public parks, playgrounds and so on—places where there are large groups of people—and then becomes furious when people stare.[68]

Grebler found a connection between the quality of the parent-child relationship and the direction of parents' anger about a mental handicap; to wit, if parents blame the actions and attitudes of the rest of the world for the frustrations they feel regarding the child, they will tend to reject him.[69] The only circumstance under which parents are inclined to accept a retarded child is if they stop looking for someone or something to blame for the handicap.[70]

The Phase of Searching for Solutions

Although a retarded child can progress developmentally, medical science has not fashioned the means to replace neurons. Mental retardation caused by brain damage is incurable. To reduce the effects of this painful realization, some parents begin to search for miraculous remedies, and where there is a demand for false hopes, a supply can always be found. There are a few hucksters who sell false hope. For example, the parents of one New Morning student were saving their money to take the child to a clinic that purported to reactivate neurons by standing retarded children on their heads!

Arrant misrepresentation is not always the problem though. Some special educators, for example, get carried away with a "miracle-worker syndrome"—promising parents more than they can deliver. Conversely, parents can misinterpret and amplify the promise represented by realistic assessments of their child's developmental potential. Special educators must be careful of any promissory statements they make, and mental retardation researchers have to be cautious about what they publish. The promise offered by even the wildest remedial speculations can snare parents in a web of false hopes. This raises another issue.

Just how abruptly should professionals dispel the unrealistic remedial expectations of parents? One can empathize with the difficulties professionals face: They endeavor to motivate parents to stimulate their children, without luring the parents into overexpectation; at the same time they try to diffuse false hopes, without causing parents to despair. The issue is further complicated by the question of just what constitutes a false hope. Historically, many important contributions were made by individuals who were seen to harbor false hopes—persons such as Itard and Seguin.

The Phase of Acceptance

It is difficult to know what is meant by *acceptance* of a retarded child; the term is used so ambiguously. As Olshansky says, "Every parent—whether he has a normal or a mentally defective child—accepts his child and rejects his child at various times in various situations."[71] What constitutes parental acceptance becomes less confusing if the concept is defined in terms of its opposite—the absence of rejecting behaviors. The latter are at least more obvious. How do parents of mentally handicapped children *reject* their youngsters?

Some do so by neglecting the children physically or emotionally. A common form of physical neglect is evident in a parent's carelessness about his child's personal appearance. A few parents camouflage their psychological neglect of retarded offspring behind a smokescreen of altruism. They will, for example, immerse themselves in a multiplicity of community activities to avoid meeting their responsibilities to the child. All parents who spend a great deal of time going to meetings and the like are not doing so to avoid contact with their retarded child. Advocacy on behalf of the youngster is the focus of many community gatherings. The parents simply have to make the hard choice between spending more time with the retarded child and spending less time with him in order to advocate his needs.

There are, of course, parents who use the child's handicap as the source of purpose in their lives. As one mother put it, "Nobody in the world ever really needed me except this one little child. Thank God that he will need me forever."[72] It is reported that some families that otherwise might have dissolved are held together because of the "helplessness and needs for special care" of the retarded child[73]—a factor that places an enormous burden on the youngster and intensifies rejecting behaviors toward him by the family.

Parental rejection occasionally manifests itself in abuse. Retarded children are more likely to be abused by their parents than those without handicaps.[74] Some retarded youngsters are so unmanageable that they require restraint, which occasionally gets out of hand. If the child cries for prolonged periods, this can precipitate an abusive event.[75] Abuse-prone parents often have low self-esteem to begin with, which is greatly aggravated by the emotional trauma of having a retarded child. This intensifies the abusive impulse, especially if there is no social support system in the house and "if prevalent attitudes favor violence as a legitimate means of solving conflicts."[76] Aside from the immediate physical and emotional damage done to the child through such abuse, he frequently assumes an exceedingly inhibited style to avoid angering parents. This intensifies the apparent severity of his handicap and the likelihood of further abuse.

Like physical abuse, emotional abuse is insidious, and nothing particularly overt need be done. Many retarded children simply pick up on antipathetic parental attitudes toward them—attitudes that are fairly widespread. For example, one body of research has shown that parents of retarded children: (1) derive less pleasure in relating to their retarded youngsters than to their normal children, (2) have more rejecting attitudes toward their retarded offspring than parents of normal children have toward theirs, and (3) tend to show much more rejecting attitudes toward their retarded youngsters than toward their own normal children.[77] Pearl S. Buck, author and mother of a retarded child, highlights the impulse that leads to these feelings in vivid terms: "All the brightness of life is gone, all the pride in parenthood—there is more than pride gone: there is an actual sense of one's life being cut off in the child. The stream of generations is stopped."[78]

Parents can also reject a retarded child by denying their relationship with him. For example, some of them isolate the child and themselves socially to avoid being discovered as the child's parents. They refuse to join parent organizations because of the shameful admission such membership entails. Kurtz describes one father who "traced an outline of his retarded child's foot on a cardboard, taking this to the store to buy a pair of shoes so that the child would not be seen in public."[79] This is not surprising in a society in which children are often regarded as means to parental ends (physical extension of self, vicarious satisfaction, immortality, and so on) rather than ends in themselves. The parent who "realizes" himself though his offspring will find the defective child an unflattering clone.

Rejection through denying one's relationship with a retarded child often goes hand-in-glove with rejection through denial of the youngster's limitations. Determining the realistic functional capacities of a retarded child is a difficult task. Many parents can only discover these through a pendulous negotiation process with the child. Some parents start by expecting too much of the child and consequently nag, become unduly critical, and push the youngster beyond his limits. Naturally, the parents are disappointed with the results, and thus swing to the opposite extreme—expecting too little, infantilizing, and understimulating the retarded child. Some parents are lucky enough to approximate reasonable expectations for the youngster in a few tries. However, when parents go through the cycle repeatedly, especially in cases where an older child is involved, this bespeaks rejection, not confusion; and it can become exceedingly frustrating, even abusive, for the youngster.

The infantilization process is not always a result of the foiled expectations of parents. Sometimes the retarded child is treated like an infant out of convenience. Parents think they can save a lot of time if they feed, dress, and bathe a retarded child, rather than going to all the trouble of teaching the youngster to do these things himself. Infantalizing a retarded child can, in turn, compound the parent's burden of guilt. Stone reports the mother of a retarded youngster saying, "You put this down in big letters, I am to BLAME for the girl's retardation as I have done too much for her."[80]

Another form of parental denial of a child's retardation can be seen in a parent's attempt to "pass" the child off as someone he is not. Like the physicians discussed earlier, these parents emphasize a handicap other than mental retardation, if the child has multiple handicaps, or say the child is "cerebral palsied" even if he is not so afflicted.[81] It is not uncommon for parents to feel they *have* to bend the truth in informing non-handicapped people about their child's retardation, because the mere mention of brain injury evokes all the old deprecatory stereotypes. Barsch quotes a typical parental account: "I used to tell everyone who was interested that he was a brain-injured child, but the words are too harsh and people who think there's something wrong with the brain usually don't understand the details. I tell those who I think might understand. The rest I tell that he lacks control over his emotions and that he is improving—this most people accept."[82]

Several New Morning staff members reported that parents denied their children's limitations by blaming them on a lack of will: "He could learn if he just wanted to." Similarly, a few parents engaged in magical thinking as a form of denial. For example, they reversed the causal link between retardation and speech.[83] It is as if these parents were suggesting "If the child could only talk, his retardation would vanish."

Even though many examples of rejection of retarded children by their parents can be chronicled, rejection, like acceptance, defies our ability to develop a precise, compact definition that reflects the reality of the parents' and children's lives. Perhaps the sentiment involved in such rejection is best summed up in the comment of one parent: "Raymond is like a small pair in poker—too good to throw in—hoping it will improve—while throwing money in."[84]

Having a better idea of how parental rejection evidences itself, it is easier to formulate a less ambiguous definition of what parental acceptance of retarded youngsters is. It is attendance to the physical and emotional needs of one's child with a genuine respect. It is a regard for the child fully cognizant of his handicap, unencumbered by the impulse to deny an affinity with him or misrepresent the handicapping condition to others. Most importantly, it is an active augmentation of the child's acceptance of himself. The latter is a particularly important dynamic because, as Svarstad and Lipton point out, mere acceptance of the handicapping condition does not necessarily mean that parents will manage the child more rationally than they did in the preacceptance phases.[85]

SOCIOLOGICAL DIMENSIONS OF ACCEPTANCE

A number of sociological factors are associated with parental attitudes toward retarded children, including related variables such as the intelligence of parents, their educational levels, and their socioeconomic status. Other factors that figure into the acceptance equation are the gender of the child, that of the parent, parental age, and religiosity.

Parental Intelligence

It is said that the greater the deviation of the child's measured intelligence from that of his parent, the less accepting, or "tolerant," the parent will be of the handicapped child.[86] Although this is a general tendency, closer examination of parent-child divergencies in intelligence shows this dimension of acceptance to be more complex. For example, Worchel and Worchel illustrated that the distribution curve for parental ratings of the acceptability of *severely* retarded children was virtually bimodal, indicating the tendency of parents to rate these youngsters on either end of a continuum of acceptance (similar ratings for normal children yielding a bell-shaped curve).[87] While the parents of severely retarded youngsters are predisposed either to accept or reject them, the parents of higher-functioning retarded children seem confused about how they feel—expressing positive attitudes one time and negative another.[88] The ambivalence here probably emanates from confused expectations. Parents have a general inclination to be more positively disposed to higher-functioning retarded children, but it is also easier to expect too much from them and to react negatively when they do not measure up to expectations.

There is, by the way, evidence that parental rejection affects the child's intelligence. Five different inquiries have shown a direct relationship between accepting parental behaviors and rising or falling increments in a child's measured intelligence. Rejecting parental behaviors were shown to accompany diminishing IQ scores in the children.[89]

Parental Education

The effects of parental education on the acceptance of a retarded child are, at best, confusing. Researchers contend that more highly educated parents are less rejecting of their retarded children than parents from less-advanced educational backgrounds,[90] although another study illustrated that highly educated parents tended to be more embarrassed at having a retarded child than those with less education.[91] We do know that highly educated parents are more likely to institutionalize their retarded children at an earlier age than less-educated parents.[92] Part of this phenomenon is doubtless explainable by the fact that parents of higher socioeconomic status (which correlates with education) recognize and classify the child as retarded at a younger age than do low-status parents.[93] And part of it comes from the tendency of highly educated parents to "respond more to the abstraction than to the actual experiences of living with a mentally retarded child"[94]—the reification of abstractions being one of education's effects. In any event, there is evidence that parents who institutionalize retarded children have more rejecting attitudes than those who do not[95] and that highly educated parents who place children in institutions demonstrate less interest in their children than less-educated parents do for their institutionalized youngsters.[96]

Social Class

A third factor affecting parental acceptance of retarded children is social class. The impact a mentally retarded child has on upper- or middle-class families is different from that experienced by lower-class families. For example, according to Farber, middle-class mothers tend to be concerned primarily about how the handicapped child will affect the family's status aspirations, this concern evidencing itself in what Farber called a "tragic crisis."[97] On the other hand, a lower-class mother more typically suffers a "role crisis," which comes from her concern that the retarded child will demand so much of her attention that she will not have sufficient time to give other family members.[98]

One can understand why higher-socioeconomic-status families are susceptible to Farber's "tragic crisis." The status aspirations of these families are closely tied to the success-oriented goals of modern industrialized society, and the retarded child is without the wherewithal to achieve most of these goals. Thus he or she is sometimes seen as useless, and as Farber implies, an impediment to the family's upward social mobility.[99] Indeed, Culver found "the earlier in a marriage a retarded child was born, the greater were the chances of his having a depressing effect on social mobility."[100] This is not inconsequential given the fact that the majority of retarded children are the first born.[101]

Cummings, Bayley, and Rie shed further light on tragic versus role crises. They found that while lower-class mothers showed equal stress with regard to mentally retarded and chronically ill children, middle-class mothers were under more stress if they had a retarded child than a child who was chronically ill.[102] Presumably, having a healthy retarded child ought not to be more "tragic" than having a child who suffers from chronic sickness. The difference for the middle- and upper-class parents seems to lie in the social stigma attached to retardation versus illness. Farber suggests that lower-class families do not have "tragic crises" because the stigma associated with the retardation label is not greatly divergent from other socially prevalent attitudes associated with low status.[103]

Not surprisingly, the statistics on early institutionalization of retarded children and the social class of parents parallel those for institutionalization and parental level of education. Parents from the middle classes are inclined to institutionalize their retarded children at a younger age than are those from the lower classes.[104] If upward social mobility is important to a middle-class family, this practice makes some sense. It was found, for example, that parents who kept severely retarded youngsters at home were more likely to be downwardly socially mobile than those who institutionalized their children.[105] *In the long run,* however, lower-class people are more receptive to institutionalization of their retarded children.[106] This is due, in large measure, to the fact that child-care problems ultimately become more acute for lower socioeconomic groups. They usually have more children to care for and less money with which to do it.

Because attitudes toward retardation differ in high- and low-status families, it is reasonable to assume that these differences would be reflected in the self-esteem of retarded children from different classes. I was unable to find research delineating such differences. For what it's worth though, there is an analog. Meadow demonstrated that deaf children from higher-status families had lower levels of self-esteem than other hearing-impaired children.[107]

Other Factors

The effect of a retarded child's gender on the marital integration of his parents has some bearing on their acceptance of the child. Retarded boys living at home were found to have increasingly disruptive effects on their parents' marriages as the boys approached adolescence.[108] Marital malintegration was much lower for the parents of mentally retarded girls.[109] Levine disclosed that parents perceived an improvement in the social competence of a mentally handicapped daughter as she reached adolescence, while no such improvement was discernible for boys.[110] Why?

The answer probably lies in parental perceptions of the handicapped child's conformity with traditional sex roles. Barry, Bacon, and Child, drawing from a survey of 110 cultures, report "a widespread pattern of greater pressure toward nurturance, obedience, and responsibility in girls, and toward self-reliance and achievement striving in boys."[111] Even though these roles are changing in our society, traditional sex roles are still prevalent, and mentally retarded boys are less likely than girls to fulfill the conventionally prescribed roles for their gender. Because of this, as retarded sons mature, their parents get an intensified perception of the boys as deviant. This is less characteristic of parental impressions of mentally handicapped daughters. Thus, the sons are more likely to be rejected by their parents.

The gender of *parents* also affects their acceptance of a retarded child. Love's research revealed that mothers had more positive overall attitudes toward retarded children than fathers,[112] although that may have owed to the fact that women generally have more favorable attitudes toward retarded people than do men.[113] In any case, the initial stress associated with recognition of the handicap is different for men and women depending on whether the child is a boy or a girl. Mothers are typically more upset if the child is a girl,[114] and Tallman reports that "fathers tend to react in extremes of great involvement or total withdrawal if the retarded child is a boy and in a limited, routine fashion if the child is a girl."[115]

Given the gender factors at work in the determination of parental attitudes toward mentally retarded children, it is reasonable to wonder whose attitudes are pervasive—the mother's or the father's? Peck and Stephens found a high correlation between the fathers' attitudes and the degree of acceptance of the child in the home, while a much lower correlation was found for mothers' attitudes.[116]

The age of parents is also a factor in their acceptance of a retarded child. Younger mothers of handicapped children "revealed more hostile rejection of the maternal role than did older mothers."[117] Parents who institutionalize a retarded child are, on the average, younger than those who do not apply for institutionalization,[118] although there are probably socioeconomic factors involved in this decision as well.

The religiosity of parents is another factor in their acceptance of mentally handicapped children. Keeping in mind that a certain amount of skepticism about self-reports on religiosity is required, we see that mothers who rate themselves as being more religious express attitudes that are more accepting of their retarded children than mothers less religiously inclined.[119] One-fourth of the parents in Zwerling's survey pointed to religion as a very important factor in their acceptance of a mentally handicapped child.[120] Several parents told me that they had become more religious since their retarded children were born—that, as one of them said, "It got us through the worst times." However, in a recent study comparing the parents of mentally handicapped and non-handicapped children, it was found that the former were actually less religious.[121]

PRACTICAL DIMENSIONS OF PARENTAL ACCEPTANCE

Even though the sociological factors already described do affect parental acceptance of retarded children, when all is said and done, more immediate, practical considerations likely play a larger role in determining how parents respond to their mentally handicapped offspring. One of the most critical of these factors concerns how disruptive the retarded child is to the family.

The evidence of marital disruption associated with a mentally retarded child is dramatic. H. D. Love reports the divorce rate for parents with retarded children to be three times higher than for those of non-handicapped youngsters.[122] In 170 families with retarded children, Holt found that approximately 10 percent of the mothers had been deserted by their husbands subsequent to giving birth to the child.[123] In keeping with this, it was suggested to me by several New Morning staff members, and by parents of retarded children, that fathers often leave the bulk of the stressful work of rearing the handicapped child up to the mother. Where this happens, marital and familial stress can ensue from the creation of an uncanny symbiosis. As one mother put it, "I have always spared my husband and my other children from taking care of my retarded child. They owe it to me to spare me from taking care of them too."[124]

All in all, there is more marital stress in families with retarded children.[125] Sometimes, though, a retarded child gets a "bum rap" in this regard, being blamed for preexisting martial stresses. Love asserted that one-third of planned pregnancies were directed at parental desires to fill the "emotional emptiness" of marriages.[126] One can imagine how such parents feel if the child is defective. Under such circumstances, the youngster is seen as doubly inadequate and his defects only exacerbate the emotional alienation between parents. Of course, a mentally retarded child can create a lot of stress even in the happiest families.

The youngster can severely disrupt a family's social life—his care requirements holding the entire family hostage. For example, if parents cannot find a respite care provider (which will be discussed momentarily) or a qualified babysitter, they cannot go out unless they do so one at a time or take the child with them. If the child's behavior is disruptive or he has a serious physical incapacity, it is very inconvenient to take him on certain outings, and I have been told that babysitters are hard to find. Forty percent of the parents in Holt's survey said it was impossible for them to go out together.[127] As a result, many parents are forced to disengage themselves from social encounters or community activities outside the home. Of course, they can always entertain in the home . . . or can they?

"Friends" of the family are sometimes reluctant to visit a home where a retarded youngster lives. Several parents told me that after the birth of their retarded child, friends deserted them. Other friends were so solicitous and patronizing about the child that the friendships faltered. Carr found that 25 percent of the mothers he surveyed felt they had made friends through their retarded children, but that 21 percent said that having a handicapped child made them lonely.[128]

Even if a socially isolated family attempts to get by on home entertainment, there can be problems associated with the retarded child. For example, if he is hyperactive and does not possess the judgment and imagination to amuse himself, the rest of the family members are precluded from enjoying simple pleasures such as reading, watching TV, or taking a nap, because of the child's constant interruptions. During the early stages of my observations, I was invited to the home of one of New Morning's students so I could be there when he got home from school and could experience for one afternoon what the child's mother encounters every day. The youngster required an enormous amount of attention. The vigilance needed to care for children such as this one breeds a state of chronic tension and fatigue among their families. Greenfeld, discussing his retarded son, says, "Noah was up all night chirping. . . . And Foumi and I, our nerves tired, insomniacal, have been on the combative verge all day long."[129] Freeman further elaborates on the problem:

> Loss of sleep can aggravate the child's behavior and the family's ability to cope in a direct manner. Some handicapped children seem to need less sleep than most youngsters and may either have difficulty going to sleep, awaken during the night, or arise early in the morning and get into trouble. The parents may have to retire early in the evening to get enough sleep so that they have little time together, cannot go out, or cannot finish projects in the evening. Occasionally, one parent will sleep with the child or try to keep him quiet while the other rests.[130]

To make matters worse, many families never get a vacation from the constant demands of these children.[131]

Fortunately, the training of paraprofessionals to provide *respite care* for families in need of it has progressed well in some locales in the last decade. This is one of the most hopeful and sensible steps in family relations that has ever been taken in the field of mental retardation. Regrettably, respite care does not exist in all communities, and it is underfunded, understaffed, and underutilized in others.[132]

Families can be economically as well as socially disrupted by the care requirements of a mentally retarded child. For example, the hyperactive tendencies of a few children necessitate extra expenditures, both to pay for things damaged and to construct the house around the needs of the child, so both are protected. In line with this, the doors in many houses of retarded children are kept locked to protect the child from wandering off into potentially dangerous situations, giving the house a fortress-like atmosphere and inconveniencing family members.[133]

It is not uncommon for a retarded child to require a great deal of medical care as a result of problems associated with his handicap. These expenses are a hardship on most families. Such financial demands can also lead to significant alterations in the interaction patterns of family

members. For example, if the father is breadwinner, escalating expenditures may force him to increase his occupational work load and
spend less time at home. Several professionals told me that this frequently
happens in homes with retarded children even when there has been
no appreciable increase in family expenses—presumably because the
father just wants to be away from the situation.

Another disruption in family integration can be seen in parental
discord that develops around the issue of "placing" a retarded child
outside the home in such places as group or foster homes or institutions.
Some parents are at odds for years over the issue, especially as it relates
to institutionalization. And even after the die is cast, the conflict is not
always resolved. One body of research shows that "there is little difference
in the quality of marital integration whether the retarded child is kept
at home or placed" in an institution.[134] The functioning of the majority
of families did not significantly improve after the child had been out
of the home for a year.[135] Perhaps the parents remained at odds about
the placement, or residuals of the child's presence in the home continued
to have a disruptive influence. Or perhaps the youngster's disruptiveness
prior to placement had been exaggerated in the first place.

While in the field, it was repeatedly suggested to me that one of
the most decisive factors in parental acceptance of a retarded child is
the attitudes of other family members such as grandparents and siblings.
The evidence on the effects grandparents have on parental acceptance
is scant, although it seems reasonable that their attitudes would loom
important. What has been demonstrated is that if either of the maternal
grandparents of an institutionalized retarded child is alive, the parents
of that youngster will take less interest in him than if the grandparents
are dead.[136] On a related topic, it is reported that, while the maternal
grandmother is usually quite sympathetic to her daughter's plight, the
paternal grandmother frequently places blame on the wife for the retarded
child[137]—blame that doubtless gets passed along to a few retarded
children.

The attitudes of siblings of the handicapped youngster also exert
considerable influence on parental acceptance of the child, and there
are many reasons why tensions develop between mentally retarded
children and their siblings. For example, siblings who are old enough
are often expected to help care for their retarded brothers and sisters.
One inquiry demonstrated that non-handicapped females who interacted
frequently with their mentally retarded siblings, especially in the performance of parent-substitute responsibilities, had much more tense
relations with mothers than those not saddled with such responsibilities.[138] Daughters who interacted frequently with retarded siblings tended
to be viewed by their mothers as "moody, stubborn, easy to anger, or

having other negative traits" more often than daughters who did not interact frequently with the retarded child.[139] At first blush, one might infer from this that the tension between mother and daughter resulted because the daughter recoiled from the added responsibilities of caring for the retarded child. This is not always the case. In fact, some of the most bitter resentments between parents and non-handicapped children develop because the latter take such pride in meeting care responsibilities for retarded siblings. It is not uncommon for a non-handicapped sibling to believe that she manages the retarded child much better than her mother and to resent maternal interference.[140] Fowle found that the tensions between mothers and daughters charged with caring for a retarded sibling were significantly reduced when the child was institutionalized.[141] Institutionalization or other placement of a retarded youngster can, however, have harmful effects on non-handicapped siblings. For example, it arouses fears of rejection in some younger brothers and sisters. When a handicapped child is "sent away," a normal sibling reasons "If it can happen to him, it can happen to me."

Even if normal siblings do little to care for their retarded brothers or sisters, many are still expected to assume extra household duties to free their parents' time for the retarded youngster. That does not bother most of them.[142] Sometimes, though, the extra time and attention parents devote to the retarded child cause the non-handicapped sibling to conclude that parents are less attentive to him because they do not love him as much. Indeed, some of these children end up getting the attention of preoccupied parents by developing psychosomatic illnesses.[143]

Non-handicapped siblings face other problems. Some may be embarrassed by retarded brothers or sisters, not knowing how to tell friends and fearful that if they do not, their duplicity will be discovered. They can translate this embarrassment into fears that they will never have dates or get married, or if they do get married, their choice of a partner will be dictated by that person's tolerance of the retarded sibling. Like parents, a few siblings question their own "normalcy," fearing genetic contamination. Normal siblings may also wonder what will happen to the retarded child in the event of the parents' death: Whose reponsibility will he be then? Further, some normal siblings believe, or are made to believe, that they ought to "make up" for the deficiencies of the retarded brother or sister by being very special. "Look at how difficult it is for your brother to learn. Think of what you could do with the same effort." These are just a few of the factors that can make non-handicapped siblings feel resentful, even angry, at their retarded brothers and sisters.

The normal child is not the only repository of sibling resentment. Retarded children could come to resent non-handicapped siblings because of the latter's greater degree of achievement and self-determination. This has an especially keen edge if the children have enjoyed an equalitarian relationship when young, which becomes asymmetrical as they grow older[144]—the one youngster's roles being redefined by parents, while the retarded child ever remains the baby of the family. This process also works in reverse, with the normal child being kept from doing the things appropriate for his peer group because of the retarded child. Several non-handicapped youngsters told me that they were prohibited by parents from doing certain social things if a retarded sibling could not do them as a result of his intellectual limitations.

Where it exists, the retarded child's resentment of the advantages enjoyed by non-handicapped siblings occasionally evidences itself in an angry outburst. Skelton found that retarded children frequently directed their aggression against their brothers and sisters, "particularly against a successful younger sibling."[145]

Mentally retarded children do not always resent their normal brothers and sisters, nor is the converse true. Indeed, most non-handicapped siblings do not succumb to any of the aforementioned problems. Graliker, Fishler, and Koch found that a sizable majority of non-handicapped siblings: (1) accepted the retarded child; (2) had good relationships with their parents; (3) agreed, for the most part, with the way parents raised the retarded child; (4) had a normal social life with positive peer relationships; and (5) had little trouble in telling people about the sibling's handicap.[146] As one sibling mentions, "I just say 'he is mentally retarded,' or 'he's a bit slow but it's not his fault.' Usually people say they're sorry, but I just tell them we love him anyhow."[147]

Even if the relationship between retarded and normal siblings is strained, the latter often profit from it by developing greater "maturity, tolerance, patience, and responsibility than is common among children their age."[148] Farber says that "children who interact frequently with their retarded siblings seem to develop a more socially conscious outlook on life," emphasizing as life goals "devotion to a worthwhile cause" or "making a contribution to mankind."[149]

NEEDS AND DEEDS

The families of mentally handicapped children face a constellation of complex problems, only a few of which have been examined here. These families, especially the parents, can deal more easily with such difficulties if they have help.

Things are better from the start if physicians relate to the diagnostic process sensitively and without excesses of circumspection. Where possible, the parents' psychological histories should be taken into account before the informing interview. If the family has a regular physician, he or she ought to be involved in the process. If physicians are certain of their diagnosis, parents have to know in no uncertain terms that their child is retarded.

Parents need as many facts as can be provided concerning the cause of the child's handicap. They need these to avoid having another retarded child if the circumstances of the youngster's handicap were avoidable or to set their minds at ease if the retardation did not result from anything they did wrong.

Parents ought to be given realistic information on what to expect from their retarded child to help them avoid victimizing the youngster through a protracted period of negotiating these capacities. Parents not in possession of realistic images of their children's functional capacities are vulnerable to "false hopesters" and other charlatans whose businesses depend upon the legitimation of misinformation.

Parents have to assume certain self-help responsibilities in their interactions with physicians. They must not let themselves be intimidated by doctors to the point of not communicating. For example, parents of children with "genetic anomalies" should insist that the physician clarify this terminology. If they cannot assimilate all the information given to them by doctors, they should take notes or tape record diagnostic encounters. Parents should not allow physicians or any other professionals to cast them in the role of passive receivers of services. This does not permit these parents to share crucial skills and knowledge regarding their retarded children. Parents should also keep the professional's role in perspective. No one can make mental retardation "go away." In standing up for their rights as consumers, parents of handicapped youngsters are not likely to realize any appreciable results from adopting a surly, denigrating attitude toward professionals such as physicians. What doctors and parents need is information on mental retardation and candid feedback on how best to use this information.

The job of accepting and raising a retarded child can be facilitated by sensitive public attitudes. It has been shown that community rejection of retarded children adversely affects parental attitudes toward them.[150] Further, parents ought to be sensitized to the erroneous attitudes they possess regarding mental retardation. Many subscribe to popular stereotypes that accentuate the tragic dimensions of mental retardation. Parents who become engulfed in their children's shortcomings fail to recognize that a great many retarded individuals turn out to be good friends, good company, good neighbors, good citizens, and, most importantly to their parents, good relatives.

To the parents of mentally handicapped children, the most important aspect of social attitudes toward retarded people is the way they are translated into services made available to help the retarded child. Parents should have a voice in determining what services are required and how they will be delivered. Moreover, parents must be encouraged to use available services. Some need prodding on this account because they are embarrassed at seeking help for their retarded children,[151] feeling this lessens them or makes them "welfare cases." Additionally, the services must be provided in such a manner that parents do not feel distrustful of, or hostile to, the service delivery system.

A few parents require help in understanding their feelings toward their mentally retarded offspring. Counseling services should be accessible to parents and non-handicapped siblings in need of them. That is not to imply that all parents of mentally handicapped children *need* counseling. In fact, many of them are rebelling against being stereotyped as emotional "wrecks" who invariably need psychotherapy. A few of these parents do require therapy, though, because of the stresses created by a retarded child in the family. For instance, Holt found that one out of every six mothers in his survey was under severe physical and mental strain in having to care for her retarded child.[152] It has been reported that the suicide rate for parents of mentally retarded children is twice that of the national average.[153]

Where psychotherapy is provided, it ought to be directed at helping parents to overcome anger they feel toward themselves, their doctors, their mates, their retarded children, and anyone else who is blamed for the child's handicap. Parents should be helped to overcome their guilt and shame and to pinpoint and eliminate rejecting behaviors, both subtle and flagrant.

Where family integration has faltered, marriage counseling can help. Perhaps the most important function of this is to ensure that parents do not blame the retarded child for preexisting shortcomings of the marriage. Where marital or other family problems *have* been occasioned by the effects of the retarded child, parents ought to share in the experiences of other families who have overcome similar difficulties. Even though solutions to the problems encountered by different families usually require different remedies, parents can draw comfort from the realization that the experiences they face are not unique. Parent encounter techniques and individual therapies have been shown to foster personal improvement for parents in areas such as patience with, and tolerance of, the handicapped child.[154] Counseling has also been shown to change parents' goal orientations from "immediate and short range to more sophisticated and long range goals."[155]

Aside from the short supply of professionals trained to do parent counseling, the major problem associated with it is getting parents who need therapy to avail themselves of it. For those who have entered a shell of shameful denial, the availability of counseling is irrelevant. The regrettable thing about this is that these people usually need the most help.

NOTES

1. J. C. Higgens, "Medicinal," in *Lindy*, Valley Forge, Pa.: Judson, 1970, p. 13.

2. Ibid., "Where?" p. 24.

3. H. Wortis, "Parent Counseling," *Mental Retardation and Developmental Disabilities*, 4:1972, p. 25.

4. L. Rosen, "Selected Aspects in the Development of the Mother's Understanding of Her Mentally Retarded Child," *American Journal of Mental Deficiency*, 59:1955, pp. 524–525.

5. C. Waskowitz, "The Parents of Retarded Children Speak for Themselves," *Journal of Pediatrics*, 54:1959, p. 322; H. L. Lipton and B. Svarstad, "Sources of Variation in Clinicians' Communication to Parents about Mental Retardation," *American Journal of Mental Deficiency*, 82:1977, p. 159; L. Rosen, p. 525.

6. B. Farber, "Family Organization and Crisis: Maintenance of Integration in Families with a Severely Retarded Child," *Monographs of the Society for Research in Child Development*, 25:1960, p. 5.

7. J. Carr, "The Effect of the Severely Subnormal on Their Families," in A. M. Clarke and A.D.B. Clarke, eds., *Mental Deficiency: The Changing Outlook*, 3rd ed., New York: The Free Press, 1974, p. 813.

8. C. Waskowitz, p. 323.

9. K. A. Anderson and A. M. Garner, "Mothers of Retarded Children: Satisfaction with Visits to Professional People," *Mental Retardation*, 11:1973, p. 37.

10. K. A. Anderson, "The 'Shopping' Behavior of Parents of Mentally Retarded Children: The Professional Person's Role," *Mental Retardation*, 9(4):1971, p. 4.

11. B. L. Svarstad and H. L. Lipton, "Informing Parents About Mental Retardation: A Study of Professional Communication and Parent Acceptance," *Social Science and Medicine*, 11:1977, p. 650.

12. C. Waskowitz, pp. 326–327.

13. A. C. McDonald, K. P. Carson, D. J. Palmer, and T. Slay, "Physicians' Diagnostic Information to Parents of Handicapped Neonates," *Mental Retardation*, 20(1):1982, p. 13.

14. N. K. Kelly and F. J. Menolascino, "Physicians' Awareness and Attitudes Toward the Retarded," *Mental Retardation*, 13(6):1975, p. 11.

15. Ibid.

16. S. Olshansky and L. Sternfeld, "Attitudes of Some Pediatricians Toward the Institutionalization of Mentally Retarded Children," *The Training School Bulletin*, 59:1962, pp. 67–73.

17. J. Intagliata, S. Kraus, and B. Willer, "The Impact of Deinstitutionalization on a Community Based Service System," *Mental Retardation,* 18(6):1980, p. 307.

18. C. Waskowitz, p. 325.

19. N. K. Kelly and F. J. Menolascino, p. 13.

20. G. L. Adams, "Referral Advice Given by Physicians," *Mental Retardation,* 20:1982, p. 19.

21. Ibid., p. 11.

22. K. A. Anderson and A. M. Garner, p. 37.

23. B. L. Svarstad and H. L. Lipton, p. 650.

24. C. Waskowitz, p. 322.

25. J. Carr, p. 813.

26. A. C. McDonald, K. P. Carson, D. J. Palmer, and T. Slay, p. 13.

27. I. Philips, "Children, Mental Retardation, and Emotional Disorder," in I. Philips, ed., *Prevention and Treatment of Mental Retardation,* New York: Basic Books, 1966, p. 115.

28. E. W. Gordon and M. Ullman, "Reactions of Parents to Problems of Mental Retardation in Children," *American Journal of Mental Deficiency,* 61:1956, p. 159.

29. M. J. Appell, C. M. Williams, and K. N. Fishnell, "Changes in Attitudes of Parents of Retarded Children Effected Through Group Counseling," *American Journal of Mental Deficiency,* 68:1964, p. 808.

30. B. L. Svarstad and H. L. Lipton, pp. 649–650.

31. R. N. Emde and C. Brown, "Adaptation After the Birth of a Down's Syndrome Infant: A Study of 6 Cases, Illustrating Differences in Development and the Counter-Movement Between Grieving and Maternal Attachment," unpublished paper, University of Colorado, School of Medicine, n.d.

32. K. P. Meadow and L. Meadow, "Changing Role Perceptions for Parents of Handicapped Children," *Exceptional Children,* 38:1971, pp. 21–29; C. Waskowitz, pp. 319–329; M. Blumenthal, "Experiences of Parents of Retardates and Children with Cystic Fibrosis," *Archives of General Psychiatry,* 21:1960, pp. 160–171; R. Barsch, "Explanations Offered by Parents and Siblings of Brain-Damaged Children," *Exceptional Children,* 27:1961, pp. 286–291; K. P. Meadow, "Parental Response to the Medical Ambiguities of Congential Deafness," *Journal of Health and Social Behavior,* 9:1968, pp. 299–309.

33. K. A. Anderson and A. M. Garner, p. 37.

34. Ibid.

35. F. Davis, *Passage Through Crisis,* Indianapolis: Bobbs-Merrill, 1963, p. 66; H. L. Lipton and B. Svarstad, p. 159.

36. C. Waskowtiz, p. 322.

37. S. Olshansky, G. Johnson, and L. Sternfeld, "Attitudes of Some GP's Toward Institutionalizing Mentally Retarded Children," *Mental Retardation,* 1(1):1963, p. 20.

38. N. K. Kelly and F. J. Menolascino, p. 12.

39. K. Fishler, R. Koch, R. Sands, and J. Bills, "Attitudes of Medical Students Towards Mental Retardation—A Preliminary Study," *Journal of Medical Education,* 43:1968, p. 68.

40. C. G. Schwartz, "Strategies and Tactics of Mothers of Mentally Retarded

Children for Dealing With the Medical Care System," in N. R. Bernstein, ed., *Diminished People*, Boston: Little, Brown and Co., 1970, p. 82.

41. H. L. Lipton and B. L. Svarstad, p. 160.

42. H. Richardson, M. J. Guralnick, and D. B. Tupper, "Training Pediatricians for Effective Involvement with Handicapped Preschool Children and Their Families," *Mental Retardation*, 16(1):1978, p. 3.

43. Ibid., p. 5.

44. Ibid., p. 6.

45. S. E. Waisbren, "Parents' Reactions After the Birth of a Developmentally Disabled Child," *American Journal of Mental Deficiency*, 84:1980, p. 350.

46. C. Waskowtiz, p. 320.

47. A. J. Solnit and M. H. Stark, "Mourning and the Birth of a Defective Child," *The Psychoanalytic Study of the Child*, 16:1961, p. 524; S. Olshansky, "Parent Responses to a Mentally Defective Child," *Mental Retardation*, 4:1966, p. 21.

48. K. A. Anderson, p. 3.

49. W. C. Keirn, "Shopping Parents: Patient Problem or Professional Problem?" *Mental Retardation*, 9:1971, p. 6.

50. J. Greenfeld, *A Place for Noah*, New York: Holt, Rinehart, and Winston, 1978, p. 254.

51. A. M. Grebler, "Parental Attitudes Toward Mentally Retarded Children," *American Journal of Mental Deficiency*, 56:1952, p. 479.

52. J. Michaels and H. Schucman, "Observations on the Psychodynamics of Parents of Retarded Children," *American Journal of Mental Deficiency*, 66:1962, p. 571.

53. N. W. Hart, "Frequently Expressed Feelings and Reactions of Parents Toward Their Retarded Children," in N. R. Bernstein, ed., *Diminished People*, Boston: Little, Brown and Co., 1970, p. 59.

54. S. Olshansky, p. 22.

55. N. W. Hart, p. 57.

56. G. Zuk, R. Miller, J. Bartram, and F. Kling, "Maternal Acceptance of Retarded Children—A Questionnaire Study of Attitudes and Religious Background," *Child Development*, 32:1961, p. 538.

57. J. Greenfeld, p. 299.

58. L. Weller, C. Costeff, B. Cohen, and D. Rahman, "Social Variables in the Perception and Acceptance of Retardation," *American Journal of Mental Deficiency*, 79:1974, p. 277.

59. B. Farber, W. C. Jenne, and R. Toigo, *Family Crisis and the Decision to Institutionalize the Retarded Child*, Washington, D.C.: Council for Exceptional Children, Research Monograph Series, no. 1, 1960, p. 7.

60. L. Rosen, p. 526.

61. K. S. Holt, "The Influence of a Retarded Child Upon Family Limitation," *Journal of Mental Deficiency Research*, 2:1958, pp. 28–34.

62. J. C. Higgens, "Invocation," p. 13.

63. R. N. Emde and C. Brown, p. 37.

64. Ibid.

65. B. L. Svarstad and H. L. Lipton, p. 650.

66. J. Michaels and H. Schucman, p. 570.

67. M. Stone, "Parental Attitudes to Retardation," in C. L. Stacey and M. F. DeMartino, eds., *Counseling and Psychotherapy With the Mentally Retarded*, Glencoe, Ill.: The Free Press, 1957, p. 420.

68. N. W. Hart, p. 55.

69. A. M. Grebler, p. 483.

70. Ibid.

71. S. Olshansky, "Chronic Sorrow: A Response to Having a Mentally Defective Child," *Social Casework*, 43:1962, p. 192.

72. J. Michaels and H. Schucman, p. 572.

73. B. M. Caldwell and S. B. Guze, "A Study of the Adjustment of Parents and Siblings of Institutionalized and Non-Institutionalized Retarded Children," *American Journal of Mental Deficiency*, 64:1969, p. 856.

74. A. Sandgrund, R. W. Gaines, and A. H. Greene, "Child Abuse and Mental Retardation: A Problem of Cause and Effect," *American Journal of Mental Deficiency*, 79:1974, p. 329; A. M. Frodi, "Contribution of Infant Characteristics to Child Abuse," *American Journal of Mental Deficiency*, 85:1981, p. 341.

75. Ibid., p. 343.

76. Ibid., p. 348.

77. C. S. Ricci, "Analysis of Child-Rearing Attitudes of Mothers of Retarded, Emotionally Disturbed, and Normal Children," *American Journal of Mental Deficiency*, 74:1970, p. 759; S. T. Cummings, H. C. Bayley, and H. E. Rie, "Effects of the Child's Deficiency on the Mother: A Study of Mothers of Mentally Retarded, Chronically Ill, and Neurotic Children," *American Journal of Orthopsychiatry*, 36:1966, p. 605; T. L. Worchel and P. Worchel, "The Parental Concept of the Mentally Retarded Child," *American Journal of Mental Deficiency*, 65:1961, p. 788.

78. P. S. Buck, "The Child Who Never Grew," *Ladies Home Journal*, May 1950, p. 134.

79. R. A. Kurtz, *Social Aspects of Mental Retardation*, Lexington, Mass.: Lexington Books, 1977, p. 11.

80. M. Stone, p. 420.

81. R. Barsch, p. 291; G. Zuk, R. Miller, J. Bartram, and F. Kling, p. 537.

82. R. Barsch, p. 288.

83. J. Michaels and H. Schucman, p. 569.

84. B. Farber, p. 7.

85. B. L. Svarstad and H. L. Lipton, p. 651.

86. J. Michaels and H. Schucman, pp. 568–569; D. B. Ryckman and R. A. Henderson, "The Meaning of a Retarded Child for His Parents: A Focus for Counselors," *Mental Retardation*, 3:1965, p. 6.

87. T. L. Worchel and P. Worchel, p. 788.

88. D. B. Ryckman and R. A. Henderson, p. 6.

89. B. Hymovitch, "The Effects of Experimental Variations in Early Experience on Problem Solving in the Rat," *Journal of Comparative Physiological Psychology*, 45:1952, pp. 313–321; W. R. Thompson and W. Heron, "The Effects of Restricting Early Experience on Problem-Solving Capacities of Dogs," *Canadian Journal of Psychology*, 8:1954, pp. 17–31; A. L. Baldwin, J. Kalhorn, and F. H.

Breese, "Patterns of Parent Behavior," *Psychological Monographs,* 58:1945, whole no. 268; J. R. Hurley, "Parental Acceptance-Rejection and Children's Intelligence," *Merrill-Palmer Quarterly,* 11:1965, p. 28.

90. H. D. Love, *The Mentally Retarded Child and His Family,* Springfield, Ill.: Charles C. Thomas, 1973, p. 175; J. R. Hurley, p. 28.

91. G. Saenger, *The Adjustment of Severely Retarded Adults in the Community,* Albany: New York State Interdepartmental Health Resources Board, 1957.

92. S. Olshansky, "Parent Responses to a Mentally Defective Child," p. 23.

93. J. Mercer, "Career Patterns of Persons Labeled as Mentally Retarded," in E. Freidson and J. Lorber, eds., *Medical Men and Their Work,* New York: Aldine, 1972, p. 440.

94. S. Olshansky, "Parent Responses to a Mentally Defective Child," p. 23.

95. M. M. Klaber, "The Retarded and Institutions for the Retarded—A Preliminary Research Report," in S. B. Sarason and J. Doris, eds., *Psychological Problems in Mental Deficiency,* New York: Harper and Row, 1969, p. 180.

96. K. J. Downey, "Parental Interest in the Institutionalized, Severely Mentally Retarded Child," *Social Problems,* 11:1963, p. 190.

97. B. Farber, *Mental Retardation: Its Social Context and Social Consequences,* Boston: Houghton Mifflin, 1968, p. 155.

98. Ibid.

99. B. Farber, "Sociology," *Mental Retardation and Developmental Disabilities,* 6:1974, p. 150.

100. M. Culver, "Intergenerational Social Mobility Among Families With a Severely Mentally Retarded Child," unpublished doctoral dissertation, University of Illinois, 1967.

101. M. Sternlicht, J. Staaby, and I. Sullivan, "Birth Order, Maternal Age, and Mental Retardation," *Mental Retardation,* 13(6):1975, p. 4.

102. S. T. Cummings, H. C. Bayley, and H. E. Rie, p. 605.

103. B. Farber, *Mental Retardation: Its Social Context and Social Consequences,* p. 154.

104. B. Farber, "Sociology," p. 150.

105. M. Culver, 1967.

106. N. D. Stone, "Family Factors in Willingness to Place the Mongoloid Child," *American Journal of Mental Deficiency,* 71:1967, pp. 16–20; G. Saenger, *Factors Influencing the Institutionalization of Mentally Retarded Individuals in New York City,* Albany: New York State Interdepartmental Health Resources Board, January 1960, pp. 45–50; L. C. Wolf and P. C. Whitehead, "The Decision to Institutionalize Retarded Children: Comparison of Individually Matched Groups," *Mental Retardation,* 13:1975, p. 3.

107. K. P. Meadow, "Self-Image, Family Climate, and Deafness," *Social Forces,* 47:1969, pp. 428–438, cited in K. P. Meadow and L. Meadow, "Changing Role Perceptions for Parents of Handicapped Children," *Exceptional Children,* 38:1971, p. 25.

108. B. Farber, "Effects of a Severely Mentally Retarded Child on Family

Integration," *Monographs of the Society for Research in Child Development*, 24:1959, no. 2, serial no. 71, p. 78.

109. Ibid.; D. B. Ryckman and R. A. Henderson, p. 6.

110. S. Levine, "Sex Role Identification and Parental Perceptions of Social Competence," *American Journal of Mental Deficiency*, 70(6):1966, pp. 822–824.

111. H. Barry, M. Bacon, and I. Child, "A Cross Cultural Survey of Some Sex Differences in Socialization," *Journal of Abnormal and Social Psychology*, 55:1957, pp. 327–332.

112. H. D. Love, *Parental Attitudes Toward Exceptional Children*, Springfield, Ill.: Charles C. Thomas, 1970, pp. 41–59.

113. H. D. Love, *The Mentally Retarded Child and His Family*, p. 174.

114. B. Farber, W. C. Jenne, and R. Toigo, cited in B. Farber, *Mental Retardation: Its Social Context and Social Consequences*, p. 156.

115. I. Tallman, "Spousal Role Differentiation and the Socialization of Severely Retarded Children," *Journal of Marriage and the Family*, 27:1965, p. 42.

116. J. R. Peck and W. B. Stephens, "A Study of the Relationships Between the Attitudes and Behavior of Parents and That of Their Mentally Defective Child," *American Journal of Mental Deficiency*, 74:1960, pp. 839–843.

117. L. C. Wolf and P. C. Whitehead, p. 4.

118. N. D. Stone and J. J. Parnicky, "Factors Associated With Parental Decision to Institutionalize Mongoloid Children," *Training School Bulletin*, 61(4):1965, pp. 166–172.

119. G. Zuk, R. Miller, J. Bartram, and F. Kling, p. 538.

120. I. Zwerling, "Initial Counseling of Parents With Mentally Retarded Children," *Journal of Pediatrics*, 44:1954, pp. 469–479.

121. W. N. Friedrich and W. L. Friedrich, "Psychosocial Assets of Parents of Handicapped and Nonhandicapped Children," *American Journal of Mental Deficiency*, 85:1981, p. 552.

122. H. D. Love, *The Mentally Retarded Child and His Family*, p. 162.

123. K. S. Holt, "Impact of MR Children on Their Families," unpublished doctoral dissertation, University of Sheffield, England, 1957, cited in T. E. Jordan, "Research on the Handicapped Child and the Family," *Merrill-Palmer Quarterly*, 8:1962, p. 245.

124. J. Michaels and H. Schucman, p. 571.

125. W. N. Friedrich and W. L. Friedrich, p. 552; A. Gath, "The Impact of an Abnormal Child upon the Parents," *British Journal of Psychiatry*, 130:1977, pp. 405–410.

126. H. D. Love, *The Mentally Retarded Child and His Family*, p. 29.

127. K. S. Holt, cited in B. Farber, *Mental Retardation: Its Social Context and Social Consequences*, p. 160.

128. J. Carr, p. 818.

129. J. Greenfeld, p. 55.

130. R. D. Freeman, "Use of Psychoactive Drugs for Intellectually Handicapped Children," in N. Bernstein, ed., *Diminished People*, Boston: Little, Brown and Co., 1970, p. 281.

131. K. S. Holt, cited in B. Farber, *Mental Retardation: Its Social Context and Social Consequences*, p. 160.

132. C. C. Upshur, "Respite Care for Mentally Retarded and Other Disabled Populations: Program Models and Family Needs," *Mental Retardation,* 20(1):1982, pp. 2–6.

133. N. W. Hart, p. 64.

134. C. M. Fowle, "The Effects of the Severely Mentally Retarded Child on His Family," *American Journal of Mental Deficiency,* 73:1968, p. 472.

135. J. B. Fotheringham, M. Skelton, and B. A. Hoddinott, *The Retarded Child and His Family: Effects of Home and Institution,* Toronto: Ontario Institute for Studies in Education, Monograph Series 11, 1971, cited in L. C. Wolf and P. C. Whitehead, p. 5.

136. K. J. Downey, p. 190.

137. B. Farber, *Mental Retardation: Its Social Context and Social Consequences,* p. 162.

138. B. Farber, W. C. Jenne, and R. Toigo, p. 89; B. V. Graliker, K. Fishler, and R. Koch, "Teenage Reaction to a Mentally Retarded Sibling," *American Journal of Mental Deficiency,* 66:1962, p. 842.

139. B. Farber, W. C. Jenne, and R. Toigo, p. 90.

140. M. Schreiber and M. Feeley, *Siblings of the Retarded,* New York: Association for the Help of Retarded Children in conjunction with National Association for Retarded Citizens, 1964, p. 16.

141. C. M. Fowle, p. 473.

142. B. V. Graliker, K. Fishler, and R. Koch, p. 841.

143. P. C. Cohen, "The Impact of a Handicapped Child on the Family," *Social Casework,* 43:1962, p. 140.

144. B. Farber, *Mental Retardation: Its Social Context and Social Consequences,* p. 159.

145. M. Skelton, "Areas of Parental Concern About Retarded Children," *Mental Retardation,* 10:1972, p. 39.

146. B. V. Graliker, K. Fishler, and R. Koch, pp. 841–843.

147. Ibid., p. 841.

148. M. Schreiber and M. Feeley, p. 7.

149. B. Farber, *Mental Retardation: Its Social Context and Social Consequences,* p. 7.

150. T. Worchel, "Attitudes of Parents Toward Mentally Retarded Children," unpublished masters thesis, University of Texas, 1955, cited in H. D. Love, *The Mentally Retarded Child and His Family,* p. 194.

151. S. E. Waisbren, p. 350.

152. K. S. Holt, "The Influence of Mentally Retarded Children on Their Families," cited in E. J. Gumz and J. F. Gubruim, "Comparative Parental Perceptions of a Mentally Retarded Child," *American Journal of Mental Deficiency,* 77:1972, p. 175.

153. H. D. Love, *The Mentally Retarded Child and His Family,* p. 162.

154. J. J. Tavormina, R. B. Hampson, and R. L. Luscomb, "Participant Evaluations of the Effectiveness of Their Parent Counseling Groups," *Mental Retardation,* 14:1976, p. 9.

155. M. J. Appell, C. M. Williams, and K. N. Fishnell, p. 182.

8
The Rights of Retarded People in an Era of Legal Advocacy: Ideals, Laws, Realities

The Law is not concerned with trifles.
—Legal maxim

BASIC RIGHTS

Mentally retarded persons have the same essential human and constitutional rights as other citizens. At least, that is the way it is supposed to be. The next few chapters will explore the sociolegal environment inhabited by mentally handicapped citizens.

In settings governed by laws, there are discrepancies in what the laws should *ideally be*, in what in actuality *is mandated*, and in how legal mandates are interpreted or *applied* in practice. Because such discrepancies are not uncommon in the legal world of mental retardation, they bear further examination. For didactic purposes, I have chosen the *Declaration of Rights of Mentally Retarded Persons*, adopted by the United Nations General Assembly in 1972, as representative of the ideal.[1] We shall look at each of the seven articles of this declaration in this and subsequent chapters. For current legislation, specific reference will be made to federal and state laws in effect as of 1982. The focus will be on Colorado state law, because that is where this study was conducted and because Colorado's legal climate for retarded persons is comparatively progressive. Published material and anecdotes based upon my own observations will be the basis of descriptions of compliance with currently existing laws. One wishes there were a way to change manuscripts as quickly as laws change. Recognizing that as a problem, I have tried to focus on social issues inherent in current laws that have an abiding nature. In other words, while the laws will change, the major issues they address will not—for the foreseeable future, anyway.

Article I of the *Declaration of Rights of Mentally Retarded Persons* says, "The mentally retarded person has the same basic rights as other citizens of the same country and same age." Mentally retarded people generally enjoy freedom of speech, religion, and most other constitutional guarantees. However, they do not do such things as serve on juries or bear arms (there being obvious exceptions among mildly retarded persons). The suggestion here is not that they should exercise these rights, only that they do not. This raises an issue.

Most bills of rights have provisions that can abrogate the guarantees contained in them. For example, while Article I of the *Declaration of Rights of Mentally Retarded Persons* holds that retarded citizens should have all the same rights as other people, Article VII provides for the selective denial of these rights. It says,

> Some mentally retarded persons may be unable, due to the severity of their handicap, to exercise for themselves all of their rights in a meaningful way. For others, modification of some or all of these rights is appropriate. The procedure used for modification or denial of rights must contain legal safeguards against every form of abuse, must be based on an evaluation of the social capability of the mentally retarded person by a qualified expert and must be subject to periodic reviews and the right to appeal.

As abstract principles, such "override" clauses are seemingly just. But when we deal with bills of rights on concrete levels, the override clauses can be used to cut too wide a swath through guarantees. Let us look at an example.

Clause 110, Article 10.5, of Senate Bill 135 *(Care and Treatment of the Developmentally Disabled)* of the State of Colorado holds that, just because a person is institutionalized, he shall not be deprived of "any other rights, benefits, or privileges."[2] Clause 111 of the same bill says, "Denial of any right shall in all cases be entered upon the facility's [institution's] record. Information pertaining to a denial of rights shall be made available, upon request, to the resident or his attorney. . . . Rights may be denied only by the professional person providing care and treatment or by any court exercising jurisdiction over the resident."[3]

All of this sounds fair. The problem is that sometimes denials of rights do not get past the stage of a professional entering them in the "facility's record," and this does not ensure that the rights have been justifiably withdrawn. If there is any question of justification, the recourse a retarded person has is to retain an attorney and get involved in a litigation, if it *occurs* to the retarded individual that he ought to seek legal advice. Legal advocates can, of course, intervene on the retarded person's behalf, but this assumes that there is an efficient monitoring

procedure for the legal rights of retarded people. There ar
and organizational legal advocates who do such monitoring,
are spread very thinly. As Switzky and Miller say, "the great d
in protection of the rights of the mentally retarded lies not in desc
appropriate procedures, but in establishing safeguards for actual p
tice."[4]

There are a number of reasons why there is such an uneasy balance
between the fundamental rights of retarded people and the abrogation
of those rights. Wald alludes to a key element of the problem when
she says,

> Our notion of law and legal obligations and rights normally operates on
> certain basic assumptions about people for whom they are formulated.
> First, that they know and understand the consequences of what they do.
> Second, that they can explain to others what they intend to do. Third,
> that they act reasonably in their own interests, and it is morally right
> that they suffer the consequences of their own actions. Our law has never
> formulated a different set of assumptions on which to deal with people
> who don't fit that profile. Such people are in the most basic sense of the
> word, the real "outlaws" of our society.[5]

Oliver Wendell Holmes put the issue slightly differently: "the chief
end of man is to frame general propositions, and . . . no general
proposition is worth a damn."[6] They certainly are not when applied
to the legal rights of retarded persons. Special difficulties arise as to
how laws are applied differently to mentally handicapped versus normal
people. Further, there are legal ambiguities as to how judicial interpretations can be applied equitably to different retarded people when
there is so much variation in the degree to which they are handicapped.
For example, is the criminal responsibility of a person with an IQ of
30 the same as that of someone with an IQ of 55? What rights does
a highly functioning retarded person have that a severely or profoundly
retarded person does not? Just because a law is tested on one retarded
individual, does that mean that the adjudicated outcome will be applicable
to all other retarded people under similar circumstances? This question
is particularly interesting, because many suits filed on behalf of retarded
people are class-action suits. Yet, when one considers the heterogeneity
of the retarded population, such suits cannot reflect the broadest interests
of the multifaceted group they seek to represent.

Let us consider two illustrative instances in which the legal and
practical rights of retarded persons do not coincide: the right to own
and control property and the right to vote. The U.S. Constitution sets
standards in the Fifth Amendment that ensure that one's property cannot

"due process of law." Thus, retarded people ⟨...⟩ or inherit property. Yet I never met a retarded ⟨...⟩roperty than the paltry belongings he had in ⟨...⟩ a matter of fact, the National Association for ⟨...⟩ retarded people's most active advocate, once ⟨...⟩, "It is generally agreed that it is undesirable ⟨...⟩ve substantial funds or to possess property."[7]

⟨...⟩g statement to be made by an advocacy orga-
⟨...⟩ one realizes a few of the underlying reasons:

[1] In many states, institutional charges [fees] are higher or applied only to those retarded persons who have estates left to them outright;
[2] It is felt that the inexperienced retarded person will have more financial responsibility than he can handle;
[3] If the appointment of a guardian is found necessary, the estate passes to the probate court where financial management will be more rigid than parents may desire.
[4] In most cases, therefore, property should not be willed directly to a retarded person. It is also felt that a retarded person should not be the beneficiary of a life insurance policy.[8]

Things have changed little since 1648, when John Milton said, "By civil laws a foole or idiot born shall lose the lands whereto he is born because he is not able to use them aright."[9]

Voting is another area in which a constitutionally guaranteed right of retarded people can be thwarted in practice. For example, the retarded person who resides in an institution typically faces prohibitions against political activities on state grounds and injunctions against institutional vehicles transporting voters to the polls.[10] Thus, if a polling place is not set up on the institutional grounds, if the retarded person cannot find his own transportation, or if he does not pursue the process of getting an absentee ballot, there is a de facto disenfranchisement. It can be asked, Is it really so bad if institutionalized "retardates" don't vote? What can they know about politics anyway? According to one study, *non-institutionalized, mildly* retarded adults (not subjected to the informational confines of an institution) only knew half as much as their non-handicapped counterparts about political issues pertaining to elections in which they voted, and they did not improve their knowledge when trained in "election matters."[11]

That notwithstanding, the Constitution and the Voting Rights Act of 1970 do not prohibit voting on the basis of political ineptitude. Many electoral issues impact the lives of retarded persons directly, precisely because they are retarded. Moreover, even if they are not politically knowledgeable, that does not mean that retarded people are any less electorally astute than their non-handicapped counterparts. In one study in which retarded persons voted in mock elections held prior to the real thing, they predicted the choices of the rest of the electorate very accurately.[12]

When dealing with the practical realities of legally mandated rights such as voting, it cannot be assumed that retarded citizens are, or ought to be, indifferent about elections because they are retarded. Self-advocacy groups of mentally handicapped persons are taking increasing interest in political action. There was, for instance, a significant increase in the participation of retarded voters in the 1976 general election over that shown in 1972.[13] Mentally retarded voters will, in the absence of flagrantly discriminatory laws, not remain a silent minority in the U.S. political arena. This factor raises an interesting issue.

We are not sure precisely what the numbers are, but mentally retarded persons represent a sizable constituency in our society.[14] As retarded people become more electorally active, it is important that their exercise of voting rights not become a multiple enfranchisement of their parents, teachers, or whoever else can most influence them. We are all subject to motivational pressures in elections; with retarded people, the subjugation of their own preferences to superficial influences or persons close to them may function to a greater degree than it does with non-handicapped voters. For example, in Mountview, it was widely rumored that some parents and advocates took retarded people to polling places, not just to help them vote, but to tell them whom to vote for. Thus, as the ideal, the law, and the reality inch closer together in one important area of democratic rights, a social problem begins to emerge—one that puts the ideal and the actuality at more than an arm's length. Indeed, the apparency of legal progress for retarded persons has been fraught with such perils.

MEDICAL RIGHTS

Article II of the *Declaration of Rights of Mentally Retarded Persons* says,

> The mentally retarded person has a right to proper medical care and physical restoration and to such education, training, habilitation and guidance as will enable him to develop his ability and potential to the fullest possible extent, no matter how severe his degree of disability. No mentally handicapped person should be deprived of such services by reason of the costs involved.

There are federal and state laws and programs designed to meet the aforementioned right to "medical care and physical restoration." Title V (Crippled Children's Services) and Title XIX (Medicaid) of the Social Security Act are two examples of federal mandates that have had an impact on the provision of medical care for mentally retarded people. Even though medical and restorative services are delineated under such laws, retarded persons do not always receive the services despite the fact that delivery systems are available.

For instance, if a retarded child needs an operation that his parents cannot afford, the federal government has provisos, such as those in the Handicapped Children's Program, that provide funds for essential medical procedures under a specified set of circumstances. If the money is made available and if the parents have access to physicians who can perform the operation in adequate surgical facilities, the child ought to get the treatment he needs. Of course, this all presupposes that someone will initiate procedures that will get the wheels of bureaucratic medicine turning. Many parents do not do so, either because seeking such help is an admission of their own inability to provide adequately for their children's needs or because the whole procedure is seen to be too much trouble. It can be very difficult to make the proper contacts in the huge service bureaucracy, and, if they are made, many parents are quickly discouraged by the torrent of forms they must fill out, the multitude of appointments they must keep, and the difficulty in "relating" to some of the lower-echelon bureaucrats who are alienated in their jobs and let it show. All of this is especially intimidating to parents who are somewhat "slow" themselves.

If the parents of handicapped children do not commence medical referral procedures, then someone else must. The task usually falls to social workers, public health nurses, or special educators—most of whom have full caseloads, eschew bureaucratic roadblocks, and do not relish spending their off-duty hours trying to secure these medical needs if they can avoid it. To special educators particularly, it is axiomatic that such involvement requires a lot of unpaid overtime. Moreover, the effort to help sometimes occurs against a backdrop of parental apathy or resistance to the intervention, which is given an especially sharp edge if the professional initiates a medical procedure hazardous to the child. If something goes wrong, even if the parents and the child were supportive of the intervention, the professional who launched it feels the onus of inevitable guilt. Thus, if the medical need is not too acute, it may be temporarily overlooked.

For retarded people living in institutions, there are special guarantees of medical services. For example, Clause 114 of Article 27-10.5 of Colorado's Senate Bill 135 says, "Each resident shall receive appropriate dental and medical care and treatment for any physical ailments and for the prevention of illnesses or disability." Related subclauses say, "Residents shall have a right to be free from unnecessary or excessive medication" and "Medication shall not be used for the convenience of the staff, for punishment, as a substitute for a treatment program, or in quantities that interfere with the resident's treatment program."

Mandates for adequate medical and dental care in institutions are important for the people living and working in them. In order to provide this care, though, there must be enough doctors and dentists associated with the institution. Scheerenberger's research points out the difficulties institutions face in attracting medical professionals.[15] Well-intentioned laws guaranteeing high standards of health and medical care in institutions have more of a rhetorical than real quality when personnel shortages and funding limitations are taken into account in the delivery of such services.

The same is true of guarantees against the use of "chemical straitjackets." The types and dosages of medications given institutional residents are listed in their files, but monitoring these drugs is problematic. Most advocates have neither the degree of pharmacological expertise needed to decide whether the medications are appropriate nor the time to plow through the files. Few doctors question the prescriptions of colleagues, and drug utilization review committees, composed of pharmacists, physicians, and advocates, are exceedingly rare in institutional settings. There is some evidence, based on a very limited sample, that indiscriminate use of the major tranquilizers on institutional populations may be declining.[16] However, other studies show that anticonvulsants such as phenobarbital (which has tranquilizing effects) are being used inappropriately on segments of institutionalized populations.[17] Where institutional budgets are low and staff members inadequately trained or overworked, chemical pacification may seem to be the best functional alternative to physical restraints or time-consuming programs of psychological restraint. In any case, with money getting tighter, it would not be surprising to see pills substituted for programs, laws to the contrary notwithstanding.

EDUCATIONAL RIGHTS

The second section of Article II of the *Declaration of Rights of Mentally Retarded Persons* provides for the education of retarded people, no matter how severe their degree of disability. A potent boost to achieving this ideal came with the passage of Public Law 94-142—the Education for All Handicapped Children Act of 1975. P.L. 94-142 went into effect on the opening day of school in 1978. Under provisions of the act, it became a violation of federal law for public educational agencies to deny an appropriate program to *any* handicapped child in need of special education. By 1980, the law was extended to cover handicapped individuals three to twenty-one years old, except in cases where state-sponsored education of those three to five years old and eighteen to twenty-one years old would be inconsistent with state laws.

While P.L. 94-142 was designed to redress the educational inequities faced by all handicapped children, the specific importance of the law to youngsters with mental handicaps is clear. As late as 1971, only 36 percent of school-age retarded children were enrolled in educational programs in the United States.[18] In some parts of the country, only 15 percent of the retarded school-age children were participating in any programs at all.[19] Such exclusions were most evident with children having severe handicaps or those with behavioral disturbances.[20] Although such problems were beginning to be rectified before the passage of P.L. 94-142,[21] the law formalized the process of redressing decades of intellectual discrimination in American education. Let us look briefly at the primary components of the law and some of the issues associated with each of them.

One part of the law requires that states and local school districts engage in extensive "child-find" and identification procedures of handicapped persons, from birth to twenty-one years of age. Child-find is a good idea, but the mandate is difficult to implement. First, school districts must make evaluation services easily accessible to the public. That means more than merely having the services; it means taking them out into the community, interfacing with physicians, human service agencies, and the like—essentially "advertising" the availability of the evaluation service. Second, even if a school district is aggressive in its efforts to identify handicapped clients, that does not mean it will succeed in doing so. Effectiveness here usually relies on the willingness or ability of parents to make use of the child-find services. Some of these parents sequester their children, rail at the thought that the child is handicapped, or are oblivious to child-find efforts. School districts can hardly be expected to go door-to-door in search of handicapped clients. Third, even if a child is "found," that does not guarantee that a program will be available to meet his needs. For example, if preschool services are inconsistent with state educational laws and no community center board preschool services are available, the primary result of a child's having been identified may be his acquisition of the retarded label.

Second, P.L. 94-142 holds that once handicapped people are identified, states are required to establish "priorities for providing free appropriate public education, . . . first with respect to handicapped children who are not receiving an education, and second with respect to handicapped children, within each disability, with most severe handicaps who are receiving an inadequate education. . . ."[22]

This element is a "can of worms," especially as it pertains to the education of severely and profoundly retarded institutionalized populations. It is an apt generalization that severely and profoundly handicapped institutionalized persons to date have not received appropriate educational services. For example, in 1979, one institution with which I became acquainted had five certified special education teachers for a population of 674 school-age clients—this four years after the passage of P.L. 94-142. As advocates press for a rectification of this inadequacy, one begins to see the emergence of certain logistical problems.

For instance, since institutions are centralized, residents come from numerous school districts. Which district is responsible for providing educational funds? Is it the district in which the institution is located, or the home district of parents of residents? If that can be decided, along with how funds can be equitably transferred from one district to another (so that one district is providing funds, and another services), which district is responsible for monitoring the IEP? Assuming such issues can be resolved, a greater controversy concerning another provision of P.L. 94-142 arises.

A third requirement of the law is that handicapped children and their parents should receive assurances of "full services." These services, as they are defined by the law, include:

> . . . transportation, and such developmental, corrective, and other supportive services (including speech pathology and audiology, psychological services, physical and occupational therapy, recreation, and medical counseling services, except that such medical services shall be for diagnostic and evaluation purposes only) as may be required to assist the handicapped child to benefit from special education, and includes the early identification and assessment of handicapping conditions in children.[23]

The crucial phrase here is "as may be required to assist the handicapped child to benefit from special education. . . ." What are appropriate educational needs and benefits for severely and profoundly retarded children? If a child's highest educational ability is the development of rudimentary motor skills, is that "educational"? The law is being interpreted in different ways in various locales. In the face of fiscal constraints, school districts feel it unfair that they should be required to provide funding for services that are not interpreted as being educational. There is no question that some low-functioning retarded persons do not profit from currently accepted educational techniques. Should school districts thus be required to foot the bill for the provision of a nurturing environment?

There are some other problems with the "full service" guarantees of the third provision of P.L. 94-142 that do not relate to institutionalized populations. Before P.L. 94-142, a multitude of agencies supplied the different educational-ancillary services needed by retarded students. In those times, even the most energetic parents could be run ragged going from agency to agency to meet all the various service needs of their children. This problem has not been totally alleviated,[24] as is manifest in the case of medical care, but the situation is getting better. If, however, we look at the "interpretive" aspects of service provision of P.L. 94-142, we see that the spirit of the law is occasionally subverted. For example, when the transition of New Morning School from the aegis of the Department of Institutions to the Department of Education was being effectuated, the first thing the director of special education of the Mountview schools recommended was a number of program cutbacks in areas such as speech therapy, occupational therapy, and classroom teaching personnel. The monies saved here were to be used to nearly double the salary of the school's newly proposed administrative position. A great deal of political pressure by parents, teachers, and other advocates halted the proposed service cutbacks. Where advocates are more complacent, though, laws such as P.L. 94-142 can be used regressively. They may not have a legal leg to stand on, but *some* financially beleaguered administrators have and will continue to test the climate of compliance with P.L. 94-142 to get a feel for how much latitude they have in its implementation. It cannot be assumed that special education administrators are necessarily chosen for their jobs because they are advocates of retarded people. Most of them probably are, but the nuts and bolts of administration put some of these individuals at odds with humanistic concerns relating to retarded persons. Thus, in terms of full services, the process of compliance is erratic and bears continuous vigilance from advocates.

There are also some logistical impediments to the full service goals of P.L. 94-142. For example, in rural areas it is difficult to attract enough qualified specialists. Where they can be attracted, the mentally handicapped population is so widely dispersed that time and distance result in infrequent encounters between specialists and clients.

A fourth component of Public Law 94-142 assures that children being considered for special education placement will be evaluated and tested in culturally and racially non-discriminatory ways. Specifically, the law asserts that materials and procedures will be provided in the child's native language or his own mode of communication and that no single procedure, such as an IQ test, will be the sole criterion for determining the child's placement in the educational system. We can get an idea of how this element of the law will ultimately translate into social reality by looking at the success of a precursive legal case. In *Diana* v. *the State Board of Education* (1970), the courts ruled against discriminatory assessment and placement practices. In the wake of the *Diana* case, Cohen did a five-year follow-up study to see if things had changed in California. His conclusion: "It appears that the schools have not incorporated the changes that were demanded by the litigation and have not changed basic practices. More importantly, there were many expressions of racial and class biases."[25] It is a difficult process to develop legitimately culture-free assessment procedures. It is even more difficult to achieve a consensus about when that has been achieved. And it does not logically follow that non-discriminatory assessment results in cultural or racial equity in placement. If services to special children who are members of cultural and racial minorities are tinged with racial prejudice or indifference to the special cultural needs of these youngsters, the non-discriminatory assessments that direct such placements are a trifle anemic in their consequences.

A fifth component of Public Law 94-142 is a complete guarantee of "due process" procedures in all placement decisions. The law is very specific in its admonition that a reasonable attempt must be made to alert parents or guardians whenever it has been decided by school authorities that a child should be placed in a special class, reassigned, or excluded from participation in the school program. The notification must be in writing, delivered by registered mail, and be in the parents' primary language or interpreted for them by a translator provided by the school district. The notification should describe what the school intends to do, tell why, and include any tests or reports related to the school's decision and all alternative educational options the school system could provide for the student in question. Further, the notifications should inform parents of their rights to:

- Contest the school's action before the State Commissioner of Education, or his designee, at a time and place convenient to them
- Be represented by legal counsel at the hearing
- Examine all of the child's records, including tests and reports, prior to the hearing
- Present evidence of their own, including expert medical, psychological and educational testimony
- Confront and cross-examine any school official who may have evidence upon which the school's proposed action is made
- Receive a complete and accurate record of the proceedings
- Appeal the decision.[26]

Some school districts are especially sensitive to communicating with parents of handicapped children about placement issues. But again, interpretive elements of the law can undermine its spirit. For example, in 1979, one Mountview family whose child was to be placed in a new special class was informed of the move by letter, after the decision to move the youngster had been made. The parents confronted school officials and were told that the similarities in the old and new classrooms were such that the move did not constitute a change in placement by the school district's definition. The parents asked for a hearing. The hearing officer, himself a special education administrator, decided in favor of the school district. The parents appealed this decision in the courts, where the outcome was reversed in an expensive, time-consuming, and energy-draining case. Not only is there a sense in which the hearing procedure allows the "fox to guard the chickencoop," but most parents would not go to the expense and trouble to guarantee that their due process rights had not been abrogated by an interpretive decision.

A sixth provision of P.L. 94-142 requires that Individual Educational Plans be developed for all handicapped children. This is rational and potentially beneficial to teacher and child. As we saw earlier, however, professionals develop the plans with widely varying degrees of enthusiasm, creativity, and competence. The major problem with IEPs is that there are really no consequences of not achieving the stated goals or not formulating the right ones in the first place. Given the subjectivity that goes into the development of IEPs, they also have a "best guess" quality; combined with their dearth of consequential punch, that makes some of them seem well-intentioned superfluities.

A seventh provision of P.L. 94-142 guarantees a special education for all handicapped children in "the least restrictive environment." This is the component of the law that generates the greatest controversy, for reasons that quickly become apparent. For one thing, no one is exactly sure what a "least restrictive environment" really means. The term is too ambiguous to be very practical on the interpretive level. Providing services in the least restrictive environment is like complying with an innuendo. As nearly as I am able to tell, when the principle is translated into practice, the least restrictive environment is whatever parents and educational representatives decide it will be.

Types of Educational Environments for Retarded Persons

The educational environments for retarded persons are varied. A mentally handicapped student can be educated in any of these settings: at home, in an institution, in a special school, in a special classroom in a regular school, in a special classroom in a regular school with integration into structured and/or unstructured activities with non-handicapped students during certain parts of the day, in a regular classroom with part-time special class or resource-room placement, in a regular classroom with additional personnel support for the classroom teacher on a full- or part-time basis, or exclusively in a regular classroom.

Homebound Education. Homebound education is considered "least restrictive" for those students who have special physical requirements that cannot be met in a school. A child on a respirator would be an example. Children with profound and dangerous behavioral problems may also make homebound education the least restrictive environment, although this is typically resorted to only after special classes for youngsters with behavioral problems have been tried and proven inadequate. The disadvantages of homebound education are high personnel costs and the child's separation from peers.

Institutional Education. Institutions responsible for the education of retarded students must comply with all the provisions of P.L. 94-142. But as we have seen, there are some unresolved problems associated with education in institutional settings that can lead to shortfalls in funding, programs, personnel, and monitoring, among other things. Moreover, some students in institutions require less restrictive educational environments than they get there. For example, in one study, representatives of institutions reported that 95 percent of parents of institutionalized students abdicated the responsibility of monitoring educational decisions about their offspring to the facilities' own review committees.[27] It has been shown that the members of such committees base their efforts to get institutionalized students into public schools on "expected community acceptance" of the students, not "educational considerations."[28] This is commendable from a humanitarian point of view, but it probably leaves many students in environments that are more restrictive than they ought to be in order for the students to progress educationally. This raises several perplexing elements of P.L. 94-142. For example, does "less restrictive" necessarily mean better? Is it possible to put a child in the least restrictive *place*, but give him a more restrictive *program* than he can get in a more restrictive setting, or the converse? Are social needs more important than academic needs in determining least restrictive environment? Or do physical needs supersede the others? How do we prioritize the most important of these elements to come up with the optimal placement? There are probably many least restrictive environments for a given child depending upon his multiple dimensions of need; but P.L. 94-142 does not give us a formula for determining which of these is the most important. We can see this when we look at special schools such as New Morning.

Special-school Education. While there has been a thrust toward integrating mentally handicappped students into regular schools—mainstreaming them—some advocates still believe that special schools are the least restrictive environment for the vast majority of retarded children. These special-school proponents turn the least restrictive definition on its head, focusing on special schools as providers of the "most expansive" environments for retarded students. For example, it is held that students in special schools have high community visibility as a cohort, with legitimate claims to special needs and in possession of special capabilities. It is argued that when they are taken out of their own schools, their interests tend to get lost in the shuffle. It is also argued that retarded students develop an esprit de corps in their own schools, which gives them a positive social identity. Other contentions go as follows: First, centralization of special services helps to abolish neighborhood boundaries, so that all handicapped children, whether they live in a poor neighborhood or not, will get the services they need. Second, special schools are centers of special education expertise; thus, the personnel share common challenges in an environment with common purposes and need not feel, as they might in integrated settings, that they are the only ones who know or care about the needs of handicapped children. Third, service delivery is more efficient in segregated schools than in integrated settings because ancillary services can be provided with less traveling about by specialists, and special medical needs are more easily met in a centralized area. Fourth, it is easier for researchers to do remedial types of research in centralized settings where there are concentrations of handicapped children. Finally, many parents and teachers of mentally handicapped children like their special schools— and not just out of complacency or a disdain for change. A lot of parents and educators have struggled for years to get their special schools functioning smoothly, and they perceive that the schools work.

Mainstream Education. Public Law 94-142 does not mandate that all handicapped children will be mainstreamed, but it does imply that mainstreaming them is appropriate in most cases:

> Each state must establish procedures to insure that to the maximum extent appropriate, handicapped children, including children in public and private institutions and other care facilities, are educated with children who are not handicapped and that special classes, separate schooling, or the removal of handicapped children from the regular education environment occurs only when the nature or severity of the handicap is such that education in regular classes with the use of supplementary aids and services cannot be achieved satisfactorily.[29]

Mainstreaming has been the most controversial aspect of P.L. 94-142. This is rather surprising, as a year before the law was passed thirty-seven states had already mandated some form of mainstreaming as the preferred mode of educating handicapped children.[30]

Before taking a closer look at mainstreaming, a couple of caveats are in order. First, the vast majority of empirical work that has been done on mainstreaming has focused on mildly retarded students. While some of the issues germane to their educational experiences are applicable to lower-functioning students, we must be aware of the risks in making generalizations about mainstreaming and its effects on the basis of such a narrow sampling. Second, there is little longitudinal evidence on the effectiveness of mainstream programs, the research generally being confined to static or one-year examinations of such programs.[31]

Promainstream Arguments and Evidence

One of the primary advantages proponents of mainstreaming cite for their advocacy of the principle is its purported human relations value. The notion is advanced that continuous contact of handicapped children with regular education programs, personnel, and students will facilitate the handicapped students' acceptance in the educational community, if not the community at large. Moreover, there is evidence that the earlier the integration is achieved, the more likely non-handicapped students are to become comfortable around handicapped peers and the less likely to succumb to pejorative stereotypes about the latter.[32] Other evidence supporting the contention that propinquity evokes positive attitudes in non-handicapped children toward those with mental handicaps can be seen in the works of Chennault,[33] Sheare,[34] and Voeltz.[35] Rynders et al. suggest the same outcome if handicapped and non-handicapped students are placed in cooperative learning groups for selected tasks.[36] Jaffe found that non-handicapped adolescents ascribed a greater number of favorable traits to retarded persons if they had previous contact with them.[37]

Other ramifications of mainstreaming allegedly go beyond its human relations value. For example, it is suggested that if retarded children in special schools only have other retarded children for behavioral models, this will occasion a self-perpetuating accentuation of all the children's abnormal mannerisms. There is a body of literature that demonstrates that segregated placement perpetuates a host of cognitive and social maladaptations.[38] On the other hand, it is said that if retarded children have normal models, they will pattern their behavior after them. Several studies hold this to be especially salient with regard to the imitative effects that such interactions have on toddlers and pre-schoolers.[39] Although it is difficult to ascertain whether modeling non-handicapped behaviors is the cause or not, it has been demonstrated in several inquiries that integrated mildly retarded pupils showed more socially appropriate behaviors in school than a matched group of segregated students.[40]

Studies based on self-reports of mildly retarded integrated students showed that they had more positive attitudes toward school than matched groups of students who remained in segregated schools[41] and that such students reported "better self concept" than matched counterparts in special schools.[42] Further, mildly retarded students who were mainstreamed into regular classes performed better academically than matched groups who remained in special classes.[43] There are several reasons posited for this. First, children in special classes are said to be impaired in their goal-setting behaviors and expectancies for achievement when compared to retarded children in regular classes.[44] Second, regular-class teachers are purported to be more demanding than special-class teachers in their efforts to get a retarded child to "try harder."[45] Third, integrated classes have more emphasis on academic work than special classes, the latter focusing to a greater extent on the development of social skills.[46]

Proponents of mainstream education cite as another of its advantages the greater probability that mainstreamed children will be placed in schools close to their homes. Some mentally retarded students do not live close to their special schools. A few New Morning students, for example, spent a minimum of two hours a day on the school bus. Moroever, the mainstreamers say, a retarded child who goes to school in his own neighborhood will be more likely to be accepted there.

Another promainstream argument inverts what is supposed to be a special-school advantage. The reader will remember that some champions of special schools viewed them as indispensable centers of expertise. Mainstreamers say that if the special problems of retarded people are dispersed across a greater range of settings and personnel, there will be a diversification of attempts to remediate the problems, or, to put it another way, special educators do not have a monopoly on good special education ideas.

Antimainstream Arguments and Evidence

The evidence is conclusive that retarded students are not as socially acceptable to their non-handicapped peers as normal children.[47] There are data indicating that segregated mildly retarded children are more accepted by non-handicapped peers than mentally handicapped children who are integrated with these normal children.[48] Familiarity does not, according to these researches, reduce stigma; it breeds contempt.[49] It is sociologically naive to equate desegregation and integration, propinquity and assimilation.

As for the notion that retarded people have their self-images improved in mainstream situations, Thompson found that integrated retarded youngsters actually felt greater distance from non-handicapped students than retarded pupils in segregated classes.[50] Some retarded children might only have their feelings of inadequacy and frustration intensified in a mainstreaming situation, either as a result of the retarded child's perception of the intellectual superiority of normal youngsters or of the cruelty of some of his non-handicapped classmates. In any event, researchers like Gottlieb say that there is no evidence of greater social adjustments for mainstreamed children.[51]

Opponents of mainstreaming argue that even if retarded students integrated into regular classes were to show more socially appropriate behavior or higher academic aspirations than they did before the integration, the personal costs exacted in achieving these are too great. For example, integrated retarded students manifest significantly heightened degrees of anxiety compared to those who are not mainstreamed.[52] For some students, this probably results from social pressures brought to bear by classmates or teachers. It remains to be seen whether regular teachers do, in fact, make retarded children "try harder" in mainstream settings than special educators do in special classrooms. What is certain is that special educators choose to work with special children and are more likely than most individuals to interact with mentally retarded students "in a patient accepting manner."[53] The issue boils down to this: a youngster who has relied on the predictability of a special-school environment can be shocked and bewildered in an integrated setting, and in some cases it is difficult to predict whether a student will adapt or crumble.

The idea that retarded students benefit from imitating the models supplied for them by normal children in mainstream classrooms was disputed in research conducted by Ray, who could not detect any appreciable cross-group positive interaction or imitation between retarded and normal toddlers.[54] Other investigations found the same to be the case for retarded and normal preschoolers.[55] If we do wish to put retarded children in environments where they have only normal models, then we have to take them out of settings they share with their handicapped friends. We saw in an earlier chapter how disconcerting that can be. The best way to avoid such jarring contrasts is to mainstream clusters of retarded children. If that is done, it does not necessarily follow that they will model normal behaviors; they might simply increase their solidarity with retarded peers.[56]

Opponents of mainstreaming try to negate the argument that integration leads to better academic performance by raising the oft-repeated criticism that too much academic work for retarded students is not appropriate anyway. For example, Childs holds that "as much as 90 percent of the mainstreamed mentally retarded child's day is spent studying academics," and that "there is not one shred of evidence which supports regular class curriculum for mentally retarded children as opposed to a practical skills curriculum approach."[57]

Mainstreaming affects lives other than those of the students. Educators of both handicapped and non-handicapped students, parents of normal and retarded children, administrators, and politicians all have a stake in the mainstreaming issue, and many of these people are concerned about the consequences of integrating retarded children into regular schools. As such integration proceeds, it will increasingly emerge as an emotionally-charged issue.

Parents of mentally retarded students wonder whether regular-school teachers have the skill to work effectively with their children, and if these teachers will spend as much time with the youngsters as they were accustomed to getting in special schools.[58] These parents are glad that their children are finally getting equal educational opportunities. But even some of the parents who lobbied for P.L. 94-142 are circumspect about mainstreaming. As we have seen with several aspects of the normalization process, resonance with a general concept does not always translate into its acceptance when it is applied to real situations.[59]

Parents of non-handicapped children have heard stories about the uncontrollable urges of retarded people. Conversely, some fear that their youngsters will victimize the retarded children. They worry that teachers will have their attention diluted by the presence of handicapped students. In mainstream situations, these parents also see the extra expenditures that go to retarded students and find them hard to justify without parity. Some worry that their children will begin to imitate the behavior of retarded children, although research has shown this not to be the case.[60]

Many teachers of non-handicapped students are less than enthusiastic supporters of the mainstream concept.[61] Some of them fear that retarded students will be "dumped" on them. School districts typically allow these teachers to participate in negotiating admission and retention criteria for handicapped students, but it is impossible for teachers to ignore the pressures they are under to comply with administrative directives. If they are told to work with a handicapped child, most teachers will, whether they want to or not. Where it exists, the enthusiasm of regular-school teachers for mainstreaming is ephemeral. One group of investigators studied the attitudes of fifty-nine regular-school teachers who had mildly retarded students integrated into their classes with the support of a resource-room teacher. (Resource-room teachers usually spend part of their days in regular classes and part in a resource room, which has a curriculum designed especially for handicapped students.) The researchers found that, as the school year wore on, regular-classroom teachers became less enthusiastic about the integration program and increased their overall negative attitudes about retarded students and the whole mainstream idea.[62] These same teachers expressed pessimism about the possibility of the retarded students ever successfully adjusting to the placement, saying that "the retarded children in their classes were among the lowest achievers, were not participating in general class activities, and frequently were teased by the other children."[63] Voeltz makes a penetrating comment about the negativity normal children show retarded classmates in mainstream settings:

> Even if researchers were to document that nonhandicapped children exhibit an intolerance for their handicapped peers that includes a willingness to engage in overtly cruel behavior, this should posit a challenge to educators rather than a limitation. Surely such behavior of presumably "normal" children is as susceptible to change as the behavior of severely handicapped children, now apparently acquiring skills once thought unattainable.[64]

It is a point well taken, but the challenges educators of normal children see in working with retarded youngsters are not always sufficient to overcome their resistance. In a sampling conducted by Gickling and Theobald in 1975, 60 percent of the regular-class teachers surveyed felt that self-contained classes were more effective than regular classes in the education of *mildly* retarded students.[65] One can imagine what the percentage might have been if more severely retarded students had been the object of discussion.

Negative educator attitudes toward mentally handicapped students slated for integration are understandable from the teachers' perspectives. The vast majority of regular educators do not feel they have the overall skills necessary to work with handicapped children.[66] Many of these educators are put off by medical problems associated with mental retardation, such as convulsive disorders and sensorimotor defects. Some of them feel that they do not have the materials or know the methods needed to teach retarded children. Given our earlier discussion of *ad hoc* pragmatism, it is not surprising that regular educators have some difficulty in finding easy access to the most effective educational methods to use with retarded students. Special educators have learned to live with procedural ambiguity, but it is intimidating to regular-classroom teachers, who are accustomed to fairly well elaborated methodological paradigms. And to make matters worse, a few special educators exaggerate the technical complexities associated with special education in an effort to enhance their own professional mystique. To regular educators, this gives special education an esoteric aura something akin to alchemy.

Research has shown that regular-class teachers can diminish their trepidation and improve their attitudes about retarded students by taking a single college special education course.[67] Procedures for personnel development and in-service training are mandated under P.L. 94-142,[68] but many regular teachers have other educational priorities in the recertification courses they do take and only grudgingly enroll in special education classes. If they do not take university training in special education, regular educators usually rely either on resource-room teachers or in-service training provided by their school districts to expand their knowledge of special students. Resource-room teachers are in short supply, although the demand for them should alter this. Where in-service training programs exist, they are often brief, static, superficial, and done on the educators' own time.

In addition to their attitudinal problems and the self-perceived dearth of knowledge about handicapped students, regular-classroom teachers have other concerns about mainstreaming. For instance, they recognize that retarded youngsters need programming the entire school day. Traditional slack times such as recess, lunch, and free periods before and after school will require the same focused attention as other instructional periods. Regular-class teachers will thus feel the unrelenting pressures that typify the workdays of special educators, as well as many of the latter's frustrations. There is also concern about whether local school districts will equitably alter student-teacher ratios to account for the extra attention retarded students integrated into regular classrooms will need. Some teacher unions have openly opposed mainstreaming because handicapped students are seen to put undue strain on regular-classroom teachers who are already overtaxed.[69] Where this occurs, it is disturbing because it has the effect of pitting educators against each other and disaffecting special educators from union affiliation. The mainstream philosophy can be divisive in another way. Where it breaks up special schools and disperses students, the power of parent lobbies can be diffused. Parents and advocates who have unified in special-school settings will have to keep their advocacy organizations vital as mainstreaming progresses if they hope to see the spirit of P.L. 94-142 carried out.

If mainstreaming is going to work, it is important that regular-classroom teachers be an integral part of the process, starting with placement decisions. Their attitudes will have to be groomed through a careful program of sensitization to the needs and potentials of retarded children. These teachers will require a lot of support from parents, special educators, and administrators.

Special education teachers will have to be considered carefully in the mainstreaming process as well. They are concerned about social reproach from parents of normal children and from regular teachers who get involved in integrated programs. Some special educators feel like unwanted outsiders forcing themselves on the public schools, although they might not even support mainstreaming themselves. They have apprehensions about the kind of interactions that will occur between retarded and non-retarded students and wonder if they are suited to the advocacy task that confronts them in the schools. They also worry about becoming itinerant in mainstreaming situations. A few will have to move about to different classrooms and different schools to do their jobs. They do not relish the travel or the sense of belonging nowhere.

Administrators can present another impediment to rational mainstreaming. Special education administrators have worked to build bigger and better special education programs for years; it has been an important survival skill. A few of these administrators have created special education empires. Now they are being asked to turn some of their power over to administrative officials in integrated educational environments. While many special education administrators are taking a cautious attitude about mainstreaming because they see the complexities associated with the process, others eschew it because they cannot stand to see their empires dismantled.

Most regular-school administrators have been just as uninformed about special students as regular-classroom teachers.[70] And if administrators do not have adequate information about mentally handicapped students, their leadership is bound to be haphazard—a fact that holds true not only for principals, but superintendents, school board members, and everyone else who will be making critical decisions about mainstreaming.

Mainstreaming is one of the most volatile issues associated with Public Law 94-142. On the basis of the evidence available to us, it is difficult to determine if it will work to achieve its ostensible social and academic goals. Indeed, there are some scholars who assert that proponents of mainstreaming are confused about what its goals are. Gottlieb, for example, contends that mainstreamers are more "involved with placing children in that least restrictive environment than with educating them in the least restrictive environment," the long-term goals of mainstream *education* having yet to be enunciated.[71] If, however, the tacit social, legal, and educational promises of mainstreaming can be realized, then skeptics will be quickly quieted—most of them anyway. There are a few whose opposition to mainstreaming will probably never be diminished, and they ask, "what do we hope to gain by placing handicapped youngsters back in the 'mainstream' if that mainstream is itself polluted with questions of efficacy, relevancy, and quality?"[72]

Eddying

There is another side to the least restrictive environment issue that concerns students who can neither be mainstreamed nor put in special classes successfully. Because these students do not really fit anywhere, they tend to get caught up in the eddies of education. For example, in Mountview, if a student in a special education class designed for mildly retarded (educable) students proved to be emotionally unstable or behaviorally intractable, or could not handle the academic demands of the educable class, he or she might be sent to New Morning School. Such moves were not always successful in their effects. A case in point was one New Morning student who had been ousted from an educable class in a regular school because he was a "troublemaker" and from a class for emotionally disturbed students because he was too "slow."

After the move to New Morning, this student's siblings, who used to tease him about being in a "dumbbell class," began to ridicule him for being in a "dumbbell school." Since many of his behavioral problems reportedly stemmed from the negative self-image of being in special education in the first place, the move to New Morning only further diminished his self-esteem and exacerbated hyperaggressive tendencies. The student was so embarrassed to be at the school that he refused to go on field trips with his classmates. He was, in a three-year period, moved back and forth several times between New Morning and various other schools that had classes for educable, emotionally disturbed, and learning-disabled students. While some individuals would declaim that his movement was only used to pacify classrooms in the various settings, he represented a cohort of students in our schools for whom there may be no suitable placement—no "least restrictive environment." They just go round and round.

Other Educational Rights

An eighth element of Public Law 94-142 guarantees that policies and procedures to protect confidentiality of data and information will be assured to students and their parents. According to several Mountview parents, there was a time when they were not allowed to read their children's educational files, even though it was relatively easy for nearly any professional or paraprofessional to have access to the files. With the passage of the Family Educational Rights and Privacy Act of 1974[73] and P.L. 94-142, the problems associated with student records have been essentially rectified. Parents can see the files, have them explained to them, and be assured they will not be destroyed, amended, or shown to anyone not specifically entitled to see them without parental permission. Further, parents have the right to request that informational inaccuracies be amended in the files. This element of P.L. 94-142, when used in conjunction with the Family Educational Rights and Privacy Act, is probably the component least subject to interpretive distortion.

A ninth guarantee of Public Law 94-142 is the right of all handicapped children to a free, appropriate public education, at no cost to parents or guardians. This component of the law intimates the last section of Article II of the *Declaration of Rights of Mentally Retarded Persons*, which says that "No mentally retarded person should be deprived of such services [medical care and physical restoration, education, training, habilitation, and guidance] by reasons of the costs involved."

Public Law 94-142 was based on a funding formula designed to meet the educational ideal expressed in the United Nations' Declaration. This formula works on an "excess costs" basis, the federal government helping to reimburse state and local educational providers for the extra costs involved in educating handicapped children. To ensure that states and localities would comply with P.L. 94-142, it was tied to Section 504 of the Rehabilitation Act of 1973. The effect of this tie-in was that states and localities out of compliance with P.L. 94-142 would be subject to loss of all of their federal monies. To advocates, this gave P.L. 94-142 the fiscal wallop that it needed.

Money talk is rhetoric. The very strongest of costly laws are highly assailable by the vicissitudes of economic reality. In 1982, as I write this, there is a mammoth contextual commotion in the fiscal bulwarks of federal, state, and local governments. Educational laws are always vulnerable, and there is much talk among advocates about de facto or more deliberate efforts to rescind P.L. 94-142. As the law is subjected to closer scrutiny by a wider public, some of its funding priorities are going to make certain people angry. Its highest priorities are, the reader will remember, financing the education of children who are not currently being served and who have the most severe handicaps within their disability categories. Thus, while the funds will be going where they are most needed, they will be going to provide services for mentally handicapped individuals who show the least immediate and conspicuous results. Moreover, there are some parents and advocates who have abused the spirit of the law. After years of inequities, these individuals demanded too much, too soon for some handicapped children—creating situations in which resources were so lavished on these youngsters that parents of normal children started to feel relative deprivation. Anecdotal evidence of such abuse will be generalized by foes of P.L. 94-142 in an effort to assail the law, and if it survives, it will be at the cost of many other non-mandated, but essential, services.

Numerous advocates have struck a "wait and see" posture. And what I believe they will see as budgets constrict and as they wait, is not only a reduction in educational services for retarded persons, but an intense exploitation of ablebodied retarded workers, a return to custodial institutionalization based on its purported economies of scale, and—with enough waiting—a new eugenics. We shall examine these in forthcoming chapters.

NOTES

1. United Nations General Assembly, *Declaration of the Rights of Mentally Retarded Persons,* G.A. Res. 2856, 26, U.N. GAOR Supp. 3 at 73, U.N. Doc. A/8588, 1972.

2. State of Colorado, Colorado State Legislature, Senate Bill 135, *Care and Treatment of the Developmentally Disabled,* Article 10.5, Title 27, Clause 110, 1973, p. 8

3. Ibid., Clause 111, p. 9.

4. H. N. Switzky and T. L. Miller, "The Least Restrictive Alternative," *Mental Retardation,* 16(1):1978, p. 52.

5. P. Wald, "The Legal Rights of People with Mental Disabilities in the Community: A Plea for Laissez Faire," in B. J. Ennis and P. Friedman, eds., *Legal Rights of the Mentally Handicapped,* New York: Practicing Law Institute—Mental Health Law Project, 2:1974, p. 1041.

6. O. W. Holmes, Jr., to Sir Frederick Pollock, 1920.

7. National Association for Retarded Citizens, *How to Provide for Their Future,* Arlington, Texas: The Association, NARC Insurance Committee, 1975, p. 8.

8. Ibid.

9. B. Farber, *Mental Retardation: Its Social Context and Social Consequences,* Boston: Houghton Mifflin, 1968, pp. 4–5.

10. G. Olley and G. Ramey, "Voter Participation of Retarded Citizens in the 1976 Presidential Election," *Mental Retardation,* 16(3):1978, p. 255.

11. S. A. Warren and D. C. Gardner, "Voting Knowledge of the Mildly Retarded," *Exceptional Children,* 40(3):1973, p. 216.

12. C. C. Cleland, C. Swartz, J. D. McGaven, L. Maureen, and K. R. Bell, "Voting Behavior of Institutionalized Mentally Retarded," *Mental Retardation,* 11(4):1973, pp. 31–35.

13. G. Olley and G. Ramey, p. 255.

14. C. C. Cleland et al., p. 34.

15. R. C. Scheerenberger, "Public Residential Services for the Mentally Retarded," *International Review of Research in Mental Retardation,* 9:1978, p. 200.

16. D. A. Silva, "The Use of Medication in a Residential Institution for Mentally Retarded Persons," *Mental Retardation,* 17(6):1979, p. 285.

17. K. R. Kaufman and L. Katz-Garris, "Epilepsy, Mental Retardation, and Anticonvulsant Therapy," *American Journal of Mental Deficiency,* 84:1979, p. 258.

18. National Association for Retarded Children, *Educational Services for Men-*

tally Retarded Students in the United States, Research Report no. 3, Arlington, Texas: The Association, 1971.

19. Ibid.

20. National Association for Retarded Citizens, *Monitoring the Right to Education,* Arlington, Texas: The Association, 1976, p. 2.

21. F. W. Litton, *Education of the Trainable Mentally Retarded,* St. Louis, Mo.: C. V. Mosby, 1978, p. 34.

22. National Association for Retarded Citizens, *The Parent/Professional Partnership. Book II: Classroom Programming: What Should be Taught?,* Arlington, Texas: The Association, 1976, p. 3.

23. J. Ballard and J. Zettel, "Public Law 94-142 and Section 504: What They Say About Rights and Protections," *Exceptional Children,* 44(3):1977, p. 179.

24. S. E. Waisbren, "Parents' Reactions after the Birth of a Developmentally Disabled Child," *American Journal of Mental Deficiency,* 84:1980, p. 346.

25. J. S. Cohen, *The Impact of Litigation—A Report of a Field Study. A Report to The President's Committee on Mental Retardation,* 1974, pp. 1–16.

26. National Association for Retarded Citizens, *The Parent/Professional Partnership. Book II,* p. 12.

27. S. Miller, T. Miller, and A. Repp, "Are Profoundly and Severely Retarded People Given Access to the Least Restrictive Environment?" *Mental Retardation,* 16(2):1978, p. 124.

28. Ibid.

29. Public Law 94-142, *The Education for All Handicapped Children Act,* November 29, 1975, Section 612, 5, B.

30. L. Corman and J. Gottlieb, "Mainstreaming Mentally Retarded Children: A Review of Research," *International Review of Research in Mental Retardation,* 9:1978, p. 252.

31. J. Gottlieb, "Mainstreaming: Fulfilling the Promise?" *American Journal of Mental Deficiency,* 86:1981, p. 123.

32. J. Blacher-Dixon, J. Leonard, and A. P. Turnbull, "Mainstreaming at the Early Childhood Level: Current and Future Perspectives," *Mental Retardation,* 19:1981, p. 237.

33. M. Chennault, "Improving the Social Acceptance of Unpopular Educable Mentally Retarded Pupils in Special Classes," *American Journal of Mental Deficiency,* 72:1967, pp. 455–458.

34. J. B. Sheare, "Social Acceptance of EMR Adolescents in Integrated Programs," *American Journal of Mental Deficiency,* 78:1974, pp. 678–682.

35. L. Voeltz, "Children's Attitudes Toward Handicapped Peers," *American Journal of Mental Deficiency,* 84:1980, p. 455.

36. J. E. Rynders, R. T. Johnson, D. W. Johnson, and B. Schmidt, "Producing Positive Interaction among Down Syndrome and Nonhandicapped Teenagers through Cooperative Goal Structuring," *American Journal of Mental Deficiency,* 85:1980, p. 273.

37. J. Jaffe, "Attitudes of Adolescents Toward the Mentally Retarded," *American Journal of Mental Deficiency,* 70:1966, pp. 907–912.

38. F. Christopolos and P. Renz, "A Critical Examination of Special Education

Programs," *The Journal of Special Education,* 3:1969, pp. 371–379; L. M. Dunn, "Special Education for the Mildly Retarded—Is Much of It Justifiable?" *Exceptional Children,* 35:1968, pp. 5–22.; G. O. Johnson, "Special Education for the Mentally Handicapped: A Paradox," *Exceptional Children,* 29:1962, pp. 62–69; M. S. Lilly, "Special Education: A Teapot in a Tempest," *Exceptional Children,* 37:1970, pp. 43–49; M. S. Lilly, "A Training Based Model for Special Education," *Exceptional Children,* 37:1971, pp. 745–749; R. Reger, W. Schroeder, and D. Uschold, *Special Education: Children With Learning Problems,* New York: Oxford University Press, 1968.

39. T. Apolloni, S. A. Cooke, and T. P. Cooke, "Establishing a Normal Peer As a Behavioral Model for Developmentally Delayed Toddlers," *Perceptual and Motor Skills,* 44:1977, pp. 231–241; T. P. Cooke, T. Apolloni, and S. A. Cooke, "Normal Preschool Children as Behavioral Models for Retarded Peers," *Exceptional Children,* 43(8):1977, p. 531; J. Blacher-Dixon, J. Leonard, and A. P. Turnbull, pp. 235–241.

40. J. Gottlieb, D. H. Gampel, and M. Budoff, "Classroom Behavior of Retarded Children Before and After Integration into Regular Classes," *Journal of Special Education,* 9:1975, pp. 307–315; S. L. Guskin, "Theoretical and Empirical Strategies for the Study of the Labeling of Mentally Retarded Persons," *International Review of Research in Mental Retardation,* 9:1978, p. 142; D. H. Gampel, J. Gottlieb, and R. H. Harrison, "A Comparison of the Classroom Behaviors of Special Class EMR, Integrated EMR, Low IQ, and Nonretarded Children," *American Journal of Mental Deficiency,* 79:1974, pp. 16–21; L. Corman and J. Gottlieb, p. 267.

41. M. Budoff and J. Gottlieb, "Special Class Students Mainstreamed: A Study of an Aptitude (learning potential) X Treatment Interaction," *American Journal of Mental Deficiency,* 81:1976, pp. 1–11; J. Gottlieb and M. Budoff, "Attitudes Toward School by Segregated and Integrated Retarded Children," *Proceedings of the American Psychological Association,* 1972, pp. 713–714; L. Corman and J. Gottlieb, pp. 265, 271.

42. A. W. Carroll, "The Effects of Segregated and Partially Integrated School Programs on Self Concept and Academic Achievement of Educable Mental Retardates," *Exceptional Children,* 34:1967, pp. 93–99.

43. R. Yoshida, D. L. MacMillan, and C. E. Meyers, "The Decertification of Minority Group EMR Students in California: Student Achievement and Adjustment," in R. L. Jones, ed., *Mainstreaming and the Minority Child,* Minneapolis, Minn.: Leadership Training Institution/Special Education, 1976, pp. 215–234; S. L. Guskin, p. 142; R. P. Cantrell and M. L. Cantrell, "Preventive Mainstreaming: Impact of a Supportive Services Program on Pupils," *Exceptional Children,* 42:1976, p. 381.

44. R. J. Zito and J. I. Bardon, "Achievement Motivation Among Negro Adolescents in Regular and Special Education Programs," *American Journal of Mental Deficiency,* 74:1969, pp. 20–26.

45. M. J. Fine, "Attitudes of Regular and Special Class Teachers Toward the Educable Mentally Retarded Child," *Exceptional Children,* 33:1967, pp. 429–430, cited in J. R. Shotel, R. P. Iano, and J. F. McGettigan, "Teacher Attitudes

Associated With the Integration of Handicapped Children," *Exceptional Children*, 38:1972, p. 678.

46. S. A. Warren, "What is Wrong With Mainstreaming? A Comment on Drastic Change," *Mental Retardation*, 17(6):1979, p. 301.

47. H. Goodman, J. Gottlieb, and R. H. Harrison, "Social Acceptance of EMR's Integrated Into a Nongraded Elementary School," *American Journal of Mental Deficiency*, 76:1972, pp. 412–417; J. Gottlieb and M. Budoff, "Social Acceptability of Retarded Children in Nongraded Schools Differing in Architecture," *American Journal of Mental Deficiency*, 78:1973, pp. 15–19; J. Gottlieb and J. E. Davis, "Social Acceptance of EMRs During Overt Behavioral Intersection," *American Journal of Mental Deficiency*, 78:1973, pp. 141–143; G. O. Johnson, "A Study of the Social Position of Mentally Handicapped Children in Regular Grades," *American Journal of Mental Deficiency*, 55:1950, pp. 60–89; L. Corman and J. Gottlieb, p. 271.

48. L. Corman and J. Gottlieb, p. 265; H. Goodman, J. Gottlieb, and R. H. Harrison, pp. 412–417; J. Gottlieb and M. Budoff, pp. 15–19; S. L. Guskin, p. 142.

49. S. F. Stager and R. D. Young, "Intergroup Contact and Social Outcomes for Mainstreamed EMR Adolescents," *American Journal of Mental Deficiency*, 85:1981, p. 497.

50. T. Thompson, "The Behavioral Perspective," *Hastings Center Report*, 8(3):1978, p. 29.

51. J. Gottlieb, pp. 121–122.

52. J. Gottlieb, D. H. Gampel, and H. Budoff, pp. 307–315.

53. S. A. Warren, p. 302.

54. J. S. Ray, *Behavior of Developmentally Delayed and Non-delayed Toddler-Age Children: An Ethological Study*, unpublished doctoral dissertation, George Peabody College, 1974, cited in T. P. Cooke, T. Apolloni, and S. A. Cooke, p. 531.

55. C. Devoney, M. J. Guralnick, and H. Rubin, "Integrating Handicapped and Non-Handicapped Preschool Children: Effects on Social Play," *Childhood Education*, 50:1974, pp. 360–364; M. J. Guralnick, "The Value of Integrating Handicapped and Nonhandicapped Preschool Children," *American Journal of Orthopsychiatry*, 42:1976, pp. 236–245.

56. S. F. Stager and R. D. Young, p. 500.

57. R. Childs, "Rebuttal," *Mental Retardation*, 17(6):1979, p. 306.

58. G. F. Aloia, J. A. Maxwell, and S. D. Aloia, "Influence of a Child's Race and the EMR Label on Initial Impressions of Regular-Classroom Teachers," *American Journal of Mental Deficiency*, 85:1981, p. 619.

59. D. M. Ferrara, "Attitudes of Parents of Mentally Retarded Children Toward Normalization Activities," *American Journal of Mental Deficiency*, 84:1979, p. 151.

60. R. P. Cantrell and M. L. Cantrell, p. 385; J. Blacher-Dixon, J. Leonard, and A. P. Turnbull, p. 237.

61. D. L. MacMillan, R. L. Jones, and C. E. Meyers, "Mainstreaming the Mildly Retarded: Some Questions, Cautions, and Guidelines," *Mental Retardation*,

14(1):1976, pp. 3–10; E. E. Gickling and J. T. Theobald, "Mainstreaming: Affect or Effect," *Journal of Special Education*, 9:1975, pp. 317–328; J. R. Shotel, R. P. Iano, and J. F. McGettigan, "Teacher Attitudes Associated With Integration of Handicapped Children," *Exceptional Children*, 38:1972, p. 682; W. M. Cruick-shank, J. L. Paul, and J. B. Junkala, *Misfits in the Public Schools*, Syracuse, N.Y.: Syracuse University, 1969; R. A. Rubin and B. Balow, "Learning and Behavioral Disorders: A Longitudinal Study," *Exceptional Children*, 38:1971, pp. 293–299.

62. J. R. Shotel, R. P. Iano, and J. F. McGettigan, p. 681.

63. Ibid.

64. L. Voeltz, p. 463.

65. E. E. Gickling and J. T. Theobald, pp. 317–328.

66. Ibid.

67. S. F. Shaw and T. B. Gillung, "Efficacy of a College Course for Regular Class Teachers of the Mildly Handicapped," *Mental Retardation*, 13(4):1975, p. 3; R. M. Glass and R. S. Meckler, "Preparing Elementary Teachers to Instruct Mildly Handicapped Children in Regular Classrooms: A Summer Workshop," *Exceptional Children*, 39:1972, pp. 152–156.

68. S. A. Warren, p. 302.

69. B. Blatt, "A Drastically Different Analysis," *Mental Retardation*, 17(6):1979, p. 304.

70. P. R. Jones and W. R. Wilkerson, "Preparing Special Education Admin-istrators," *Theory Into Practice* 14:1975, p. 108; T. Bullock, "An Inquiry Into the Special Education Training of Elementary School Administrators," *Exceptional Children*, 36:1970, pp. 770–771.

71. J. Gottlieb, p. 122.

72. H. W. Heller, "The Resource Room: A Mere Change or Real Opportunity for the Handicapped?" *Journal of Special Education*, 6:1972, p. 371.

73. National Association for Retarded Citizens, *The Parent/Professional Part-nership. Book I: The Right to Education: Where Are We and How Did We Get Here?*, Arlington, Texas: The Association, 1976, p. 18.

9
The Occupational World of Mentally Retarded Workers

When the handicapped individual's abilities are matched with the requirements of the job, he is no longer handicapped.
—R. T. Collins[1]

If he finds out what a crazy bastard you are, we won't get no job, but if he sees ya work before he hears ya talk, we're set.
—J. Steinbeck[2]

Article III of the *Declaration of Rights of Mentally Retarded Persons* says, "The mentally retarded person has a right to economic security and a decent standard of living. He has a right to productive work or other meaningful occupation." Generally speaking, retarded citizens are entitled to the same occupational guarantees as other U.S. citizens. A job is not considered a right. Unlike such countries as Britain and the Netherlands,[3] the United States does not set quotas for the hiring of handicapped workers. And while our beleaguered affirmative action policies do address the needs of most handicapped workers, mentally retarded persons are tacitly regarded as a special case, because intellectual deficits are seen to preclude so many occupational activities. Our laws are "bent" sometimes to accommodate the special needs of retarded workers. For example, the federal government can hire a retarded person without his having to take a civil service test, which has made it possible for thousands of mentally handicapped workers to be employed in federal offices in America.[4] Such special provisions notwithstanding, it is reported that retarded citizens are grossly underemployed.[5] Where they do have employment opportunities, there is a continuum of work settings that includes institutional labor, sheltered workshops, sheltered employment in the community in so-called work stations, and competitive community employment. Let us examine each of these.

INSTITUTIONAL LABOR

Historically, institutional labor has been one of the most legally abrasive areas of employment for mentally retarded people. In the past, many retarded persons worked in institutions as virtual slaves. This institutional peonage was litigated in the case of *Dale* v. *New York*,[6] in which a woman named Dale sued the state of New York for back wages and interest after being released from an institution where she had worked without compensation for sixteen years. The state contended that her work had been therapeutic, but the woman testified that when she did not work, her privileges were taken away, and that her work had been an implied condition of her release. The plaintiff held that her Thirteenth Amendment rights against involuntary servitude had been violated. She won her suit, and courts have begun to rectify some of the other problems in this area. For example, in *Wyatt* v. *Stickney*,[7] the court ordered payment to institutional residents who volunteer for maintenance duties in the institutions. It is being recognized legally that while work is "therapeutic," such therapy cannot be accomplished through exploitation of the worker. In Colorado, it is the law that institutionalized workers must: (1) give their work voluntarily, (2) not be required to work as a condition of their release, (3) be compensated, and (4) not have the compensation applied to offset costs of their institutionalization.[8] This, and other state laws like it, provides a legal basis for the eradication of institutional peonage. What such laws do not mandate is a sense of purpose in retarded persons' work in institutional settings. Even profoundly retarded individuals can be trained to acquire the necessary skills for performing complex jobs.[9] Thus they should not be given "busy work" in the name of creating occupational opportunities. If they can produce, they ought to produce meaningfully.

SHELTERED WORKSHOPS

The second kind of work setting for mentally retarded laborers is in sheltered workshops. Most of these workshops are private, non-profit corporations from which state governments purchase services. The clientele of a typical workshop is made up of moderately and severely retarded persons. Most of the workshops I visited were like small factories.

With institutionalized workers, a move to a sheltered workshop (and presumably to community-based residential placement) can run into unforeseen roadblocks. For example, the President's Committee on Mental Retardation reported in 1973 that certain institutional superintendents would send unqualified laborers into newly opened, community-based workshops to fill them up, while keeping the best workers in the institutions.[10] Such activities would be unlikely today, but as one moves along the continuum toward greater occupational independence, there is an increasing likelihood that good workers will have their mobility curtailed precisely because they are good workers. The directors of sheltered workshops like a good employee. The efficiency of their operations hinges on the output of the best workers, and while most of the workshops are non-profit, they must stay in the black. The directors may mouth platitudes about placing their workers "in the community," but when workshop personnel, rather than independent vocational counselors, are charged with this placement, the effort may be less than wholehearted, particularly when the relocation of the best workers is at stake. This raises the question of whether there should be a "least restrictive environment" provision for occupation as well as education.

Getting into a workshop can be just as difficult as getting out of an institution for some retarded workers. Since most workshops are private corporations, their acceptance of clients is, within certain limits, discretionary. The limits are set by the Vocational Rehabilitation Act of 1973 and amendments attached to that act in 1978.[11] These say that no agency receiving federal funds may discriminate against a handicapped person solely on the basis of the handicap. Nonetheless, if a potential workshop client is likely to be very disruptive in the work setting because of severe behavioral problems or has such profound functional limitations that the workshop staff cannot provide the continuous attention he or she needs, this would-be client is occasionally refused entrance to the workshop. States can threaten to stop purchasing services from workshops that become too elitist, but this rarely happens. If a worker is turned down for admission into one workshop program, an attempt will generally be made by vocational rehabilitation counselors and parents to find a more appropriate placement. The skills development and life enrichment programs mentioned in an earlier chapter have begun to take up some of the slack in vocational programming for more severely retarded workers who are not living in an institutional setting, but cannot get into community-based workshops. However, some mentally handicapped adults have nowhere to go during the workday and thus spend this time at home, much to the consternation of their parents, or in nursing homes.

Students who have attended schools under the aegis of P.L. 94-142 have typically had some preparation for the working world. The law requires that states spend a minimum of 10 percent of their total federal allotment of funds under the law on vocational education for the students.[12] In addition to promoting the productivity of clients, the purpose of sheltered workshops is ostensibly to continue the educational and habilitative programming begun in school. In all of the workshops I am familiar with, the productivity element is stressed: Workshop administrators work hard to land contracts, and clients are expected to produce first, habilitate later. Indeed, during "down time" in several workshops, clients arrived at the work site, but spent most of the day in the coffee lounge rather than receiving habilitative or instructional services. In the earliest stages of my observations, several rehabilitation counselors and supervisors attributed this to the low wages and consequent lack of rehabilitation training of many of their colleagues. In the last few years, as wages rose, more trained counselors had been hired at workshops in and around Mountview. Still, though, when clients were between contracts, many were idle.

The emphasis on productivity in workshop settings has led to a fair amount of thinking about how to improve it. Research has shown that mentally handicapped laborers work most efficiently in small-group situations.[13] The small-group element of the work environment is important because it produces stronger interpersonal cohesiveness, leads to more rapid socialization of new workers, and establishes a more intimate relationship between clients and supervisors.[14]

Monetary incentives also lead to significantly increased production rates for retarded workers.[15] Retarded workers in sheltered employment are usually paid on one of two bases. Most receive a piecework wage. The normal production standard for each job is generally established by having one of the workshop's non-handicapped supervisory staff perform the task in question for a specified time. This output norm becomes the basis for determining the retarded worker's wage. Thus, if the normal laborer turns out ten pieces of work in an hour for $2.20, the handicapped worker will receive $0.44 if he produces two units in an hour. There is at least one drawback to this system for the handicapped laborers. Unless the supervisors who establish production norms work *for a sustained period,* the rates they set do not act as good barometers of expected productivity for workshop clients. In the workshops with which I became familiar, the supervisors typically worked for about an hour to arrive at productivity norms. Had they done the same thing all day long for a week, their productivity norm might have been more realistic.

A few mentally retarded workers receive an hourly wage. This is rare, and such workers scarcely ever get the minimum wage. Despite the fact that the Rehabilitation Act of 1973 says that workers should receive equal pay for equal work, the Wage and Hour Office of the Department of Labor has established a special minimum wage that is approximately half of that paid to normal workers or to workers with handicaps other than mental retardation ("normal handicapped workers"). This, and the fact that numerous workshop facilities have antiquated production equipment that undermines productivity,[16] leads to substandard wages for many workshop employees.

Even those retarded laborers who are very productive and on a high wage base, relative to their peers, do not always get to enjoy the full fruits of their labors. For example, in Colorado (as of 1979), retarded workers in sheltered workshops could keep only the first $80 of their monthly earnings, the rest going back to the state to defer living expenses. Thus, while persons earning less than $80 could keep everything they made, the most productive workers—some of whom were earning upwards of $450 a month—saw little of what they earned. The $80 arrangement seemed ill conceived from the standpoint of providing work incentives. Many normal workers would have earned their $80 and rested for the duration of the month. Most of the retarded workers I knew did not mind producing extra units for no extra reward, though. Having a job was the important thing—a sentiment both virtuous and amenable to exploitation. (There have been recent changes in Colorado procedures to give workers a fairer share of their earnings.)

Because many retarded workers received so little money from what they earned, they were very limited in purchases they could make for essential personal needs. For example, retarded adults in Mountview had to pay for their own eye examinations and eyeglasses, hearing examinations and hearing aids, clothing, entertainment, transportation, laundry, over-the-counter drugs, and yearly physicals, among other things. The poorest of them were at an obvious disadvantage unless parents, friends, or government intervened. The monetary deficiencies of retarded persons go a long way in explaining why some of them are aesthetically unappealing. They may not have the money to get stylish glasses, to buy a new dress, or to remedy unsightly dental flaws.

In line with the criticism that retarded laborers do not earn enough for what they do is the objection that they are not permitted to do as much as they could to boost their earnings and enrich their work environments. Several authors have concluded that mentally retarded workers are not allowed to work up to their productive potential, either qualitatively[17] or quantitatively.[18] Gold, the most outspoken occupational advocate, holds that "more should be done to increase the level and value of the work of the retarded instead of trying to develop bigger and better reinforcement systems for simple, low paying work."[19] One implication of Gold's admonition is that just because workshop clients are retarded, it does not necessarily follow that they should do the work no one else in our society wants to do. With proper training many retarded persons can do the same jobs as non-handicapped laborers, just as productively.[20] This suggests that they should have opportunities to do these jobs and that when they do them well, they ought to be paid the prevailing rate in the mainstream market rather than the "retarded wage."

WORK STATIONS

Work stations are a third type of work environment for mentally handicapped laborers. Most of the work stations I visited were mini-workshops in separate rooms or buildings, within the confines of larger factories owned by private corporations. On one of these visits, I watched workers recycling assembly-line parts. These workers, all of whom reported that they were pleased to be working on "the outside," took a lot of pride in the work, their exactitude lending it special dignity despite its menial character. The tour guide said that the company was "pleasantly surprised" at the handicapped workers' job performance, as well it should have been. It got the best graduates of workshop training to do tedious, low-status jobs for $1.12 an hour. The tour also had some surprises.

After leaving the building that housed the work station, the tour director asked our group if we would like to see the rest of the factory. We said we would, and on our meanderings, passed through a section of the plant where military equipment was manufactured. The handicapped workers did contribute in minimal ways to this manufacture, although only one of them knew about it when I asked them. This individual had no sense of any moral subtleties involved in the work.

The example here is innocuous enough in its immediate ramifications, but it does raise the provocative issue of using mentally handicapped workers in morally questionable work environments. Such use intimates Huxley's discussion of the "Epsilons" in *Brave New World*. Taken to a malevolent extreme, unmonitored use of retarded workers could have very serious consequences for them. They could be subjected to danger or unwittingly particpate in ethically reprehensible kinds of productivity. They could be used as strikebreakers in labor disputes. And in spite of the fact that an untoward precedent was being set at the work station mentioned above, the board of directors who oversaw the employment of the handicapped workers (who had approved the program without seeing it) refused to discuss the military-equipment issue at a meeting when a concerned board member raised it. It *was* awkward. One of the directors was also a manager at the company that manufactured the equipment.

Occupational advocates often find themselves in untenable positions when circumstances they find questionable arise for retarded workers in the private sector. If someone threatens to tarnish a corporation's carefully manicured public relations image, it will simply terminate the contracts upon which the work station programs are based. Retarded workers need to work in the private sector, and when one corporation terminates a work station program, the employment of retarded workers gets a lot of "bad press" among other potential employers. The quandary suggests two things.

First, labor unions should organize mentally handicapped workers. They are the most exploitable group of laborers in our society, although it could be argued that their exploitability is precisely what gets them contracts in the first place—there being an inverse relationship between the protections afforded retarded workers and their ability to get these contracts. Not incidentally, it is not always the private sector that takes advantage of retarded workers. For example, in 1978, it became a state policy for a brief period that retarded workers in Colorado could only keep the first twenty-five dollars of their monthly earnings, rather than the first eighty dollars. The decision "came down" overnight and without consultation with retarded workers or workshop directors. It took a great deal of effort to get it reversed. The whole confrontation probably never would have happened if the handicapped workers had been organized.

Second, laws should be passed establishing ground rules for the utilization of the productive energies of mentally retarded workers. These laws ought to provide for informed consent on the part of the workers engaged in controversial forms of production and ensure that the labor practices of employers are monitored by advocacy organizations.

COMPETITIVE COMMUNITY EMPLOYMENT

The fourth type of work program for retarded laborers is unsheltered competitive employment in the community. This most closely corresponds to the basic views of the normalization principle, although finding this kind of employment is very difficult for retarded workers, even with the help of vocational counselors and special programs that reimburse employers a sizable segment of entry wages.[21] Getting a job is one of our society's most critical rites of passage, and retarded people have three strikes against them on this account because of their handicap, even if they have been very productive in other work environments. This is regrettable because, by some accounts, retarded workers can do very well in the occupational mainstream. As president of the W. T. Grant Company (which operates over a thousand variety stores across the country), Louis Lustenberger described his company's experiences with mentally handicapped workers this way: "After two years of concentrated effort in the placement of trained mentally retarded persons in our stores and offices . . . I am more than ever impressed with their ability to do a good job. . . . I recommend this employment force to any company interested in securing eager and dependable employees for jobs where turnover is steadily increasing."[22] If a mentally handicapped worker does get a competitive job on "the outside," he often faces community prejudices that erode his morale or threaten his job. For instance, two retarded men who had been trained as janitors at New Morning School were given jobs in one of Mountview's department stores. The non-handicapped janitors in the same store were incensed and threatened to quit if the retarded men were not dismissed. They were.

Retarded workers in competitive employment are sometimes regarded as threatening by non-handicapped workers. Occasionally the threat is economic; at other times, as was the case with the janitors, people feel that their intellects are impugned by being compelled to work with retarded workers, or at the same jobs.

Other problems are associated with community employment for mentally retarded workers. For example, a few get stuck in careers they did not want in the first place or no longer covet. One handicapped worker employed at a laundry in Mountview recounted his work experience in this fashion: "I'm a pretty good worker, but I'm tired of it. I worked at a laundry in_____. I worked at a laundry at_____. I worked at a laundry in_____. Phew! Boy, I've had my share of laundries. I'm still workin' in 'em."

One of the paradoxes faced by retarded workers is the expectation that they will be so glad to have a job that they will not become vocationally restive, despite the fact that they work at some of the most unstimulating, low-status jobs society has to offer. Indeed, retarded workers' heightened boredom threshold is often used as a selling point to get them employment. Witness the following statement: "Employers have begun to realize the benefits of hiring mentally retarded persons. In general, a mentally retarded individual usually proves his reliability and desire for doing his job well. In addition, he has less of a propensity toward boredom than others when he is hired for repetitious labor."[23] It is true that mentally handicapped people tend to relish continuity in their routines. It may even be true that they do not need much to stimulate them. But there is no basis in fact for assuming that retarded workers do not get bored on the job.[24] They do.

Measures can be taken to diminish the likelihood that retarded people will be stuck in boring, unrewarding jobs. They can be rated vocationally and their aptitudes ascertained in prevocational programs to find out what they are likely to do well and enjoy.[25] They can receive prevocational training that gives them some inkling of what will be available for them to do in the community and what these jobs will be like. Retarded people need to be given some choices in making their career determinations, rather than just being "placed." To that end, Gold's admonition to enrich the "level and value" of jobs for retarded persons in workshops ought to be extended to apply to competitive employment.

What do mentally handicapped workers do for a living in competitive employment situations? Becker surveyed 1,438 *mildly* retarded workers to find out.[26] Nearly 34 percent of the respondents were concentrated in hotel and restaurant occupations, working as dishwashers, bus boys, and motel maids. The latter is, by the way, a particularly important source of community employment for retarded women, since there are far fewer occupations opened to them than men in the community.[27] About 13 percent of the workers in the Becker survey were janitors; approximately 8 percent were in "retail trade occupations," such as stockboys or grocery baggers; 7 percent in "auto service occupations," acting as service station attendants, car washers, or parking lot attendants; 6 percent in construction work; and 5 percent in agricultural work, including grounds keeping or farm labor. The remainder were engaged in an array of services, ranging from laundry work to shoe shining. Despite some occupational variability here, the concentrations in certain areas are notable and would have been more striking had *moderately* retarded workers been included; their options were more limited. If one were to compile a list of jobs mildly and moderately retarded people could do and compare it with what they actually do, the potential skills would greatly outweigh the available options. The narrowness of perspective on vocational possibilities does not always come from resistant employers, either.

There has, for example, been a reluctance on the part of some vocational advocates to place mentally handicapped workers in rural job settings. This is probably a residual reaction to the wholesale institutionalization of retarded people on so-called farms during the period of the eugenic scare.[28] No one can blame vocational advocates for their aversion to anything that smacks of "out-of-sight-out-of-mind" programming. Activists such as Jacobs,[29] however, have taken the position that there are some very good rural occupations for retarded workers. For instance, he points out the advantages of gleaning (picking up crops that have been missed by mechanical harvesters). These advantages are that many retarded workers find outdoor settings quite agreeable; that costs are 50 to 80 percent below those of more traditional workshop programs;[30] and that workers can make more money gleaning than they can in most other occupations. Vocational advocates should consider following Jacobs's bold lead in diversifying occupational possibilities for mentally handicapped workers. This will take a rethinking about some old ideas concerning appropriate placement and a readiness to examine seemingly preposterous notions such as the ownership of businesses by retarded persons.

I have watched many retarded people work under a variety of conditions. Some of them are featherbedders and relatively useless to employers. Conversely, many are loyal, conscientious employees who produce, pay taxes, and approach their work with dignity and grace. It makes good economic sense to promote their production of goods rather than their consumption of services.

NOTES

1. R. T. Collins, quoted in *Give an Opportunity. Gain an Asset*, published by National Association for Retarded Citizens, Arlington, Texas: 1976.

2. J. Steinbeck, *Of Mice and Men*, New York: Bantam Books, 1937, p. 6.

3. P. Wald, "The Legal Rights of People With Mental Disabilities in the Community: A Plea for Laissez Faire," in B. J. Ennis and P. Friedman, eds., *Legal Rights of the Mentally Handicapped*, New York: Practicing Law Institute— Mental Health Law Project, 2:1974, p. 1081.

4. National Association for Retarded Citizens, *Give an Opportunity. Gain an Asset*, Arlington, Texas: The Association, 1976.

5. M. McInerney and O. C. Karan, "Federal Legislation and the Integration of Special Education and Vocational Rehabilitation," *Mental Retardation*, 19(1):1981, p. 21.

6. *Dale v. New York*, cited in *Silent Minority*, The President's Committee on Mental Retardation, Washington, D.C.: U.S. Government Printing Office, Department of Health, Education, and Welfare, 1973, pp. 16–17.

7. *Wyatt v. Stickney*, 334 F. Supp. 13141 (M.D. Ala. 1971).

8. State of Colorado, Senate Bill 135, *Care and Treatment of the Developmentally Disabled*, Article 10.5, Clause 118, p. 13.

9. J. L. Morris, A. S. Martin, and M. B. Nowak, "Job Enrichment and the Mentally Retarded," *Mental Retardation*, 19(6):1981, p. 291.

10. The President's Committee on Mental Retardation, *Silent Minority*, Washington, D.C.: U.S. Government Printing Office, Department of Health, Education, and Welfare, 1973, p. 16.

11. *Amendments to the Rehabilitation Act of 1973*, Public Law 95-602, Superintendent of Documents, 1978.

12. M. McInerney and O. C. Karan, p. 22.

13. D. Huddle, "Work Performance of Trainable Adults as Influenced by Competition, Cooperation, and Monetary Reward," *American Journal of Mental Deficiency*, 72:1967, p. 198.

14. E. S. Zaharia and A. A. Baumeister, "Technician Turnover and Absenteeism in Public Residential Facilities," *American Journal of Mental Deficiency*, 82:1978, p. 587.

15. D. Huddle, p. 211.

16. The President's Committee on Mental Retardation, p. 31.

17. J. E. Crosson, "A Technique for Programming Sheltered Workshop Environments for Training Severely Retarded Workers," *American Journal of Mental Deficiency*, 73:1969, pp. 814–818; M. M. Dolnick, "Sheltered Workshop Programs in the Netherlands," *Rehabilitation Record*, 12(2):1971, pp. 35–38; M. W. Gold, "Factors Affecting Producing by the Retarded: Base Rate," *Mental Retardation*, 11(6):1973, p. 41.

18. L. Brown, S. Johnson, E. Gadberry, and N. Fenrick, "Increasing Individual and Assembly Line Production Rates of Retarded Students," *Training School Bulletin*, 67:1971, pp. 206–212; J. Zimmerman, T. Stuckey, B. Garlick, and M. Miller, "Effects of Token Reinforcement on Productivity in Multiple Handicapped Clients in a Sheltered Workshop," *Rehabilitation Literature*, 30:1969, pp. 34–41.

19. M. W. Gold, p. 44.

20. D. Huddle, p. 211.

21. National Association for Retarded Citizens.

22. Ibid.

23. The President's Committee on Mental Retardation, p. 31.

24. K. Wehbring and C. Ogren, *Community Residences for Mentally Retarded Persons*, Arlington, Texas: National Association for Retarded Citizens, 1976, p. 24.

25. R. L. Becker, C. Schull, and K. Cambell, "Vocational Interest Evaluation of TMR Adults," *American Journal of Mental Deficiency*, 85:1981, p. 355.

26. R. L. Becker, "Job Training Placement for Retarded Youth: A Survey," *Mental Retardation*, 14(3):1976, p. 7.

27. J. Tobias, "Vocational Adjustment of Young Retarded Adults," *Mental Retardation*, 8(3):1970, p. 15.

28. M. E. Frampton and H. G. Rowell, *Education of the Handicapped*, vol. 1, Yonkers, N.Y.: World Book Co., 1938, p. 18.

29. J. W. Jacobs, "Gleaning: Sheltered Employment for Retarded Adults in Rural Areas," *Mental Retardation*, 16(2):1978, pp. 118–122.

30. Ibid., p. 121.

Lives of
...ded People:
...o Humble

...cess hearing before a parent placed a retarded ...But all of us would require a full due-process ...nt placed a retarded child in a state prison. *The question, then is whether our state institutions for the retarded are closer to prisons or weekend respite centers.*

—B. Ennis[1]

Article IV of the *Declaration of Rights of Mentally Retarded Persons* states, "The mentally retarded person has a right to live with his own family or with fosterparents, to participate in all aspects of community life, and to be provided with leisure time activities. If care in an institution becomes necessary, it should be in surroundings and under circumstances as close to normal living as possible." This article does not encompass the whole spectrum of residential services for retarded persons. As was the case with education and occupation, there is a continuum of independence in residential settings.

THE RANGE OF RESIDENTIAL SERVICES

First, and most restrictive, are the total institutions. In these, the residents' medical, educational, occupational, recreational, nutritional, and emotional needs are supposed to be addressed in a single locality that separates them from the rest of the community. Institutions vary by size, the degree of autonomy given residents, physical layout, and effectiveness in meeting habilitative needs. An institution can have a dormitory style of living, with large groups concentrated in a few buildings, or a cottage system, which allows residents to live in smaller, more intimate, settings on institutional grounds. Although they are not supposed to be, some institutions are custodial. Others try to be habilitative and work toward normalizing residents' lives, including preparing them for deinstitutionalization.

Second, there are nursing homes. The term evokes visions of elderly persons. It is true that some older mentally retarded persons live in nursing homes, but younger clients can also be found living in them, especially if they have physical disabilities that require nursing care unavailable in other residential settings.

Third on the continuum are large community-based residential facilities. Some of the these are much like total institutions set down in the middle of a community; according to detractors, they are merely mini-institutions. These facilities may allow residents quite a bit of autonomy, or very little. There are large group homes exclusively for children, or for adults only, while a few mix all ages.

Fourth, there are the small group homes. These are usually located in regular residential areas in the community and rarely have more than seven or eight residents. As a rule, they have a more homelike atmosphere than large group homes, although I have been in large group homes that were homey and small group facilities that were institutional. Like their larger counterparts, small group homes are typically age-specific in their clientele; thus there are homes for young clients and homes for adults.

Fifth is a variant of small group homes called the group foster home. Here youngsters live in groups with state-certified foster parents rather than residential counselors. These settings are not unlike other small group homes, except that a familial atmosphere tends to prevail, with residents looking at foster parents as parents and other residents as quasi-siblings.

Sixth, retarded youngsters can live with foster parents in regular family settings, either being the only child or sharing in family life with non-handicapped siblings who are the natural offspring of the foster parents. Retarded adults can also move into foster homes, which are called family-care homes or host homes. These are a relatively new concept and are said by people in the developmental disability service system to require smaller state expenditures for residents than if they live in group homes.

Seventh, retarded children and adults may reside with their own parents or other relatives. With increased daytime programming in communities, institutionalization of retarded children is much less prevalent than it once was. Most retarded youngsters live with their own parents until they reach adulthood, when they move into other facilities. A few retarded adults go on living with their parents, although this can create problems for them in adapting to new residential settings when their parents die or are no longer able to take care of them.

Finally, a few retarded adults move into supervised or unsupervised apartments of their own. Proponents of normalization, recognizing that home ownership is unlikely for retarded persons, view unsupervised apartment living as the epitome of normalized residential placement.

There are permutations of the elements along the independence continuum. Most of the variations will, however, incorporate the essential features of one of the types.

INSTITUTIONS

It would require volumes to scratch the surface of the controversies that have surrounded institutions. The earlier discussion of Willowbrook intimated many of the problems historically associated with them. In recent years, there have been several important legal decisions designed to eliminate the worst elements of institutional life.

In *Wyatt* v. *Stickney*,[2] a class action suit was brought on behalf of all involuntarily committed mentally ill and mentally retarded persons in Alabama state institutions. The plaintiffs alleged that if they were going to be locked up for the expressed purpose of treatment, they had a right to that treatment. Judge Johnson ruled, "To deprive any citizen of his or her liberty upon the altruistic theory that the confinement is for humane therapeutic reasons, and then fail to provide adequate treatment violates the fundamentals of due process."[3]

In the case of *Halderman* v. *Pennhurst*, Judge Broderick concluded the following about confinement of retarded people in the Pennhurst Center, an institution for retarded individuals in Pennsylvania: "The evidence has been 'fully marshalled' and we find that the confinement and isolation of the retarded in . . . Pennhurst is segregation in a facility that clearly is separate and not equal."[4] Although not stated specifically, in effect the *Pennhurst* ruling makes confinement in settings that are less than "the least restrictive environment" a breach of the equal protection clause of the Fourteenth Amendment.

Such legal decisions are important for institutionalized populations. For instance, *Wyatt* v. *Stickney* has been the basis of "right to treatment" suits on the state level. As of this writing, it is too early to tell if all the appeals, counterappeals, motions to modify, and the like will uphold the spirit of such decisions as *Wyatt* v. *Stickney* and the *Pennhurst* case. There are, however, earlier parallel cases that indicate that the practical effects of these decisions could turn out to be less than profoundly consequential.

Take the Willowbrook case. The reader will remember that the suit that brought the sordid conditions in that institution to light resulted in a Consent Judgment containing provisions designed to eliminate the worst ills of the facility. That was in 1972. Despite specific legal decrees, a special review panel, great expenditures of tax money, and an almost ideal outline for improvement, it was observed in 1977 by Hansen that "life has not changed significantly for most of the 5,200 plaintiffs."[5] Hansen held that it was not for want of money, knowledge, or administrative skill that the Consent Judgment had so little impact. He echoed the oft-stated notion that there are severe limitations on the creation of social change through litigation and went on to say,

> There are really no effective means for lawyers to force recalcitrant or incompetent state officials to obey a court order such as the Willowbrook Consent Judgment. The only apparent recourse for the lawyers, faced as in Willowbrook with massive noncompliance, is to seek to have state officials held in contempt. Even if the court does find them in contempt, it is limited in what it can do. It can fine state officials, taking away money which should be used to implement change.[6]

Grunberg, who had at one time been deputy commissioner of mental retardation in the New York State Department of Mental Hygiene (the chief state official responsible for the implementation of the Consent Judgment), explained the deficiencies in compliance this way: "A court can make an individual or an organization take specific remedial actions under threat of sanctions for noncompliance, but it cannot order an organization such as a bureaucracy to become 'competent' at changing a system on a grand scale within a limited time span."[7]

Getting compliance with court-ordered directives or legislation requiring institutional improvement depends on competent implementation, adequate funding, continuous monitoring, and an ability and willingness on the part of advocates to litigate non-compliance. Achieving an adequate balance of these factors is not easy. While I was in the field, many professionals conveyed the sense that institutions could never comply with habilitative laws, not because of malintent, but because the idea of institutions was a conceptual disaster.

Whether or not this is the case, some things are changing for the better with regard to institutionally based habilitative programming. Even though it is still very difficult to attract personnel to institutional settings,[8] staff-client ratios for professionals such as physicians; dentists; registered nurses; recreational, occupational, physical, and speech therapists; and psychologists are showing signs of improvement over the last two decades.[9] Regrettably, there has been a dearth of applications for paraprofessional staff positions in many institutions.[10] There is a tendency for persons who are employed by institutions to view the work as temporary, which adversely affects their motivation to become involved with clients.[11] Absenteeism and turnover rates are very high for those paraprofessionals who are already on the payroll,[12] leading to high costs for personnel replacement.[13] These problems will persist until salaries for paraprofessionals are adequate to attract a more stable work force. Despite the implication here, our society has not been excessively miserly in funding institutions during the past decade. In a national survey, Scheerenberger found a mean per diem increase per client for public residential facilities (PRFs—another name for institutions) from $24.43 in fiscal year 1973–74[14] to $60.10 in fiscal year 1978–79.[15] The problem is that money does not necessarily resolve shortcomings in institutional services. Observe, for example, the effects of increased funding on staff-client interaction.

In 1969, based on a survey of six institutions, Klaber said, "Roughly between one-third and one-half of the time of the severely retarded resident of a typical institution is spent doing nothing (not even watching television)."[16] In 1980, Reuter and her associates studied a private institution that had experienced a threefold increase in funds in three years. The researchers found that the severely and profoundly retarded residents spent 50 percent of their waking hours alone and in bed.[17] If institutions are inherently a bad idea, it makes little difference how much money we pump into them. That argument notwithstanding, careful observers such as Scheerenbeger have noted a definite "positive movement" toward institutional reform in the recent past,[18] and dein-stitutionalization has progressed with enough dispatch that institutions are becoming less of a factor in the residential continuum. In 1974, it was estimated that 3 percent of the nation's mentally retarded population lived in institutions.[19] Owing to an increase in community-based resi-dential programming and a reduced birthrate, there has been a nationwide decrease in institutional resident populations of nearly 4 percent since 1976.[20]

The makeup of institutional populations has also been changing. In 1976, 73 percent of the persons in institutions were labeled as severely and profoundly retarded.[21] This had changed to 77 percent by 1979.[22]

In addition to becoming lower functioning, the average age of in-stitutional populations has increased in recent years. Approximately 70 percent of the persons residing in institutions are above the age of twenty-one.[23] Although this may testify to community-based program-ming deficiencies for adults, it more likely illustrates the difficulties some older residents with "institutionalized personalities" have in adapt-ing to community placement during their adult years.[24] Having adjusted to institutional dependency patterns, some retarded persons simply cannot deal with the increased autonomy of non-institutional life. Transition shock[25] results from an array of problems these persons face. They must process a lot of new and incomprehensible environmental stimuli; they must adjust to differences between institutional and non-institutional values; they must make adjustments in their sleep and eating patterns; and, most importantly, they must negotiate a completely altered emotional landscape. Institutionalized retarded individuals are much more fearful and wary in social interactions with other people than are handicapped persons who do not live in institutions.[26] Thus, community-based settings frighten these people. For instance, the director of one community-based group home told me that his staff had to invent errands for newly deinstitutionalized residents just to get them to go outside the house, because of their fears of what was out there. It is little wonder a few of these individuals retreat into idealizations of the old institutions and even get homesick for them.

For the deinstitutionalized adult, serious failure to adapt to any of hundreds of new contingencies on "the outside" can result in readmission to institutions. Although general readmission rates to institutions have dropped, the readmission rates for residents from community-based intermediate care facilities have more than doubled in recent years.[27] I would speculate that many of these persons have developed institutional personalities that preclude effective community integration. They have been involved too long in what I call the protection cycle, which works this way: Retarded people are put in institutions because of arrested development. Isolation exacerbates delayed social development and also minimizes the contact non-handicapped citizens have with retarded persons, forcing normal individuals to rely on mechanisms of conventional ignorance in forming attitudes about people with mental handicaps. Where such stereotypes portray "the retarded" as dangerous, fears are aroused that lead to an intensification of the impulse toward isolation. Isolation, in turn, intensifies the qualities in retarded people upon which the fears are based, especially if the retarded individual's self-control relies solely on maintenance of the institutional regimen. Stereotypes are therefore escalated, which intensifies fear, which increases the thrust toward isolation, which makes retarded people more dependent on institutional controls, which arrests development, and so on.

The transition shock of deinstitutionalization is not always restricted to the retarded persons themselves. Their families can have adjustment difficulties as well, even at the thought of deinstitutionalization. Some parents are quite satisfied with institutional services (although it has been suggested that a few exaggerate the virtues of the institutional life[28]). There are many reasons for this satisfaction. On the most superficial level, parents may be taken in by the way institutional visits are orchestrated—these always starting with the lowest-functioning residents and gradually drifting toward the highest functioners, so the parents can see progress right before their eyes.[29] In other cases parents need to have their child out of sight, feel that the institution provides abiding security, or are reluctant to criticize available institutional services for fear that these will be curtailed. Many are afraid that if community-based residential facilities are established at the cost of threatening the existence of institutions, their children will have no place to go if the former fail.

Whatever the cause of their concern, parents can become very troubled when changes are made in their youngsters' residential placement. One investigation showed that nearly 50 percent of the families sampled experienced a release crisis attendant upon deinstitutionalization of their child or relative.[30] A few of these parents find themselves in a double bind. If the handicapped offspring returns home from the institution, there is parental concern over his potentially disruptive behavior; if he goes to live in a group facility, there is parental guilt that he did not come home.[31] And one can imagine the confusion and guilt felt by those parents who were once told institutionalization was the right thing to do with their children and are now told it was wrong.

Although the numbers indicate that deinstitutionalization has been progressing steadily, questions concerning the efficacy of actual outcomes for residents have been raised. Advocates ask if the ardor of certain "deinstitutionalizers" to get mentally handicapped clients out of public residential facilities has not caused them to be less than discriminating in where they ultimately relocated the residents.[32] For example, moving someone from a habilitatively deficient institution to a habilitatively deficient nursing home does little to promote normalization. I do not mean to imply that all nursing homes are inadequate to the needs of retarded persons. Where they are, though, deinstitutionalization is really transinstitutionalization or, as it has been less euphemistically referred to, "dumping."[33] Turnbull and Turnbull talk of the importance of there being an "obligation of equivalency" that would compel the develop mental-disability service system to provide for deinstitutionalized individuals community-based services that are "the quantitative and qualitative equivalents of services at the discharging institution."[34]

The latest hoopla about institutions illustrates how hard the old ideas about housing retarded people die. In 1978, in the case of *Wyatt* v. *Hardin*,[35] a committee of mental retardation experts attempted to explain the reasons underlying the failure of Alabama's Partlow State School to meet the treatment standards mandated in the original *Wyatt* v. *Stickney* decision. The Partlow Committee reported the following conclusions:

1. That the growth potential for a substantial number of Partlow residents is so low that training programs seem inappropriate "even for living within the sheltered environment of the institution" . . . ;

2. that persons who are not trainable should be assigned to programs for enriched daily programs . . . ;

3. that community living is a "serious injustice" for most Partlow residents who are unable to live adequately outside a highly sheltered environment such as the institution. . . .[36]

In criticizing the Partlow report, Menolascino and McGee held it to be unconscionable to terminate habilitative training for any retarded person. Further, they argued that even the lowest-functioning persons are served better in community-based environments, which are more effective and humane and less expensive than enriched institutional programs.[37]

Along with their assertion that there are some institutionalized persons who do not profit from habilitative training, the Partlow Committee members suggested channeling resources that would have been ill spent on habilitation into enriching the lives of institutionalized persons, with emphasis on such things as leisure time, work activities, exercise, and anything else that is said to give dignity to the clients' lives.[38] The primary implication here is that some sort of pleasure model should be applied on institutionalized persons who cannot be habilitated. It is understandable that the committee was too timid to call explicitly for a pleasure model. It does not "play well' from the public relations standpoint, but if we are going to give up on habilitating people, the very least that can be done is to make them feel comfortable. No apologies are necessary.

The issue of costs raised in the Partlow controversy is an old one. For years, the economies-of-scale argument used to promote the cost-effectiveness of institutional placements has been pitted against the idea that community-based services are less expensive and have a greater habilitative yield. This controversy has taken on added salience as developmental-disability budgets have become tighter, with the result that fiscal gains for community-based residences have diminished part of the resource base of institutional facilities.

Who is right in all these matters? Are there people who cannot profit from habilitative services? Are community-based facilities less dehumanizing than institutions? Is it less expensive to house all retarded people in the community than in institutions?

First, I believe that nearly anyone who has spent time with certain profoundly retarded persons has asked himself if any amount of habilitative training could be useful. Menolascino and McGee hold that it is, and they present evidence indicating the superiority of community-based residential facilities in promoting adjustment and growth for even the lowest-functioning persons.[39]

Second, there is the question of what is the most humane environment for profoundly retarded residents. The Partlow Committee says of institutional habilitative training, "To pursue a daily regimen of training with those who are not profiting from such training, and who do not participate by choice is punishing, even demeaning."[40] The assertion is true, but it does not address the issue of whether similar training in a community setting would be less demeaning to an individual. The same training in two completely different environments could have very different results.

There also tends to be a leap of faith in the Partlow Committee's conclusions—a belief that enriching the institutional environment makes the lives of residents better than force-feeding them "a daily regimen" of ostensibly useless habilitative programming. As we have seen, severely and profoundly retarded institutionalized residents spend a lot of their time doing nothing. One wonders just how much programming has, in fact, been forced on them—how many institutions actually have such daily regimens. Moreover, it has been suggested by Reuter et al. that severely and profoundly retarded children in *deinstitutionalized* environments get about four times the social interaction they get in an institutional setting.[41] How does enriching an institutional environment necessarily increase interaction time? To put it differently, does enriching institutions make them less custodial? If so, how?

Third, the issue of the costs of institutional versus community-based residential programming is a muddle. If one accepts Menolascino and McGee's figures, institutions are three times more expensive than community-based programs.[42] Other scholars say that when certain variables are considered, such as the fact that many community-based residential facilities do not provide daytime training activities and only minimal medical support services, community-based costs are comparable to those of institutions.[43] Conversely, advocates of community-based programs cite unnecessary expenditures tied to institutional settings. For example, as self-sufficient communities, institutions do not take full advantage of the parks, schools, and hospitals that already exist in the community. The duplication of these so-called generic services is often done at tremendous expense by institutions.

The most careful analysis of cost differential between community-based and institutional services indicates that costs in the different settings are much the same.[44] This raises an obvious question. If retarded persons, no matter what their degree of handicap, can get essentially the same kind and quality of services for the same price either in or out of institutions, why provide the services in institutions?

NURSING HOMES

It is more difficult to generalize about nursing homes than any other segment on the residential-service continuum. The range of types is quite broad. Although many nursing homes render appropriate and adequate habilitative and residential services to mentally retarded residents, investigators such as Brown and Guard[45] show that this is not always the case. In their examination of eight nursing homes, they concluded, "All homes fell short of the levels of patient autonomy and activity predicated for a therapeutic community."[46] Further, they said, "[Nursing] homes appear to perform more adequately in custodial and medical matters of sanitation, hygiene, and safety than in matters relating to the education, social life, and personality development of retarded persons."[47]

GROUP HOMES

Group homes, sometimes called community residential facilities (CRFs) or intermediate care facilities for the mentally retarded (ICFMRs), proliferated as a result of the deinstitutionalization movement. The number of these facilities nearly doubled between 1973 and 1977.[48] Although there are large dormitory types of CRFs, residential advocates keen on normalization prefer to see retarded persons living in smaller group residences of no more than seven or eight persons. These advocates take the position that residential facilities should never be intended for a greater number of people than is commonplace for other residences in the surrounding neighborhood. In keeping with this, it is said that group homes ought to look like regular homes, without signs and other indicators that retarded people live in them.

The seven- or eight-resident figure is generally cited because it represents the lowest number of clients that residential programmers can have in a group home and provide with adequate services, while still breaking even financially. Smaller settings do have certain economic advantages associated with the physical plant. They are usually more easily kept up to codes than larger structures and less difficult to sell when residential needs change.

Smaller residential settings also tend to provide more intimate, homelike atmospheres than larger structures. Moreover, the effectiveness of habilitative personnel is said to be enhanced when dealing with fewer clients, even if the same staff-client ratio obtains as in a larger setting.

Klaber explains the phenomenon this way: "One attendant with ten children will be more involved with them than will ten attendants with one hundred children."[49] This factor is probably one of the reasons Hemming and her associates found more staff-client interaction in CRFs than in PRFs (institutions).[50]

Obviously, it is a mistake to jump to the conclusion that smaller is always better in residential settings. The size of the facility is less important than what goes on in it in terms of programming, personnel, privacy, and protection of the property of residents.

It is also an unwarranted leap in logic to assume that community-based residential facilities are not without problems. For example, like institutions, community-based group homes have a difficult time attracting and retaining qualified staff.[51] Staff members typically "burn out" in one or two years.[52] These persons are frequently underpaid, inadequately trained, and expected to work excessive hours, sometimes without remuneration, in an atmosphere where communication along the staff hierarchy often leaves a lot to be desired.[53] As with institutions, employee turnover in CRFs is costly and leaves many retarded residents bewildered and with a continuous sense of loss, as their "friends" come and go.

Another problem community-based facilities encounter is the imposition on them of inappropriate accountability standards. Moen and Aanes contend that regulations and standards first developed for large institutions have been applied without much modification to community-based group homes.[54] The upshot of this is that compliance with transplanted standards pushes group homes to emulate institutional models of service delivery. Further, some group homes have been forced to reduce direct-care personnel resources in order to hire supplementary employees just to comply with the complex documentation standards designed for PRFs.[55]

Probably the most serious problem confronting community-based residential facilities is community resistance. Prospective neighbors can seriously impede construction and maintenance of community-based group homes. Among other things, neighbors fear declining property values, vandalism, and sexual assaults by retarded persons. Since many of these neighbors have nothing but deviant stereotypical imagery upon which to base their expectations, the concerns are understandable, but largely unfounded. For example, property values have not been shown to decline in neighborhoods with CRFs,[56] and, as we shall see, retarded people are no more likely to deviate from the law than anyone else.

Neighbor resistance is illustrated in the following quotes, which were excerpted from letters sent to the planning department considering a zoning variance for a small group foster home in a suburban area of Mountview:

- In recent months we have remodeled our home in the amount of $5,000. With the proposed Group Care Home we wonder and are in doubt that we could regain our investment in our property.
- We feel that a rural development is not the place for a care home. It is not a commercial zoning and as these people [the foster parents] are paid for their services, it qualifies as a business. We prefer to keep this neighborhood residential.
- If one business is allowed to operate here then that would be an excuse for more. Even we would reopen our business that we had in our own home before living here.
- From previous experience we also know that sound carries extremely well from the residence and that 8 active children will create a high level of noise which will carry to the surrounding property. One of the reasons that we bought our home here was the relative quiet of this area.
- As I have said we have many other reasons but I see no reason to list all of them. Only that we as property owners and residents of this neighborhood do OBJECT.

The impact of such letters can be very potent where zoning ordinances are determined by individuals unfamiliar with retarded people, as can the "lynch mob" mentality that often prevails at meetings held to discuss the establishment of these facilities.[57] I attended a number of these meetings, and the tone of opposition was desperate and vindictive. A single hysterical neighbor can amplify the inevitable anxieties that accompany the news that a group of retarded strangers is moving into the neighborhood. The board of directors of one advocacy agency located in a particularly resistant area close to Mountview told me that threats had been made against their lives, the lives of the prospective residents, and against the proposed facility itself.

Not all retarded persons make good neighbors, but most of them are carefully socialized to the role of being a good neighbor. As a result, they tend to be unobtrusive and friendly. This goes a long way in explaining why neighborhood resistance to CRFs diminishes when neighbors find out what it is really like to live by retarded people.[58] Kastner and her colleagues hold that attitudes improve in these circumstances primarily because of a "disconfirmation of expectancies"— a shattering of all the untoward stereotypes.[59]

Resistance to mentally handicapped people living in community-based group settings can be seen also in the interpretation of certain zoning ordinances. For example, "single family" ordinances have been invoked when a small group of retarded people wished to live together, although unrelated non-handicapped persons were able to live together in exactly the same neighborhoods and were considered "single house-keeping units."[60]

Zoning ordinances often push residential facilities into crowded commercial or industrial areas. I know of several nice group homes that allow residents considerable autonomy in coming and going, but because these places are located in sleazy neighborhoods, far from adequate public transportation, there is really nowhere for the residents to go.

Other impediments to the establishment and maintenance of group homes are associated with certification and licensure problems and with meeting fire and other safety regulations in older buildings.[61] In the latter case, service providers face a "Catch-22". On the one hand, they may have to buy an older building because of funding limitations. On the other, they might end up having to remodel it radically to meet modern, ever-changing code requirements. Variances on these codes are available that still protect the safety of residents, but if there is neighborhood resistance or the zoning board is sensitive to charges of intellectual blockbusting, these variances are difficult to obtain.

FOSTER HOMES

A retarded youngster living with foster parents can live either as a foster child within the bounds of a conventional family structure or in a foster group home. Living with a foster family of the first variety is not unlike living with one's natural family, although there is an instability built into the placement—a conditional belongingness.

Foster group homes are like small CRFs except that the atmosphere in them is more family oriented. The children in a foster group home have more stable, and generally deeper, relationships with foster parents than they would with the transient staffs of small group homes. They also have more of a sibling-type relationship with other foster children than would be likely with peers in a regular group home.

A lot of foster homes do have warm and accepting environments. Nonetheless, it is difficult to find foster placement for handicapped children, and although more refined systems of parent selection, training, and support are being developed, many foster placements still do not work out. For example, some foster parents agree to accept a handicapped child without very realistic understandings of the limitations placed upon him by his handicap.[62] Parents (and siblings) who are inadequately informed about mental retardation have great difficulties in meeting the handicapped youngster's needs. Incompatibilities of this kind lead to frequent placement changes[63] that can aggravate unstable elements of the retarded child's personality and further undermine the possibility of successful foster placement in the future. A succession of foster placements confuses a child, making subsequent adaptations more difficult.

There are other more sordid problems that can develop with foster care. Let us look at a couple of examples. Foster parents receive a per diem for each child under their care, usually an amount adequate to meet a youngster's basic needs. Although the money is earmarked, it is nearly impossible to monitor how foster parents spend all of it. While in the field, I heard that there were foster parents who cut corners in spending per diems by serving low-cost, marginally nutritional, meals and by clothing the children in thrift store items. A number of foster parents who were privy to the gossip of the foster-parent network told me that "the retarded child business" was not all that uncommon and that they suspected other foster parents of using "excess funds," accrued from cutting corners, for self-serving purposes. The detection of such malfeasance would require detailed audits of every expenditure made in these homes, which would be a difficult and expensive undertaking.

A particularly disturbing phenomenon that I observed was the closure of a foster group home near Mountview because the parents who operated it were purportedly abusing residents. This is probably not widespread, but retarded children are safe "game" for abusive individuals, especially if the youngsters have sensorimotor problems or convulsive disorders that can be used to explain away cuts, abrasions, and other signs of abuse. Of course, this could apply in all residential settings, not just foster homes, but the checks against it are somewhat less effective in the foster-home setting than in others along the residential continuum, precisely because the foster homes are more private.

The difficulties associated with foster care are not solely attributable to foster parents. For instance, foster children's natural parents occasionally ignore their youngsters' needs for some semblance of a stable family environment and stifle good foster parents' efforts to provide such stability. Thus, the natural parents insist upon having their children spend birthdays or other holidays with them, which foils foster parents' efforts to make their own special plans with the child for those days. Where there are no legal prohibitions against it, such well-intentioned thoughtlessness on the part of natural parents disrupts the stability of the foster-family situation and upsets the children. Some become very undone when they see their own parents after a long hiatus, all the more so if they are taken to visit their own homes and then not allowed to stay.

Despite the difficulties associated with foster care, where it works, it is a windfall for retarded children. Not only does it give them the comfort of an understanding environment, but in being part of a family, they have opportunities to interact more normally in the community than they would as a resident of an institution or other group home.

APARTMENT LIVING

A few retarded persons in Mountview had begun to move into apartments. In all of these cases, they needed the help of non-handicapped advisers. In some instances, a residential counselor actually moved into the apartment with the retarded individuals long enough to get them started. Even though the handicapped people were socially adept in sheltered environments, they usually needed extra help to figure out things such as purchasing necessities, learning new transportation routes, storing perishables, cooking, dealing with medications, working a thermostat, relating to door-to-door salesmen and religious proselytizers, and so on. When handicapped apartment dwellers had these kinds of tasks fairly well under control, the counselor moved out and thereafter only made periodic consultation visits. In other cases, residential counselors lived in close proximity to a series of apartments and were available when retarded residents needed help.

No matter what the arrangement, living in an apartment is easier said than done for retarded people. As is the case with group homes, there are problems of community resistance. Most landlords are less than enthusiastic to rent an apartment to a retarded person. Trippi and associates surveyed 100 landlords who advertised apartments for rent. Fifty-two of them said that the apartment was no longer available when they found that the prospective tenant was a retarded person, despite only moments before telling a research confederate over the telephone that it was available.[64] Forty seven of the subjects tried to make the apartment sound unattractive when told the tenant was retarded. Eight raised the rent. Twelve refused to rent because of their doubt that a retarded person could live in an apartment. Although they were told that the handicapped individual was holding a responsible job in the community, the landlords said things such as "These persons would play with matches and be likely to start fires" or "They would damage property or steal."[65]

Resistance to independent living for retarded individuals does not always come from landlords. Crnic and Pym documented extreme rises in the anxiety levels of retarded persons as the time approached for them to move into independent living situations.[66] Indeed, these anxieties led some individuals to regress behaviorally "to pre-training levels of skill development."[67]

Another problem associated with independent living is the disappointment of a failed attempt to make it on the outside. Schalock, Harper, and Carver studied sixty-nine clients who had moved into independent living environments (individual or shared apartments) in 1974. As of 1981, fifty-five of these people were still in the same or similar independent living arrangements.[68] The fourteen persons who failed did so because of "inappropriate social behavior or inadequate nutrition and home maintenance."[69] Such failures, no doubt, carry a fairly heavy burden of embarrassment.

In Mountview, the residents who failed in independent living did so because they were generally unable to manage their money or health. Nonetheless, all of them talked of the day when they could try again. The persons who were making it in their own apartments were the envy of many of their old residential friends; the apartments were objects of pride for the former and sanctuary for some of the latter who visited them.

It is notable that many retarded persons who are quite capable of moving into apartments will not do so. Anxiety contributes to this decision in some cases, but it is not the only factor at work. Several people who had demurred on the independent living idea in Mountview told me that their friends were in the group home, and they wanted to stay with them. For many of these people, the others with whom they shared residences were the closest things to families they would ever have, and they liked communal living. It was not lost on them, either, that some of their friends who had moved into apartments were lonely.[70]

I believe there is considerable projection on the part of residential advocates when they assume that independent living is necessarily the best option for every handicapped person capable of it. If a communal environment allows a resident appropriate autonomy and respects his private needs, the communal life can be very rich. As a matter of fact, one wonders if many of us without handicaps would not lead more fulfilling lives if we became part of extended families or lived communally, rather than living the private, atomized, isolated lives so characteristic of our culture.

NOTES

1. B. Ennis, quoted in The President's Committee on Mental Retardation, *Silent Minority*, Washington, D.C.: U.S. Government Printing Office, Department of Health, Education, and Welfare, 1973, p. 15.

2. *Wyatt* v. *Stickney*, 334 F. Supp. 1341 (M.D. Ala., 1971).

3. Quote from Judge Johnson, in M. J. Cohen, "The Right to Treatment," *Mental Retardation and Developmental Disabilities,* 8:1976, p. 3.

4. *Halderman* v. *Pennhurst,* discussed in National Association for Retarded Citizens, "Believed To Be A Landmark Decision," *Mental Retardation News,* 27(1):1979, p. 1.

5. C. A. Hansen, "Willowbrook," *Mental Retardation and Developmental Disabilities,* 9:1977, p. 15.

6. Ibid.

7. F. Grunberg, "Willowbrook: A View from the Top," *Mental Retardation and Developmental Disabilities,* 9:1977, p. 48.

8. R. C. Scheerenberger, "Public Residential Services for the Mentally Retarded," *International Review of Research in Mental Retardation,* 9:1978, p. 205.

9. Ibid., p. 201.

10. E. S. Zaharia and A. A. Baumeister, "Technician Turnover and Absenteeism in Public Residential Facilities," *American Journal of Mental Deficiency,* 82:1978, pp. 584–585.

11. E. S. Zaharia and A. A. Baumeister, "Technician Losses in Public Residential Facilities," *American Journal of Mental Deficiency,* 84:1979, p. 39.

12. E. S. Zaharia and A. A. Baumeister, "Technician Turnover," p. 580.

13. Ibid., p. 584.

14. R. C. Scheerenberger, p. 199.

15. R. C. Scheerenberger, "Public Residential Facilities: Status and Trends," *Mental Retardation,* 19(2):1981, p. 60.

16. M. M. Klaber, "The Retarded and Institutions for the Retarded—A Preliminary Research Report," in S. B. Sarason and J. Doris, eds., *Psychological Problems in Mental Deficiency,* New York: Harper and Row, 1969, p. 174.

17. J. Reuter, F. M. Archer, V. Dunn, and C. White, "Social Milieu of a Residential Treatment Center for Severely and Profoundly Handicapped Young Children," *American Journal of Mental Deficiency,* 84:1980, p. 371.

18. R. C. Scheerenberger, "Public Residential Facilities: Status and Trends," p. 60.

19. National Association for Retarded Citizens, *Avenues to Change: Book III: Effective Advocacy,* Arlington, Texas: The Association, 1974, p. 20.

20. R. C. Scheerenberger, "Public Residential Facilities: Status and Trends," p. 59.

21. R. C. Scheerenberger, "Public Residential Services for the Mentally Retarded," p. 191.

22. R. C. Scheerenberger, "Public Residential Facilities: Status and Trends," p. 59.

23. Ibid.

24. The President's Committee on Mental Retardation, *Mental Retardation: Trends in State Services,* Washington, D.C.: U.S. Department of Health, Education, and Welfare, 1976, p. 32.

25. T. L. Coffman and M. C. Harris, "Transition Shock and Adjustments of Mentally Retarded Persons," *Mental Retardation,* 18(1):1980, pp. 3–8.

26. E. Zigler and S. Hartner, "The Socialization of the Mentally Retarded," in D. A. Goslin, ed., *Handbook of Socialization Theory and Research,* Chicago: Rand-McNally, 1969, p. 1087.

27. R. C. Scheerenberger, "Public Residential Facilities: Status and Trends," p. 60.

28. J. E. Payne, "The Deinstitutional Backlash," *Mental Retardation,* 14:1976, p. 45.

29. J. Greenfeld, *A Place for Noah,* New York: Holt, Rinehart, and Winston, 1978, p. 29.

30. B. S. Willer, J. C. Intagliata, and A. C. Atkinson, "Deinstitutionalization as a Crisis Event for Families of Mentally Retarded Persons," *Mental Retardation,* 19(1):1981, p. 29.

31. Ibid.

32. F. J. Menolascino and J. J. McGee, "The New Institutions: Last Ditch Arguments," *Mental Retardation,* 19(5):1981, p. 218.

33. Ibid.

34. H. R. Turnbull and A. P. Turnbull, "Deinstitutionalization and the Law," *Mental Retardation,* 13:1975, p. 16.

35. *Wyatt v. Hardin,* Civil Action No. 3195-N, U.S. District Court, Middle District of Alabama, October 18, 1978.

36. F. J. Menolascino and J. J. McGee, p. 215, quoting from N. R. Ellis , D. Balla, O. Estes, J. Hollis, R. Isaacson, R. Orlando, B. E. Palk, S. A. Warren, P. S. Siegel, in *Wyatt v. Hardin,* Memorandum of Balla et al.

37. F. J. Menolascino and J. J. McGee, pp. 215–219; F. J. Menolascino and J. J. McGee, "Rejoinder to the Partlow Committee," *Mental Retardation,* 18(5): 1981, pp. 227–229.

38. N. R. Ellis, D. Balla, O. Estes, S. A. Warren, C. E. Meyers, J. Hollis, R. L. Isaacson, B. E. Palk, and S. Siegel, "Common Sense in the Habilitation of Mentally Retarded Persons: A Reply to Menolascino and McGee," *Mental Retardation,* 19(5):1981, p. 221.

39. F. J. Menolascino and J. J. McGee, "Rejoinder to the Partlow Committee," p. 228, citing J. W. Conroy, J. S. Lemanowicz, L. Sokol, and M. Pollack, "Development of Seventeen Former Pennhurst Residents Who are Now in Community Living Arrangements in Montgomery County, Pennhurst Study— Brief Report #1," Philadelphia: Temple University, October 1980.

40. N. R. Ellis et al., "Common Sense in the Habilitation of Mentally Retarded Persons," p. 222.

41. J. Reuter, F. M. Archer, V. Dunn, and C. White, p. 372.

42. F. J. Menolascino and J. J. McGee, "The New Institutions: Last Ditch Arguments," p. 219.

43. R. H. Bruininks, F. A. Hauber, and M. J. Kudla, "National Survey of Community Residential Facilities: A Profile of Facilities and Residents in 1977," *American Journal of Mental Deficiency,* 84(5):1980, p. 477.

44. J. Mayeda and F. Wai, *The Cost of Long-Term Developmental Disabilities Care,* Pomona: University of California at Los Angeles, Research Group at Pacific State Hospital, for the Office of the Assistant Secretary of Planning and Evaluation, U.S. Department of Health, Education, and Welfare, 1975.

45. J. S. Brown and K. A. Guard, "The Treatment Environment for Retarded Persons in Nursing Homes," *Mental Retardation*, 17(2):1979, pp. 77–82.

46. Ibid., p. 77.

47. Ibid., p. 81.

48. R. H. Bruininks, F. A. Hauber, and M. J. Kudla, p. 476.

49. M. M. Klaber, p. 184.

50. H. Hemming, T. Lavender, and R. Pill, "Quality of Life of Mentally Retarded Adults Transferred from Large Institutions to New Small Units," *American Journal of Mental Deficiency*, 86(2):1981, p. 166.

51. K. Wehbring and C. Ogren, *Community Residences for Mentally Retarded Persons*, Arlington, Texas: National Association for Retarded Citizens, 1976, p. 21; A. Parkes, "A Model for Psychological Consultation to Community Residences—Pressures, Problems, and Program Types," *Mental Retardation*, 16(2):1978, p. 149.

52. K. Wehbring and C. Ogren, p. 21.

53. M. J. George and A. A. Baumeister, "Employee Withdrawal and Job Satisfaction in Community Residential Facilities for Mentally Retarded Persons," *American Journal of Mental Deficiency*, 85:1981, pp. 639–647.

54. M. G. Moen and D. Aanes, "Eclipse of the Family Group Home Concept," *Mental Retardation*, 17(1):1979, p. 17.

55. Ibid., p. 18.

56. National Association for Retarded Citizens, "Study Shows Group Homes Don't Hurt Land Values," *Mental Retardation News*, 28(5):1979, last page.

57. "They Voted Thumbs Down in DeKalb County," *Mental Retardation News*, 28(5):1979, last page.

58. K. Wehbring and C. Ogren, p. 19.

59. L. S. Kastner, N. D. Reppucci, and J. J. Pezzoli, "Assessing Community Attitudes Toward Mentally Retarded Persons," *American Journal of Mental Deficiency*, 84(2):1979, p. 142.

60. The President's Committee on Mental Retardation, *Silent Minority*, Washington, D.C.: U.S. Government Printing Office, Department of Health, Education, and Welfare, 1973, p. 23.

61. A. Parkes, p. 149.

62. J. A. Browder, L. Ellis, and J. Neal, "Foster Homes: Alternatives to Institutions?" *Mental Retardation*, 12(6):1974, p. 36.

63. Ibid.

64. J. Trippi, R. Michael, A. Colas, and A. Alvarez, "Housing Discrimination Toward Mentally Retarded Persons," *Exceptional Children*, 44(6):1978, p. 433.

65. Ibid.

66. K. A. Crnic and H. A. Pym, "Training Mentally Retarded Adults in Independent Living Skills," *Mental Retardation*, 17(1):1979, p. 15.

67. Ibid.

68. R. L. Schalock, R. S. Harper, and G. Carver, "Independent Living Placement: Five Years Later," *American Journal of Mental Deficiency*, 86(2):1981, p. 171.

69. Ibid., p. 175.

70. Ibid.

11
Mentally Retarded People in the Judicial and Penal Systems: Guardianship and Due Process

Those I guard I do not love.
—W. B. Yeats[1]

Simply stated, due process will be available to those members of a community who can read, who share middle-class values, and who will aggressively assert their rights despite intimidating institutions and personnel. Since this country has a rather large number of citizens who do not and cannot meet these criteria, due process will not function under the equal protection clause of the Constitution.
—L. Katz-Garris[2]

GUARDIANSHIP

According to Article V of the *Declaration of Rights of Mentally Retarded Persons*, "The mentally retarded person has a right to a qualified guardian when this is required to protect his personal well-being and interest. No person rendering direct services to the mentally retarded should also be his guardian." The appointment of a guardian for a retarded person presupposes that he has been found incompetent to guard his own interest. The history of incompetency hearings for mentally handicapped persons has been replete with minutes-long, uncontested proceedings that were parodies of justice.[3] Judges who made the final adjudications of competency usually did not have much information about mental retardation, and still do not, for that matter.[4]

One particularly unfortunate chapter in the history of guardianship proceedings was the use of plenary (total) guardianships where they were unnecessary. Since there are degrees of retardation, it logically follows that there are degrees of incompetency, and therefore gradations of guardianship should be tailored to a ward's particular needs. However, to determine precisely those areas in which a person was incompetent, the judge had to conduct a full-scale hearing. Until the recent past, it was more expeditious just to declare a person totally incompetent and set up a plenary guardianship. This had two primary effects. First, most retarded persons who had guardians were subject to their virtually absolute control. Second, plenary guardianships had the effect of reinforcing the equation of mental retardation with total helplessness, victimizing higher-functioning people in possession of many areas of competency.

In response to a growing recognition that limited guardianships are appropriate in many cases, the idea of the conservatorship has gained legitimacy. Conservatorships do not require a declaration of total incompetency, specifying instead circumscribed areas of supervision. It is not uncommon for a retarded person to have two conservators, one to take care of personal matters and another for financial interests.[5] One of the primary responsibilities of the personal conservator is to secure the ward's progress toward greater competency, as there is no quid pro quo for taking away an individual's rights to manage his own affairs unless habilitative plans are made and adhered to. I could find no data on the performance of guardians in promoting habilitation, but my limited observations indicated that unless the ward lived with his guardian, there was minimal contact between them, the guardians becoming active only in crisis situations.

The caveat in Article V of the *Declaration of Rights of Mentally Retarded Persons* that specifies that a care provider should not be a guardian was attached primarily to prevent the surrender of retarded people's rights to institutions. Under the legal theory called *in loco parentis*, it was asserted that institutions acted in the best interests of the residents or, as the name implies, just as a parent presumably would if the handicapped person were living at home. As we have seen, this has not always been the case.

MENTAL RETARDATION AND CRIMINALITY

Article VI of the *Declaration of Rights of Mentally Retarded Persons* says, "The mentally retarded person has a right to protection from exploitation, abuse, and degrading treatment. If accused, he has a right to a fair trial with full recognition being given to his degree of responsibility." There is no need to belabor the point that exploitation, abuse, and degrading treatment are difficult to prohibit by legislation.

The section of Article VI that holds that a retarded person who is accused of a crime has a right to a fair trial is already covered in the "due process" and "equal protection under the law" guarantees of the Fourteenth Amendment. Yet retarded people have seldom fully enjoyed either guarantee when they have broken the law or been accused of doing so.

Mental retardation has a history of being equated with criminality. Goddard, the old-time eugenicist, was a spokesman for this position. He said,

> If we wish to save our teachers from the possibility of being murdered by their pupils, or our daughters from being killed by their wooers, or businessmen from being struck down by the blows of feeble-minded boys, we must be on the watch for symptoms of feeble-mindedness in our school children. When such symptoms are discovered, we must watch and guard such persons as carefully as we do cases of leprosy or any other malignant disease.[6]

Such statements have contributed to a historical cloud that still obscures the relationship between mental retardation, deviance, and criminality.

There is some dated research suggesting that, proportionate to their numbers in society, retarded persons commit more antisocial acts and a greater variety of crimes than non-handicapped people.[7] Conversely, there is a considerable body of inquiry that points to no significant correlation between mental retardation and criminality.[8] While this evidence is manifold, it is not conclusive enough to disprove unequivocally the reported relationship between mental retardation and elevated levels of criminal behavior. What is certain is that retarded individuals occasionally break the law as a direct result of their mental deficiencies.

A few retarded people have difficulty discriminating "right" from "wrong." A person who does not abstract very well may not foresee the consequences of his deviant actions and is unlikely to be deterred by the abstract threat of punishment. Retarded persons who have been socially isolated come to find their hypothetical understandings of norms on "the outside" inadequate when confronted with the subtleties of the reality. Mentally handicapped individuals with malleable personalities (as many have) are easily influenced by non-handicapped delinquent peers, and as Menolascino points out, "retarded individuals more frequently are reared in families and neighborhoods where their early and ongoing identification with delinquent models is common."[9]

Other social factors probably explain the deviant behavior of certain retarded persons. For example, since they have fewer occupational roles available to them than normal individuals, some—particularly mildly retarded persons who lose touch with the occupational or vocational rehabilitation service systems—are forced into crime to survive. Further, when retarded people whose handicaps are not very evident are subjected to societal pressures to compete occupationally, they may rebel against their frustrations in criminal ways. Such economic and competitive factors, in conjunction with *mildly* retarded persons' greater autonomy in the community, help to explain why that group has been found to be disproportionately represented in the deviant category by one research tandem.[10]

Whether retarded people commit crimes deliberately or without criminal intent, their deviant acts are almost automatically attributed to mental defects.[11] This is an epiphenomenon of what has been called "the patronization effect," which prompts non-handicapped persons to see those who are retarded as less blameworthy when they fail and less praiseworthy when they succeed.[12] As we shall see, social and legal factors are more salient features in a retarded person's offender status than his intelligence,[13] but the patronization effect raises an interesting issue. For one thing, it conflicts with a basic premise of the normalization principle, which taken to its logical conclusion promotes societal privileges for retarded persons only to the extent that they can assume corresponding responsibilities. The dilemma advocates face in this regard is whether they really want to normalize retarded persons' participation in the criminal justice system or want to seek special considerations for them based upon their intellectual limitations. It cannot be both ways. Not fully blaming retarded individuals for deviant behavior reduces their motivation to avoid such behavior in the future.[14] However, retarded people are playing the life game at a considerable disadvantage. Perhaps they should be given some special legal considerations to make it a fair contest.

DUE PROCESS

Actually, retarded people do get special considerations, just the wrong kind. For example, according to a number of New Morning School's staff, retarded children do not have the same latitude as normal youngsters when they make mistakes on "the outside." "When retarded kids get out in the community," one teacher said, "they have to act better than normal people." People watch them, and mistakes in behavior substantiate negativistic stereotypes. The problem is really more acute than this, though. When a deviation is serious enough, the retarded offender is more likely to be convicted,[15] less likely to be given probation,[16] and "will probably be incarcerated longer than the non-retarded offender."[17] And, yes, they are incarcerated, not just in institutions, but in jails and prisons.

We do not have very reliable statistics on the number of mentally retarded persons incarcerated in the United States, but the number is probably significant.[18] Brown and Courtless did the most systematic collection of data on this subject.[19] Their survey, conducted in 1963, involved all the correctional institutions in the United States. Using an IQ of 70 or below as the cutoff point for mental retardation, they found that 9.5 percent of the prisoners upon whom information was available had IQs in the retarded range, with 1.6 percent of the population having IQs below 55, thus putting these individuals in the moderately to profoundly retarded range.[20] In light of the widely accepted 3 percent prevalence figure for mental retardation, it was concluded from the 9.5 percent datum that mentally retarded people constituted a considerably greater number of incarcerated offenders than was proportionate to their numbers in the general population. In 1972, it was estimated that there were approximately 21,000 mentally retarded inmates in our nation's prisons.[21]

There were several problems with the Brown and Courtless statistics. For example, the researchers based their estimates on IQ scores derived from an array of different intelligence tests that did not lend themselves well to comparison. Further, eight out of ten inmates in the study were black or Hispanic American,[22] people for whom standard IQ tests are notoriously poor barometers of actual intelligence. Despite such problems, the Brown and Courtless study did seem to indicate that there were some persons in prison who did not belong there because of the severity of their handicaps. That this is still the case can be expected, given certain social characteristics of mentally retarded persons and quirks of the criminal justice system. What are these?

First, because they are not very smart, retarded persons are more likely than non-handicapped individuals to get caught when committing crimes.

Second, mentally handicapped individuals sometimes get blamed and ultimately imprisoned for things they have not done or have participated in only at the instigation of someone else. If a retarded person is in the immediate vicinity of some transgression, he may be accused automatically. Several New Morning School staff members recounted stories in which their students were blamed for mistakes of playmates or siblings. Edgerton describes the more extreme aspect of the phenomenon. He says, "one girl was literally left holding the bag of articles stolen by the others. A boy repeatedly wrote bad checks in his name and then turned all the money over to a gang which otherwise ignored him. Several other boys were used by a gang to steal for them."[23]

Third, when arrested, a retarded person may not be able to understand the charge, know nothing about constitutional rights to legal counsel, have no idea what an incriminating question is, and be totally oblivious to the import of the *Miranda* warnings. Of thirty-one cases of retarded offenders studied in a second important inquiry by Brown and Courtless, there was evidence of incriminating statements being made before the trial in twenty cases.[24] Also, a mentally retarded person probably will not be very eloquent in telling his side of the story and can be easily confused by interrogators.

Fourth, retarded persons are more likely to confess than normal people.[25] According to the President's Panel on Mental Retardation, "The retarded are particularly vulnerable to an atmosphere of threats and coercion, as well as to one of friendliness designed to induce confidence and cooperation."[26] If a confession will please, it will be given. One story describes this fairly well:

> A janitor confessed to the murder of a girl and her roommate and recounted facts to the police which only the murderer could have known. It was found, however, that the police subconsciously or consciously infused these facts into the purported confession. The young man was innocent.
>
> The young man's attorney discovered the level of his client's retardation. As it was noted later, his client would have confessed to the murder of Julius Caesar if the police had asked him. He was overjoyed at having his words listened to with great interest by a group of adults and men in uniform.[27]

Fifth, the competency level of an accused person who is retarded is occasionally overlooked. According to the Supreme Court's judgment in *Pate* v. *Robinson*, it is the duty of the prosecution and/or defense to raise the issue of the accused's competency if there is any suspicion in this regard.[28] In Brown and Courtless's survey of thirty-one retarded "offenders," the competency question was raised in only three cases.[29] Unless the person who has been apprehended for a crime acts in a way that coincides with justice officials' stereotypes of retarded people, his handicap can go unnoticed, or worse, ignored. For example, in interviews with trial judges, prosecutors, and defense counsel, Allen found that "evidence of retardation is rarely presented on the issue of the admissibility of a confession."[30] A few quotes from this research will illustrate some of the attitudes Allen encountered. A prosecuting attorney said, discussing a person he prosecuted who, it was later discovered, had an IQ of 57, "We all thought he was dumb, but he was a mean_____, and we were all a little afraid of him." A public defender who had had several retarded clients said, "I don't recall that any of my clients were retarded." A judge in a case in which a mentally retarded defendant had been convicted of first degree murder said, "He did appear somewhat slow, but most of these migrant farm workers are retarded to a certain extent anyway."

When defendants plead guilty or confess, the judicial process can progress so quickly that no one will spend enough time with the convicted person to notice that he is a trifle slow. And 95 percent of retarded prisoners have been reported either to confess or plead guilty.[31]

Incidentally, if the competency of the accused is not raised in the pretrial phases of a case, so that a competency hearing can be conducted, there is no guarantee that the defendant will get special consideration during the trial because of his diminished capacity. According to Tygart, "No state law in the United States has specific provisions that grant special diminished capacity status to mentally retarded offenders."[32] In some states, lawyers are not precluded from making a diminished capacity defense. As of 1981, however, mental retardation per se was not seen to be a legally extenuating circumstance in criminal actions,[33] despite this view's apparent contradiction with the Durham Rule. This rule is a part of the U.S. legal code that states that a "defendant must be held not guilty if the jury finds that his act was the product of mental disease or defect."[34]

Sixth, the inequity in the justice system for retarded people is evident at times in their procurement of inadequate legal advice. If the accused is poor or does not have a legal advocate, it is common for him to be defended by a court-appointed attorney. In Brown and Courtless's survey of thirty-one retarded defendants, only six had private counsel.[35] Overworked public defenders cannot spend much time with individual clients. If the accused has confessed, as is so common in the case of retarded people, the counselor may not question the validity of the confession.[36] Another way to avoid time-consuming trials is to plea bargain—a strategy that plays upon retarded people's susceptibility and acquiescence to suggestions.[37]

There are other problems with court-appointed attorneys and retarded defendants. Under *Dusky* v. *U.S.*, the test of competency to stand trial was based on whether the defendant had sufficient ability to consult with his attorneys and a rational and factual understanding of the proceedings against him.[38] This implies a reciprocal relationship between a defendant with diminished capacities and an attorney who typically has a limited knowledge of mental retardation. Unless the latter gets help from special legal advocates, pretrial consultations can be very difficut for counselor and client alike. Thus, some attorneys see added incentives to plea bargain the cases of retarded clients. It not only saves time, but potential embarrassment; the gambit can always be justified by saying the trial would have been too hard on the retarded person anyway . . . as well it might. There is no legal rule that requires that prosecuting attorneys wear kid gloves when they cross-examine "slow-witted" defendants. A hard-hitting examination can easily intimidate, confuse, and discredit a retarded person. With all the aforementioned factors at work, it should come as no surprise that it was once reported that mentally retarded individuals were twice as likely as normal persons to be convicted of crimes when apprehended.[39]

DOING TIME, ONE WAY OR THE OTHER

Retarded people have an especially difficult time in prison. They are targets of physical and sexual abuse, exploitation, and extortion.[40] Because they have difficulty comprehending prison rules, and thus have more violations than other inmates,[41] they are looked upon with jaundiced eyes by guards. Since parole is based upon a prisoner's comportment and likelihood of success after release, the troublesome behavior of retarded inmates, coupled with their difficulty in getting jobs on the outside, often earns them longer periods of incarceration than those of non-handicapped prisoners convicted of the same crimes.[42]

That there are mentally handicapped persons in prisons at all is a result of the shortage of reasonable sentencing alternatives available to judges. A judge usually has one of four choices when sentencing a retarded offender. First, he can do nothing. For instance, in 1977, a New Morning student went on a spree of setting off fire alarms. Not wishing to send this repeat offender to a reformatory or institution, the judge released him to the custody of his parents, who had been completely unsuccessful in curbing the boy's fascination with fire alarms. It is not uncommon for retarded people to deviate in simple ways that give them a sense of power and create a great deal of excitement. In releasing the boy, the judge did not alter the psychological conditions that led to the spree, but what alternative did he have? The boy was eventually moved to a residential facility in which he had a lot of supervision and where . . . he set off fire alarms.

Second, judges can grant probation to sentenced retarded offenders. This seems sensible and humane, but repentance and rehabilitation imply that there was criminal intent in the first place. Where there was not, and where no qualified probation officers exist, probation is more ritualistic than instrumental.

Third, a judge can sentence retarded criminals to reformatories or prisons. If incarceration of retarded persons is not to be seen as "cruel and unusual punishment," the justification for the imprisonment ought to be the habilitation and/or rehabilitation of the offender. Hence, retarded prisoners should be entitled to the same "right to treatment" as mentally handicapped persons in public residential institutions. That is not usually the case. As a rule, there are only a few retarded inmates in any single prison, so the cost benefits of trying to provide special programming for them are questionable.[43] Prisons already face enough financial problems; thus, prison officials are understandably reluctant to operate two programs—one for handicapped and one for non-handicapped inmates. This explains the paucity of special education classes in our nation's penal institutions.[44] Indeed, retarded inmates in prison programs designed for non-handicapped prisoners enjoy the ironic fate of being in the vanguard of mainstream education in the United States.

Although mentally retarded prisoners may not get special education in prison, that does not mean they do not get extraordinary educations. In their eagerness to be accepted by other inmates, retarded prisoners assume the deviant life-styles inherent in prison values with the same mechanical devotion that well-socialized retarded persons assume toward normal values on the outside. This, of course, intensifies the retarded offender's deviant proclivities, making it all the more difficult for him to get out of prison and stay out.

A fourth choice judges have is to send retarded offenders to institutions—a brand of "sentencing" that occasionally happens before the accused person ever comes to trial. For example, some retarded people accused of crimes, but not considered competent to be tried, are put in maximum-security institutions until they are able to stand trial or, in other words, until they "recover" from their retardation. This thwarts a defense against allegations; in the past, it resulted in "life sentences" without trial. The Supreme Court, in *Jackson* v. *Indiana*,[45] found such practices to be a denial of due process, and states have passed laws overturning indeterminate sentencing of retarded offenders[46] in prisons or institutions. Nonetheless, it is still possible for a retarded person to be *institutionalized* for committing a crime, either with or without the benefit of a full-scale trial, for a much longer period than had he been tried, convicted, and *imprisoned* for the same offense.

It has been suggested that the conundrum of dealing judiciously with mentally retarded offenders could be reduced if there were exceptional offenders' courts,[47] with judges specifically trained to deal with retarded persons. This is a good idea, although it might be difficult to find judges who are willing to go through the extensive training required. Moreover, it would be senseless if the penal system cannot offer judges better rehabilitative options for retarded offenders.

More data ought to be gathered on the numbers of mentally handicapped people in this nation's prisons and what they have done to get there. Such research could point the way in helping our society minimize the possibility of incarcerating incompetent people who have not committed the crimes of which they are accused, have not known they were committing a crime, have not received full due process guarantees, or have not been the beneficiaries of rehabilitiation where it is necessary and possible.

NOTES

1. W. B. Yeats, "An Irish Airman Foresees His Death," in *The Collected Poems of W. B. Yeats,* New York: Macmillan, 1919, p. 154.

2. L. Katz-Garris, "The Right to Education," *Mental Retardation and Developmental Disabilities,* 10:1978, p. 18.

3. R. Allen, E. Z. Ferster, and H. Weihofen, *Mental Impairment and Legal Incompetency,* Englewood Cliffs, N.J.: Prentice-Hall, 1968.

4. F. X. Gibbons, B. N. Gibbons, and S. M. Kassin, "Reactions to the Criminal Behavior of Mentally Retarded and Nonretarded Offenders," *American Journal of Mental Deficiency,* 86:1981, p. 235.

5. K. Martin, "Guardianship," *Mental Retardation—An Annual Review,* 3:1971, p. 23.

6. H. H. Goddard, *The Criminal Imbecile: An Analysis of Three Remarkable Murder Cases,* New York: Macmillan, 1915, p. 105.

7. R. J. Kennedy, 1948, cited in H. D. Love, *The Mentally Retarded Child and His Family,* Springfield, Ill.: Charles C. Thomas, 1973, p. 193; J. V. Morris, "Delinquent Defectives—A Group Study," *American Journal of Mental Deficiency,* 52:1948, pp. 345–369; R. C. Allen, "The Retarded Offender, Unrecognized in Court and Untreated in Prison," *Federal Probation,* 32(3):1968, p. 22.

8. A. E. MacEachron, "Mentally Retarded Offenders: Prevalence and Characteristics," *American Journal of Mental Deficiency,* 84:1979, p. 175; D. P. Biklen and S. Mlinarcik, "Criminal Justice," *Mental Retardation and Developmental Disabilities,* 10:1978, p. 176; D. Balastik, "Some Curiosities of Intellectual Level in Juvenile Delinquents," *Psychologia a Patapsychologica,* 5(1):1970, pp. 21–50; E. A. Blackhurst, "Mental Retardation and Delinquency," *The Journal of Special Education,* 2(4):1968, pp. 379–391; B. S. Brown and T. F. Courtless, *The Mentally Retarded Offender,* Washington, D.C.: The President's Commission on Law Enforcement and Administration of Justice, 1967; S. Levy, "The Role of Mental Deficiency in the Causation of Criminal Behavior," *American Journal on Mental Deficiency,* 58:1953, pp. 455–464; F. J. Menolascino, "The Mentally Retarded Offender," *Mental Retardation,* 12:1974, pp. 7–11; A. Shapiro, "Delinquent and Disturbed Behavior Within the Field of Mental Deficiency," in A. V. de Renck and R. Porter, eds., *The Mentally Abnormal Offender,* Boston: Little, Brown and Co., 1968; D. E. Silber and T. F. Courtless, "Measures of Fantasy Aggression Among Mentally Retarded Offenders," *American Journal of Mental Deficiency,* 72(6):1968, pp. 918–923.

9. F. J. Menolascino, p. 7.

10. L. Nihira and K. Nihira, "Jeopardy in Community Placement," *American Journal of Mental Deficiency,* 79:1975, p. 543.

11. E. Goffman, *Stigma: Notes on the Management of Spoiled Identity,* Englewood Cliffs, N.J.: Prentice-Hall, 1963, p. 15.

12. F. X. Gibbons, L. G. Sawin, and B. N. Gibbons, "Evaluations of Mentally

Retarded Persons: 'Sympathy' or Patronization?" *American Journal of Mental Deficiency,* 84:1979, p. 130.

13. A. E. MacEachron, p. 175.

14. F. X. Gibbons, L. G. Sawin, and B. N. Gibbons, p. 130.

15. T. Ferguson, "A Young Delinquent in His Social Setting," *Social Medicine,* 52:1952, cited in M. Foale, "The Special Difficulties of the High Grade Mental Defective Adolescent," *American Journal of Mental Deficiency,* 60:1956, p. 874; R. C. Allen, p. 25.

16. R. L. Marsh, C. M. Friel, and V. Eissler, "The Adult MR in the Criminal Justice System," *Mental Retardation,* 13(2):1975, p. 22.

17. R. C. Allen, p. 25.

18. A. E. MacEachron, p. 165.

19. B. S. Brown and T. F. Courtless, cited in D. P. Biklen and S. Mlinarcik, p. 175.

20. B. S. Brown and T. F. Courtless, "The Mentally Retarded in Penal and Correctional Institutions," *American Journal of Psychiatry,* 124(9):1968, p. 1166.

21. D. E. Haggerty, L. A. Kane, and D. K. Udall, "An Essay on the Legal Rights of the Mentally Retarded," *Family Law Quarterly,* 6:1972, p. 62.

22. R. L. Marsh, C. M. Friel, and V. Eissler, p. 22.

23. R. B. Edgerton, "A Patient Elite: Ethnography in a Hospital for the Mentally Retarded," *American Journal of Mental Deficiency,* 68:1963, p. 375.

24. B. S. Brown and T. F. Courtless, "The Mentally Retarded in Penal and Correctional Institutions," p. 1168.

25. D. E. Haggerty, L. A. Kane, and D. K. Udall, p. 62.

26. D. L. Bazelton, E. M. Boggs, H. E. Hilleboe, and W. W. Tudor, *Report of the Task Force on Law: The President's Panel on Mental Retardation,* Washington, D.C.: U.S. Government Printing Office, 1963, p. 155.

27. The President's Committee on Mental Retardation, *Silent Minority,* Washington, D.C.: U.S. Government Printing Office, Dept. of Health, Education, and Welfare, 1973, p. 19.

28. *Pate* v. *Robinson,* 383, U.S. 375 (1966).

29. B. S. Brown and T. F. Courtless, "The Mentally Retarded in Penal and Correctional Institutions," p. 1168.

30. R. C. Allen, pp. 25–26.

31. Ibid., cited in D. P. Biklen and S. Mlinarcik, p. 177.

32. C. E. Tygart, "Effects of Religiosity on Public Opinion About Legal Responsibility for Mentally Retarded Felons," *American Journal of Mental Deficiency,* 86:1982, p. 459.

33. F. X. Gibbons, B. N. Gibbons, and S. M. Kassin, p. 241.

34. Ibid., p. 235.

35. B. S. Brown and T. F. Courtless, "The Mentally Retarded in Penal and Correctional Institutions," p. 1168.

36. R. C. Allen, p. 26.

37. D. P. Biklen and S. Mlinarcik, p. 178.

38. *Dusky* v. *U.S.,* 362 U.S., 402, 805 Ct. 788, 4 L.Ed 2d 824 1960.

39. T. Ferguson, cited in M. Foale, p. 874.

40. D. P. Biklen and S. Mlinarcik, p. 179.

41. The President's Committee on Mental Retardation, p. 20.

42. D. P. Biklen and S. Mlinarcik, p. 180; The President's Committee on Mental Retardation, p. 20.

43. A. E. MacEachron, p. 175.

44. R. C. Allen, p. 23.

45. The President's Committee on Mental Retardation, pp. 19–20.

46. D. P. Biklen and S. Mlinarcik, p. 181.

47. F. J. Menolascino, p. 9; R. Allen, "Toward an Exceptional Offenders Court," *Mental Retardation*, 4:1966, pp. 3–7.

12
Sexuality, Marriage, Parenthood, and Sterilization: Affective Dimensions of the Retarded Life

In some societies, the retarded are so restricted that they are said to be denied any sexual experience. Thus, the Nyakyusa of East Africa say that "halfwits" have neither heterosexual nor homosexual intercourse . . . and the Balinese exclude the retarded along with lepers from legitimate access to any sexual activity.

—R. B. Edgerton[1]

There is an issue not enumerated in the *Declaration of Rights of Mentally Retarded Persons* that ought to have been. It is retarded people's right to lives of affection and mutuality through their adult years, which includes the issues of their sexual expression, their right to marry, and, most controversially, the possibility of their becoming parents.

SEXUALITY

Retarded people face many difficulties in finding opportunities to express their sexuality appropriately. Indeed, the question arises as to whether society, and more specifically, the developmental-disabilities service system, perceives there to be *any* kind of appropriate sexual expression for retarded persons.

In institutions, retarded residents are frequently sexually segregated, not only from each other, but from direct care personnel of the opposite sex.[2] The attitudes of institutional attendants discourage the sexual expression of residents. For example, Hall found that half the institutional personnel surveyed would punish a resident caught masturbating.[3] Mulhern's results indicated that: (1) most institutions had no guidelines covering the sexual practices of residents; (2) allowable sexual practices for residents were determined *ad hoc* by ward attendants; and (3) for the most part, these attendants enforced very prohibitive sexual norms for residents, even if they stated otherwise.[4] There is an irony in this, for even though 67 percent of the attendants in the Mulhern survey believed that the sexual frustrations of residents led to serious adjustment problems, the only forms of sexual release that received the endorsement of the majority of attendants were private masturbation and public kissing. Mulhern comments on this, "Thus, a scurry of retarded persons briefly kissing and quickly retreating to private masturbation for final fulfillment emerged as the majority's preference for dealing with the clearly recognized problem of retarded persons' sexual frustration."[5] In a more recent work, Mitchell, Doctor, and Butler found that even though staff members knew that a lot of autosexual, heterosexual, and homo-sexual activities were going on in their facilities, "a large percentage" felt that "no sexual behavior on the part of residents" was acceptable.[6]

The sexual urges of retarded residents in community-based residential facilities are also suppressed, although the role residential counselors play in this situation is difficult to discern. Saunders found that, as was the case in institutions, explicit definitions of sexual policies for residents in community-based facilities were vague or absent. However, staff members in the residences he studied "expressed a high degree of tolerance for residents' sexual behavior and expressed significant interest in assisting residents to cope responsibly with their sexual feelings."[7]

It was clear from my own experiences in residential facilities that all staff members were not so tolerant. Several told me they had personal convictions against residents experiencing their sexuality and would certainly not act as facilitants of such experiences. A few said they did not want to get involved or did not want to complicate their jobs by helping to activate all the interpersonal dynamics that accompany the sexual expressions of residents—jealousies, heartbreaks, lovers' quarrels, and the like. Others were concerned that non-permissive parents or residential directors would get angry at them if they were on duty and "something happened."

It is difficult to generalize about the permissiveness of residential directors in allowing their clients to express sexual feelings with each other. There is evidence that staff members in group homes have more tolerance of sexual behavior by retarded residents than administrators have.[8] One residential director explained his reticence on the matter this way, "The sexual issue is important to residents, but I hate to open the door to it. It's better if they just don't do anything at all. If just one resident goes out of this place and does anything sexually ques-tionable, the whole place could be closed up."[9] All residential directors do not share this view. For example, one said, "I don't know what other directors do because we don't communicate much about it, but I try to encourage my night shift to be very liberal." Another residential director turned the sexual facilitation issue back on residential staff: "Many staff get violently upset when they see residents masturbating. Sometimes they are just like parents who shake a child when he gets out in the street. They are not geared for it, and when they realize what they have done, they get embarrassed, even the best staff."

Parents often play important roles in impeding the sexual expression of *adult* offspring in residential settings by putting intense pressure on directors and staff to ensure that sex is curtailed. One residential director said, "I suggested a co-ed floor at [names facility]. One parent insisted that if her daughter was to live on it, all the men had to have a vasectomy." Another director said, "Some parents yank residents out of the setting even when they find a sex education program is going on. You can imagine how unglued they get if they find there's been sexual activity." And they do find out, according to a third director: "Parents find out about their kids' [21 years old and above] sexuality in residences. The grapevine is amazing. Sometimes they grill their kids' roommates."

One of the primary parental concerns about the sex lives of their sons and daughters is fear of pregnancy, which is not always without foundation. Having to care for a child puts a severe burden on retarded individuals,[10] and when they cannot take care of the youngster, their own parents usually end up doing it.[11]

Parental fears of pregnancy are apocryphal in some cases. For example, I knew of one mother who seemed to be preoccupied with the pregnancy issue despite the fact her retarded daughter had been sterilized. Conversely, other parents are so genuinely frightened about pregnancy that, even though they find homosexuality reprehensible, for their offspring they prefer homosexuality rather than heterosexuality in conjunction with closely monitored birth control. They want to take no chances.

Parents also fear that permissive sexual atmospheres increase the probability that their sons and daughters will be sexually exploited. Such exploitation is not unknown, but is probably more widespread outside the confines of residential facilities. For example, very passive retarded adolescents make ideal victims for sexual assaults,[12] which occasionally occur at the hands of non-handicapped offenders on "the outside." If one examines the files of retarded persons, it is not uncommon to run across reports of sexual victimization or exploitation. What these files almost invariably fail to report is whether the retarded person was really being exploited or just cooperating in an act that he or she enjoyed very much, and perhaps initiated.

I recall one incident in this regard that occurred while I was in the field. I had taken a man new to the service bureaucracy to visit a small group home. He was going to be making a number of high-level decisions on behalf of retarded people and thought he ought to meet some. We met all the residents of the home, and as we were sitting in the living room talking, one little girl plopped herself in the man's lap and put her arms around him. Her affection was somewhat provocative, but the official was being very careful not to appear too standoffish to her. As it turned out, she was sixteen (just small and young looking for her age) and was really "coming on" to the man, as one of the directors of the home later told me. I suppose the issue of who exploited whom could have been the subject of debate if the encounter had happened under less-sheltered circumstances and had led to allegations.

Another case of pseudo exploitation would be that of the retarded person who, having met with constant failure in life, turns to sex as the only device he or she has of being "accepted" by non-handicapped peers. To the observer, such acceptance is not real and is blatantly exploitative, but it may feel real and thus seem a fair exchange to the retarded person.

CAUSES AND CONSEQUENCES OF SUPPRESSED SEXUALITY

As we have seen, the suppression of retarded persons' sexuality was articulated by the early eugenicists, culminating in the historic *Buck* v. *Bell* decision. The effects of this are still with us, resulting in the stereotypical view held by a few people that retarded persons are "oversexed," maniacal in their sexual urges, and dangerous—especially to children. There is no evidence to support the claim that retarded persons are child molesters.[13] Generally speaking, the sexual offenses of retarded individuals are disproportionately low relative to those of non-handicapped people in society[14] and typically restricted to deviant acts such as voyeurism, exhibitionism, or public masturbation. Indeed, the infrequency of retarded people's sexual offenses bespeaks a remarkable sense of self-control on their part, given the power of the sexual instincts that are suppressed. There is no question that mentally handicapped persons do occasionally engage in serious sexual offenses, but those cases cannot be generalized to the whole retarded population and should not be sensationalized, as they sometimes are.

Retarded persons face a dual stereotype regarding their sexual proclivities that further confuses social attitudes. While the sex-maniac stereotype is one component of retarded persons' sexual suppression, another errant view with similar consequences is that they have no sexual interests at all.[15] This position is intimated in a comment made by the director of a residential facility: "Most retarded children are lovingly responsive and enjoy the opposite sex, but usually they can be made happy by companionship, dancing, and parties so that they do not feel any real lack. Like the child, he is easily distracted."[16] It is true that many severely and profoundly retarded people are permanently retarded in their sexual development.[17] Yet, most moderately and mildly retarded adolescents begin puberty according to normal developmental timetables and have sex drives comparable to their peers.[18]

Parents sometimes repress the recognition of this maturation by acting as though the sexual needs of their retarded sons and daughters will go away if these needs are ignored. Hall reported that "many parents relied on their child to ask questions regarding sexual topics; when questions did not come, this was taken to reflect little interest in sexuality."[19] This view is facilitated by the eternal child stereotype, which can be conveniently applied, for a time at least, to the youngster's body as well as his mind. Even seasoned special educators slip up from time to time and call retarded adults "kids."

Other parents recognize their youngsters' sexual needs are growing, but avoid discussing these for fear of stimulating sexual experimentation—a concern shared by some special educators. One New Morning staff member said, "Too much information leads to too much curiosity," while a colleague of hers described another of the by-products of sex education this way: "More romances develop; but along with this, there is more competition, more jealousy. I'm not sure that that is necessarily desirable." A residential director, in commenting on some of his staff, said, "They put questions about sex off with roundabout answers. They can always justify it by saying other things are more important than sex" and ought to be attended to first.

Not *all* parents of retarded children are opposed to sex education for their youngsters. In fact, it has been shown that, as a group, parents of mentally handicapped sons and daughters have more concern for, and are more willing to participate in and promote, sex education programs than parents of non-handicapped children.[20] Such support also is the case with special educators and residential personnel. For instance, most of New Morning School's staff were enthusiastic about its sex education program, and the vast majority of residential personnel favor sex education in their facilities.[21] The need for such education is obvious.

Although many retarded people know more about sex than they let on,[22] in the absence of sensitive sex education programs, they must rely upon what knowledge they get from magazines, films, and peers who are not particularly well informed themselves. If they are not taught that they have certain responsibilities attendant upon their sexuality, retarded individuals may pick up just enough information about sex to get into some sex-related trouble.

If ignorance leads to sexual irresponsibility, it does not necessarily follow that informed, sexually responsible attitudes by retarded people will lead to sexual opportunities. One of the most serious problems associated with the sexual education of mentally retarded persons is the vacuous hope it inspires in the trainees. On the one hand, they are taught what to do sexually; on the other, they have virtually no outlets for their knowledge. As one research team put it, "We found that all individuals in our study group were over-educated but under-experienced about sex, and that education had apparently been used as an excuse for ignoring their sexual development."[23]

Thus, even those retarded adults who are willing to exercise discretion in their sexual activities often are prevented from making love. Those who are must become confused, then embittered, if they have worked to acquire a high degree of sexual responsibility and then are denied the rights associated with that responsibility because of prohibitive oversupervision, lack of privacy, and constrained mobility. A sex educator described the problem this way: "All we give them is the image of the real thing . . . I feel shackled as a sex educator. I'd like to be able to let the kids know that someday they'll be getting away from home and will be able to have sex. I could never say that though. I'd lose my job."

At one progressive school in which I observed, a well-established sex education program was discontinued immediately when a parent became upset because two twenty-year-old students had a "sexual encounter." There was no intercourse, and the woman involved had been sterilized. Within the constraints they faced, the couple, who had no car and were not allowed to date, were being quite discreet. So much for sex education.

The contradiction between sexual responsibility and sexual opportunity retarded people confront is only one frustrating dimension of the confusing or "double messages" they get about sex. Consider the retarded child who lives in a normal neighborhood where he has been provisionally accepted by other children and their parents until he begins to mature physically, then suddenly becomes taboo as a playmate.

The sexual frustrations of mentally handicapped people are exacerbated by the surfeit of sexually charged messages that permeate our culture. Because retarded persons do not abstract very well, some of them take the superabundance of sexual stimulation in the social environment very literally, which can create problems. The director of a residential facility addressed the issue this way: "Retarded people are imitative.

In the community, they see sex everywhere. Yet at home, or in residential settings, they get neutral or negative views of sex. So they are getting double messages and don't know what to do."

Such double messages are commonplace. For instance, retarded persons see non-handicapped people touching each other all the time. When a retarded individual touches someone who is not handicapped, he is often rebuffed; indeed, sometimes it is construed as an attack. As the director of one residential facility stated it, "They see sex everywhere and assume maybe it's okay after all, and then they get in trouble. Our poor male residents get out on the streets and "come on" to somebody and get rejected and frustrated, and some of them become too direct. . . ." The problem is not just peculiar to men either. Sexual behavior of retarded women over the age of fourteen is the greatest single cause of their institutionalization.[24]

What we come to see is that the sexual suppression of retarded persons precipitates the very kind of social deviance it is designed to prevent. This is apparent in the account of a special educator: "Some of my male students walk around with an erection all day, but get no release because they don't know what to do and wouldn't have any place to do it if they did. If they had some release, maybe they could get to work and learn something."

Masturbation would relieve some of the tensions here, but a few retarded persons have to be taught what to do, and there is not always an abundance of non-handicapped personnel eager to help. The results of neglect on this account can be dangerous, though. One special educator with extensive experience in institutional settings said, "A lot of retarded women, you know, hurt themselves with bottles and sticks . . . stuff like that."

Besides self-pleasuring, homosexuality is the only outlet for retarded individuals living in sexually segregated environments. This victimizes those persons with heterosexual preferences, leading some of them to feel a lot of guilt. Indeed, the whole constellation of sexual oppression retarded people face leads to guilt surrounding sex. A residential director said, "Many residents get very uncomfortable when I talk about sex even though they know they can trust me. Some say, 'I didn't do it,' any time the subject is brought up." A professional sex therapist added the following, "They get so browbeaten they won't point to a penis on a picture when identifying a man."

Other manifestations of sexual deviance by sexually oppressed retarded persons are reported. For instance, prohibition of sexual activities under "normal" circumstances results in some retarded people engaging in tearoomlike sexual encounters of both homosexual and heterosexual varieties. A special educator told a story of how a large group of retarded people who lived in a closely supervised and sexually prohibitive residential facility worked it out so that members of their group, usually couples, could have sex on their weekly visits to the movie theater. The teacher said, "They were very well organized, taking turns watching out for each other so that no one would get caught." She went on, "You just can't stifle sex. You see how strong the impulse is when you consider these 'kids' are normally very compliant in other things."

The sexual needs of retarded adults are not suppressed in all residential settings. In one large facility I visited, this was how sexual facilitation worked: Sexual liaisons were discouraged in residents' rooms to avoid inconveniencing roommates, but there was a special "privacy room" for residents. There was only one key to the room, so persons who wanted to use it while it was occupied had to wait. If individuals who had not been sterilized wished to use the room, they were counseled about contraception, and it was provided if they so desired—although it was tacitly assumed that the key would be impossible to obtain unless there was no chance of conception. The system, I was told, worked quite nicely for residents, who seemed not to be embarrassed by the unusual circumstances. It was all any of them had ever known, and they were glad to have a place to make love without feeling and acting like outlaws. While privacy rooms are not the ideal, they are a sensible step in normalizing the sexual lives of retarded persons and reducing deviance born of suppression. As one sex educator saw it, "MRs are creatures of habit. If they have a place to have sex which is appropriate, they will make love there habitually."

The whole issue of the prohibitions on sexuality for retarded persons runs deeper than we have seen in examining parental and professional fears and eugenic specters. The heart of the issue has to do with four sociological factors.

First, retarded people are not seen by those who are normal as having the ability to give reciprocal returns in sexual exchange. This is part of the reason most non-handicapped individuals would not consider making love with a retarded person. Such a viewpoint overlooks the adequacy of sexual exchange value mentally handicapped people have for each other and is an obstacle to one of the few activities wherein retarded persons can achieve normal levels of personal satisfaction.

Second, retarded persons do not accord with our images of the kind of people who should be allowed to make love. A special educator stated it this way: "We have certain images about who can make love. In books and on TV, the people are always dashing and beautiful. You never see two ugly people making love, and mental retardation is associated with ugliness. We grew up seeing only perfect people making love." As we have seen, this problem is compounded by societal expectations that retarded persons cannot be physically attractive—let alone sexy. Well, they are sexy to each other.

Third, retarded people are often seen as buffoons in the sexual rituals of our society. A residential director explained it by saying, "Sexual rituals are supposed to be played skillfully and the MR brings flaws to the ritual." Sex rituals are one of the heavily "scripted" activities of our society, and retarded persons cannot learn the lines unless they are allowed to rehearse.

Fourth, retarded sexuality is viewed as somehow being subhuman. A residential director said, "Retarded people's sexuality is seen as animal behavior because they aren't seen to have human intelligence."

Retarded persons can engage in responsible sexual expression. As a matter of fact, their intense socialization on this matter probably makes many of them more responsible than some of their non-handicapped counterparts. When we erect barriers to a responsible retarded person's sexual expression, this bespeaks a hauteur normal society has toward marginal beings.

MARRIAGE

Greater acceptance of marriage for mentally retarded persons could legitimize their sexual expression, but it has never been easy for them to get social permission to marry. The Mental Deficiency Act passed by Congress in 1913 made it illegal for retarded people to marry,[25] and by 1972, marriage was still prohibited for them in one-fourth of the states.[26] Currently, the general rule governing the marital rights of a mentally retarded person rests on his or her ability to understand the special nature of the contract of marriage and the duties and responsibilities it entails.[27] This is taken on a case-by-case basis and is subject to rather broad interpretations.

Whatever the interpretation, retarded persons rarely marry,[28] and special obstacles to success confront those who do. Mentally handicapped couples have lower than average incomes. If they were institutionalized as children, they have had no family model, and they often fail to have the support of their own families in the marriage.[29] They lack foresight and planning abilities, and some of them have very unusual problem-solving skills. Andron and Sturm report an event that gives us some insight into this phenomenon: "Of note is one young wife's solution for a marital problem. She came home one day to find her husband in bed with a friend. She announced that she wanted to move up into the hills, near his parents, and change their phone number so that the friend could not find them."[30]

Such problems notwithstanding, several studies indicate that marriage has salutary stabilizing influences on retarded persons.[31] The most frequent reason retarded individuals give for the satisfaction they derive from their marriages is companionship,[32] which contrasts with the social isolation they experienced before marrying. Many become more self-accepting than they were before the marriage.[33] There are also practical benefits. For example, one partner can help another who might have seizures, aid a spouse in learning to handle money, and pitch in with cooking and housekeeping chores (a much more egalitarian division of household labor than is considered traditional has been observed with retarded couples[34]). Social workers have also reported that retarded partners who had drinking problems reduced them significantly after marrying and that spouses with poor verbal abilities improved these greatly in the marital relationship.[35] Although a selection factor may be responsible, there is also a significant association between successful marriage and vocational adjustment of mentally handicapped people.[36] Given these and other factors, it is little wonder that several studies have found that the majority of retarded persons express satisfaction with their marriages.[37]

If people with mental handicaps are denied the right to marry, they not only miss out on the practical and psychological lifts that can accrue, but they are consigned either to celibacy or extramarital sexual encounters, which are viewed in some quarters as another sign of their overall deviancy. One wonders whether the chief proponents of the family in our society will support the profamily philosophy as it relates to retarded citizens.

PROCREATION

A great deal of opposition to sexual expression and marriage for retarded people is generated by the eugenic fear that "defectives" will beget more inferior babies and thus genetically contaminate society. There is no area of mental retardation that has been so thoroughly studied as the probability of retarded persons giving birth to retarded children, and none quite so inconclusive in its findings.

In 1911, Charles B. Davenport declared, "In view of the certainty that all of the children of two feebleminded parents will be defective, how great is the folly, yes, the crime of letting two such persons marry."[38] Hall presented the findings of thirty-one inquiries on the likelihood of retarded parents having retarded offspring—the figures ranging from 2.5 percent of all children of retarded persons being retarded, to 83 percent.[39] The most comprehensive of these studies was done by Reed and Reed.[40] Using a sample of 7,773 children, they concluded that retarded parents produce approximately 17 percent of all mentally retarded children.[41]

In the case of *Eisenstadt* v. *Baird*, procreative rights were found to be fundamental in our society,[42] but the increased risk that mentally retarded parents will produce children with mental handicaps brings into question the rights of many people besides the would-be parents. There are the grandparents, who might have to care for the child should the retarded parents find the task overwhelming. If the child is likely to become a ward of the state, the rights of everyone who pays taxes are threatened. Most importantly, though, there are the rights of the child himself. Is he or she entitled to live in an environment free from the limitations and hardships typical of households headed by retarded parents? To answer that we must first answer another question: what kind of parents do mentally retarded people make?

Vitello holds that "social science data shows an absence of positive correlation between IQ scores and parental capabilities."[43] This assertion flies in the face of common sense and does not accord with Davis's contention that people with IQs less than 55 or 60 "are seldom able to provide proper care of children."[44] Mickelson concluded that 58 percent of the mentally handicapped parents in his survey were either "unsatisfactory" or "inadequate."[45] Scally held that 62 percent of the children of retarded parents were not being cared for "adequately" in their homes.[46] Peck and Stephens found four out of five retarded fathers in their survey were overwhelmed by the responsibilities of parenthood.[47] Of course, the determination of what "satisfactory" or "adequate" means in these studies is very subjective, and the courts have been rather vague in defining what constitutes a "proper environment" for children.[48] Such ambiguities notwithstanding, there are many specific problems associated with parenting for mentally retarded adults: They have difficulty in deferring gratifications for the long-term benefit of the child, they frequently encounter economic problems, and they are likely to provide a lower level of intellectual stimulation for their child than most normal parents. And there is a social stigma automatically proxied to the children of retarded parents.

It could be argued that a lot of non-handicapped parents do a terrible job of raising their youngsters; ergo, the possibility of that with retarded people should not forestall their procreative rights. The logic here is too simplistic, though; for while the basic premise is true, the risks to the children of retarded parents are endemically greater.

Of course, adoptive parents can be found for the offspring of retarded persons who cannot take care of them, and evidence indicates that "in above average adoptive homes," adopted children whose natural mothers were retarded "have an average chance of normality, subnormality, or superiority."[49] Nevertheless, the stability of the adopted child's life is disrupted, to say nothing of the lives of his natural parents and those of the adoptive parents, who still have to endure the discomfiture of their gamble on a child whose genetic endowment may eventually lead to developmental problems.

One thing that is important to note in this discussion of procreation is the fact that not all retarded persons can have or want to have children. For example, "only some 23 affected Down's Syndrome females have been reported, in the world medical literature, to have had children, and no fully affected Down's Syndrome male is known to have been a father."[50] Further, retarded persons can be realistic about parenting. Andron and Sturm found that several of the handicapped people in their small sample said they would be "nervous" about caring for a child, and some recognized that the parenting responsibilities for their children would probably fall to their own parents, something the retarded persons said they would not want to happen.[51] One women involved in another inquiry said, "What if we had kids and they weren't retarded and they came home from school and asked us something we couldn't answer? What would they think of us then?"[52] Sometimes the reaction is more severe. A retarded woman, in commenting about another who had become pregnant, said, "What chance will her baby have anyway, with her being retarded herself, so I hope she and the baby both die!"[53]

Conversely, there are mentally retarded persons who do want to have children. Gan and associates found that 61 percent of the *mildly* retarded persons they surveyed "believed they should have children."[54] One retarded man in another study said, "That's what regular people do. . . . They get married and have children and a house. That's what we wanted too."[55] Mentally handicapped people who are trained to emulate the activities of normal persons are understandably perplexed when they are enjoined from having the experiences that reflect conformity with community norms.

I have yet to meet a professional in the field of mental retardation who promoted the procreative rights of retarded persons. I have, however, met some who were nonplussed at the way the reproductive issue was used to thwart sexual and marital opportunities for people with mental handicaps. I do not believe that retarded people should have children, but I do think it is very important for them to be around children to enrich their own lives, and perhaps those of the children. Yet once a retarded person leaves school, he is likely to enter a residential and occupational milieu in which he will be with children infrequently. Many retarded people fill this void by interacting with child surrogates; for example, some collect dolls with whom they form intense, almost filial, relationships. Most like pets and are very affectionate with gentle animals. Residential facilities usually do not allow pets, however, which is sad and a case in which bureaucratic considerations should be subordinated to humanistic concerns.

STERILIZATION

There is an interesting history of court cases involving involuntary sterilization of mentally retarded persons, starting in 1927 with the oft-mentioned *Buck* v. *Bell* case and including *Skinner* v. *Oklahoma* (1942)[56] and *Cook* v. *The State of Oregon* (1972).[57] To understand modern sterilization laws regarding handicapped persons, one should read the decisions in these cases; however, the first real breakthrough in protecting the rights of retarded individuals against arbitrary involuntary sterilization came in 1974 in the case of *Wyatt* v. *Aderholt*.[58] Here, Judge Johnson curtailed the legal guardian's (parents in many cases) participation in the sterilization decision, saying that no third party ought to have the right to give consent for sterilization on behalf of a retarded person. In essence, this prohibited involuntary sterilizations,[59] putting the decision-making power in the hands of the individual being sterilized. There have been cases subsequent to *Wyatt* v. *Aderholt* in which the constitutionality of involuntary sterilization was upheld under very strict limitations,[60] but this has been under the same constraints regarding the participation of guardians that were established in the *Wyatt* v. *Aderholt* case.

The issue of excluding third parties from participation in sterilization decisions goes deeper than constitutional concerns relating to personal autonomy. The matter can be brought into better focus by looking at the results of a couple of studies. In one of these, Bass found that 60 percent of a sample of 132 parents of retarded offspring favored sterilization of their children,[61] while Whitcraft and Jones discovered that 85.5 percent of 652 parents surveyed favored or strongly favored sterilization, albeit voluntary, for retarded offspring.[62] Needless to say, parental participation in the sterilization process might not prove very judicious when it relates to their own children.

The prohibition of involuntary sterilizations inherent in *Wyatt* v. *Aderholt* was important for reasons that go beyond the procreative issue. In the past, it was held by eugenicists that retarded persons looked upon sterilization "in a remarkably matter-of-fact way."[63] Not so. In a survey of retarded people, most of whom had been involuntarily sterilized, Sabagh and Edgerton found that 62 percent disapproved of the sterilization.[64] These people had many reasons for objecting to the operation. First, it can have adverse psychological effects on them. Some recalled "the operation vividly and in many cases saw it as a humiliating process."[65] Second, sterilization has been equated with punishment in the minds of some retarded persons. One woman said, "I still don't know why they did that surgery to me. The sterilization wasn't for punishment was it? Was it because there was something wrong with my mind?"[66] Roos says that sterilization that is equated with punishment is sometimes seen as being tantamount to castration in the minds of retarded people.[67] A man who had been sterilized said, "It makes a man weak, and what woman would want a weak man?"[68] Third, retarded people have been told on occasion that the operations were appendectomies or were for some reason other than sterilization.[69] If they discovered this not to be the case, they felt betrayed and became unwilling to trust service providers and other professionals in the future.

The maleffects of involuntary sterilization make *voluntary* sterilization a progressive and humane step in the rights of mentally retarded persons. Under the guidelines of voluntary sterilization, mentally handicapped persons can choose to be sterilized if they give an informed consent. For example, one informed consent law says,

> Consent shall always be preceded by the following: (I) A fair explanation of the procedure to be followed, including an identification of those which are experimental; (II) A description of the attendant discomfort and risks; (III) A description of the benefits to be expected; (IV) A disclosure of alternative procedures that would be advantageous; (V) An offer to answer any inquires concerning procedures; and (VI) An instruction that the person giving consent is free to withdraw his consent . . . at any time.[70]

Moreover, under the same law, not only must the person who is to be sterilized give consent, but certain consultants must certify that he gave an "informed" consent. These consultants are "(1) A psychiatrist or psychologist who consults with and interviews the mentally retarded person; and (2) A person who works in the field of mental retardation, who is knowledgeable in it, and who consults with and interviews the mentally retarded persons."[71]

The intent of this last part of the law is that the "neutral" consultants' counsel will lead to consents that are more informed than they have been in the past. Impressionable retarded persons or those anxious to be approved by "significant others" have been unduly influenced by close friends and relatives in their decisions to be sterilized. Indeed, I know of instances in which supposedly neutral professional consultants worked diligently to convince a retarded person to be sterilized, despite their ostensible roles as buffers.

Involuntary sterilizations can no longer serve as the legal precondition for "release from an institution, or for exercise of any right, privilege, or freedom."[72] That does not, however, mean that some retarded persons have not tried to enhance their chances of release from an institution by acquiescing to *voluntary* sterilizations. The possibility of this has been reduced as a result of the ruling in *Kaimowitz v. Department of Mental Health for the State of Michigan,*[73] which said that noncoercive consent under institutionalized circumstances is essentially impossible. This created a problem, though: while it protects some institutionalized residents from implied coercion leading to sterilization, it can also impede the efforts of others to be sterilized if they really want to be.

Such problems of curtailed consent are even more acute for persons outside of institutions. For example, it is impossible for some low-functioning individuals to give an informed consent for sterilization even if there is no question that they would be benefited by the operation. This was apparent in one case[74] in which three Connecticut families went to court seeking approval to have their severely retarded, deaf, and blind daughters sterilized on the grounds that the girls could not utilize birth control or cope with pregnancy. Further, the families said that they had great difficulties in dealing with the girls' menstruation. Everyone involved in the case, except the girls (who could not communicate a preference), agreed that the sterilizations were warranted, yet the hospital refused to perform the operations because there were no state laws covering voluntary sterilization of *non-institutionalized* retarded people and no third party could give consent on the girls' behalf.[75]

Even voluntary sterilizations involving people capable of informed consent are often difficult to get these days. The laws are precarious enough that doctors are reluctant to perform such operations because of potentially litigious consequences. For example, in 1979, one of my mentally handicapped friends tried to get sterilized. She wanted to have an intimate relationship with her boyfriend without the physical and procreative risks of other forms of birth control. According to the woman, all six of the doctors with whom she consulted refused to perform the operation.

CONTRACEPTION

Obviously, mentally retarded people could use birth control if they wished to be sexually active without having children, but there are problems here as well. First, questions tend to arise in residential facilities as to whether birth control is coercively administered. Second, it is difficult to find residential counselors who are willing to help with instruction involving the use of birth control devices such as condoms. Lessons demand a level of intimacy that embarrasses many people.

Third, one of the most effective forms of contraception, the pill, has been found to be dangerous to certain women, particularly those predisposed to heart disease. Aside from the fact that many retarded women fall into this category, a lot of them take other medications that have bad synergistic effects when taken in conjunction with oral contraceptives. Fourth, the government has done its part to complicate things. A three-month contraceptive injection of a substance called Depo-Provera has been approved on two occasions by the Food and Drug Administration's (FDA) Obstetrical and Gynecological Committee and been used in sixty-five countries for the equivalent of 5-million patient-years without any serious side effects. Depo-Provera was banned in the mid-seventies by the FDA[76] and was still illegal as of this writing. A mentally handicapped friend of mine, in addressing all the prohibitions she faced in her desire to have a moderately mature sex life, gave about the best commentary on the whole issue I have heard: "Sometimes when you're retarded, a person can't win."

NOTES

1. R. B. Edgerton, "Mental Retardation in Non-Western Societies: Toward a Cross-Cultural Perspective on Incompetence," in H. C. Haywood, ed., *Social-Cultural Aspects of Mental Retardation: Proceedings of the Peabody-NIMH Conference*, New York: Appleton-Century-Crofts, 1970, p. 535.

2. National Association for Retarded Citizens, *Residential Programming for Mentally Retarded Persons: A Checklist*, Arlington, Texas: The Association, 1972, p. 12.

3. J. E. Hall, "Sexual Behavior," *Mental Retardation and Developmental Disabilities*, 6:1974, p. 203.

4. T. J. Mulhern, "Survey of Reported Sexual Behavior and Policies Characterizing Residential Facilities for Retarded Citizens," *American Journal of Mental Deficiency*, 79:1975, p. 672.

5. Ibid.

6. L. Mitchell, R. M. Doctor, and D. C. Butler, "Attitudes of Caretakers Toward the Sexual Behavior of Mentally Retarded Persons," *American Journal of Mental Deficiency*, 83:1978, p. 295.

7. E. J. Saunders, "Staff Members' Attitudes Toward the Sexual Behavior of Mentally Retarded Residents," *American Journal of Mental Deficiency*, 84:1979, p. 208.

8. Ibid., p. 207.

9. This quote and most of the rest of the unfootnoted quotes that appear in the "Sexuality" section of this chapter were gleaned in tandem interviews conducted with Dr. Richard Skeen of The University of Northern Arizona.

10. J. R. Peck and W. B. Stephens, "Marriage of Young Adult Male Retardates," *American Journal of Mental Deficiency*, 69(6):1965, p. 287.

11. M. Bass, "Surgical Contraception: A Key to Normalization and Prevention," *Mental Retardation*, 16(6):1978, p. 402.

12. N. Bernstein, "Intellectual Defect and Personality Development," in N. Bernstein, ed., *Diminished People*, Boston: Little, Brown and Co., 1970, p. 182.

13. J. E. Hall, p. 189.

14. N. Bernstein, p. 183.

15. R. B. Edgerton, *The Cloak of Competence: Stigma in the Lives of the Mentally Retarded*, Berkeley: University of California Press, 1967, p. 112.

16. E. M. Stabler, *Primer for Parents of a Mentally Retarded Child*, Arlington, Texas: National Association for Retarded Citizens, 1975, p. 6. (The sentiments inherent in this quote do not reflect those of the Association for Retarded Citizens.)

17. J. E. Hall, p. 203.

18. E. J. Saunders, p. 207; L. Mitchell, R. M. Doctor, and D. C. Butler, p. 289.

19. J. E. Hall, p. 202.

20. L. Goodman, S. Budner, and B. Leah, "Parents' Role in Sex Education for the Retarded," *Mental Retardation*, 9:1971, p. 45.

21. E. J. Saunders, p. 208; L. Mitchell, R. M. Doctor, and D. C. Butler, p. 294.

22. B. Edmonson, K. McCombs, and J. Wish, "What Retarded Adults Believe About Sex," *American Journal of Mental Deficiency*, 84:1979, p. 11.

23. M. Aninger, B. Growick, and K. Golinsky, "Individual Community Placement of Deinstitutionalized Mentally Retarded Adults: Some Personal Concerns," *Mental Retardation*, 17(6):1979, p. 308.

24. M. Begab, "Adopting Techniques in Social Work and Mental Retardation," in M. Schreiber, ed., *Social Work and Mental Retardation*, New York: John Day, 1970, p. 339, cited in M. Bass, p. 399; B. Edmonson, K. McCombs, and J. Wish, p. 17.

25. P. Morris, *Put Away: A Sociological Study of Institutions for the Mentally Retarded*, London: Routledge and Kegan Paul, 1969, p. 11.

26. C. H. Krishef, "State Laws on Marriage and Sterilization," *Mental Retardation*, 10:1972, p. 37.

27. *Corpus Juris Secundum*, vol. 55, p. 825.

28. E. S. Gendel, *Sex Education of the Mentally Retarded Child in the Home*, Arlington, Texas: National Association for Retarded Citizens, 1975, p. 11.

29. L. Floor, D. Baxter, M. Rosen, and L. Zisfein, "A Survey of Marriages Among Previously Institutionalized Retardates," *Mental Retardation*, 13(2):1975, p. 33; J. E. Hall, p. 202.

30. L. Andron and M. L. Sturm, "Is 'I Do' in the Repertoire of the Retarded?" *Mental Retardation*, 11(1):1973, p. 32.

31. L. T. Hilliard, "Discussion on Community Care of the Feebleminded," *Proceedings of the Royal Society of Medicine*, 49:1956, pp. 837–841; C. H. Shaw and C. H. Wright, "The Married Mental Defective, A Follow-Up Study," *Lancet*, 278:1960, pp. 273–274; J. M. Abbot and G. M. Ladd, " . . . any reason why this mentally retarded couple should not be joined together," *Mental Retardation*, 8(2):1970, pp. 45–48; L. Andron and M. L. Sturm, p. 32.

32. L. Andron and M. L. Sturm, p. 32.

33. J. E. Hall, p. 195.

34. S. S. Hartman and J. Hynes, "Marriage Education for Mentally Retarded Adults," *Social Casework*, 56(5):1975, p. 282.

35. L. Andron and M. L. Sturm, p. 33.

36. M. Mudd, B. Melemed, and H. Wechsler, *Post School Vocational Adjustment of Educable Mentally Retarded Boys in Massachusetts*, Boston: The Medical Foundation, 1968, cited in L. Andron and M. L. Sturm, p. 32.

37. M. Bass, p. 399; P. Mickelson, "Can Mentally Deficient Parents Be Helped to Give Their Children Better Care?" *American Journal of Mental Deficiency*, 53:1949, pp. 516–534; M. S. Bass, "Marriage for the Mentally Deficient," *Mental Retardation*, 2(4):1964, pp. 198–202; J. Mattinson, "Marriage and Mental Handicap," in F. F. de la Cruz and G. D. La Veck, eds., *Human Sexuality and the Mentally Retarded*, New York: Brunner/Mazel, 1973, p. 174.

38. L. Kanner, *A History of the Care and Study of the Mentally Retarded*, Springfield, Ill.: Charles C. Thomas, 1964, p. 130.

39. J. E. Hall, p. 196.

40. E. W. Reed and S. C. Reed, *Mental Retardation: A Family Study*, Philadelphia: W. B. Saunders, 1965.

41. J. E. Hall, p. 197.

42. *Eisenstadt* v. *Baird*, 405 U.S. 438, 92 S. Ct. 1029, 31 L. Ed. 2d 349 1972.

43. S. J. Vitello, "Involuntary Sterilization: Recent Developments," *Mental Retardation*, 16(6):1978, p. 406.

44. J. E. Davis, "Birth Control By Sterilization," in C. A. Frazier, ed., *Is It Moral To Modify Man?*, Springfield, Ill.: Charles C. Thomas, 1973, pp. 75–76.

45. P. Mickelson, "The Feebleminded Parent: A Study of 90 Family Cases," *American Journal of Mental Deficiency*, 51:1947, pp. 644–653.

46. B. G. Scally, "Marriage and Mental Handicap: Some Observations in Northern Ireland," in F. F. de la Cruz and G. D. LaVeck, p. 193.

47. J. R. Peck and W. B. Stephens, p. 827.

48. S. J. Vitello, p. 406.

49. A. M. Clarke and A.D.B. Clarke, "Adoption and Fostering of Children of the Mentally Subnormal," in A. M. Clarke and A.D.B. Clarke, eds., *Mental Deficiency: The Changing Outlook*, 3rd ed., New York: The Free Press, 1974, p. 210.

50. J. M. Berg, "Genetics and Genetic Counseling," *Mental Retardation and Developmental Disabilities*, 8:1976, p. 44.

51. L. Andron and M. L. Sturm, p. 33.

52. R. Meyers, "A Couple That Could," *Psychology Today*, November 1978, p. 107.

53. S. E. Slivkin and N. R. Bernstein, "Group Approaches to Treating Retarded Adolescents," in F. J. Menolascino, ed., *Psychiatric Approaches to Mental Retardation*, New York: Basic Books, 1970, p. 447.

54. J. Gan, A. J. Tymchuk, and A. Nishihara, "Mildly Retarded Adults: Their Attitudes Toward Retardation," *Mental Retardation*, 15:1977, pp. 5–9.

55. R. Meyers, p. 107.

56. *Skinner* v. *Oklahoma*, 316 U.S. 535, 62 S. Ct. 1110, 86, L. Ed. 2d 1655 1942.

57. *Cook* v. *The State of Oregon*, Or. App. 496 P. 2d 768 1972.

58. *Wyatt* v. *Aderholt*, 368 F. Supp. 1383 (1974), cited in R. Soskin, "Voluntary Sterilization—Safeguarding Freedom of Choice," *Amicus*, February 1977, p. 43.

59. A. R. Cavalier and R. B. McCarver, "*Wyatt* v. *Stickney* and Mentally Retarded Individuals," *Mental Retardation*, 19(5):1981, p. 210.

60. *North Carolina Association for Retarded Citizens* v. *State of North Carolina*, 450 F. Supp. 459 (M.D.N.C.) 1976.

61. M. S. Bass, "Attitudes of Parents of Retarded Children Toward Voluntary Sterilization," *Eugenics Quarterly*, 14:1967, pp. 45–53.

62. C. J. Whitcraft and J. P. Jones, "A Survey of Attitudes About Sterilization of Retardates," *Mental Retardation*, 12:1974, p. 33.

63. P. Popenoe, "Study of 6,255 Sterilized Patients," *New England Journal of Medicine*, 201:1929, p. 880.

64. G. Sabagh and R. B. Edgerton, "Sterilized Mental Defectives Look at Eugenic Sterilization," *Eugenics Quarterly*, 9:1962, p. 217.

65. J. E. Hall, p. 181.

66. G. Sabagh and R. B. Edgerton, p. 220.

67. P. Roos, "Psychological Impact of Sterilization on the Individual," *Law and Psychology Review*, 50:1975, p. 45.

68. G. Sabagh and R. B. Edgerton, p. 218.

69. *Stump et al.* v. *Linda Kay Sparkman and Leo Sparkman*, cited in *Law Week*, March 28, 1978, p. 4255.

70. State of Colorado, Colorado State Legislature, Senate Bill 135, *Care and Treatment of the Developmentally Disabled*, Article 10.5, Clause 102(2), 1975, p. 12.

71. Ibid., Clause 128:II and III, p. 16, and Clause 130, p. 17.

72. Ibid., Clause 132, p. 18.

73. *Kaimowitz* v. *Department of Mental Health for the State of Michigan*, No. 73-19434-AW.

74. "Parents of Three Retarded Girls Fight Hospital Refusal to Sterilize," *New York Times*, October 2, 1977.

75. M. Bass, "Surgical Contraception, " p. 400.

76. Ibid.

13
Geriatrics, Euthanasia, and Legal Advocacy: Living Long, Living at All?

What is the worst of woes
that wait on age?
    —Lord Byron[1]

When we switch to the rubric of who constitutes persons and non-persons, we
have opened the door to a form of ideation that has acted as a common denominator
in all of man's mindless slaughters. . . .
                                                        —J. A. Robertson[2]

Although it is not mentioned in the *Declaration of Rights of Mentally Retarded Persons*, the right of mentally handicapped people to live out their lives to the end in dignity ought to be assured. Such a guarantee raises two issues: the needs of elderly retarded people, and euthanasia.

GERONTOLOGICAL DIMENSIONS

In the past, aged retarded persons were something of a curiosity. More often than not, people with mental handicaps died before they reached old age.[3] This is changing because of better medical and health care. Between 1949 and 1971, for instance, the mean age of mortality for mentally retarded persons rose by fifteen years.[4] Society must now address the needs of more people who are both old and retarded.

In a sense, retarded individuals are better equipped than non-handicapped persons to cope with some of the attendant difficulties of aging, because they confront many of them before they get old. As Kriger points out, retarded persons often have had early life experiences of: (1) severance of family ties or rejection by family members, (2) low income potential, (3) a surfeit of "leisure time with no means of utilizing it," and (4) physical or social dependence.[5] The societal tendency to regard old people as useless is less likely to disillusion and embitter an elderly retarded person than someone who has not had a lifelong handicap. Retarded persons have a lifetime to get used to their stigma.

There are other elements that augur well for elderly retarded persons. Out of sheer necessity, many develop a spirit of mutual aid in their early years, which helps them as they get old. The brighter learn to guide the dimmer. The physically able have practiced being the eyes, ears, hands, and legs of those with physical handicaps. This, coupled with most retarded people's readiness to accept help without embarrassment or self-effacement, contributes to a dignified attitude toward aging.

Retarded persons are also more likely than non-handicapped aged peers to adjust to group living situations. Non-retarded people usually live as part of a nuclear family prior to entering residential facilities such as nursing homes, while most retarded persons have spent some time in an institution or other kind of group-living setting. It may be difficult for retarded people to move from a group home or institution to a nursing home (especially if it separates them from old friends), but they do not face quite the jarring contrast non-handicapped persons do who have never had to live with a larger aggregate. The fact that many retarded persons are seasoned communal residents probably explains why they have been shown to mix well with other residents in nursing homes, make more expeditious use of community social opportunities and therapeutic services,[6] and generally cause less trouble for staff than non-handicapped residents.[7] Having a mentally handicapping condition has little to recommend it, but it does, in some cases, serve as a primer for the travails of old age. In my opinion, it is this buffering effect that partially accounts for the overall life satisfaction reported by elderly mentally retarded persons.[8] That is not to say their latter years are problem free.

It is widely believed in some nursing homes that retarded residents who were accustomed to dull environments in institutional settings should fare no better in the new milieu. Thus, nursing home staffs are not seen as requiring any special training to help retarded residents, who are considered unborable[9] and therefore easily warehoused. Such transinstitutionalization may, in fact, result in the geriatrically mainstreamed resident getting less attention in the nursing home than in the institution.[10]

Like transinstitutionalization, deinstitutionalization can do old retarded citizens a disservice. Although it has been shown that the overwhelming majority of elderly retarded persons are eligible for community placement[11] and probably adapt to it better than younger retarded people,[12] a too zealous implementation of deinstitutionalization creates problems. It uproots some people who do not want to live on "the outside."[13] It creates culture shocks for elderly institutional residents who have not had the benefit of community living education that younger handicapped persons get in places such as New Morning School. If older persons are deinstitutionalized suddenly, they have to develop a new array of survival skills. Such crash courses in reality overwhelm some of them. Several professionals charged with imparting these skills to elderly retarded individuals confided to me that the prospects were overwhelming to them as well.

The issues surrounding older retarded people are going to require increasing attention in the next few decades. I did not see much evidence, in the field or in the literature examined, that these matters are being given serious consideration by mental retardation professionals.

EUTHANASIA

We have seen that during certain periods of human history it was considered a social obligation to kill mentally retarded people. This idea is not bandied about in our society with any regularity except by extremists, whom most people denounce as "idiotic" themselves. That is why it distressed me, when visiting a terminal-profound ward of an institution, to discover that I felt an eerie compulsion to put some of the people I encountered out of their apparent misery. In talking with professionals in the field, I found that the issue of euthanasia crosses their minds with greater regularity than one might expect on the basis of their daily conversation, where, understandably, the topic is considered to be in bad taste. One does encounter an occasional article or reference to euthanasia in the mental retardation literature. Here a frequently discussed issue is what constitutes humanness—the attendant implication of some discussants being that "non-humans," or "sub-humans," or "pseudo species" are somehow less entitled to life than humans. What does constitute humanness?

One approach to the determination of species legitimation is the neurophysiological bent—neocortical functioning being seen as the essence of humanness.[14] Accordingly, just because the brain stem and midbrain continue to regulate the autonomic functions of the organism, that does not mean it is human.

Another perspective on the key to humanness is the psychometric approach. Walmsley cites a professor of medical ethics at the School of Medicine in Toronto who had deduced that "an IQ of 40 is the cutoff for humanness and that certainly anyone with an IQ of 30 or less is, for all intents and purposes, sub-human."[15]

Neither the neurophysiological nor the psychometric viewpoints advocate doing away with "sub-humans," although the implication is evident. Neocortical malfunction and low IQ bespeak one's status as mere organism, and even herbivores show no compunction about dispatching vegetables.

The "Who is human?" controversy also takes on a philosophical hue. Some scholars hold that humanness is constituted by the ability of consciousness to ponder itself as consciousness, or, as Heidegger called it, *dasein*.[16] Tooley takes the concept a step further, maintaining that a human who has neither self-identity (self taking itself as an object of its own ponderings) nor a self-conscious desire to go on existing should have its indifference to life accommodated.[17] Tooley says, "So an entity that lacks such a consciousness of itself as a continuing subject of mental states does not have a right to life."[18] This reasoning, taken to its *reductio ad absurdum*, requires that individuals who are sleeping, comatose, deranged, suicidal, in a state of spiritual bliss, or watching most daytime television would all be candidates for extinction.

A fundamental question in the euthanasia issue is whether the preservation of any life is a sufficient end in itself, or if such a view is merely irrational vitalism. Individuals who hold the latter point of view believe that life is valuable only insofar as it leads to other ends, such as self knowing self, humans knowing other humans,[19] or man knowing or being capable of unity with a deity. All three of these prerequisites of humanness are seen in a report on the subject made by an Anglican Church of Canada committee composed of a physician, a surgeon, a canon of the church, a professor of law, a head nurse of a neurosurgical ward, a hospital chaplain, a Presbyterian minister, an Anglican priest, a fourth-year medical student, a gerontologist, and a professor of religion. The committee members concluded that "The capability of man to relate to himself, with his neighbor, and with God encapsulates all the minimal criteria set down by theologians and scientists alike. It would follow, therefore, that without any of these minimal criteria, actual or potential, a living body is not human."[20] The committee continues, "The severely defective new-born infant which has no chance of gaining a modicum of spiritual or intellectual life deserves special consideration. The medical attendants may hope that the infant will contract some infection which, without treatment, will cause death. . . ." Luther would have been proud.

Some euthanasiasts insist that killing certain retarded individuals is warranted so that they will not have to suffer the tribulations of their handicaps. Such a conclusion is an audacious bit of intersubjectivity. Since the causes of joy and other human pleasures are so radically varied and idiosyncratic, it is presumptuous of an observer to assume the presence of another person's death wish. An individual who has engaged in pleasurable social interaction and then been thrown into a world of loneliness may wish to die, as do some people who have known freedom from pain, only to face terrible suffering. But a person who has no basis of comparison cannot wish to die as a result of pining for that which he or she has never known. Profoundly retarded people who seem to be miserable may be enraptured. Moreover, it is never suggested that those of us who have not shared the consciousness of the genius or saint should no longer wish to live for want of that experience.

Other euthanasiasts are less motivated in their position by the suffering of retarded persons than by the costs handicapped people represent to society. Because retarded individuals are seen to have no utility, they are held to have no social viability and, accordingly, no reason for living. In a recent article in a popular periodical, a highly respected physician who decries the skyrocketing costs of medicine suggests that "expensive and heroic medical care might also be denied those unfortunate babies born with Down's Syndrome. . . ."[21] Walmsley holds that a euthanasic ethos will develop that equates "fiscal viability with humanness."[22] Is life, too, to be reduced to cost-effectiveness? In articles written as recently as 1967, we can read the ideas of perverse humanitarians who call for "sacrifice of mentally defective humans, or human vegetables . . ." to provide organ transplants and "increase the intellectual betterment of mankind."[23]

While one disdains such extremes of utilitarianism, it is naive not to recognize that harsh economic realities of the future will eventually force us to develop a public policy directing difficult life-and-death decisions regarding retarded people. How will these decisions be guided? Say, for example, two people—one normal and one retarded—need a life-saving respirator. Both will profit equally from the use of the machine and can be expected to make full recoveries. Who should get it?

As we develop medical technologies that can sustain nearly any life indefinitely, we shall have to decide what the appropriate level of expenditures on these technologies will be for our handicapped citizens— particularly those with severe handicaps. As neonatal mortality rates plummet in hospitals with infant intensive care units,[24] it must be decided which infants' lives are worth saving.

In the absence of a formalized public policy, we quietly (and gratefully) abdicate our responsibility in these matters to physicians, parents, and judges. Doctors face the most onerous task; yet most of them make their decisions about who is worth saving on the basis of personal prejudice rather than scientific knowledge,[25] and their prejudices are not unlike those of other citizens uninformed about mental retardation.

Thus, some of these doctors wrongly assume that the quality of life for all retarded persons is bad, that the infant before them can hope to make no contributions to society, and that he will disrupt, if not destroy, his family.[26] It should not surprise us then that researchers like Duff and Campbell found widespread de facto euthanasia that resulted from physicians withholding treatment in a special care nursery.[27] Wolfensberger says, "Euthanasia is already being committed in various forms and guises—and not rarely at all. Physicians today lean strongly toward denial of life supports to handicapped new-borns. . . ."[28] The decision "not to resuscitate" is purportedly so common in some hosptials that special "Code 90" stickers to that effect are placed on selected patients' charts.[29]

There are still some physicians—17 percent by one account—who would respect the idea of doing "everything humanly possible" to preserve a seriously defective infant's life and convince the parents to go along with this.[30] It is a rare physician, though, who would try to block parental refusal to consent to life-saving procedures for a retarded infant.[31] Letting one's retarded baby die is currently a parental prerogative.

The prototype of this was the well-known Johns Hopkins case. Here, the parents of a baby born with Down's Syndrome and a duodenal obstruction withheld their permission for simple surgery that would have corrected the obstruction. The baby starved to death fifteen days later. What of the child's rights? In the case of "Baby Boy Houle," the presiding judge responded to the parents' refusal to give permission for a life-saving operation by ruling, "At the moment of live birth there does exist a human being entitled to the fullest protection of the law. The most basic right enjoyed by every human being is the right to life itself."[32] It has never really worked that way, though. In 1975, Robertson was able to say, "Although a clear basis for prosecution exists, no parent or physician has ever been criminally prosecuted for withholding ordinary medical care from a defective infant. . . ."[33] In 1980, the Surpeme Court ruled in the case of Philip Becker that "even absentee parents who had divested themselves of their handicapped child at birth may withhold permission for life-saving medical procedures for such a child. . . ."[34] This does not correspond with the American Association on Mental Deficiency's position on euthanasia, which holds that "the existence of mental retardation is no justification for the terminating of the life of any human being or for permitting of such a life to be terminated either directly or through the withholding of life sustaining procedures."[35] In turn, this position is not reflected in the attitudes of all mental retardation specialists. For example, four of the fifteen special educators with whom I had conversations about the subject of euthanasia said that mercy killing might be applicable to the grossest levels of retardation. They were, however, uncertain as to who would be vested with the decision-making power and assured me that they would never be a party to such a decision. Their uncertainty is well founded.

If decisions to withhold treatment from retarded infants are going to be made, who should be making them? Physicians—despite their general lack of knowledge about mental retardation? Parents—with their vested interests? Courts—which are socially distant from the child? Attorneys, maybe,—theologians—some kind of committee structure? Further what should be the legal liabilities of those who make such decisions? What ought to be the objective basis of a decision to let someone die? Whose best interests should be paramount? The retarded person's? His parents'? Society's? Does one mercy killing make the next seem easier and more merciful, resulting in what Greenfeld calls "the domino theory of societal morality?"[36] It is all exceedingly complex.

What *is* sure is that euthanasia for one retarded person because of his handicap casts a pall over all retarded people. This highlights a fundamental element of the retarded life that has been slowly emerging throughout the previous pages. The reader will remember the literal death of Spartan tardocide (and all its parallels) and the figurative forms of death inherent in retarded persons' separation from society, their treatment as unchanging entities, and the mourning that accompanies their births. Throughout history, a symbolic association has developed between mental retardation and death—between mental handicap and grief. I believe that many retarded individuals feel the aura of this association—that they sense the grief they evoke—but they do not have the cognitive abilities to grasp the precipitating loss. Hence, they experience a loss-grief disjunction[37] in which a diffuse sense of grief precedes the understanding of what has been lost—which is, of course, the intellectual abilities they do not have the intellectual capacity to miss. Because retarded people have no causal antecedents to explain the grieving process they become the focus of, they are left with no reasonable course of adaptation short of bereavement becoming something of a lifestyle, which I believe happens to many of them.

LEGAL ADVOCACY

The issue of euthanasia and many of the other issues that have been discussed in previous chapters have obvious legal ramifications. Because of this, the legal profession will be called upon to take an increasingly active role in all aspects of the law pertaining to mental retardation. The profession's history is less than august in this matter. In 1970, it was concluded by the Law and Ethics Work Group, sponsored by the

President's Committee on Mental Retardation, "that a reasonable estimate of those lawyers who had some familiarity with the legal problems of retarded people was perhaps one-half of one percent."[38] Interest in securing legal rights for mentally handicapped people does, however, appear to have been growing slowly in the legal community over the last decade. The American Bar Association formed a Committee on the Law and the Mentally Retarded; the American Civil Liberties Union Foundation established the Mental Health Law Project; the Association for Retarded Citizens has a National Legal Advocacy Committee. Literature on the law and mental handicaps is more in evidence now, and more states have legal centers for handicapped people. These factors bode well for mentally retarded citizens, but the legal profession's awakening regarding mental retardation has not been problem free. For example, time and again I saw attorneys who served as legal advocates bring an unwarrantedly harsh adversary tone to their interactions with governmental representatives and service providers, creating a polemic atmosphere where specific realities did not necessitate it. In certain situations, it was clear that this attitude prejudiced the best interests of a client. Perhaps cantankerousness goes with the profession, and certainly lawyers are the vanguard of legal reform for retarded persons, which calls for tough-mindedness in some cases. Conversely, these lawyers should be mindful that although temperance and finesse cannot move mountains, they do occasionally move bureaucrats.

Lawyers are not alone in their responsibility to promote legal advocacy. Special educators and other scholars in the area can provide vital data on retardation, designed to inform attorneys and aid legislators in framing necessary and cogent laws. If special educators such as those on the staff of New Morning School were barometers of progress in this regard, the prospects are not bright. At New Morning, and in several other special education settings, virtually every educator I talked with knew only as much of the law as was required to do his or her daily tasks—which is not very much. Given the exhausting nature of their work, this is not startling, nor was the assumption by most of them that somebody else was taking care of legal advocacy. If, however, special educators abdicate their participatory rights in formulating the direction legal advocacy takes, there will be no room for sour grapes if this direction does not mirror their professional interests or those of their students.

The parents of mentally retarded youngsters I came to know were, for the most part, motivated to take part in legal advocacy activities only in crisis situations. This is understandable, particularly in the case of the "oldtimers," most of whom had boarded the legal bandwagon at least once in their lifetimes, only to be disappointed by the practical ramifications of their efforts. As I write this, massive cuts in federal and state expenditures for retarded persons are being effectuated, oversight hearings on the viability of P.L. 94-142 are once again being conducted, and New Morning School has been dismantled. The struggle to hold the line on past advances is continuous, and the parents who have waged it are weary. As one mother put it,

> We are tired. We have kept our children at home and raised them ourselves, with all the extra demands on time and energy which that implies—often without much help from the community, neighborhood, professionals, friends, or relatives, and in fact commonly against their well-intentioned advice. We have founded parent groups and schools, run them ourselves, held fund raising events to pay teachers and keep our little schools afloat, organized baby-sitting groups, and summer play groups. We have built and repaired special playground equipment for our children's use at home and at school. We have painted classrooms and buildings; we have written legislators and educated them about our children's needs and rights. We have collated and stapled hundreds of newsletters, attended school board meetings, lobbied at the state legislature for better legislation for handicapped children, informed newspaper reporters about inhumane conditions in institutions, and written letters to editors. All this we have done for a decade or more.[39]

One widely publicized group working toward procuring legal rights for mentally handicapped people is called Citizen Advocacy. It is defined as "an independent movement of consumers and their allies to monitor and change human service agencies."[40] As an advocacy movement, Citizen Advocacy has promoted progressive laws and better human services through methods such as demonstrations, letter-writing campaigns, newsletters and other educational or consciousness-raising forums, boycotts, and lobbying.[41] The most important activity of Citizen Advocacy is, however, the pairing of a non-handicapped sponsor with a handicapped person, called a protégé. For retarded persons lucky enough to live in a community that promotes Citizen Advocacy with funds and a cadre of active sponsors, it is a windfall concept. Not only does the protégé have a "friend," but if his legal rights are threatened, there is someone to protest on his behalf. (Because of political machinations that have resulted in funding cuts and reallocations, the Citizen Advocacy programs of several states have been dismantled.)

Lawyers, special educators, parents, and citizen advocates are not alone in their attempts to secure legal rights for mentally retarded persons. Some of the most active legal advocates in Mountview came from the ranks of retarded people themselves, and self-advocacy groups are slowly gaining momentum around the country. This is a heartening sign to proponents of normalization, yet there have been some disquieting consequences of the self-advocacy and retarded-rights movement.

Although a few retarded individuals were articulate spokespersons for their minority in Mountview, others, in trying to advocate their cause, acted very retarded in public forums, thus intensifying negative public imagery about all retarded persons. Further, a new breed of boorish politico emerged. In Mountview, two of the most active self-advocates would not address any topic other than the political issues associated with mental retardation. Their preemptory pontifications consisted solely of cliches culled from the rhetoric of legal advocacy and self-serving statements concerning their own involvement in the advocacy movement. One could understand why people who had consistently failed in society would seize the notoriety that resulted from their conversance with a set of political issues, although one could not escape the impression that these people were automatons, programmed to a constricted perspective of themselves and the world. Moreover, one had to question the motivations of the non-handicapped individuals who did the programming. While in the field, I met many extraordinary non-handicapped advocates. Occasionally, though, I would encounter the piteous marginal being who, for lack of purpose in his own life, sought it in the lives of others. The disturbing thing about this was the great power these persons wielded over their retarded constituencies.

Another problem that has accompanied the legal advocacy movement was intimated by a social worker who said she had become very circumspect in view of the litigious atmosphere that has developed as retarded persons assert their legal rights to the fullest extent. As a result, this woman refused to restrain retarded clients physically even if such restraint was the only way to prevent physical injury to a third party. To restrain a belligerent retarded person was, according to her, to leave oneself open, not only to personal injury, but to a lawsuit. Although it is rare, some retarded people misconstrue their newfound rights as carte blanche to manipulate the legal system in an irresponsible manner. As another social worker put it, "Some of them are beginning to find that they can get away with murder." A New Morning teacher who had been active in the early stages of the legal advocacy movement registered her reservations on the rights issue in this way: "In some cases, you can't give these people too many rights. They're like rope; if you give them too much, they're bound to hang themselves."

Legal advocacy is an important facilitant of the normalization movement. As we have seen, there are problems in mustering an effective force for the never-ending skirmishes that surround effectuating and maintaining progressive laws and getting realities to correspond with legal guidelines. Moreover, as each successive generation of legal advocates "burns out" in these struggles, there is an inevitable social regression that leaves the succeeding generation with a sense of having to start over. A commitment to legal advocacy should not be made lightly nor abandoned too easily in the face of the disappointments or fatigue of being a legal advocate. The payoffs are few and almost always intangible; but advocates must remember that mentally handicapped persons need the help of those without handicaps to ensure their legal rights, and there are few more selfless deeds a man or woman can engage in than helping people who can use so much help.

NOTES

1. Lord Byron (George Noel Gordon), *Childe Harold's Pilgrimage,* Canto II, 1812, st. 98.

2. J. A. Robertson, "Involuntary Euthanasia of Defective Newborns," *Stanford Law Review,* 27(2):1975, p. 247.

3. B. Sayder and S. Wollner, "When the Retarded Grow Old," *Canada's Mental Health,* 22:1974, pp. 12–13.

4. B. H. Kirman, "Clinical Aspects," *Mental Retardation and Developmental Disabilities,* 3:1971, p. 16.

5. S. F. Kriger, "Geriatrics," *Mental Retardation and Developmental Disabilities,* 8:1976, p. 165.

6. L. DiGiovanni, "The Elderly Retarded: A Little-Known Group," *Gerontologist,* 18:1978, p. 264.

7. P. D. Cotten, G.F.P. Sison, Jr., and S. Starr, "Comparing Elderly Mentally Retarded and Non-Mentally Retarded Individuals: Who Are They? What Are Their Needs?" *Gerontologist,* 21(4):1981, p. 363.

8. P. C. Chinn, C. J. Drew, and D. R. Logan, *Mental Retardation: A Life Cycle Approach,* St. Louis, Mo.: C. V. Mosby, 1975, p. 342.

9. L. DiGiovanni, p. 264.

10. B. Stotsky and J. Dominick, "Mental Patients in Nursing Homes: II. Intellectual Impairment and Physical Illness," *Journal of the American Geriatrics Society,* 17:1969, pp. 45–55.

11. G. O'Connor, R. S. Justice, and N. Warren, "The Aged Mentally Retarded: Institution or Community Care?" *American Journal of Mental Deficiency,* 75:1970, p. 360.

12. L. DiGiovanni, p. 264.

13. M. Dickerson, J. Hamilton, R. Gaber, and R. Segal, "The Aged Mentally Retarded: The Invisible Client—A Challenge to the Community," paper presented at the Annual Meeting of the American Association on Mental Deficiency, Toronto, 1974, cited in P. C. Chinn, C. J. Drew, and D. R. Logan, p. 340.

14. J. F. Fletcher, "Four Indicators of Humanhood—The Enquiry Matures," *The Hastings Center Report, Institute of Society, Ethics and the Life Sciences,* 4(6):1974, pp. 4–7.

15. S. A. Walmsley, "A Life and Death Issue," *Mental Retardation,* 16(6):1978, pp. 387–388.

16. M. Heidegger, *Being and Time,* New York: Harper and Row, 1962.

17. M. Tooley, "Abortion and Infanticide," *Philosophy and Public Affairs,* 51:1972, p. 37.

18. Ibid., quoted in J. A. Robertson, p. 248.

19. M. Buber, *Between Man and Man,* London: Collins, 1947, p. 224.

20. Committee of the Anglican Church of Canada, Report to General Synod, "Considerations Concerning Passage From Life to Death," p. 5, cited in S. A. Walmsley, p. 389.

21. H. Schwartz, "We Need to Ration Medicine," *Newsweek,* February 8, 1982, p. 13.

22. S. A. Walmsley, p. 389.

23. *The Atlantic Monthly,* October 1967, p. 49, cited in W. Wolfensberger, *Normalization,* Toronto: National Institute on Mental Retardation, 1972, p. 17.

24. C. J. Duff and A. Campbell, "Moral and Ethical Dilemmas in the Special-Care Nursery," *New England Journal of Medicine,* 289:1973, p. 890.

25. A. A. Baumeister, "Mental Retardation Policy and Research: The Unfulfilled Promise," *American Journal of Mental Deficiency,* 85:1981, p. 453.

26. G. G. Affleck, "Physicians' Attitudes Toward Discretionary Medical Treatment of Down's Syndrome Infants," *Mental Retardation,* 18:1980, pp. 79–81.

27. C. J. Duff and A. Campbell, p. 892.

28. W. Wolfensberger, "The Extermination of Handicapped People in World War II Germany," *Mental Retardation,* 19(1):1981, p. 6.

29. J. Fletcher, "Ethics and Euthanasia," in R. H. Williams, ed., *To Live and To Die,* New York: Springer-Verlag, 1973, pp. 113–122, cited in M. Hardman and C. Drew, "Life Management Practices With the Profoundly Retarded: Issues of Euthanasia and Withholding Treatment," *Mental Retardation,* 16(6):1978, p. 394.

30. A. A. Baumeister, p. 453.

31. W. Wolfensberger, "The Extermination," p. 6.

32. R. A. McCormick, "To Save or Let Die," *Journal of the American Medical Association,* 229(2):1974, p. 172.

33. J. A. Robertson, p. 243.

34. W. Wolfensberger, "The Extermination," p. 6; "Six Days in the Life of a Deformed Baby," *Newsweek,* April 26, 1982, p. 59.

35. American Association on Mental Deficiency, "The Right to Life—Proposed Statement," *Mental Retardation,* 11(6):1973, p. 66.

36. J. Greenfeld, *A Place for Noah,* New York: Holt, Rinehart, and Winston, 1978, p. 105.

37. D. Evans, "Death and Mentally Retarded Persons," *Mid-American Review of Sociology,* 6(2):1981, p. 57.

38. D. E. Haggerty, L. A. Kane, and D. K. Udall, "An Essay on the Legal Rights of the Mentally Retarded," *Family Law Quarterly,* 6:1972, pp. 59–71.

39. K. A. Gorham, "A Lost Generation of Parents," *Exceptional Children,* 4:1975, p. 523.

40. B. Biklen, "Advocacy Comes of Age," *Exceptional Children,* 42(6):1976, p. 310.

41. Ibid., pp. 310–312.

14
Prevention

While we wait for the napkin,
   the soup gets cold,
While the bonnet is trimming,
   the face grows old.
When we've matched our buttons,
   the pattern is sold.
And everything comes too late—
   too late.
                          —F. Ludlow[1]

Past hopes for betterment of the lives of retarded persons have inched their way toward realization in the era of normalization and legal advocacy despite the discrepancies in ideals, laws, and social realities. Hope should not be fueled exclusively with the promise of remediation, though. Given the preventive advances that have been developed in the last few years, there is reason for cautious optimism that the incidence of mental retardation can be reduced. Let us examine a few of the potentialities that exist to prevent mental retardation and some of the impediments to the attainment of these potentials.

GENETIC CAUSES

Metabolic Defects

Retardation resulting from inborn errors of metabolism such as phenylketonuria (PKU) can be minimized with effective neonatal care. PKU is an enzyme disorder leading to mental retardation as a result of the newborn's inability to oxidize phenylalanine, a substance found in most high-protein foods. With early diagnosis, the child is put on a special diet that restricts foods that contain phenylalanine. There are some dangers to the low-protein diet itself,[2] but the risk is miniscule compared to the inevitable damage caused by PKU. If the diet is carefully monitored, most PKU babies will develop "near normal" intelligence.[3] Since the 1960s, when PKU tests began to be mandated in various states, mental retardation caused by the disorder has been reduced.[4] Such mandates are an encouraging sign, but only a beginning. Other neonatal tests exist to detect treatable disorders such as galactosemia, maple syrup urine disease, histidinemia, homocrystinuria, and hypothyroidism (cretinism). If tests for these retarding disorders were given to all newborns, the additional cost per child would be about two dollars and the testing could be done on the same blood sample used to detect PKU.[5] Yet these procedures are not mandated in all states.

Chromosomal Abnormalities

Significant strides have been made in the prenatal detection of chromosomal abnormalities such as Down's Syndrome. This has been accomplished through the development of procedures referred to as genetic counseling. Genetic counseling involves: (1) identifying parents who have a high risk of having babies with retarding conditions; (2) testing the high-risk people to see if the suspicions are substantive; (3) providing information on the probability of a child being born with certain retarding conditions where specific tests are not available; (4) explaining the clinical characteristics of conditions that are diagnosed, including prognosis, mortality, and so on; and (5) clarifying the options available to parents to prevent handicapping conditions.

Let us look at some of the considerations the genetic counselor would take into account in counseling parents on a specific disorder such as Down's Syndrome. First, the counselor would look at the risk factors. If a mother has a chromosomal translocation (the attachment of a fragment of one chromosome to another structurally dissimilar chromosome), there is a 9 percent chance her child will have a chromosomal abnormality, while the probability is 4 percent if the father has the translocation.[6] If a woman has already had a Down's Syndrome child, her risk of having another is significantly greater, particularly at younger maternal ages.[7] Older parents also have a higher risk of having children with Down's Syndrome. Each ovum a woman will release for her entire reproductive life is already present in her at puberty. Over time, the risk that ova will recompose with other genetic material in a mutant form is elevated. Women between thirty-five and forty years of age have a 1.5 percent rate of offspring with chromosomal abnormalities, but this goes up to 3.5 percent for women between forty and forty-five and 10 percent for those over forty-five.[8] The "genetic material" of men is subject to decomposition as well.[9] Other signs that a couple is at risk of having a baby with a chromosomal abnormality are a high rate of fetal wastage, including such things as multiple (three or more) spontaneous abortions[10] or stillbirths, and problems of infertility.[11]

The most frequently performed procedure to get data on high-risk women is called amniocentesis. Between the thirteenth and sixteenth weeks of pregnancy, a needle can be inserted through the mother's abdominal wall into her uterus and a small amount of amniotic fluid withdrawn. This fluid contains a few free-floating cells from the fetus. These can be used for three kinds of testing: (1) chromosome analysis, to detect disorders such as Down's Syndrome; (2) alphafeto-protein quantification, which can act as an indicator of congenital malformations, such as hydrocephalus (a condition characterized by abnormal accumulation of cerebro-spinal fluid within the skull and atrophy of the brain), and fetal neural tube defects, such as anacephalus (failure of the skull to form); and (3) enzyme-level analysis, which can point out metabolic defects such as Tay-Sachs Disease or Hurler's Syndrome.[12]

Amniocentesis is becoming accepted as a routine obstetrical procedure for high-risk patients,[13] as well it should. Every known chromosomal abnormality and threescore inborn errors of metabolism can be diagnosed through amniocentesis,[14] with little risk to the fetus and an accuracy of 99.4 percent.[15]

The most volatile objection to amniocentesis emanates from its association with abortion. One study showed a sizable majority (forty of fifty-four) parents chose this option when they were found to have a high probability of delivering a baby with a handicapping condition.[16] A special problem associated with these abortions is their late-term nature. Because earlier there is not enough amniotic fluid, amniocentesis cannot be done until the end of the first trimester of pregnancy, and the results of the tests take from two to four weeks.[17] Some people find late-term abortions objectionable, even if they do not disapprove of abortion in principle. There are other arguments against abortion based upon the findings of amniocentesis. The most obvious of these concerns how aborting genetically defective fetuses will affect our view of those retarded persons who escaped the net of detection. The implication is that all retarded persons would have been better off not being born, which is a questionable assertion on many grounds. There is also the problem of the "unexpected result." This can be seen in Karp's example of a forty-seven XYY chromosomal arrangement discovered in some male fetuses. About 1 out of 800 men have the extra Y chromosome, most of them with no ill effects.[18] It is true, however, that some of these so-called supermale karyotypes show very aggressive antisocial behavior patterns. Thus, should all XYY fetuses be aborted because a few will have severe difficulties?

Despite the abortion-related objections to amniocentesis, the procedure is, for the most part, life affirming. It has been reported that 96 percent of the people who have amniocentesis get normal results from the laboratory,[19] thereby reducing the likelihood that untested prospective parents will seek abortion because they are anxious about being in a high-risk category and have no information on probable outcomes.

A bizarre sidelight on amniocentesis and abortion is the appearance of so-called wrongful-birth lawsuits. These are brought by parents on behalf of defective offspring who are misdiagnosed *in utero* by genetic counselors as having no risk of being defective.[20] The doctor is sued because of the child's ostensible right not to have been born.

ACQUIRED PHYSIOLOGICAL CAUSES

Maternal Infection

An example of good health care abetting the prevention of mental retardation is in the control of maternal infections such as German measles (rubella). If a mother contracts rubella during the first three months of pregnancy, her child runs a high risk of being born blind, deaf, with a convulsive disorder, with cerebral palsy, or mentally retarded. Rubella vaccines are not effective if administered to a woman who is already pregnant, so they must be given preconceptually. The vaccines are inexpensive, risk free, and take seconds to administer, yet every year babies are born with handicaps that result from the disease.

Maternal venereal diseases can also retard children. The requirement of blood tests as a prerequisite for marriage has helped to reduce *in utero* transmission of diseases such as syphilis.[21] Where the disease is not detected before conception, the mother can be treated safely with antibiotics while she is pregnant. Herpesvirus, Type II, another form of venereal disease, is typically transmitted from mother to infant during a vaginal delivery. Between 40 and 60 percent of these infants become infected.[22] Because the newborn's immunological system has not fully matured, the infection usually spreads and results in death or serious disorders, including mental retardation, in about 80 percent of the cases.[23] The transmission of the infection can be prevented if the baby is delivered by cesarean section.

Physical Agents: Irradiation

Doctors have stopped the practice of X-raying women during the first three months of their pregnancies, and other less-risky techniques of getting a picture of the fetus, such as ultrasonography, have been developed. With ultrasound pictures, the physican can locate the placenta, measure the diameter of the fetus's skull, determine whether the baby lies in breech position, and so on. If a problem of fetal dimension or position is detected, appropriate procedures can be employed to reduce hazards such as paranatal trauma to the baby. One area that demands the special attention of researchers interested in the prevention of mental retardation is to gain a better understanding of the effects of *preconceptual* X-irradiation on mothers. It has been shown to put some of the women, especially those in the late reproductive years, at risk.[24]

Blood Incompatibilities

Mental retardation from Rh blood incompatibilities can be brought under total control if the preventive techniques currently available are utilized. A woman with Rh negative blood and a man with Rh positive blood run a high risk of producing a mentally retarded child. In most cases, the fetus in such a matching inherits the father's blood type. The couple's first child will not experience any difficulties as a result of the Rh factor, because the circulatory systems of the mother and baby are separate and their blood does not mix. Future children can face problems as the result of a sequence of events. If, at the delivery of the first child, some of the blood in the placenta mixes with the mother's blood, it causes her to form antibodies to Rh positive blood. During the next pregnancy, these antibodies can cross the placenta, entering the fetus's circulatory system. This triggers a process that destroys the red blood cells in the newborn, resulting in an interference with the brain's ability to utilize oxygen carried by the blood, as well as the destruction of brain cells. Prompt exchange transfusions, which give the newborn an entirely new supply of blood, can usually prevent brain damage, but such last-ditch efforts are not necessary. A vaccine that keeps the mother from forming antibodies that threaten future children can be given to her within seventy-two hours after the birth of each child.

Cerebral Defects plus Malformation of the Skull

Neonatal examinations reduce the risk to infants caused by anatomical malformations of the skull. A case in point is craniosynostosis. This is a condition in which the sutures of the baby's skull are fused together at birth or in the early postnatal period, not allowing the expanding brain to grow. Surgeons can create sutures when the skull is already fused and prevent others from fusing prematurely by putting polyethylene strips on their edges.

Maternal Ingestion of Toxins

Occasionally, pregnant women ingest toxins inadvertently, but what is most vexing are those mothers who deliberately consume poisons that put their unborn babies at risk. We know, for example, that pregnant women who smoke heavily are more likely than non-smokers to have low-birth-weight babies. In these women, there is also an increased likelihood of premature separation of the placenta, causing fetal anoxia, or improper attachment of the placenta to the uterus in front of the fetus, which blocks the baby's way out of the womb.[25] We also know the heavy toll Fetal Alcohol Syndrome takes on babies born to mothers, particularly those who are teenagers, who cannot control excessive alcohol consumption.[26] What we do not know is how to get these mothers to stop the overindulgence that damages their babies—an impotence that, ironically, is grounded in the very power of our medical service system. What do I mean?

SOCIAL CAUSES

Health and Medicine at Odds

Unlike therapeutic medicine, in which cures are vended in a seller's market, prevention takes place in a buyer's market, in which the physican has very little leverage on consumers. Prevention rests on the power of persuasion, and most physicians are taught to treat sick patients, rather than persuade them to stay healthy in the first place. In that this has become the medical norm, it is not surprising that those physicians who do try to practice preventive medicine are often confronted by consumer attitudes more attuned to response to medical crises than to preservation of health.

There is a great reciprocity of medical stupidity in our culture. Doctors, who have fostered the idea of treating sick people with modern technologies while ignoring prevention, have no room to rail about the pregnant woman who smokes or drinks too much or to lament the ignorance of parents who bring them a once normal child suffering the ravages of something such as hypernatremic dehydration. Consumers, so quick to protect the shine on their automobiles and the sanctity of their goods, often ignore simple preventive measures that can protect the health of their born or unborn babies. As late as 1976, 25 percent of the women who gave birth in public hospitals in the United States had *no* prenatal care.[27] Indeed, one survey showed that the majority of people—not just poor people—did not even know that mental retardation could be prevented.[28]

Poverty

The poor health of poor people cannot be blamed solely on their lack of adequate health facilities or their refusal to use the ones they have. Even in societies like Britain, where socialized medical services are made use of by the majority of citizens, there is still a disproportionate correlation between poverty and the incidence of mental retardation.[29] Medical care cannot prevent poverty, but intelligent health and medical care can help to reduce some of the intellectually debilitating by-products of it.

For instance, one health service that could reduce mental retardation in the children of poor people would be to ensure that their mothers get a proper diet during pregnancy. Women with inadequate diets have up to five times as many low-birth-weight babies as those who get proper nutrition.[30] Regrettably, food stamps have not been totally successful in reducing such important nutritional problems. Indigent pregnant mothers receiving the coupons were shown to be protein deficient and calorie poor even in the heyday of food stamps.[31] There are ways to make the food stamp program work toward better prevention, though. For instance, more rigid standards governing purchases made with the coupons ought to be combined with diet counseling to ensure that indigent mothers-to-be reduce the nutritional risks to their babies. Diet counseling does help. A study conducted at the Montreal Diet Dispensary between 1963 and 1972 indicated that when lower-class mothers were given such counseling, their incidence of low-birth-weight babies dropped significantly.[32]

Another way in which mental retardation of youngsters from poor families can be reduced is through early developmental intervention with children whose home environments are especially poor in proper stimulation.[33] It has been asserted that as much as 50 percent of human development has taken place by the time we are four years old.[34] And yet, as we have seen, our educational system—by intervening too late—ignores the developmental needs of the very persons who require the greatest help and have the highest likelihood of profiting from it.

Child Abuse

The sickness of abusive parents can destroy their children emotionally, physically, and intellectually. We do no one a favor in ignoring suspected abuse. We only exacerbate the burdens abusive parents and their children must bear and, ultimately, our own burden, for all of us end up paying the economic price of brain-injured children. There should be no equivocation, no temporizing, no politenesses when we suspect that a child is being abused. The person responsible for the abuse should be reported immediately to social service agencies empowered to remove children from dangerous environments.

The Physical Environment

It is here that our society is most remiss in its responsibility to its progeny. The problem is simple: If we do not get a grip on our mindless environmental husbandry, we shall witness the creation of whole generations of mutant children, whose primary adaptation to the destructive technological brilliance of their predecessors will be that they are not smart enough to carry on. We have seen only the first of the "Love Canal" situations. Sadly, I fear, mental retardation, instead of being reduced, will become "a growth industry."

UNKNOWN CAUSES

Because so many of the causes of mental retardation are unknown, a great deal of research must be done to find them and to develop preventive, diagnostic, and remedial measures. Some of these discoveries will be so "space age" as to make amniocentesis, ultrasonography, and fetography seem prosaic. Current advances already portend the trends. For example, erythroblastosis fetalis, a form of hemolytic anemia associated with Rh blood incompatibilities, is being treated *in utero*.[35] There will doubtless be many other advances in fetology in the coming decade, including, I suspect, genetic reengineering of defective fetuses through replacement therapy.

Pharmacy and pharmacology are areas of remedial and preventive potential for the future. It is reported that Dr. de Wied of the Netherlands has enhanced the memory, as well as the learning ability, of mentally retarded persons by giving them a concentrated dose of a protein substance manufactured in the brains of humans.[36] We are a long way from popping pills to enhance intellectual functioning, but if we make the commitment, pharmacological applications to reduce the deficiencies of unprevented retardation will be developed.

Another area into which research should carry us is the development of techniques that enable undamaged portions of a retarded individual's brain to assume functions that should be performed by damaged portions. Obviously, there are certain areas of the brain that cannot be compensated for if damaged, and there will be significant limitations on compensatory recircuiting, but there are glimmers of hope in this area. For example, speech clinicians have had some success with what is called *melodic intonation therapy*—this for patients with brain damage to the left hemisphere. The therapy uses music to activate the right side of the brain, which sends signals to the left side in such a manner that the damaged portion of the left hemisphere is bypassed.[37] This therapy is not used to treat retarded persons, but the application of parallel measures is worth considering.

Genetic tune-ups, "smart pills," synaptic bypasses—it all sounds a trifle too futuristic. We must, however, consider the benefits of modern technologies to retarded persons and keep our minds open to new ways of thinking about thinking. The ethical problems that will be faced in applying such preventive and remedial technologies will be immense. Nonetheless, professionals in the field of mental retardation should continue to cultivate alliances with researchers in the scientific and technological communities, so that the former can impact the applications of research rather than simply react to discoveries and consume the technological consequences. This will require a new scientific synthesis of the medical and developmental models, which have been seen as incompatible only because of the reductionistic intractability of some of the more narrow-minded proponents of the two views.

THE COSTS OF NOT PREVENTING

The development of preventive advances will be an awesome task, requiring a great deal of money and human effort in a society of diminishing resources. Harried legislators face the conundrum of appropriating the funds they have to work with, either for prevention or for developmental services to persons who are already retarded. The need for the latter is undeniable, and lawmakers gain little political capital for doing the former. The prevention lobby is conspicuously silent—most professionals in the field being service oriented.

There is a logical flaw in underfunding preventive policies, though, because not preventing mental retardation is enormously expensive. In 1973, Conley calculated the costs of institutions, residential facilities, hospitals, prisons, special education programs, regular education programs servicing retarded people, personnel training, employment programs, research, clinical programs, construction, and agency operating expenses, and concluded that the United States spent $4,725,800,000 on mental retardation that year.[38] After adding the loss of earnings, homemaking services, and other productive activities to Conley's figures, Kurtz estimated in 1977 that "a figure of $9,557,800,000 . . . represented the total observable retardation-related economic loss to the nation."[39] Neither of these figures included such things as economic losses represented by homebound parents of homebound retarded children nor accounted for inflation and the ever-escalating demands for better services. It is ironic and rather pathetic to hear politicians who are supposedly working in the public interest tout the importance of cost-effectiveness and yet limit the concept's applicability to the short period encompassed between elections.

The cost of mental retardation should not be calculated only in dollars, but also in terms of the personal tragedies it occasions. While in the field, I had many experiences that highlighted the extent to which retarded people recognize the tragic elements of their lives. None was so poignant as an encounter I had with a sixty-eight-year-old, moderately retarded woman. On the day we met, she was lying in bed while her wheelchair "aired out" because she had been incontinent. The chair was important to her because one of her legs had been amputated when cerebral palsy made both legs so rigid that they could not be pried apart. As I stood alone with her in her room, she said to me with a toothless grin, "When I get heaven, I want be cowgirl." She then added, as she scanned her body with an eerily sagacious expression, "There, I won't be *like this.*"

THE PARADOX OF PREVENTION

Throughout this chapter, there have been intimations of the tension that exists between remedial-service delivery and prevention. The latter is predicated upon the notion that mental retardation is a bad thing. Remedial services, on the other hand, are based on the tacit assumption that people afflicted with this "bad thing" ought to be accepted in our society. I have gone to several meetings over the years at which speakers on the subject of prevention addressed audiences composed of both retarded and non-retarded persons. As I sat at one of these meetings, listening to a so-called expert decry the horrors of mental retardation, I wondered how the handicapped members of his audience must have felt. We have a long way to go on the path of prevention and must choose our steps and our words very carefully.

NOTES

1. F. Ludlow, "Too Late," Stanza 2, quoted in J. Bartlett, *Familiar Quotations,* Boston: Little, Brown and Co., 1882, p. 770.

2. R. N. Schimke, *Inheritance and Mental Retardation,* Arlington, Texas: National Association for Retarded Citizens, n.d., p. 6.

3. C. J. Sells and F. C. Bennett, "Prevention of Mental Retardation: The Role of Medicine," *American Journal of Mental Deficiency,* 82:1977, p. 124.

4. B. R. Gearheart and F. W. Litton, *The Trainable Retarded: A Foundations Approach,* St. Louis: C. V. Mosby, 1975, p. 34.

5. R. Koch and J. H. Koch, "Retarded Children," *Psychology Today,* December 1976, p. 93.

6. C. J. Sells and F. C. Bennett, p. 119.

7. J. M. Berg, "Genetics and Genetic Counseling," *Mental Retardation and Developmental Disabilities,* 8:1976, p. 43.

8. A. Milunsky, "Prenatal Diagnosis of Genetic Disorders," *New England Journal of Medicine*, 295:1976, pp. 377–380.

9. B. Farber, *Mental Retardation: Its Social Context and Social Consequences*, Boston: Houghton Mifflin, 1968, p. 32.

10. J. G. Davis, "Ethical Issues Arising from Prenatal Diagnosis," *Mental Retardation*, 19(1):1981, p. 13.

11. H. T. Lynch, G. M. Mulcahy, and A. J. Krush, "Genetic Counseling and the Physician," *Journal of the American Medical Association*, 211:1970, p. 650.

12. C. J. Sells and F. C. Bennett, p. 120.

13. T. M. Powledge and J. Fletcher, "Guidelines for the Ethical, Social, and Legal Issues in Prenatal Diagnosis," *The New England Journal of Medicine*, 300:1979, pp. 168–172.

14. J. D. Smith, "Down's Syndrome, Amniocentesis, and Abortion: Prevention or Elimination?" *Mental Retardation*, 19(1):1981, p. 8.

15. J. G. Davis, p. 12.

16. J. M. Berg, p. 50.

17. Massachusetts Association for Retarded Citizens, *Uncovering Birth Defects During Pregnancy—Amniocentesis*, Newton Upper Falls, Mass.: The Association, n.d., p. 3.

18. L. E. Karp, "The Prenatal Diagnosis of Genetic Disease," in T. A. Mappes and J. S. Zembaty, eds., *Biomedical Ethics*, New York: McGraw-Hill Book Company, 1981, p. 462.

19. A. Milunsky, *The Prenatal Diagnosis of Hereditary Disorders*, Springfield, Ill.: Charles C. Thomas, 1973, cited in J. G. Davis, p. 13.

20. A. Press, J. Contreras, and L. Walsh, "Suing for Being Born," *Newsweek*, March 8, 1982, p. 53.

21. B. R. Gearheart and F. W. Litton, p. 31.

22. C. J. Sells and F. C. Bennett, p. 126.

23. Ibid.

24. Ibid., pp. 122–123.

25. American College of Obstetricians and Gynecologists, *Cigarette Smoking and Pregnancy*, Bulletin No. 53, Chicago: Resource Center, ACOG, 1979.

26. The National Foundation/March of Dimes, *When You Drink, Your Unborn Baby Does Too!*, White Plains, N.Y.: The Foundation, n.d., p. 3.

27. R. Koch and J. H. Koch, p. 88.

28. R. Latimer, "Current Attitudes Toward Mental Retardation," *Mental Retardation*, 8(5):1970, p. 32.

29. C. M. Drillien, "Complications of Pregnancy and Delivery," *Mental Retardation—An Annual Review*, 1:1970, p. 294.

30. R. Koch and J. H. Koch, p. 90.

31. The President's Committee on Mental Retardation, *Silent Minority*, Washington, D.C.: U.S. Government Printing Office, Dept. of Health, Education, and Welfare, 1973, pp. 2–3.

32. A. C. Higgens, E. W. Crampton, and J. E. Moxley, "A Preliminary Report of a Nutrition Study on Public Maternity Patients 1963–1972," unpublished report, Montreal Diet Dispensary, Montreal, 1973, cited in S. A. Perkins,

"Malnutrition and Mental Development," *Exceptional Children*, 43(4):1977, p. 216.

33. S. A. Kirk, "The Effects of Early Intervention," in H. C. Haywood, ed., *Social-Cultural Aspects of Mental Retardation: Proceedings of the Peabody-NIMH Conference*, New York: Appleton-Century-Crofts, 1970, pp. 494–495.

34. B. Bloom, *Stability and Change in Human Characteristics*, New York: Wiley, 1964, p. 88.

35. J. G. Davis, p. 14.

36. L. Edson, "Superbrain," *Think*, March/April 1978, p. 41.

37. C. I. Berlin, "On Melodic Intonation Therapy for Aphasia by R. W. Sparks and A. L. Holland," *Journal of Speech and Hearing Disorders*, 41:1976, p. 299.

38. R. Conley, *The Economics of Mental Retardation*, Baltimore: Johns Hopkins University Press, 1973, p. 143.

39. R. A. Kurtz, *Social Aspects of Mental Retardation*, Lexington, Mass.: Lexington Books, 1977, p. 85.

15
Society's View of Retarded People: The Challenges of Third-Class Citizenship in a New Era

From the Carbon of
  Despair
    Later
      Diamonds
—J. C. Higgens[1]

SOCIOLOGICAL ANTECEDENTS

Social attitudes toward mentally handicapped citizens are grounded, in part, in the values of our culture. Sociologist Max Weber traced the development of what I believe to be one of the most basic of our social values in his work *The Protestant Ethic and the Spirit of Capitalism*.[2] Here, Weber showed how Calvinist thought motivated capitalist economic organization and explained the attendant social preoccupation with what William James once called the "bitch goddess success." Briefly, Weber's argument goes as follows: The Calvinists had a strong belief in predestination; hence, a life of good works could not ensure that a person would be saved. Admission to the Protestant heaven was already decided. One could, however, show his peers he was one of the elect if he lived a very successful life—God presumably not lavishing success on the damned. Of course, in seeking success, individuals fell into the productive (some would say, overproductive) work habits that promoted capitalist development.

Although the religious connotations associated with the success ethos disappeared long ago, our society is still engulfed in its homage to the goddess. This has had regrettable consequences for retarded citizens.

By conventional standards, mentally handicapped people have never been very successful. Indeed, many of them inadvertently challenge the legitimacy of the success value because they do not aspire to it. A few eschew the sacred tenet because they recognize the futility of trying to succeed, while others are simply oblivious to the importance of doing so. A special stigma is reserved for members of the latter group. Not only are they marginal in their achievements and aspirations, but their failure to participate in the learning rituals that teach social values threatens the inviolability of the socialization process. This, in turn, conflicts with another sacrosanct value of the culture, which admonishes all of us "to take advantage of the opportunity to be equal,"[3] whether or not that opportunity really exists.

Yet another of our society's primary values is utilitarianism. Although some resources and even more lip service are given to the idea that social organization should be adjusted to the people who live in the society, the American socioeconomic system is fundamentally based upon the utilitarian premise that individuals should be fit into roles and statuses that maintain the preexisting social and economic structure. When people are regarded as the servants of the socioeconomic system rather than the converse, there is an inevitable creation of surplus populations.

As we have seen in the preceding pages of this work, many retarded persons have a great deal of social utility as workers, friends, neighbors, and citizens. Nonetheless, there are those who function at such low levels that, with the exception of the fact that they provide a lot of people with jobs (and writers with subjects), they have no apparent social utility. The unfortunate thing here is that these persons' surplus population status is frequently generalized to all retarded people. Thus, it should come as no surprise that during times when the material environment becomes austere enough[4] and during periodic purges of the species,[5] retarded populations are the first to go.

Socioeconomic values are inadequate in explaining social attitudes toward retarded people. Cultures not steeped in the success tradition—cultures that are agrarian rather than industrialized, socialist and humanistic instead of utilitarian—still evidence the same kinds of stigmatic attitudes toward retarded people that exist in our own culture.[6] For example, in the People's Republic of China, although "blunted children" (the Chinese term for *mild* retardation) fit well into the farm and factory system, more severely retarded youngsters reportedly are kept at home and given no schooling or special services.[7] Indeed, the only cross-cultural evidence of severely retarded persons' not being seriously stigmatized was reported in Thompson's early study of the Vietnamese Annam, who allowed retarded individuals to marry and inherit property.[8]

If differing socioeconomic values, social structures, and organizational principles result in comparable attitudes toward retarded persons, then something much more deeply ingrained in the human psyche must be at work in explaining the contempt with which mentally defective people are regarded by many of those without handicaps. Perhaps it is too easy to cop a sociobiological plea when sociology itself fails to explain social phenomena, but the many analytic perspectives of the sociological discipline only give us varying degrees of inadequacy in explaining the social dynamics that typify interaction between handicapped and non-handicapped individuals in human societies. Thus I wonder if one of the prime motivating factors in this interaction is cerebral pride, a genetic hauteur that non-handicapped persons invoke instinctually to protect the continuity of a long and difficult evolutionary process? Reasoning from this position, I wonder if our pity and contempt for mentally defective people, and their consignment to the status of ontological deviants, are fired by a primordial instinct to cull the weak from our bands? Perhaps retarded people are disturbing to us because their own truncated development brings us face-to-face with the primitive within us—reminds us how close we are to our primate ancestors and shows us that in many ways we are still simians at heart and at head.

CIVILIZATION AND ITS DISCONTEMPTS

Even if there is an innate human contempt for mental "defectives," the social order is malleable enough that more humane sentiments regarding retarded persons can be generated through well-conceived appeals. Sometimes, though, individuals who wish to help most on this score help least. For example, in their efforts to raise community consciousness, some advocates deepen the public's confusion about mental retardation by presenting inaccurate information. One special educator said, "The greatest misconception the community has about retarded children is that they are somehow different." Retarded youngsters are developmental beings to be sure, but they *are* different. To assert that their experiences do not set them apart from the majority of the non-handicapped population only distorts public consciousness.

Another special educator told me that retarded people "must be made to appear better than they really are to gain community acceptance." This attitude frequently results in saccharine claims about how loving and compassionate mentally handicapped persons are and how wonderful they are at bringing out the good qualities in others. This cannot be generalized. Like other humans, some retarded individuals are spiteful and mean and bring out the worst in anybody they are around.

Overglorification of mentally handicapped people is also evident in the amplified perpetuation of a notion called *idiot savant*. The idea here is that a person can be deficient in all but a single aspect of his intellect, and in this respect be a genius.[9] There are retarded savants, but the phenomenon is exceedingly rare, and when it is used as a component of the overglorification gambit, it hurts retarded people more than it helps them. An overestimation of the number of savants and/or mis-representation of the magnitude of their pinpoint precocity only makes non-handicapped individuals distrustful of legitimate claims made re-garding the abilities of mentally handicapped persons.

A major issue associated with public information about mental re-tardation centers on who will do the informing. Where they possess adequate social skills, retarded persons make their own best informational advocates, because when non-handicapped people understand them in a more personally intimate way, it is difficult not to empathize with them.

One of the best-known vehicles through which retarded persons disclose themselves to large segments of the general public is participation in the Special Olympics sports program. Special Olympiads get hand-icapped and non-handicapped people together in normalized settings where they can communicate with each other. Although press and broadcast media coverage of the Special Olympics is often sentimen-talized, non-handicapped citizens have an opportunity to learn through these presentations that retarded people experience the same range of human emotions that are part of everyone else's psychological repertoire. The scope of activities of the Special Olympics is quite limited, though. Mentally handicapped people can do a great deal more than run and jump and throw things. The real difficulty retarded persons face in disclosing themselves to the nonhandicapped public is showing the many other abilities they possess. If these skills are not examined in natural settings such as schools and work places, the formats that such presentations of self follow occasionally take on the quality of degrading little sideshows. It is all very quaint when mentally handicapped people give show-and-tell demonstrations at the local service club's afternoon meeting, but it is difficult to celebrate one's marginal status publicly without exacerbating it, no matter how remarkable the show. If retarded people do not shoulder the major portion of responsibility for educating the non-handicapped population about themselves, who will?

Parents obviously have a big stake in fostering community under-standing and acceptance of their handicapped children, but it is difficult for many of them to get involved in community information programs. Some are embarrassed and ashamed of their children. A few cannot even talk about the youngsters with friends without becoming over-wrought, let alone go public. Others ask how much can be expected of them. Just meeting the responsibilities of raising a retarded child carries obligations that can be emotionally, physically, and economically draining. Must they also make the rounds of civic organizations, churches, businesses, and so on to ask that their children be accorded a modicum of human dignity? Do they have to confront the pointers and starers in the supermarket with information packets or explanations of the appearance and behavior of their children? Some do; most cannot.

There are advocacy organizations that could provide the impetus for informational advocacy—the most well known of these being the Association for Retarded Citizens. Unfortunately, however, many local chapters of this important organization have been shown "to have significant problems of identity and operational effectiveness," including low memberships, inactivity of all but a few of those who are members, poor membership-retention rates, and difficulties in attracting young constituents.[10] This kind of an organizational milieu is not particularly fruitful ground for formulating goals and implementing objectives pertinent to consciousness-raising efforts. Against this backdrop, the Association for Retarded Citizens faces the difficult task of spearheading a national public information effort to coordinate and decide what information will be circulated, how the programs to do so will be financed, who the target audiences will be, and what formats will be most effective for disseminating advocacy messages.

In my estimation, the gist of informational campaigns should aim at highlighting the important link between the well-being of retarded citizens and that of persons without handicaps. It is fine to talk about the problems and potentials of retarded persons, but it is most important to appeal to the self-interest of one's audience. Even the most fiscally conservative person is more apt to resonate with what is being said about programming for retarded persons if that programming has undeniable, verified financial benefits for himself. One need only look at the cost benefits of educating most retarded persons and helping them to find employment, versus warehousing them in institutions, to make a very powerful case for the former.[11] The message here is simple and true and has both practical and affective components. Obviously, there will be different messages that pertain more appropriately to other retarded populations (such as those who function at very low levels), but for now the advocacy movement ought to lead its trump card.

Where organizational constraints do not impede getting the advocacy message out, fiscal constraints sometimes do. Mentally retarded people must compete with many powerful interests for the public and private funds they get. What is appropriated is usually required for direct services; there is never an excess to spend on anything that smacks of public relations or image building. Unless advocacy organizations find public or private benefactors or engage in entrepreneurial activities that provide a stable source of income, they may have to carry on their informational advocacy very quietly and cheaply. It is regrettable that this happens, because all the best efforts of professionals to facilitate retarded people's entry into their communities, as well as the public expenditures that go into these efforts, are exercises in futility if these communities are not prepared for the handicapped person's entry. This fact should become part of the advocacy message.

The scope of community education about mental retardation ought to be wide, because everyone's lives will be increasingly impacted by the issues surrounding mental handicaps. Specific cohorts should, however, be targeted for special consideration. These would include physicians and allied health personnel, expectant parents, educators, legislators and governmental officials, executives of volunteer agencies, labor leaders, civic groups and service organizations, clergy, social workers, psychologists and other counselors, people making career choices, lawyers, judges, police, architects, employers, realtors, and, most importantly, children.

There are many ways to spread information about mental retardation. Newsletters, direct mailings, and speakers' bureaus may not be very inspired methods, but they do reach some individuals effectively and without great expense.

The news media have enormous power in molding public opinion and reach a broad audience, although complications easily develop when certain media are used. For example, as one newspaper reporter who was working on a story about mental retardation told me, "I get paid for writing fast, not well." Newspapers *are* limited with respect to the time and space they can spend on a story. If a reporter takes a superficial glance at nearly any aspect of a field as complex as mental retardation, there is a good chance he or she will misrepresent retarded people. Moreover, the press tends to be most attracted to those aspects of mental retardation that sell newspapers—a factor accounting for the sentimentalization and sensationalization that inhere in some news accounts.

Books, television, and films have been virtually untapped in molding public opinion about mentally handicapped people. There are few factual books on mental retardation written in a style that has mass appeal, Josh Greenfeld's diaries about his handicapped son Noah being obvious exceptions.[12]

The best-known fictionalizing that has been done about mentally retarded people distorts, rather than elevates, public consciousness. Steinbeck's brilliant *Of Mice and Men*[13] depicts an oafish giant who inadvertently kills mice, puppies, and people. Keyes's *Flowers for Al-*

gernon,[14] which was the basis of the movie *Charly,* is fascinating and touching, but it is science fiction.

TV dramas on the subject of retardation have been more in evidence in the last five years, with mixed results. One of the problems that has beset these presentations is the use of non-handicapped actors to portray retarded persons. These actors can sometimes be seen grunting and squinting in an exaggerated struggle to act retarded, transforming sensitive material into caricature. Further, these shows often perpetuate the very stereotypical images they are presumably designed to sensitize audiences to. I recall watching one of these made-for-TV films which was a drama about the Special Olympics. The lead character made faces, stuttered, had bouts of cerebral palsy and epilepsy, as well as being retarded— a fairly heady brew in great special olympians. In 1981, Mickey Rooney gave a remarkable performance with his portrayal of a retarded man in a TV movie called *Bill.* Such successes notwithstanding, the most sensible course of action in staging presentations about retarded persons is to let mentally handicapped actors play mentally handicapped persons. The medium really should be the message.

Documentary films on the subject of mental retardation abound, but they tend to be seen by people who need the least sensitization—the people who already work in the field. *Best Boy,* winner of the Academy Award for the best documentary film of 1979, was an extraordinary work, but, as a documentary, it did not have the mass appeal that a feature-length drama would have. Unfortunately, there has been a woeful dearth of good material in the area of feature-length dramas.

One of the most sensitive feature-length movies about handicapped people was *The Heart Is a Lonely Hunter,* and even it intensified stereotypes. The film begins with a middle-aged retarded man breaking the front window of a bakery to steal a model cake, as he childishly clutches a teddy bear. He comes across as an infantile and pitiable simpleton. Feature-length dramas are expensive, and studios are reluctant to take huge financial risks on topics that many non-handicapped persons enjoy the luxury of not having to see or hear about. It is time, though, for advocacy groups to promote the creation of a masterful feature-length film about mental retardation. If the "cinementality" that underlies this work does not degenerate to the bland or sickly-sweet palaver that seems to characterize most films about handicapped persons, a genuine contribution to the advancement of public consciousness about retardation can be made. A remarkable film, *Coming Home,* compelled the attention of a whole nation that had never really thought about paraplegia. There is no reason the same thing cannot be done on the subject of mental retardation, and while the effects of art are certainly ephemeral, they plant the seeds that begin to change the social landscape.

No matter what motifs are used in disseminating information, special caution will be required on several accounts. First, advocates must be mindful that tales about retarded people are like Greek desserts—a little bit can go a long way. Programs should be coordinated so that resources are channeled into the most effective methods of opinion molding, without inundating the public in mental retardation stories.

Second, public information advocates must be prepared to recognize that their efforts may result in an informational backlash. Just getting some latter-day Social Darwinists thinking about the expenditure of tax monies on retarded people can create opposition to current levels of spending. Then, too, advocates may have to face the frustration of the opposite reaction: the message gets across, but no one cares.

Third, it is important that public consciousness programs inform and elevate the people at whom they are directed, not debase them. This will be difficult, for one of the messages inevitably has to be that retarded people are victimized by the society. Public opinion must, however, be molded, not bludgeoned. Many non-handicapped people do not know if or how they wrong retarded persons, because no one has shown them appropriate interaction rituals or explained that contradictions in their interactions with mentally handicapped persons are normal. For example, at least half of the parents of retarded youngsters with whom I talked said that they could not stand the way people "stared" at their children. The other half said that the thing they could not stand was the way people "looked away." When such conflicting sentiments are funneled into the public arena, the average person is bound to become confused and recoil from further interaction.

Fourth, advocates will have to be sure not to become ponderous about the kind of interactive standards they set to govern non-handicapped people's encounters with those who are mentally retarded. The process whereby retarded people will be assimilated into the social mainstream is going to require that everyone concerned tolerate the faux pas of everyone else. That is going to oblige all of us to have a sense of humor.

PARTING THOUGHTS

Throughout the course of doing this study, one of the most striking features I noted about retarded persons was the curious paradox inherent in their need structure when compared with that of normal people. Most non-handicapped persons' desires seem to exceed their needs, while the reverse is true of retarded people, who need so much and want so little from the rest of us. Perhaps the whole constellation of their wants can best be summed up in the responses of three of my mentally retarded friends to the question, "If you could tell the people on 'the outside' anything about yourself, what would you say?" One said, "That we're nice, we're friendly company and all that stuff." Another, "I do have some feelings. I have feelings for myself; I got pride and dignity in me. . . . Really!" Finally, "Tell 'em to come out and visit sometimes."

NOTES

1. J. C. Higgens, "Mine," in *Lindy: My Retarded Child*, Valley Forge, Pa.: Judson Press, 1970, p. 56.

2. M. Weber, *The Protestant Ethic and the Spirit of Capitalism*, New York: Charles Scribner's Sons, 1958 (originally published in 1904).

3. L. A. Dexter, "On the Politics and Sociology of Stupidity in Our Society," *Social Problems*, 9:1962, p. 225; see also his articles "Towards a Sociology of the Mentally Defective," *American Journal of Mental Deficiency*, 61:1956, p. 15 and "A Social Theory of Mental Deficiency," *American Journal of Mental Deficiency*, 62:1958, pp. 922–923.

4. R. B. Edgerton, "Mental Retardation in Non-Western Societies: Toward a Cross-Cultural Perspective on Incompetence," in H. C. Haywood, ed., *Social-Cultural Aspects of Mental Retardation: Proceedings of the Peabody-NIMH Conference*, New York: Appleton-Century-Crofts, 1970, p. 535.

5. W. Wolfensberger, "The Extermination of Handicapped People in World War II Germany," *Mental Retardation*, 19(1):1981, p. 1.

6. R. B. Edgerton, p. 534; L. G. Peters, "Concepts of Mental Deficiency Among the Tamang of Nepal," *American Journal of Mental Deficiency*, 84:1980, pp. 352–356; B. Farber, *Mental Retardation: Its Social Context and Social Consequences*, Boston: Houghton Mifflin, 1968, p. 16.

7. N. M. Robinson, "Mild Mental Retardation: Does It Exist in the People's Republic of China?" *Mental Retardation*, 16(4):1978, p. 298.

8. V. M. Thompson, *French Indo-China*, New York: Macmillan, 1937, cited in R. B. Edgerton, p. 534.

9. A. L. Hill, "Savants: Mentally Retarded Individuals With Special Skills," *International Review of Research in Mental Retardation*, 9:1978, pp. 277–298; A Morishima, "Another Van Gogh of Japan: The Superior Artwork of a Retarded Boy," *Exceptional Children*, 41:1976, pp. 92–96; R. Restak, "Islands of Genius," *Science 82*, May 1982, pp. 62–67.

10. R. J. Flynn, P. L. Berck, and S. Lepan, "Evaluating the Effectiveness of Local Voluntary Associations for Mentally Retarded Persons with the LAMP," *Mental Retardation*, 18(6):1980, pp. 279–280.

11. R. W. Conley, *The Economics of Mental Retardation*, Baltimore: Johns Hopkins University Press, 1973, p. 297; R. W. Conley, "The Economics of Mental Retardation—An Economist's Approach," *Mental Retardation*, 14:1976, p. 24.

12. J. Greenfeld, *A Child Called Noah: A Family Journal*, New York: Pocket Books, 1973; J. Greenfeld, *A Place for Noah*, New York: Holt, Rinehart, and Winston, 1978.

13. J. Steinbeck, *Of Mice and Men*, New York: Bantam Books, 1937.

14. D. Keyes, *Flowers for Algernon*, New York: Bantam Books, 1966.

Index

About the Book and Author

The Lives of Mentally Retarded People
Daryl Paul Evans

What is it like to be mentally retarded in a society that places a high premium on competence? Although mentally retarded people are becoming more integral participants in our society than they once were, they still, in many respects, inhabit worlds of their own. This book examines those worlds, as well as the increasing role of mentally retarded individuals in mainstream society and the needs and problems this integration has produced. Dr. Evans explores the ways in which professionals, governments, communities, and families attempt to meet these needs and cope with the attendant problems. He also probes the special adaptations people make to being mentally handicapped and offers glimpses of their feelings, their fears, and their frustrations.

Dr. Evans's book is the culmination of several years of observation in the field, extensive conversations with professionals, parents, and retarded people themselves, and an intensive examination of the literature. Addressing such practical issues as education, sexuality, law, and prevention, as well as social attitudes toward these issues, he presents a cohesive view of what it means to be mentally retarded and invites professionals and students in the field of developmental disabilities, families of retarded people, and interested lay readers to share in a unique sociological perspective on mental retardation.

Daryl Paul Evans is an assistant professor of sociology at the University of Kansas. He has been involved in numerous activities with mentally retarded people—serving on state task force committees and the boards of service agencies—and was instrumental in the production of the film *Commencement*, recently aired on public television.